Creative Psychotherapy:
A Source Book

Creative Psychotherapy:
A Source Book

Edited by
Anthony G. Banet, Jr., Ph.D.
Human Relations Consultant
La Jolla, California

University Associates, Inc.
7596 Eads Avenue
La Jolla, California 92037

Preface

The readings in this book were chosen to outline the dimensions of contemporary humanistic psychotherapy. Sections defining the goals of psychotherapy, the personal characteristics of the effective psychotherapist, and the task of the person seeking help are included, as well as presentations of new approaches and discussions of significant psychotherapeutic issues. As such, the volume is intended as an introductory text for the student and an update review for the practicing therapist.

Selecting relevant articles is always problematic; ultimately, the selection is based on personal biases. Many of the articles presented here have proved useful to me (and to my students) in my teaching and supervisory work; others were chosen because they said clearly and succinctly what needed to be said about the subject. Still others were selected because they introduce insightful and provocative points of view.

The major credit for this book belongs to the authors of the original articles. I am grateful to them and their publishers for permission to reprint their materials in this collection. Arlette Ballew and the editorial staff of University Associates were generous with their assistance, although none of them have learned to decipher my handwriting. Bill Pfeiffer, president of University Associates, has been a source of constant support and encouragement to me in planning and developing this book.

Anthony G. Banet, Jr.

La Jolla, California
January 1976

CONTENTS

Introduction

"Psychotherapy—including its most extensive form, psychoanalysis—is repair work. This view cannot be overemphasized. A psychotherapist should not expect great transformations equivalent to a psychological rebirth or a complete reorganization of the patient's personality. The results which can be achieved in this repair work are limited by the caliber of the original material (CONstitution plus ego), the degree of damage (infantile traumas and adult frustrations), and what remains to be worked with (adult ego plus the reality situation). In people, as in clothes, some materials are finer to begin with and a repaired article is never as good as the new one."

Kenneth Mark Colby, mentor to a generation of psychotherapists, expressed the conventional wisdom when he wrote this caveat in 1951. In his wise and humane *A Primer for Psychotherapists*, Colby defined psychotherapy as a verbal transaction between one psychotherapist and one patient, a transaction intended to analyze transference, work through resistances, and prepare the patient for what Freud described as the "ordinary unhappiness of life."

Colby's view was supported by the psychiatry and psychology textbooks of the time, which reported a chain of studies attempting to measure, qualify, and evaluate the outcome of the verbal transaction. Psychotherapy, it seemed clear, was striving to be an applied science. Like science, psychotherapy at its best was thought to be impersonal, manipulative, and precise, a treatment applied to a suffering person to reduce discomfort. Psychotherapy had its critics, to be sure—novelist Peter de Vries described it as the application of "a poultice of polysyllables to a wound the therapist neither sees nor understands"—but most practitioners viewed their craft as an already-established body of knowledge that was theirs to practice but not to tinker with. When Colby instructed his students how to repair the "material"—like tailors—few psychotherapists seemed prepared for the explosion of forces that would sweep psychotherapy off the consulting-room couch and into groups and storefronts and onto the naked cliffs at Esalen.

The explosion had many sources and took many forms. From the late 1940's on, a series of books, therapeutic experiments, scientific discoveries, and social movements impacted the world of mental illness and mental health and changed its topography. Some of the explosion's force was a reaction to the creeping scholasticism of orthodox psychoanalysis, but most of the energy came from a fresh appreciation of old concerns. Rogers, Perls, Lewin, and Maslow pumped idealism into traditional images of humanity and saw the potential for growth and transformation. The discovery of chlorpromazine promised a humane, if chemical, "strait jacket" to calm the most violent psychosis, outside hospital walls. Discoveries in neurology, the community-mental-health-center legislation, the experimental communities of R. D. Laing, the criticism of Thomas Szasz, the emergence of the feminist movement and gay liberation, the counterculture, growth centers, the encounter movement, the Eastern meditations systems: all contributed to the birth of a "third force" in psychotherapy, a force that is now generally known as humanistic psychology.

"Humanistic" is used here to describe those innovative, fresh, and nontraditional styles of helping that have come to be identified with the term. Unlike its predecessors, the humanistic psychotherapy movement encourages individual experimentation and expression. For the humanistic therapist, psychotherapy is less an applied science, more an individual work of art—a creative relationship with the power to rechart life directions and alter states of consciousness. There is some presumption involved in labeling anything "creative," especially when it is as amorphous and ill defined as psychotherapy. Within the humanistic movement there are nearly as many psychotherapies as there are psychotherapists; and all are creative and original to some degree.

Because the humanistic movement has made creativity possible for the psychotherapist as well as for the client (no longer "patient"), seeker, or collaborator, changes are as possible for the therapist as they are for the person who comes for help. Humanistic psychotherapy can be characterized by its emphasis on individual responsibility, risk taking, integration, and the search for synergy. Perhaps the most apparent hallmark of the movement is its here-and-now focus; as Maslow indicated, the ability to become "lost in the present" seems to be essential for creativeness of any kind.

Creative humanistic psychotherapy is not necessarily better than other approaches; it is different. Creative psychotherapists engage in therapeutic relationships according to different rules from those followed by more traditional psychotherapists. The different rules, as

Leavitt and Doktor (1970) have pointed out, make it easier to do something original, but make it harder for the world to evaluate that originality. Humanistic psychotherapy has not abolished human suffering —there are still back wards, distorted relationships, and street violence—nor has it diminished the philosophical concerns related to psychotherapy: Does it work? Who benefits? How do you know? What is just a fad and what is genuine? But more than older approaches, creative psychotherapy offers hope, idealism, and the excitement of potential evolutionary change.

The selections chosen for this source book reflect the creative activity of a broad range of practicing psychotherapists. Collectively, the authors belong to no school of theory and technique, but they share a commitment to growth, change, and experimentation, and a willingness to search in novel places for creative resolutions to problems. Few of the authors here accept Colby's definition of psychotherapy as "repair work," but they share and manifest his concern for engaging in a warm and authentic relationship with those they serve.

The readings in this book are grouped into sections, according to their orientation or intent. The first selection provides a journalistic overview of the people, places, techniques, and theories thriving today in the humanistic psychotherapy culture. The section on The Goals of Psychotherapy contains various definitions of psychotherapy and ways of regarding the psychotherapeutic process. In The Psychotherapist, the focus is on the personal characteristics of the psychotherapist and the creative challenge of forging a helping relationship. In The Patient as Collaborator, descriptions are offered of the patient's participation in his own growth. Various psychotherapeutic strategies and techniques are detailed in the Creative Approaches section, and the use of groups in psychotherapy is the focus of Group Approaches. A final section, Issues, presents discussions of the moral, ethical, and scientific concerns of humanistic psychotherapy.

REFERENCES

Colby, K. M. *A primer for psychotherapists.* New York: Ronald Press, 1951.

Leavitt, H. J., & Doktor, R. Personal growth, laboratory training, science and all that: A shot at cognitive clarification. *Journal of Applied Behavioral Science,* 1970, 6, 173-179.

New Psychology: New Image of Man

by Eleanor Hoover

John Brodie, the articulate former quarterback for the San Francisco 49'ers, reports an ecstatic interlude when "time stood still" while he was dropping back to throw a pass.

A young man working his way through medical school by drumming in a jazz band reports many years later, that in all his drumming he had three peaks when he suddenly felt like a great drummer and his performance was perfect.

Experience—any experience—once was ignored in psychology as "unscientific." Particularly these, which the late psychologist, Abraham Maslow, called "peak experiences."

They are vivid moments when things fall into place, one's vision is clear and life is meaningful.

They happen, it was thought, only to artists, poets, mystics or saints. But Maslow found they also happen to the healthiest, most creative and happy people.

Now a new study indicates they are "widespread, almost commonplace in American society today." Nobody talks about them "because somehow they seem odd, illogical—inexplicable," says the Rev. Andrew M. Greeley, the sociologist who conducted the study for the National Research Opinion Center.

It seems that such moments are linked to feelings of self-fulfillment, creativity, achievement—or simple at-one-with-the-universe reverie. Apparently, they can happen to anyone. Interest in them is part of something loosely called the "new psychology."

"The core of the new psychology," says Hugh Redmond of Johnston College at the University of Redlands, "is based on a new image or vision of Man—on what he is and what he can do."

From *Los Angeles Times*, April 6, 1975, pp. 1, 5, 20-22. Copyright, 1975, Los Angeles Times. Reprinted by permission.

If the new psychology needs a label, "humanistic" probably fits best.

What humanistic psychology has triggered is a growing interest in expanding Man's awareness—to enhance creativity, health, learning, problem solving and to produce what one brain researcher calls "intrinsically rewarding ecstatic experiences."

Much of what is happening is still outside the ivied halls of the academy. But not for long.

The curriculum committee of Harvard University recently approved an undergraduate course in altered states of consciousness.

"Students," one professor says, "are coming into the colleges and demanding that these experiences be recognized."

Humanistic psychology grew out of opposition to the major expressions of traditional psychology—mainly, Skinnerean behaviorism and Freudian psychoanalysis.

"For as long as I can remember—until now—if it didn't have pink eyes, a long tail and a twitchy nose and run in a maze, it wasn't psychology," an older psychologist says.

It has been called everything from a "post-Freudian revolution," to a "brain revolution" and "a revolution in consciousness."

If such terms seem to overstate the case for humanistic psychology (and they do to many), they are not strong enough for a few who, in the words of one observer, see it as nothing short of "a Reformation slouching to meet its Luther at a yet undiscovered cathedral door."

Taken as a whole, humanistic psychology consists of a loose but important network of approaches, disciplines, techniques, and areas of mind and brain research which see Man from all sides—wholly different from the one we are used to.

Its main aspects, which tend to overlap, are these:

—Where once Man was seen as merely a bundle of responses to stimuli, moldable in any direction, there is a focus on individuality, the person and the intrinsic complexity, richness and power of mind and consciousness.

—Where once mind and body were split, there is a "coming together," a regard for wholeness and the way the mind affects the body and the body affects the mind. This "holistic" approach can be found today in education, medicine and sports as well as psychology.

—Where thought, logic and rationality were once dominant, there is more recognition of emotions as well as "spiritual" feelings. The goal is to be a whole person who is a harmonious blend of all his parts.

—Where once "objectivity" meant banishing subjective experience from science, it is now being allowed back in. The belief of humanistic psychologists is that there is no basic contradiction and that a new science can be built which also includes the observer's experience.

—Where once Man was seen as blindly buffeted by instinctual forces such as the id, superego and ego, there is a new belief in man's built-in capacity for growth, self-transcendence or self-actualization.

—Where once, under the old Freudian "medical model," Man was seen as either "sick" or "well," he is now seen as having a natural ability to make changes in himself rather quickly, once he sees what needs to be done. "The basic idea is," says James Fadiman of Stanford, "that you are capable of being more than you are and you know how to do it."

—Where once Man was seen as a more or less static or "fixed" system, there is a new interest in "energy flow" and "energy fields"—in Eastern meditation and yoga, seen as a means of releasing energy. A new polarity therapy is based on this idea of energy and the "natural ability of the body to balance itself."

—Where once the idea of will and willpower was so loaded with guilt and repression that generations rebelled against it, there is a renewed interest in the will and in responsibility for self as a positive, natural and liberating force.

—Where once purpose of meaning was seen as "religious," it is finding its way back into psychology. This recognition of a "spiritual dimension" to Man is a major change. Esalen's founder, Mike Murphy, calls this "the cutting edge—the psychology of the future."

Humanistic psychology began with the work of Abraham Maslow more than 20 years ago, grew and expanded in the Human Potential Movement for about 10 years, and became a full-fledged "psychology" only two years ago.

That was when humanistic psychology was accepted by the American Psychological Association as its newest and 32nd branch—along with experimental, physiological, clinical, educational, child and other such venerables, some of which go back almost 65 years.

To some unregenerate members of the Association for Humanistic Psychology—remembering its bitter turbulent history as a "third force" movement—recognition by the American Psychological Association may be "death by victory." They are proud, but they hope their "joyous movement" will not be diverted.

That there were tensions between the two groups is understandable. The American Psychological Association is made up largely of psychologists with university affiliations. Many Association for Humanistic Psychology members work outside the academy—many as therapists—or in university departments other than psychology. Lacking university support, they developed much of the new psychology at "growth centers" around the country (like Esalen at Big Sur).

To understand humanistic psychology, there must be an understanding of classical behaviorism and Freudian psychoanalysis—the two traditional psychologies to which Maslow's work, humanistic psychology and the Human Potential Movement stand more or less opposed.

A main point at issue is the notion of an "inner man."

Behaviorism (which, since its founding, has evolved into Skinnerean behaviorism, from B. F. Skinner of Harvard, its most famous spokesman) takes the view that all we can know or scientifically study about an organism is what it does, how it behaves—hence the name behaviorism. Its tools are stimulus-response and reward-punishment, and its body of knowledge is called learning theory.

The experimental schema is simple. A hungry rat is put in a maze. Hunger is its stimulus. Reward is a food pellet at the end of the maze. To get the food, the rat must learn for example, to overcome obstacles put in his way.

How the rat behaves—what it does and how it learns—is what is important to doctrinaire behaviorists. Nothing more. And nothing further is inferred. The rat model is, of course, an analogy to human behavior.

A therapy based on this system—behavior modification—is well thought of by most psychologists. At least it isn't often challenged. It has had good success in reducing obesity, phobias, and in helping cases of autism—a disorder in which a child remains regressed at early stages of development.

Behavior modification assumes that disorders, sicknesses, ills —whatever one wishes to call them—are learned, and can be changed by methods worked out in the labs. That is, undesired behavior can be stopped through punishment and desired behavior increased through reward.

Another name for this is operant conditioning, which, simply put by one therapist is, "people do what they are rewarded for doing." As Skinner told a Reed College symposium on "Behavior Control" two weeks ago, "inner man is an illusion."

The humanists deplore this view and all else in psychology that fragmentizes and reduces.

Freudianism is more concerned with what goes on inside the individual. In fact, it sees Man as buffeted by internal unconscious drives and the battlefield of instinctual drives like the id, ego and superego, with "neurosis" (a term less used today) the almost inevitable result.

Psychoanalysis, of course, was the "sole" time-honored way of alleviating such complaints until the newer, freewheeling humanistic-oriented "therapies" came along.

But sexual repression was a pressing problem in Freud's day. It is less so now. And nowhere did Freud have much to say about what has become one of today's most pressing problems—a sense of meaninglessness in life.

Freud's was a pessimistic view. He once wrote to a friend, "I have always confined myself to the ground floor and basement of the edifice called Man." Aldous Huxley once said he should have said the basement-basement.

If Freud is the basement, the humanists see themselves as the attic or penthouse. Rollo May, a founder of the Association for Humanistic Psychology, sounded the clarion call at the beginning of the movement.

"We represent the New Underground in psychology," he said. "I see a crucially important value for the (association) if we are able to find and be the kind of psychology that speaks out of the being of Man, rather than out of techniques."

May thinks psychology owes Freud a debt of gratitude for bringing "repressed hostilities, irrational urges" and other "dark" areas of the unconscious out into the open. But he feels Freud's system left out too much that is human.

He warns the behaviorists they run the risk of creating a totally mechanical society. The title of Skinner's latest book, "Beyond Freedom and Dignity," suggests just that to most humanists. The Skinnerian reply is that Man's "freedom" is illusory and leaves him abandoned to uncontrollable forces in his environment.

This issue has political overtones. The battle continues.

Maslow was the first major American psychologist to postulate that Man is an *evolutionary* creature whose higher nature is just as "instinctoid" (his word) as his lower nature . . . and to see problems, difficulties and "sickness" arising when this upward-evolution—this need for "self-actualization"—is blocked.

"This higher nature," Maslow said, "includes the need for meaningful work, for responsibility, for creativeness, for being fair and just, for doing what is worthwhile and for preferring to do it well."

Peak experiences are way stations along the path of this upward evolution—way stations that are both necessary and desirable, Maslow believed.

"Maslow's importance," explains British author-psychologist Colin Wilson, "is that he places these experiences of transcendence at the core of his psychology. Peak experiences are moments of meaning which enhance our self-image and stimulate our will. ". . . As the meaning pours in, you ask yourself, 'Why doesn't this happen all the time?' . . . and the answer is obvious: 'Because I allow the will to become passive and the senses close up. If I want more meaning then I must force my senses wide open by an increased effort of the will. . . .'"

One of those with reservations about peak experience is Sam Keen of the Association for Humanistic Psychology. He favors a more "Zen, homogenized way of living . . . Some neurotics reach the point where they need peak experience all the time."

"We can't assume our own experiences are always correct either," says Stanford's Fadiman.

"By that I mean that my gut feelings may be no more accurate than my intellectual feelings. I've made as many mistakes being led by my gut or my gonads as by my mind. That's where a lot of encounter got stuck."

Humanistic psychology is already way ahead of any simple definitions. Its adherents—or, at least, its avant-garde—say that Man, as we usually think of him, is far too narrow a concept.

The language of the humanists now takes on a "spiritual," almost mystical tone—something unheard and unheard-of in scientific circles before.

But then the humanists have been outrageous right along. Once after Maslow had delivered a paper at an American Psychological Association meeting, a famous psychologist rushed at him shouting, "Maslow—you are an evil man—you want to destroy psychology."

Ironically, Maslow went on to become the association's president a few years later.

What is different today is that humanistic ranks—although small —include so many well credentialed and influential scientists that they can no longer be dismissed as merely "misguided," "misled," "unscientific"—or, least of all, "kooky."

Nor can these new ideas be credited to the "squishy California atmosphere" or California's "tolerance for peculiar life-styles" as some writers do. They seem to be everywhere.

Anyone who remembers the flashy, flamboyant Human Potential Movement of a few years back may have trouble reconciling it with humanistic psychology's newfound respectability.

The Human Potential Movement (which was to blend with, and finally become indistinguishable from, the Association for Humanistic Psychology) was born out of the cultural upheaval of the 60s.

Affluence, the sexual revolution, the campus revolt, changing life styles, women's liberation, drugs, the flower children, television, more leisure and rising middle-class expectations all played a part. For whatever reason, thousands of people found their lives somehow flat and self-limiting.

Much earlier, after World War II, the GI Bill of Rights had brought thousands of ex-GIs onto the campuses where, with the newfound existential wisdom of war, many went into clinical psychology.

"Until then, the practice of psychotherapy had been limited almost exclusively to professionals having an M.D. degree—owing to the accidental historical fact that Freud just happened to be an M.D. himself. No other reason," says Dr. Tom Greening, a humanistic therapist.

With the flood of clinical psychologists into the marketplace, psychotherapy ceased to be the monopoly of the M.D.'s and the luxury solely of the rich. It unleashed a floodgate of self-exploration, self-examination and self-awareness.

Much of this had begun before Maslow and the humanists appeared on the scene. Astrology, I Ching, Tarot cards, esoteric religions and meditation were flourishing.

And encounter—that crucible of honest, bruising group plain talk, where people "can drop their masks and express true feelings"—was on everyone's lips if not in their living rooms.

"What happened," says Fadiman, the Stanford psychologist, "is we learned that being 'well-bred' meant dying slowly. 'Well-bred' in the sense of suppressing our real feelings. What has finally come across is that emotional honesty is necessary for mental health."

He adds, "And there were an awful lot of dead people walking around."

Encounter was big business. Corporations like TRW had major programs aimed at "sensitizing" employes, believing this resulted in more productive work. (Now some of them offer yoga classes at lunch.)

By the end of the 60s, National Training Laboratories could claim that more than half the presidents of the 500 largest U.S. corporations had exposed themselves to group experience. Encounter finally filtered down to churches, schools, police departments, the Army—and around the world.

At the same time, Esalen was deep in its far-out forays in self-exploration. Some called it "freaky audacity and a willingness to try anything that stretches the self."

Whatever it was, it met a real need of the time (and still does: there are Esalen-like growth centers now in Scotland, London, Amsterdam, Munich, Paris, the Costa del Sol in Spain—and—Japan.

Esalen and humanistic psychology met officially when Murphy, Esalen's founder, had a first, "chance" meeting with Maslow who "just happened" to be lost in the hills above Big Sur one day in the early '60s—a story Murphy tells which is positively eerie in coincidence.

But nowhere else could one glimpse the real "cutting edge" of change as readily as at Association for Humanistic Psychology conventions.

Its members tended to greet each other with bear hugs, lie around on convention floors and create culture shock at famous hotels by skinny-dipping in the early hours of the morning.

They danced to bongo drums by the pool, held workshops on "play" where they romped and cavorted like children, and practiced what they preached—a celebration of life.

("The battle to maintain a balance between the theoretical and the experiential still rages," says one member today.)

This freewheelingness cost them some of their most eminent members some years ago. After an episode where students pitched a tent in the lobby of the elegant Fairmont Hotel in San Francisco to protest high room rates, Rollo May, Gardner Murphy and some others resigned.

But May rejoined two years later with a simple statement:

"Somewhere, there has got to be a psychology that includes poetry, art, a movement toward social justice and that will help me understand myself—and nowhere does it exist—even beginningly—outside the (association)."

Packed seminars and workshops introduced professionals, and the lay public who attended in large numbers, to the latest developments in new techniques for self-discovery: aikido, gestalt, rolfing, autogenic training, bioenergetics, transactional analysis, sensory and body awareness, Zen meditation, Tibetan Buddhism, sensual massage, transpersonal workshops, biofeedback, psychosynthesis and much more.

Many seminal ideas and subjects got their first airing at Association for Humanistic Psychology forums, among them the now famous seminar on "Should a Professional Therapist Go to Bed with His Patient if Mutually Attracted?"

"It was an attempt," explains Eleanor Criswell, a California State College, Sonoma, psychology professor, "to bring certain things out in the open that are well known in the profession but seldom talked about. Actually, it was more or less engineered by a psychiatrist who had written a book on the subject which was being released that day.

"Many of our people—among them Albert Ellis, the famous sexologist and onetime firebrand—argued against the practice, warning that it could interfere with people getting well, totally disrupt the therapeutic situation and easily be exploitive on the part of the therapist."

Members of the audience—some women—wanted to know if the therapist would, with equal impartiality, sleep with an old and homely female patient or say, a male patient "who needed it."

"The press went wild," continues Criswell. "It was in every magazine and newspaper . . . People were aghast. But the next year, at their meeting in Hawaii, the American Psychological Association held a seminar on the same subject and it wasn't mentioned anywhere in the media."

This point about the trend-setting capacities of the Association for Humanistic Psychology is well taken. For years, since its founding in 1962, it has always held its convention in the same city as the American Psychological Association—only a few days before or after, so that psychologists who wished to attend both meetings could do so conveniently.

It was always a study in contrasts. The button-down academicians would file in, university-style, with decorum, and listen to formal papers formally delivered at a lecture.

"But," said one observer, "it was clear that, with each successive year, more and more of their colleagues turned up bearded and bra-less, and some even enrolled in the 'touchie-feelie' seminars run by that 'wild bunch'—the Association for Humanistic Psychology."

Now the "movement" seems to be settling down, its youthful exuberance curbed, if not peaked. At last year's Association for Humanistic Psychology convention in New Orleans, observers noted fewer "thrill seekers," fewer crowds and a growing trend toward the transcendental—and a mystical language.

Humanistic psychology is working a change in the traditional academic fare long taught to psychology students in the universities.

Words like love, consciousness, values, meaning and purpose are creeping back into the textbooks. For a long time, the only chapter on love was to be found in a standard text by Harry Harlow—and that was on love between primates.

Now human love comes under scrutiny. So do trust, altruism, self-esteem. One of psychology's leading learning theorists, Ernest R. Hilgard, is studying hypnosis at Stanford.

While animal experimentation is not necessarily on the wane, Claremont College Graduate School phased out its rat laboratory—in deference to new priorities.

Courses in the new psychology, including parapsychology, are turning up on campuses in all parts of the country. Experimental Johnston College at the University of Redlands bases an entire four-year course around new transpersonal psychology—which combines the humanistic with the "spiritual." Students use encounter at the beginning of each semester to decide on their course of study.

At Northern Illinois University, psychologist-educator Thomas Roberts uses an imagery technique much used in the new psychology called "fantasy journey" to instruct electric shop teacher trainees. He asks students to relax and begins, softly:

"Now imagine you are an electron in a wire . . . you are hopping, swirling, leaping, brushing around with other electrons, all pushing and

bumping against each other—rapidly, heatedly . . . now you are outside
the wire, feel the force, the pull and intensity of the electronic field . . .
now take a trip down an electric coil itself, feel yourself sliding, bumping, intertwining with other electrons in the rush of forces . . ."—and it
goes on.

"It's been very successful," Roberts says, "because people learn
better when they have the experience of something."

Symbolic visualization, twilight images and directed daydreams are
beginning to be used in classrooms, mind-dynamic and creativity workshops, the newer "spiritual" disciplines (once called "therapies") like
transpersonal psychology and psychosynthesis, and memory and hypnosis courses.

For centuries, of course, they have been part of many ancient systems of Eastern meditation, notably Tibetan Buddhism—all of which are
attracting growing numbers of people in the West, particularly among
students of the new psychology.

Psychology has always had an identity crisis.

As an outgrowth of philosophy and wanting to earn its spurs as a
"real" science, a young psychology needed the security of imitating
medicine and physics.

From medicine, it took the sickness model and studied pathology.

From early physics, it took the mechanistic idea of studying the
parts and not the whole.

It chopped behavior into segments like reaction time and worked
with worms, rats, dogs and apes that could be managed and controlled.

The results were often criticized—in the profession and out.

Ten years ago, writer-critic Gerald Sykes called psychology "a raw
ungainly science" and declared:

"We know less about ourselves than about any other portion of
society, and our lack of self-knowledge is now our most acute social
problem . . . I would like to know what the psychologists have done to
help us."

Now, the debate between the "new" psychology and the "old"
raises the same basic questions: What is science, what is psychology and
what should it be studying? Most crucial—what is man?

Neuropsychologist Robert Ornstein, author of the best-selling
"Psychology of Consciousness," threw out this battle cry to a UCLA
audience last year:

"Somehow, academic psychology got diverted from the study of
the most interesting areas and into the most trivial. It was a terrible
mistake but this kind of meeting marks the end of that kind of diversion.
We're here to turn the mainstream of psychology back to the time when

methods and techniques were devoted to the study of real phenomena such as mind and how people experience the world to the fullest."

Donald Hebb, though, speaking at a recent American Psychological Association convention in Montreal on "What Psychology Is All About," assailed misguided people "who want us to deal directly with the mystery of existence now. Some of this is simply antiscience . . . which we needn't bother with here. When someone thinks a science can be run that way, there is much to be said. Subjective science? There isn't such a thing."

Can psychology, in fact, be humanistic and scientific at the same time? A growing number of professionals are saying yes.

But since, in the "new psychology," man is being redefined, it may require a redefinition of scientific method.

The scientific method has always demanded "objectivity" (that the experimenter see impartially what is there), verifiability (that the experiments can be repeated by others) and predictability.

At issue, of course, is "objectivity." Humanistic psychologists demand that this term be reexamined and that the subjective be let back in—where they believe it has always been anyway.

They say that overwhelming evidence shows that we "choose" what we see or perceive as surely as we choose our words or a new pair of shoes.

What the humanists call for is a new science of ordinary and extraordinary subjective experience.

And, they say, it isn't so extraordinary after all—hypnosis has been studied scientifically for a century and a half.

Charles Tart of Davis proposes a new method. He calls it "specific science." In it, scientists do research by entering into the research area themselves. Instead of remaining outside and "objective," they go into states like meditation, hypnosis, sensory deprivation and other altered states of consciousness.

Then their collected reports can be tested against one another to verify the validity of the knowledge obtained.

This, he says, is not really different from the way science now works with normal consciousness to achieve consensus on certain observable data.

Tart's point is that all knowledge is basically experiential.

This is the belief of John Lilly—the M.D.-biophysicist, neurophysiologist-psychoanalyst who did the famous work with dolphins. He sees it as the best tradition of an older science. He quotes British biologist J. B. S. Haldane's advice to his students: "You will not understand what is necessary in the way of scientific control unless you are the first subject in your experiment."

In what is surely the most remarkable and little known scientific meeting of its kind in the world, a diverse group of psychologists, medical doctors, holy men, physicists, philosophers and anthropologists from everywhere converge on Council Grove, Kansas, once a year for a special conference.

It is cosponsored by the Association for Humanistic Psychology and the Menninger Foundation.

Its purpose? The study of experience involving an expansion or extension of consciousness beyond the usual ego boundaries and the limitation of time and space. It is by invitation only.

Some psychologists still feel that such areas as altered states of consciousness are off limits, off base and too far out.

But to Andrew Weil, M.D., author of "The Natural Mind," the desire to alter consciousness periodically is an innate, normal drive comparable to hunger or the sex drive. He believes it is visible in 3- and 4-year-olds when they whirl themselves into dizziness or squeeze each other around the chest until they lose their breath.

Some evidence for this seems to come from research on a part of the brain called the limbic system. Sensations which range from mild pleasure to intense joy or euphoria come from electrical stimulation of the limbic.

James Olds has found that hungry rats will give up on getting food if they have to cross an electric grid containing 60 microamperes of electricity, but to obtain this brain stimulation, they will cross grids charged with 450 microamperes.

To the behaviorists, the humanists are fuzzy-minded, romantic and unscientific—and are leading us to disaster with the "carrot" of freedom and no controls. Some behaviorists say they are the true humanists.

To the humanists, behaviorists, by and large, are scripting a "Clockwork Orange" future for mankind. Some admire behavior modification therapy and would like to see it adapted to humanistic goals —but (and it is a big but) with the control coming from the person himself.

Fortunately, the humanists overall show a talent for the self-awareness they preach.

Psychologist Richard Farson, for example, cautions that "peak experiences" may only have meaning in terms of valleys. "The fact that we can't always sustain such moments shouldn't make them invalid. We must learn to appreciate them while they last. Art and education also make life better—but, by the same token, make it more complicated and difficult."

In "Power and Innocence," Rollo May once wrote: "The Human Potential Movement has fallen heir to the form of innocence prevalent in

America, namely that we grow toward greater and greater moral perfection." He means, he explains, that the darker side of Man must be faced too, and sensitivity developed to both.

"A sense of wonder . . .," Maslow has said of happy, creative people, "like that of an unspoiled child . . ."

The children's story, 'The Wizard of Oz," tells how the Tin Woodman, the Cowardly Lion and the Scarecrow already have what they traveled so far to ask from the wizard–brains, courage and a heart. All the wizard could do for them was to make them aware that they already owned what they wanted so badly.

The Goals of

Psychotherapy

The goal of psychotherapy has been defined in different ways: Freud's psychotherapeutic ambition was to make the unconscious conscious; for Perls, psychotherapy's objective was learning "to wipe your own ass." Self-understanding, reducing distortions, improving relationships, becoming a person, getting along with others, living rationally, controlling anxiety, adjusting—all have been proposed as the kind of result that is available from a psychotherapeutic relationship.

Currently, there is confusion and overlap among the disciplines that attempt to provide a context for change in human behavior. Healing, development, and enlightenment were once thought to be the respective functions of medicine, education, and religion; but in the contemporary world, these functions have become intertwined and fused. As Naranjo notes in his paper in this section, there is a rediscovery of the "unity of ultimate concern" beyond the temporal purposes of psychotherapy, personal growth, and transformation. Yet, real differences remain in methods, objectives, and the change processes involved. Table 1 illustrates these differences.

In this diagram, psychotherapy is seen as a healing process that assists an individual in overcoming deficiencies. The primary deficiency of the person seeking psychotherapy is that his self has been defined for him by others—parents, family, and the culture and society into which he is born. This other-defined person is motivated by need (what Maslow termed deficiency motivation). The therapeutic process consists of ego-building, i.e., developing a personal sense of self so that the objectives of adjustment and socialization can be attained. The methods employed for this healing, focused on the individual, include the varieties of traditional psychotherapy—hospitalization, chemotherapy, directive and supportive psychotherapy, and psychoanalysis.

Personal growth is an educational and developmental process that enhances the ego of the individual so that movement toward full potential can occur. The person seeking personal growth is in the process of defining himself through a series of choices and decisions. The objectives of personal growth are self-actualization and liberation from social and cultural restraints. Personal growth methods are largely group focused; they include human relations training, encounter, Gestalt, sensory awareness and psychosynthesis.

Transformation, until recently, has been regarded as a spiritual process in which the individual surrenders his selfhood in order to achieve union with some ultimate. The person, surrendering himself, goes through a process of ego-destruction (the "death of self" and rebirth common to many religions) to achieve the objectives of union and salvation. The usual methods provided for personal transformation occur within support communities such as monasteries. Communal methods include Arica, Zen, Yoga, and Christian and Buddhist monasticism.

The blurring of distinctions between psychotherapy, personal growth, and spiritual transformation creates, as Naranjo indicates in his article, exciting possibilities for the psychotherapist and the person seeking to change.

The selections in this section provide a range of definitions of psychotherapeutic goals. Naranjo discusses reuniting the roles of teacher, priest, and medicine man in the person of the psychotherapist. He sees the goal of psychotherapy as a promise of "something more" if the risky leap into the unknown is taken.

For Hammer, psychotherapy's goal is the individual's union with the universe, through a process of self-communion. His article reflects the influence of Buddhist and Taoist views of reality; only when the suffering seeker perceives oneness beyond polarity and dualistic thinking does the journey to "home" begin.

Choice, faith, and authenticity are central concepts for Sidney Jourard, who describes psychotherapy as an invitation to become whole and authentic. Psychotherapy is not a technique or a process, but a way of being with another person. The psychotherapist's way of being involves a belief in the capacity for self-transcendance, and if that faith can be communicated, both therapist and patient can attain the freedom necessary to pursue ultimate goals.

Kopp suggests that psychotherapy may be nothing at all, but only a "humbug" in which suffering persons need to believe until they discover within themselves the sources of self-healing. Courage, perception, and the capacity to love cannot be bestowed by any wizard, but it seems useful for those seeking help to believe that wizards—or psychotherapists—can provide the necessary support and direction for transformation.

Humanistic psychotherapy seems to accept the definition provided by the Radical Therapist Collective: psychotherapy means change, not adjustment. These papers discuss the evolutionary personal change now believed possible as the result of a psychotherapeutic relationship.

Table 1.   A comparison of methods of personal change

	PSYCHOTHERAPY	PERSONAL GROWTH	TRANSFORMATION
Self	I am defined by others	I define who I am	I am defined by the Other
Motivation	Need	Choice	Surrender
Personal Goal	Adjustment	Self-Actualization	Union
Social Goal	Socialization	Liberation	Salvation
Process	Healing—Ego-Building	Development—Ego-Enhancement	Enlightenment—Ego-Reduction
Traditional Role of Helper	Physician	Teacher	Priest
Representative Method	Hospitalization Chemotherapy Psychoanalysis Directive Therapies Transactional Analysis	T-group Gestalt Therapy Encounter Sensory Awareness Psychosynthesis	Zen Yoga Arica Altered Consciousness Mysticism Monasticism
Focus	Individual	Group	Supportive Community

The Goals of Human Transformation

by Claudio Naranjo

The philosophers, logicians and doctors of law were drawn up at Court to examine Nasrudin. This was a serious case, because he had admitted going from village to village saying: "The so-called wise men are ignorant, irresolute and confused." He was charged with undermining the security of the State.

"You may speak first," said the King.

"Have paper and pens brought," said the Mulla.

Paper and pens were brought.

"Give some to each of the first seven savants."

They were distributed.

"Have them separately write an answer to this question: 'What is bread?'"

This was done.

The papers were handed to the King, who read them out:

The first said: "Bread is a food."

The second: "It is flour and water."

The third: "A gift of God."

The fourth: "Baked dough."

The fifth: "Changeable, according to how you mean 'bread.'"

The sixth: "A nutritious substance."

The seventh: "Nobody really knows."

"When they decide what bread is," said Nasrudin, "it will be possible for them to decide other things. For example, whether I am right or wrong. Can you entrust matters of assessment and judgment to people like this? Is it or is it not strange that they cannot agree about something which they eat each day, yet are unanimous that I am a heretic?"

From *The Exploits of the Incomparable Mulla Nasrudin* (23)

To but one goal are marching everywhere
All human beings, though they may seem to walk
Divergent paths; and that Goal is I.

From the *Bhagavad-Gita* (17)

Three institutions are overtly concerned with eliciting change or facilitating a change process in the minds and behavior of human beings: education, medicine, and religion. The nature of the change process that is the focus of each may at first glance seem quite specific to the institution: *development* being the province of education, *healing* that of medicine, and *salvation, liberation,* or *enlightenment* that of religion. Yet, the three were one in the past—when the shaman or primitive mystic was a medicine man, a wise man, a counselor, an initiator, and an artist. Today we seem to be rediscovering the unity of "ultimate concern" beyond the temporal purposes and the irrelevant concerns of education, psychiatry, and religion. Indeed, if we examine closely the nature of the separate quests for growth, sanity, and enlightenment, we may discover enough of a meeting ground among them to warrant the ambition of a unified science and art of human change. Since this book is in the nature of a contribution toward that goal and cuts across the different domains of endeavor that have given rise to the various ways of growth, we may do well to show some aspects of the commonality that exists among their aims. It is a commonality too often forgotten when we think of their specific means, fields of application, and terminologies.

THE GOAL OF EDUCATION

Let us first take the notion of development, the goal of education. Implicit in the art of education is the belief in a spontaneous growth process that may be influenced by environmental conditions. Just as the body needs nourishment and vitamins, exercise, and a certain amount of protection to survive and develop into what it can potentially become, the mind too needs its proper food, exercise, and care.

To become what? Here the discrepancies begin. If the answer is "what it can potentially become," we have a humanistic approach in the true sense of making man the measure: to each according to his individual goals and inclinations. Education becomes the task of giving each individual what he thirsts for, without any attempt to mold him into a pre-established pattern. Just as a gardener trusts that the shape of every plant will proceed from within if he only provides it with the optimum conditions, the educator believes in the innate goodness of man and sees himself as an aid to this intrinsic growth process.

The very word *education* contains the notion of a development of the person from within. The Latin *educare* derives from *educere*, "to extract or lead forth, to draw out something hidden or enclosed into the open." The conception implied in this etymology is that of the human being as engaged in a *growth process* that may be facilitated by the agency of others.

Needless to say, we are here speaking of an approach that probably cannot be found in pure form in reality, just as a perfect circle cannot be found outside the world of ideas. We can find it as a component of education in general though, and in some instances as its major component, as in A. S. Neill's *Summerhill* (14), in the Montessori approach (13), or in the example of Pestalozzi, who inspired so much of the educational re-evaluation of this century. The following lines of this Swiss educator are as explicit as any statement about an inner-directed growth process:

> Sound Education stands before me symbolized by a tree planted near fertilizing water. A little seed, which contains the design of the tree, its form and proportion, is placed in the soil. See how it germinates and expands into trunk, branches, leaves, flowers, and fruit! The whole tree is an uninterrupted chain of organic parts, the plan of which existed in its seed and root. Man is similar to the tree. In the newborn child are hidden those faculties which are to unfold during life. (16)

A belief in the self-regulation of the organism—including the psyche—has grown steadily in the psychology of the last three decades or so. The old view of man as an intrinsically amoral or evil being who needs to be brainwashed is being superseded by another that sees man as a self-actualizing being, and I believe that this view is flowing in part from psychology into the culture at large.

In the domain of religion the notion of an unfolding from within is found in every great tradition, though it is often obscured by the authoritarian structures (and rationalizations) of religious institutions. For instance, in Zen, we see the trust in the Buddha nature within each creature which in essence is no different from the Christian's vision of himself as a prodigal son of the Heavenly King, destined to return to His Kingdom. The difference in this case is principally one of emphasis, for the Christian notion has become a purely theoretical one, while in Mahayana Buddhism we find a living attitude of trust in the workings of the universe. How this type of attitude has generated specific ways of growth is something that we will have occasion to examine in other articles.

In contrast to the open-ended, humanistic view of man's development, seen as a fulfillment of man's inner trend, is any pre-established view of what man's end is, of where his unfolding leads, and of what his most desirable state of being is. The answers to these questions have been the concern of philosophers and prophets through the ages, and as Aldous Huxley has attempted to show in his *Perennial Philosophy* (8) their answers are not as different as might be expected. Beyond culture-bound notions of right and wrong, the wise ones of all lands throughout history seem to agree as to the existence of a *way* or *path* leading to man's fulfillment and the finding of his true place in the world, not according to a theoretical construction but as a realization. According to such views the development of a child is but a first stage in a long developmental process the end of which may well not be attained within an individual's lifetime.

Those who share this positive conception of man's destiny see the first stages of life as not only the natural time for the beginning of his evolution, but also as the time of his thwarting. In both religion and psychiatry we find, along with the exposition of ideals, a pervasive awareness that man's reality falls short of such ideals, and a lamentation that during his formative years of life a person not only fails to develop but is distorted by pressures in his environment.

The bearing of this perspective on a conception of human development is that, once we regard man as straying from his path because of his social conditioning, we can discriminate between two phases in the journey toward the desirable goal: the treading of the path and, before that, the process of finding it. The development of the child as it actually proceeds is thus seen as a thwarting of his true direction in the midst of a culturally disturbed environment. Consequently, a conversion will be necessary to reorient his life in view of the true path, a "death" to his outward nature, a renunciation or separation (as in Christ's "And a man's foes shall be they of his own household"), or an awakening. Such notions are inseparable from the mythical accounts in all religions of the fall of man, for the condition of fallen man—humanity—is that of "sin," "illusion," "sleep," "blindness," and his first aim is that of undoing his "fall."

Thus, the first stage in the attainment of spiritual fullness according to Taoism is to become a "true man"; only after this can man become a "universal man." In Sufism, too, we find the notion of two successive stages in a developmental process, the first of which is in the nature of reowning something that was forgotten or lost. The notion of "forgetting" a higher world is so important in Plato's philosophy that even the word he uses for "truth" (*a-letheia*) means no-forgetting. And in the poetic monument of Christianity, Dante's *Commedia*, two stages of attainment are depicted. In the first, man reaches "earthly paradise," his original abode. Here he is healed, and Dante says of himself:

> I came back from those holiest waters new, remade, reborn, like a sun-wakened tree that spreads new foliage to the spring dew in sweet freshness, healed of winter's scars; perfect, pure, and ready for the Stars. (3)

Beyond this, a man can still venture into "Paradise," a world of transcendence, where he experiences a unity with the cosmos as conceived of by religious thought.

Just as in religion we find that the ideas of a corrective and of a maturational process go hand in hand (the *via purgativa* and *via unitiva* of Christianity), in psychology too we find acknowledgment of a need for corrective work and of a developmental process that may take place when not unnaturally obstructed. In other words, psychiatry and psychology share with the religious view both the notion of a wrongness in the condition of average humanity and that of a developmental process that goes much beyond the school years. In the terms of dynamic psychology, the process of maturation has been arrested in childhood years and much of the psychotherapeutic process amounts to a liberation from childish fixations or blocks to growth. Furthermore, psychology has moved more and more in the direction of seeing an aim beyond that of healing. Beyond the correction of a wrongness the psychotherapist has come to recognize the existence of a void that needs to be filled, an urge for more that his patient wants to satisfy and that cannot be fulfilled by material ambitions, by his family life, or his work. The answers to such a challenge vary, so that Frankl speaks of search for meaning and logotherapy, Jung speaks of analytical psychology as the modern process of initiation, and Maslow points out that the peak-experiences most people have during their lifetimes indicate the possibility of a more satisfactory way of being which is impeded by unfulfilled basic needs such as those for safety, love, and respect. Healing, according to these authors, falls short of making a man complete or mature in more than a conventional sense; its nature is that of liberating him to his essential concern which is precisely that of further growth. The religious notions of a *way* or *path, Tao,* and *dharma* find an echo in some contemporary psychological formulations such as that of the self-actualizing drive of the organism (Goldstein) or Jung's description of the individuation process.

As the history of education amply shows, the danger of an educational approach that has in view a preconceived notion of man's goal is in its potential rigidity. In this, as in other fields, a truth that is learned and repeated is not a truth any more but a mechanical act. A statement of man's desirable goal or path may very well be accurate and yet there is a difference between intellectual statements and the understanding that can lead to the application of a truth. Without such understanding, all systems can become ways of thwarting the development that they want to foster.

How much of what we call education is only a pale shadow of activities that had a purpose long ago? The main trait of contemporary education, for example, is its emphasis upon amassing information. This trend received its impetus in the Renaissance, when men turned to a forgotten antiquity in their thirst for wisdom, and the acquisition of wisdom came to be seen as inseparable from understanding the writings of Greek and Latin classics. At first there was sense in this expression of humanism, and we may grant Erasmus that he was still thinking functionally when he designed a method of teaching that would make the child into a Greek and Latin scholar and a pious man. He was no Ciceronian: Latin was to be taught so as to be of use. And, most important of all, he saw that education would have to follow nature to achieve the best results.

But it seems to be a law of history that every good becomes an ought, every God an idol, every meaningful practice an empty ritual. It was perhaps the influence of Sturm, above that of any other single individual, that was responsible for the transition leading from true humanism to the gentleman's polite tipping of the hat. As the tutor of Queen Elizabeth and first great headmaster, he has been regarded as the introducer of "scholarship" into the schools. The means that once served the purpose of human development came more and more to be pursued as ends in themselves; what were tools of certain tasks became objects of worship; and scholarship turned into an imitation derived from what once was learning as a means to deeper understanding. As the contents of scholarship changed with the years, science and history took the place of the classics, but the attitude remained the same: learning things had become the goal of education and taken the place of self-understanding. Learning things for what? The question was never pursued too far; nor was it demonstrated that this was "to train the mind" or "prepare for life."

We could draw a parallel here between the two approaches to human development and parental love, as described by Erich Fromm (5). The unconditional mother's love finds its parallel in the first (inner-directed) approach, trusting and unconditional; the demanding father's love corresponds to the second (outer-directed) approach, which guides the individual toward the highest ideals. The balance between these two approaches is always an inescapable issue in the educational process. It is a balance between the individual and tradition, the unknown and the known, creativity and the wisdom of the ages.

There is still a third "answer" to the goal of human development, more implicit than explicit, even though, for this very reason, it is perhaps the most powerful. The goal of this third approach to education is neither that chosen by the individual nor that inspired by tradition, but consists in the adaptation of the individual to the habitual (or modal) way of being in a given culture. Just as the humanistic attitude trusts and encourages the development of feelings and the idealistic approach is predominantly intellectual, this third attitude may be regarded as predominantly mechanistic. Not only does a child mechanically imitate what he sees and hears, from language and gait to personality styles, but much of his socialization process consists of the positive and negative reinforcement that he receives in terms of what adults like. Behind each command or prohibition there is an implicit statement of "this is right" which most often does not stem from thinking or decision but from having been exposed to the same dogma in earlier years. Thus, it is right to use the fingers in eating in India but not in England; it is right for an Eskimo to share his wife on occasion but not for a Jivaro Indian; it is right to be future-oriented in the United States today but not in present-oriented areas of Mexico or tradition-oriented circles in Japan. Regardless of what may actually be right in terms of human needs, there are societal notions of what is right, the obvious rationalization of a process of conditioning. The source of the cultural traits that are thus transmitted may be in an ideal that became automatized, in economic circumstances, or in the emotional needs of parents. A child's demand for affection, for instance, may give rise to guilt feelings in parents who are falling short of filling his need and cause them to say that it is not nice to cry, that grownups do not complain, etc., and thus contribute to the perpetuation of traits of both independence and affectlessness.

The pervasiveness of the socialization process cannot fail to color the educational endeavor, and it may even become a goal of education to produce the kind of "people that the country needs." Yet this molding process should not be really considered as an approach—adequate or not—to development, but rather as an "impurity" in the approach itself. Conditioning does not posit a growth process or anything like a "human nature." Its goals are those of convenience, its ways may be ways of change but are not ways of growth. This does not exclude that principles of conditioning may be used in the service of human development, but such use generally takes the form of a deconditioning ("desensitization") that allows for increased flexibility and choice, and a reinforcement of the natural developmental process until it is experienced as self-rewarding. This is how behaviorists currently interpret psychoanalysis and client-centered therapy, in which the therapist encourages the act of self-disclosure and expression.

Though the notion of development is the concern of education more than of any other institution, it is also a core concept in religion, when we reach for the true significance of this term, and in psychiatry and psychology.

THE GOAL OF PSYCHOTHERAPY

The idea of psychological disease was at first a purely descriptive one, defined by the presence of certain symptoms. Later it became a statistical notion according to which "neuroticism" or even "psychoticism" are present in some degree in everybody. Furthermore, psychological disease became divorced from its external signs or symptoms. Thus in dynamic psychology a neurotic personality or action is judged from the point of view of its motivation rather than from its behavioral reality or even the individual's subjective state of well-being or discomfort at the moment. Also, in reaching for a deeper understanding of neuroticism, psychiatry has become more and more concerned with matters such as authenticity and estrangement, the real self, responsibility, and other issues that were formerly the concern of philosophy or religions. In fact, what psychiatry is presently doing is not just curing physical or emotional symptoms of psychic origin, but helping the individual to find the good life for himself—as philosophy and religion had been doing for centuries, prior to becoming riddled with abstract speculation and authoritarian dogma.

Just as psychiatry today tends to see symptoms as the outer manifestation of the failure to meet life with the right attitude, religions at the time of their greatest aliveness have seen man's behavioral and moral shortcomings as outward expressions of his original sin which is not essentially a moral but a spiritual mistake and is a disease, a source of suffering. *Salvation* comes from the Latin *salvare* which has the same root as the word *salus* (health, safety); in French too, *salut* (salvation) comes from the Latin *salus*. The same connection is seen in the German *heilig* (holy, saintly) and *heilen* (to heal). In the Old Testament and in rabbinical literature, sin is frequently described as folly or madness. In Buddhism, too, the question is one of deliverance from the suffering that man experiences as a result of his ignorance, a condition which is indifferently called sin or disease.

Regardless of whether we accept the formulations of psychiatry or of religion, one thing is clear: the recognition of the interrelatedness of physical and moral health or illness. Psychiatry today stresses the inability to cope with certain moral issues (i.e., responsibility, perception of values, genuineness) as the sources of psychological or psychosomatic symptoms. And both psychology and religion, in different terms, have also pointed out the cognitive issues at the root of the moral ones: understanding, consciousness, awareness of real attunement to the truth.

However, there is apparently no consensus among present-day psychiatrists or psychologists as to the boundaries of "mental disease" or its defining criteria. The concepts of different schools still range from the strictly symptomatic one of *dis-ease* to those of humanistic or dynamic psychology. It is to the former, restricted sense of disease and sanity that Thomas Merton is referring in the following paragraphs from "A Devout Meditation in Memory of Adolph Eichmann."

One of the most disturbing facts that came out in the Eichmann trial was that a psychiatrist examined him and pronounced him *perfectly sane.* I do not doubt it at all, and that is precisely why I find it disturbing.

If all the Nazis had been psychotics, as some of their leaders probably were, their appalling cruelty would have been in some sense easier to understand. It is much worse to consider this calm, "well-balanced," unperturbed official conscientiously going about his desk work, his administrative job which happened to be the supervision of mass murder. He was thoughtful, orderly, unimaginative. He had a profound respect for system, law and order. He was obedient, loyal, a faithful officer of a great state. He served his government very well.

He was not bothered much by guilt. I have not heard that he developed any psychosomatic illnesses. Apparently, he slept well. He had a good appetite, or so it seems.

And later in the same essay:

I am beginning to realize that "sanity" is no longer a value or an end in itself. The "sanity" of modern man is about as useful to him as the huge bulk and muscles of the dinosaur. If he were a little less sane, a little more doubtful, a little more aware of his absurdities and contradictions, perhaps there might be a possibility of his survival. But if he is sane, too sane . . . perhaps we must say that in a society like ours the worst insanity is totally without anxiety, totally "sane." (12)

Contrast the view of mental disease in the above quotation to that presented in the following passage by a psychiatrist:

. . . Let us begin with a very extreme case. Let us take, for instance, one of advanced senile dementia. Why does everyone agree to regard such a person as diseased? What first strikes us is the loss of his essential psychological faculties; he cannot do what others can do; he cannot, for instance, orient himself in time or space, attend to his physiologic needs, control his sphincters, and so on. Yet it is clear that such an individual is not considered to be sick merely because he cannot fulfill such functions, for if this were the case, an infant would have to be considered just as diseased. What is pathological here is not his inability but inability where we would expect ability.

After considering other instances, this author concludes that:

We always evaluate an individual's psychological activity in terms of his optimal potential, and do not regard as mentally ill he who behaves in this or that manner, but him whose optimal potential for performance is altered from within. In other words, his potentialities are prevented their full unfolding because they are hindered from within and in spite of himself, so that they are thwarted and deviated from full expression. (1)

According to such a view the notion of mental disease becomes correlative to our understanding of man's potential, for only in terms of the latter can we say whether an individual is falling short of his optimal functioning. So at this point a medical conception becomes inseparable from a conception of man's nature, man's purpose and destiny, and particularly the direction and goal of his development. In fact, the issues of health and development, the concerns of medicine and education, become one.

It would seem that the existential and ever-present foundation of the quests for both healing and enlightenment is in a dissatisfaction on the part of a fraction of humanity, a thirst that cannot be quenched by objective achievements. A traditional psychiatrist would look upon such an urge as abnormal and think, "Here is a person who cannot enjoy the given and is therefore unsatisfied. He must be cured of his inability to enjoy to the fullest." From the religious, spiritual, or esoteric point of view, the same person may be regarded instead as one who is no more sick (or removed from God, divided from his deeper self, etc.) than average humanity, but who has not become anesthetized to his suffering. Just as physical pain signals a physical damage, psychological distress may be taken as the functional signal of a psychological wrongness, and many a neurotic may be simply more awake to the problem than a completely automatized, "adjusted" human being.

The individual, too, may interpret his own urge according to different alternatives presented by the culture and feel, for instance:

"I lack something, I feel unfulfilled, empty; I should study, acquire a wider culture and understanding of things, or travel, and then I would feel satisfied."

"I lack something, my life is not rich enough; I know the answer is in love. I have not found somebody to whom I can give all my love, and who loves me. Warmth and caring is what is missing from life."

"I lack something, I feel unfulfilled. Nothing that I do or acquire will give me the sense of fulfillment that I seek; this I know from experience. The answer lies in myself. I am very far from God. I have been neglecting the inner quest, forgetting that this is what I really want."

"I lack something. No matter what I do, I feel unfulfilled and empty. Is this what psychiatrists call depression, or perhaps neurasthenia, or simple schizophrenia? I should do something about myself, and go into treatment."

The last two answers are similar, in that the dissatisfaction is interpreted as a sign of the pursuit of inner change, but they differ in that one is cast in religious language and the other in medical or psychological terms. The difference between the religious and the psychological interpretations of dissatisfaction is not that between a theistic and an atheistic view, as typically evidenced by atheistic religions (such as Buddhism or Taoism). The difference lies more in the relative stress on the ideas of lack and wrongness. The urge directing the quest for enlightenment is interpreted as a lack of fulfillment, a separation from God or higher faculties, and the process of attainment is frequently depicted as a reaching of another shore, crossing a bridge, climbing up to the heights or down into an abyss. Man's sickness and sins are the outcome of his lack: that of being removed from the presence of God, which he must become conscious of and repair in becoming one with God. Though the concept of disease is that of a wrongness in the organism or mind, in the psychological view, too, man's sickness and its symptoms are the outcome of a lack which different writers have presented in different ways: a lack of consciousness, of self-love, of contact with the real self, etc. Such a lack stems from a "wrong" pattern of psychological functioning that resists being altered and sets up defenses. Whatever language we choose to describe the inner events that are the issue of both psychiatry and religion, we can see that wrongness (illness) and deficit (de-ficiency) are interdependent. For the emptiness to be truly filled, it is necessary first of all that it be acknowledged as emptiness by removing defenses and substitute contents, much as the Zen worker Nan-in indicated to the European university professor who visited him at the turn of the century:

> Nan-in served tea. He poured his visitor's cup full, and then kept on pouring.
> The professor watched the overflow until he no longer could restrain himself. "It is overfull. No more will go in!"
> "Like this cup," Nan-in said, "you are full of your own opinions and speculations. How can I show you Zen unless you first empty your cup?" (18)

This may be enough to indicate that the concept of mental health, just as the idea of development, is only one element in the understanding of a process of human change that is the common concern of education, medicine, and religion. And just as the practical goal of education represents a compromise between a nurturing of the individual's development and the demands of society, so psychiatry and psychology, too, serve two masters: the individual patient, and the local culture. Also, as in the domain of education we can contrast the view of a development from within and the belief in such a thing as human nature with another view of cultural relativity in which the good can only be defined in terms of the needs of society, so, too, in psychiatry we can discern a developmental view that stresses some constancies in human nature and self-actualization, and another that stresses cultural relativity and the goal of adaptation. It is undoubtedly the latter that has led many humanists and those concerned with the spiritual endeavor to question the relevance of psychiatry to their own interests, and has put the term *head shrinker* in the mouth of many a common man.

THE GOAL OF RELIGION

Let us now turn our attention to the nature of the religious quest associated with expressions such as salvation, deliverance, enlightenment, union with or rejection of God.

As in psychiatry and in education, we find here many "schools" which differ from one another not so much in their essential goal, but in their symbolic and conceptual language; in the admixture of elements, other than the concern for whatever man's ultimate concern may be, into the complex phenomenon called religion. Even more than in the domains of education and psychotherapy, perhaps, the invisible power of socialization has seized religion, using it for its own end of molding people into conformity. It is because of the local ethical and dogmatic difference in religion that some prefer to speak of mysticism when referring to the common core of religious experience out of which the different religions have sprung. Others speak of mysticism in connection with a particular modality of religious experience and development and use the word *esoteric* in reference to "the transcendent unity of religions" (21). Furthermore, within some religions such as Taoism or Buddhism an esoteric or inner circle is found where the essence of religion and man are the issue, and there are other esoteric groups (of varying authoritativeness and quality) that are not bound to any single "religion."

According to the esoteric tradition, many world religions have originated from a single stream of transmission of living understanding in which their leaders were initiated, a stream which remains independent of each of them and is still alive today.[1]

Whatever the historical truth concerning the idea of a single stream of teaching behind the diversity of religions, we may still accept the existence of a single stream of meaning and intent beyond the diversity of religious forms. The deterioration of such forms is feelingly expressed in a tale by Ahmed-el-Bedavi (died 1275) who, "according to dervish lore, was accused by Moslems of preaching Christianity but repudiated by Christians because he refused to accept later Christian dogma literally." This is how the story begins, according to the version of Idries Shah:

> Once upon a time a man was contemplating the ways in which Nature operates, and he discovered, because of his concentration and application, how fire could be made.

---

[1]This idea runs through the books of Guénon (7), for instance, or from a journalistic point of view, through the pages of Pauwels' *The Dawn of Magic* (15). Interesting documents concerning a surviving and ever renewed science of man are Lefort's *The Teachers of Gurdjieff* (11), and Roy Davidson's compilation *Documents on Contemporary Dervish Communities* (4).

This man was called Nour. He decided to travel from one community to another, showing people his discovery.

Nour passed the secret to many groups of people. Some took advantage of the knowledge. Others drove him away, thinking that he must be dangerous, before they had time to understand how valuable this discovery could be to them. Finally, a tribe before which he demonstrated became so panic-stricken that they set about him and killed him, being convinced that he was a demon.

Centuries passed. The first tribe which had learned about fire reserved the secret for their priests, who remained in affluence and power while the people froze.

The second tribe forgot the art and worshipped instead the instruments. The third worshipped a likeness of Nour himself, because it was he who had taught them. The fourth retained the story of the making of fire in their legends: some believed them, others did not. The fifth community really did use fire, and this enabled them to be warmed, to cook their food, and to manufacture all kinds of useful articles.

After many, many years, a wise man and a small band of his disciples were travelling through the lands of these tribes. The disciples were amazed at the variety of rituals which they encountered; and one and all said to their teacher: "But all these procedures *are* in fact related to the making of fire, nothing else. We should reform these people!"

The teacher said: "Very well, then. We shall restart our journey. By the end of it, those who survive will know the real problems and how to approach them."

The tale goes on telling the failure of this attempt, tribe after tribe, until the wise man and his disciples returned to the lands "where fire-making was a commonplace and where other preoccupations faced them." There the master said to his disciples:

You have to learn how to teach, for man does not want to be taught. First of all, you will have to teach people how to learn. And before that you have to teach them that there is still something to be learned. They imagine that they are ready to learn. But they want to learn what they *imagine* is to be learned, not what they have first to learn. When you have learned all this, then you can devise a way to teach. Knowledge without special capacity to teach is not the same as knowledge and capacity. (22)

If "fire-making" is what we are speaking of when we talk of growth-healing-enlightenment, the fable is telling us that many of the concerns of humanity are inspired by it and yet they only mimic or substitute the real accomplishment. We hope that our survey of ways of growth may be as free as possible of such idolatries.

Some of the religious concepts associated with the goal of the human quest are implicitly negative: salvation is salvation from sin, liberation and deliverance imply something to be liberated from, and nirvana (extinction) implies that there is an illusion to be extinguished.

Other concepts are positive, like enlightenment, awakening, or union (with the divine). Yet the positive and negative aspects are interdependent. Thus, enlightenment, according to Buddhism, puts an end to the "three evil roots"—delusion, craving, and hate. Sin, in Judaism, is a rebellion in the face of God's Law (man's duty toward the Law being inherent in the doctrine of God's kingship). And God's Law, behind the six hundred thirteen Commandments delivered unto Moses on Mount Sinai, is one: "Seek the Lord and Live."[2] It would be futile to attempt to define in a few paragraphs the ineffable goal of religious endeavor, but we can probably agree that in its negative aspects it is closely related to the notions of healing and outgrowing, while in its positive aspect it is in the nature of a growth or evolution of the mind. Indeed, the symbolism of generation and development pervades all religious thought; rebirth, emanation, and the tree of life are only a few examples of the central role held by these symbols.

On the whole, the West has laid greater stress upon the negative formulation of the religious goal—salvation—and, accordingly, Christianity has emphasized the *via purgativa,* purification, and the experience of repentance. The East, on the other hand, has emphasized more the positive aspect of the religious goal—living in the Tao—in attunement with one's nature and one's true place in the cosmos. Enlightenment and full awakening of the intrinsic Buddha nature are concepts of the *via unitiva* rather than of the *via purgativa.* Yet both aspects, at the conceptual as well as the practical level, are really two sides of the same coin.

A realization of the commonality between psychotherapy and religion has had to await a deepening in the understanding of emotional disorders and a "de-dogmatization" in the grasp of religious phenomena. Increased communication with the East has been a factor in the process, as well as the work of those who have expounded the essential unity of religions.[3] We are taking for granted the existence of a meeting ground and a common direction of intent among the different formulations though not necessarily implying an identity in the goal, for the ultimate goal of spiritual regeneration—"universal" or "cosmic" man—seems more ambitious than the goal of the minor mysteries and of psychotherapy. And we shall not be mainly concerned with the convergence of theoretical formulations in various streams of thought but with that of the practical ways to the unfolding of man which have

---

[2]For a commentary of this, see the chapter entitled "The Torah in Its Aspect of Law" in Schechter's *Aspects of Rabbinic Theology* (20).

[3]See Bhagavan Das, for instance, and the works of Mircea Eliade. For discussions of the relevance of Eastern disciplines to psychotherapy, the interested reader might refer to Watts (24), Boss (2), Fromm (6), Jacobs (9), Jung (10), and Zimmer (25).

originated within the different spiritual disciplines, therapeutic schools, and educational approaches.

We have seen both psychotherapy and education as composites of two conflicting attempts, one toward socialization and the other toward liberation of the individual from the ills of his culture. Similarly, in religion we find a discrepancy between the One Quest and the attempt to indoctrinate people into a given cultural pattern—through fear of hell, hope of heaven.

How far "religion" today is from fulfilling the function it purports to serve may be seen in the fact that, despite the convergence of its goals with those of psychotherapy, no piece of psychological research has yet established a positive correlation between "religiosity" and well-being, humanitarianism, or sanity (19). In view of this, we might consider not using the term "religion" at all for what is commonly regarded as a religious issue, or else restrict "religion" to the degraded cultural forms of the phenomenon and not use it when speaking of the quest for growth. Yet, if we were to do this we should also, for consistency, do the same with the terms "education" and "psychotherapy."

To what extent is our education, for instance, a case of *educere*, a "leading forth" or drawing out?

All three—education, psychotherapy, and religion—at the same time pursue and are hostile to the One Goal of human growth. To the extent that they serve the One God they are one; to the extent that they serve Caesar, they are specialties. Yet, paradoxically, Caesar has the best intentions. If we examine his motives, we find that he also serves God, only with little understanding. His decisions are based upon insights that once constituted wisdom but fail to apply any longer; his institutions are the echo of others that once served their true function.

According to one story, when God created the world and saw that it was good, Satan joined him in his appreciation, and exclaimed, as he gazed from one wonder to another, "It is good! It is good! Let us make it an institution!"

REFERENCES

1. Blanco, Ignacio Matte, "El Concepto de Enfermedad Mental," in *El Concepto de Enfermedad*. Santiago de Chile: Ediciones de la Universidad de Chile, 1963.

2. Boss, Bedard, *A Psychiatrist Discovers India*. Chester Springs, Pa.: Dufour, 1965.

3. Dante, *The Divine Comedy, Purgatorio* (John Ciardi, Trans.), canto XXXIII, 142-46. New York: Appleton-Century-Crofts, 1971.

4. Davidson, Roy W., *Documents on Contemporary Dervish Communities*. London: Hoopoe, 1966.

5. Fromm, Erich, *The Art of Loving: An Enquiry into the Nature of Love*. New York: Harper and Brothers, 1956.

6. Fromm, Erich, Suzuki, Daisetz T., and de Martino, R., *Zen Buddhism and Psychoanalysis*. New York: Grove Press, 1963.

7. Guénon, René, *Man and His Becoming According to the Vendanta* (Richard C. Nicholson, Trans.). London: Luzac & Co., 1945.

8. Huxley, Aldous, *The Perennial Philosophy*. London: Chatto & Windus, 1950.

9. Jacobs, H., *Western Psychotherapy and Hindu Sadhana: A Contribution to Comparative Studies in Psychology and Metaphysics*. London: Allen and Unwin, 1961.

10. Jung, Carl G., Psychological Commentary to *The Tibetan Book of the Dead*, by W. Y. Evans-Wentz (Ed.). New York: Oxford University Press, 1957.

11. Lefort, Rafael, *The Teachers of Gurdjieff*. London: Gollancz, 1966.

12. Merton, Thomas, *Raids on the Unspeakable*. New York: New Directions, 1964.

13. Montessori, Maria, *The Absorbent Mind*. Madras: Adyar, 1949.

14. Neill, A. S., *Summerhill: A Radical Approach to Child Rearing*. New York: Hart, 1963.

15. Pauwels, Louis, and Bergier, Jacques, *The Dawn of Magic*. London: Anthony Gibbs & Phillips, 1963. Published in paperback edition under the title *The Morning of the Magicians* (New York: Avon Books, 1968).

16. Pestalozzi, Johann H., "Address on Birthday, 1818." Quoted in the *Encyclopedia of Religion and Ethics* (James Hastings, Ed., s.v. "education"). New York: Charles Scribner's Sons, 1908-27.

17. Prabhavananda, Swami, and Isherwood, Christopher (Trans.), *The Song of God, Bhagavad-Gita*. London: Phoenix, 1953.

18. Reps, Paul (Ed.), *Zen Flesh, Zen Bones: A Collection of Zen and Pre-Zen Writings*. New York: Doubleday & Co., 1961.

19. Sauna, Victor D., "Religion, Mental Health and Personality: A Review of Empirical Studies," *American Journal of Psychiatry*, 1969, *125*: 1203-1213.

20. Schechter, Solomon, *Aspects of Rabbinic Theology: Major Concepts of the Talmud*. New York: Schocken Books, 1961.

21. Schuon, Frithjof, *The Transcendent Unity of Religions*. London: Faber and Faber, 1953.

22. Shah, Indries, *Tales of the Dervishes: Teaching-Stories of the Sufi Masters over the Past Thousand Years*. London: Jonathan Cape, 1967.

23. Shah, Indries, *The Exploits of the Incomparable Mulla Nasrudin*. New York: Simon & Schuster, 1966.

24. Watts, Alan, *Psychotherapy East and West*. New York: Pantheon Books, 1961.

25. Zimmer, Heinrich, "On the Significance of the Indian Tantric Yoga," *Papers from the Eranos Yearbooks: Spiritual Disciplines*, Bollingen Series XXX, No. 4. New York: Pantheon Books, 1960.

The Essence of Personal and Transpersonal Psychotherapy

by Max Hammer

Sail forth, steer for the deep waters only . . .
I with thee and thou with me.

Walt Whitman

Through the influence of Eastern philosophy upon Western psychotherapy, as expounded by writers such as Watts (1961), Assagioli (1965), Maslow (1969) and more recently by this writer (Hammer, 1971, 1972, a & b), the interest of psychotherapists in the *Transpersonal* or *Transcendent* aspects of human consciousness has been increasing enormously, and one function of this paper is to help provide the reader with a more basic realization of the nature of the Transpersonal. However, what has been less recognized and understood, and what this paper also seeks to demonstrate, is that the process which most expeditiously leads to the awakening of consciousness to its *Transpersonal* or *Transcendent* essence is also the *same process* which most expeditiously leads to the transcendence of personal psychopathology. This growth process is what is here referred to as "Transpersonal Psychotherapy." Transpersonal psychotherapy is not so much a technique for doing psychotherapy as much as it represents the essential thread that underlies all psychological growth and therapeutic effect whenever they occur.

Transpersonal psychotherapy concerns itself, ultimately, with helping consciousness transcend its identification with the various limiting and relative self-defined personal labels, concepts or images which comprise the apparent and illusional ego and awaken to itself, in what is referred to as the Transpersonal Awakening experience, as the real

Reprinted from *Psychotherapy: Theory, Research and Practice*, 1974, *11*(3), 202-210. Used with permission of author and publisher.

"I-Principle" or "Transpersonal Self," which is what Consciousness is when It is in Its most essential and natural condition of being a perfect Unity, i.e., an unlabeled, indivisible, unbounded Whole which is not a sum of labels or parts but an absence of parts. The Transpersonal may also be alluded to in other ways as well by saying that It is that absolute Truth, which is the perfect Silence of pure Consciousness, which serves as the essential background, support, or substance, which composes and from which arises all personal forms and objectifications of consciousness, such as thoughts and feelings, and which underlies all of the various states of consciousness, such as wake, dream and deep sleep; It is that pure Subjectivity or most subjective Subject which is beyond all subject-object duality and relativity; It is that true and intrinsic nature of Consciousness which comprises, as a unity, the triune of absolute Peace-Love-Joy, (which shall here be subsumed under the single unifying term of "Bliss") and from which source arises their corresponding equivalents on the relative, objective, or personal plane of consciousness in the form of sensations of calm, eroticism, and elation or pleasure.

Because Transpersonal Consciousness is pure subjectivity and cannot be objectified or made into some-thing known by some more subjective subject or knower, the terms used above in the discussion of the nature of the Transpersonal are meant only to focalize psychological vision to point in Its direction and are in no way meant to suggest that the indefinable Reality pointed to, from different points of views, through the words and labels, is something which can be limited and grasped cognitively or conceptually, for It clearly cannot. In truth, nothing at all can be said or known about that Reality. Only labels can be known or experienced and the Transpersonal cannot be objectified or labeled. It is for that reason that those Masters, in whom Consciousness has become fully Awakened, when asked about the nature of the Transpersonal, quite often "respond" only with their own Silence of Consciousness and do not offer any verbal response at all, which is the only really correct "reply." For the same reason the reader must understand that the Transpersonal is not something which can be reduced to a feeling and can be experienced or known in the conventional sense of the term "to experience" which means as the dualistic and relative subject standing outside of some-thing labeled and objectified. There is another form of "knowing," which is by *being* that Reality, i.e., by being one with, or in unity or identity with that Reality in its self-luminous state. That which is self-luminous does not require the help of anything else in order to be known. This is the only way the Transpersonal can be "known." It is only through one's own direct realization of this Silence or Bliss Consciousness that brings a permanent end to the false identification by consciousness with the personal ego.

There are two fundamental aspects to the Transpersonal Awakening which help to explain how It leads consciousness to the complete surrendering and transcending of its identification with the personal ego. One basic aspect of Transpersonal Awakening is the direct realization that the "all" of diversity is not a reality, as such, but has only apparent and illusional existence and is underlied [sic], as its essential substance, by the one Reality which is the Unity of pure Consciousness. There is the direct realization that objects, as such, are never really directly related to or known, but rather it is only the *knowledge* of objects, as it takes place within consciousness, that is ever experienced or known. Therefore all objects are essentially only objectifications of, and reducable to, pure Consciousness, the one and only Reality. In other words, what is known is not essentially different from the process of knowing or awareness of the known, and knowing is not essentially different from the knower, so that one realizes that the world is, essentially, the knower himself or pure Consciousness and so all is One. Therefore, all objectivity and diversity is realized as being merely a thought-form.

The capacity to recognize and experience what is referred to as the duality of the self and the world depends upon labels. Both are essentially only objectifications of the perfect Unity of pure Consciousness and gain apparent existence only through the superimposition of labels upon that one Reality. With the application and experience of a label both the external world and the sense of self arise simultaneously as relative and mutually interdependent realities with the world serving as the object and the personal self as its subject. If one or the other of these mutually interdependent relative realities drops out then the other also drops out.

There are actually three basic ways in which the ego or sense of self tries to affirm its illusional personal existence. The first, as discussed above, is as a *subject,* in its role as the thinker, perceiver, doer, knower or experiencer of its relative labeled experiences, which include not only the experiences of the world but also of its own experiential and conceptualized self. The second is as an *object:* by constructing and identifying itself as being some labeled and objectified physical, experiential or conceptual self, it relates to the world and itself as that object and seeks to absolutely affirm, enhance and protect the particular objectified self through the validating or affirming responses of others. The third basic means by which the personal sense of self tries to affirm itself is through its identification of itself with desire or the *will* and its potency or capacity to control or influence what it puts itself on the line to influence. The operations and yearnings of egoistic consciousness will be discussed in more detail throughout this article, because, only by a complete under-standing of the nature and function of the ego, can its relative and illusory nature be realized, which ultimately enables consciousness to come to dis-identify from all of the ego's many manifestations and thereby transcend it and awaken to its own Transpersonal nature.

Another basic aspect of Transpersonal Awakening involves the di-rect realization that Consciousness is already what egoistic desire seeks to fulfill through its pursuit of various objects. Regardless of what ob-jects the ego desires and pursues, it is ultimately for their capacity to yield a sense of peace or joy that the object is desired. Consciousness is, intrinsically, that absolute Peace and Joy already when it is Transper-sonal, which it is when it is totally free of egoistic desire. Desire only takes consciousness away from its realization of itself as Paradise or Bliss. Thus, a real and lasting sense of gratification and fulfillment can never come from any desired object. The only true fulfillment of desire is the ending of desire.

Thus, Transpersonal psychotherapy recognizes that the most basic yearning of personal consciousness is to discover the ultimate answer to the question, "Who am I?," not in the relative or egoistic plane in terms of an objectified personal identity, which, because of its relativity, is never real, but rather in the most subjective, essential or Absolute sense. The thwarting or frustration of this most basic of all psychological yearn-ings is the basis for the development of all forms of psychopathology. Psychopathology begins with the rejection of the unity of consciousness for which is substituted the identification by consciousness with the various labels or fragments that comprise the dualistic psychological ego. Duality of consciousness arises in man because he is not content just to *be* himself, he wants to *know* himself so as to be able to assuage his fear that he is truly a no-thing void. Man, being essentially a unity of consciousness or pure subjective consciousness, cannot make an object of himself as he truly is and therefore cannot really experience himself. So man proceeds to make himself an object or some-thing known through the identification, by his consciousness, with the various labels by which he defines himself. By objectifying and experiencing these labels of himself, he then believes that he has created a self and is now able to experience himself as being both this objectified self as well as the subject or experiencer of those objectified labels. This is, essentially, what is meant by the dualization of consciousness.

When consciousness becomes identified not only as being the self which is the experiential reality (e.g., emotions, feelings, desires, im-pulses) that arises from moment to moment in consciousness but it also identifies itself as being the self which is the observer, judger, or censor of that feeling from the standpoint of some apparently fixed and conceptualized or idealized entity—that is the beginning and essence of duality and the pathological process.

The essence of Transpersonal psychotherapy involves helping the patient learn to live in the desireless state of Being or Unity of Consciousness which means making no identification of self with any labeled thing, but rather centering oneself between all pairs of relative opposites such as strong-weak, worthy-worthless, male-female. This puts an end to the dualistic contradiction of making consciousness both a subject and object and also puts an end to the egoistic drives for an absolute sense of self-enhancement, self-protection and self-affirmation and, further, puts an end to the chronic states of anxiety and frustration and their consequential negative experiential states such as hostility, depression, loneliness and tension which accompany the continuous threat of the non-fulfillment of these strivings for absoluteness. One is then not nothing, but only no-thing, for one is still that something which is pointed to, and represented by, the label of "pure Consciousness," which is also one with pure Being.

To establish that perfect Unity, consciousness must first unify itself in terms of all of its personal aspects by rejecting no-thing which is experientially real in itself. In order to accomplish that, consciousness must first dis-identify from all fixed conceptual selves with which it has identified itself, because, if it holds to being some fixed and enduring conceptual self, there will be no tolerance for those experiential realities which are in contradiction with that fixed conceptual self. Thus, for example, if I hold myself to be a "kind" person, I will not be able to permit myself to recognize and accept angry feelings when they arise in consciousness, because kind people just do not get angry. Therefore, to bring about a personal unity in consciousness, I must first take my stand as being no-thing fixed or enduring but hold myself to be only the moment to moment experiential reality which arises in consciousness. Thus, some moments I am anger, then sadness, then elation, then tenderness, etc.

In helping the patient to quickly identify his rejected experiential realities so that he may be in the position to unify with them, it is helpful for the therapist to identify the patient's psychological needs and strivings or the things he is trying to prove about himself, and to be aware of the fact that psychological needs are not real, as such, and therefore cannot be filled, but only represent escapes and compensatory opposites for those negative experiential realities which the fixed concept of self rejects and disowns and tries to pretend do not exist by trying to actualize their more positive compensatory opposite. For example, the striving or need for power compensates for the need to escape from feelings of impotence, weakness, helplessness, or vulnerability; the need to secure from others a feeling of being loved or valued often compensates for, and seeks to deny, one's more basic conviction and feelings of worthlessness or unlovableness; the need is not for independence, but rather the need is to deny or compensate for one's more basic dependency yearnings or fear of being controlled and helpless; the need to find security attempts to deny and compensate for one's more basic rejected feelings of insecurity, etc.

The therapist must help the patient to confront and integrate with those rejected experiential aspects of self which he actually is, at any given moment, instead of trying to help the patient actualize its compensatory opposite or what the patient feels that he *ought to be*, or that which he is trying to protect, enhance, or affirm about himself. As peculiar and contradictory as it may sound, peace is to be found only in the midst of (i.e., in communion, non-duality, or at oneness with) pain and never by struggling against or running away from what is considered to be the negative or painful. *Only communion with psychological pain opens the door for its liberation and transcendence;* only a yielding letting be or full acceptance is its ending. Psychological pain does not exist just because of the mere presence alone of some stimulus or reality which is termed "painful." Rather, the pain is produced by the interpretation of that fact or reality which produces the tendency to avoid or resist that fact. Only when the mind recoils from a fact or reality is there pain. *Psychological pain is part and parcel of the process of escape and resistance.* Pain is not inherent in any feeling but arises only after the intent to reject it arises. Essentially, the feeling of psychological pain is created by the attempt to fragment or separate consciousness from itself; the splitting of the unity of consciousness into the duality of a conceptual observing entity which tries to run from, distort or overpower the rejected feeling and the observed feeling itself. *If consciousness in duality is the cause of the pain, then only consciousness in unity can be the elimination of the pain.* Therefore, it is only in full communion with the formerly rejected feeling, in which conscious awareness is fully accepting and totally merged into it so as to re-establish a non-dualistic reunification with it, that there is the ending of pain.

Thus, for example, the patient reports that his girl friend caused him pain by rejecting him. However, that rejection is only a fact; intrinsically there is no pain in it. But the patient's mind recoils from that fact and he feels psychological pain because his consciousness is recoiling from the interpretation that he has applied to the rejection which is related to some kind of threat to his sense of self as reflected in his need for self-enhancement, self-protection or self-affirmation. Thus, if his need for self-enhancement has been threatened, then likely he has interpreted the rejection in such a way as to arouse and confirm feelings of worthlessness in himself which already existed there as a basic conviction. Because total lack of self-esteem and worthlessness tends to be equated with nothingness, his sense of being a psychological self becomes threatened with extinction, and so he rejects this feeling in himself and pain ensues. If, however, he lets be that feeling which he is labeling as worthlessness and does not try to strive to gain a compensatory feeling of worth, but rather just yields and merges with the feeling and lets it speak for itself totally, then he will find that both the feeling and the pain related to that feeling have been transcended. Thus, the therapeutic rule is always help the patient unify with what he actually is experientially from moment to moment but never encourage him to pursue some compensatory ideal of what he believes he ought to be.

Ultimately the therapist will discover that all of the patient's compensatory needs are reducible to, and merge, essentially, into the one most basic compensatory need which is to affirm oneself as being absolutely something, which serves as the compensatory opposite and defense that attempts to help consciousness avoid that one most painful experiential reality and fearful realization—that one is essentially nothing (i.e., no labeled thing), which is equated with nothingness or psychological extinction. Thus, consciousness attempts to avoid the recognition of itself as a void by identifying itself with various labels which serve to define itself and thereby pretends to give itself some personal reality. Consciousness then becomes totally devoted to the service of making this conceptualized labeled self some kind of absolute something instead of the relative some-thing that it really is.

Egoistic consciousness, because it is totally devoted to making and proving itself as being some-thing absolute, which is referred to as living in Becoming, is invariably in a state of discomfort because it is always operating within a framework of threat and frustration in regard to its needs for protection, affirmation and enhancement and so negative experiential states such as anxiety, tension, hostility, depression, and loneliness are always a part of a consciousness when it is living in Becoming. The constant devotion and desire of egoistic consciousness to actualize what can never be in its grasp, because the personal self composed of relative labels, can never attain absoluteness, guarantees that frustration, tension and unhappiness will be chronic. Whereas a consciousness which lives in Being is free of all the negative experiential states and finds that peace, love and joy are naturally intrinsic to itself. In essence, then, the greater the degree of self-preoccupation, caused by threats to, and frustration of, the ego and its drives for an absolute sense of enhancement, protection and affirmation, (which is related to the perceived tenuousness of the ego's sense of existence), the greater is the degree of psychopathology.

Transpersonal psychotherapy recognized that the various negative experiential realities are all related to threats to the sense of self and frustrations of its ambitions to make itself absolutely validated, thereby reflecting its basically illusory nature. Therefore, the treatment of these symptoms alone is superficial and in the long-run ineffective, because they must ultimately return in view of the fact that the identification with the illusional ego, which is their basic cause, still exists and therefore is a threat to it, and frustration of its drives is inevitable. Transpersonal psychotherapy takes the position that *the identification, by consciousness, with the ego must be transcended, and then all of the negative experiential states and symptoms will also immediately be transcended* because there is then no longer any labeled or personal self to be threatened with frustration and extinction. If transcendence of the ego is to be the end of psychotherapy, then the process itself, as its means, must also involve the transcendence or surrender of the ego, which Transpersonal psychotherapy does accomplish through the process of non-dualistic awareness or self-communion which involves consciousness being in a state of at-one-ness with its moment to moment experiential realities.

Another way to quickly identify what experiential realities you are rejecting in yourself is to sensitively observe what aspects of the world you are rejecting, or find absolutely intolerable. If you cannot accept some aspect of the world then what you are really saying is that you cannot accept what that thing does to you, which means more basically that you cannot accept being that experiential reality or response to that aspect of the world. You cannot accept the experiential self that you are that moment. When I am totally self-accepting and self-communing, I am free to let the world be whatever it has to be, because I am prepared to be and accept whatever it is that the world may trigger in me. I no longer disown but rather call all my responses my own, and therefore, my world and my ability to make contact with it is significantly broadened and enhanced. Thus, psychopathology begins with the first self-rejection of anything that is experientially real, which produces a sense of division and duality to consciousness; whereas what may be called psychological health is that state of consciousness in which it is free of a judgmental self-concept and therefore is a totally self-accepting or self-communing unity. Therefore, until the patient has learned that only he, alone, and not the world is responsible for his own experiential state of mind, he cannot be considered as being psychologically healthy.

To discuss the process of self-communion or non-dualistic awareness in greater detail, it is first essential to understand that when the dualistic self-concept entity is silent or inoperative, then the mind is without movement on the surface and the process of imagination is stilled, and there is no distracting opposition to prevent the clear contact, hearing and understanding of what arises spontaneously. In that state of non-duality, consciousness is in its Transpersonal condition or the state of Being which is the natural self-healing and creative condition of consciousness. In that state there is no dualistic entity operating as the judger or controller of the spontaneously arising contents of consciousness and so, being unimpeded, the rejected aspects of consciousness are free to arise spontaneously and creatively reunify themselves into the unitary whole that consciousness naturally is.

In self-communion or non-dualistic awareness one makes no conceptual reaction or interpretation of any kind to the experiential reality that arises spontaneously, but rather one should adopt an attitude of silent witnessing or quiet mind observation or listening to that which arises, and therefore consciousness is then in a non-dualistic state of being one with what is and not pursuing some imaginal [sic] what ought to be. Consciousness is then in the Transpersonal state of Being instead of the egoistic state of Becoming. Letting be and being one with what is the moment to moment spontaneously arising experiential content of consciousness is the immediate end of duality and conflict within consciousness.

Thus, to be in this non-dualistic state of consciousness one must not label, judge good or bad, or have any kind of desire or goal in regard to what arises in consciousness. There must be no sense of avoidance, resistance, condemnation, justification, distortion or attachment in regard to what arises but only a *choiceless awareness*, because any such reaction is a response of a self-concept entity which puts consciousness into the pathological state of duality and therefore consciousness is no longer in the non-dualistic state which is the only condition of consciousness in which real therapeutic effect can take place. Without the full integration which non-duality yields, the rejected still remains short of being fully assimilated. Without the occurrence of self-communion, consciousness is still in the pathological state of duality, division, and conflict so self-unification or self-healing cannot take place. The rejected painful experiential realities are not free to spontaneously arise and creatively be integrated and so no healing effect or growth is possible.

Therefore, one need only yield to and merge with the experiential reality just as it is, letting it pervade one's awareness entirely and permitting it to speak for itself to completion. Sometimes closing the eyes may assist the complete focusing of attention on, and its total absorption into, full identify [sic] with the feeling that is arising. The therapist can help the patient to understand and establish himself in the state of non-duality by encouraging him to speak as though he were the feeling itself. This can be done by simply asking the patient, "what would the feeling (e.g., anger, fear, depression, loneliness, etc.) say if it could speak?"

To achieve the creative and self-healing state of self-communion most expeditiously, it is also helpful if one takes the creative stance in consciousness that consciousness is a natural unity and not a duality and therefore there is only one self and not two. Because there is no real enduring or conceptual me that operates as the entity which is the observer-controller-judger of that which arises in consciousness, one should, therefore, take the stand that one is only that varying experiential reality that arises in consciousness and changes from moment to moment. Some moments it may be elation, other moments it may be sadness, tenderness, destructiveness, fear, loneliness, etc. Thus, for example, one should not say that this moment "I am hostile" or "I have hostility" but rather, "I am hostility" because the first two statements imply a second, dual, or additional self to which the experiential reality of hostility belongs. In reality, *there is no other self to whom the particular feeling is happening.* There is only the feeling itself. All other selves are only conceptual and illusional ideals of what ought to be. Thus, nothing can be done about what is experientially arising this moment. One can only adopt an attitude of choicelessness in regard to what is and therefore there is nothing else to do but just let it speak for itself and tell its own whole, complete story or message.

Thus, two basic forms or degrees of duality and pathology have been implied. The first is that duality and pathology are necessary to give birth to and affirm the ego. What may be referred to as the *universal pathology* is the initial or *fundamental duality* common to all non-Transpersonally Awakened persons and that is the duality which involves the separation in consciousness between self as subject and self as object, in its various forms such as the observer and that which is observed, the experiencer and that which is experienced, the judger and that which is judged, the controller and that which is controlled, or the conceptual self and the experiential self. The *secondary duality*, which follows after the establishment of the fundamental duality and which is the more severe or advanced degree of duality or pathology, is the personal or diagnostic pathology which relates to one's personal repressions. It is that duality within consciousness between what is personally acceptable and unacceptable, or between what is conscious and unconscious, and is based upon what threatens the ego's sense of existence, which is related to the ego's needs for a sense of potency, worth, integrity, and affirmation of its labeled identifications. This determines the particular form and severity that the individual's pathology will take.

These various forms and degrees of duality and pathology may be most efficaciously and expeditiously transcended through a process referred to here as Transpersonal psychotherapy. *Transpersonal psychotherapy may be succinctly defined as the attempt to restore consciousness* to its natural state of being a unitary whole through the process of self-communion. *Self-communion is the essence of all therapeutic effect* regardless of the system of therapy under which it occurs. It is the essence of what is meant by integration or reunification. It is the whole-ing process of consciousness which is essentially what is meant by healing. In most systems when self-communion does happen to occur, it is usually rarely and most fortuitously achieved; whereas in Transpersonal psychotherapy the achievement is deliberate and most direct.

There is no real psychological healing without self-communion and whenever any process of therapy has been successful it is only and always because in some way the patient has been helped to be in a state of communion or unity with whatever painful experiential reality he was formerly rejecting. If the ego, as the observer, is surrendered and consciousness takes its stand as being one with the observed, then in that moment has integration or growth occurred. No more expeditious or effective form of therapy is possible than that.

At times, it is possible that intellectual interpretations by the therapist may facilitate the arousal of some particular rejected experiential reality in the patient, but that alone is not sufficient to guarantee that the patient will then go ahead and fully accept and permit himself to merge and integrate his consciousness with that particular aroused experiential reality which is what is essential if psychological healing and growth is to occur. Intellectual interpretations by the therapist which lead to the patient perceiving his experiential self from the point of view of some distanced and dualistic observer or having just an intellectual grasp or set of theoretical explanations of his psychodynamics still maintains the patient's consciousness dualistically outside of himself and are therefore not sufficient of themselves to produce the condition of self-communion or integration which is necessary to yield a therapeutic effect. In fact, in the long run such intellectual interpretations may be permanently inhibiting to growth because they only serve to teach and condition the patient to look outside of himself for the truth of himself and thereby maintain the patient's consciousness in a state of duality. Strangely enough, there are some systems of therapy currently in vogue that actually set out deliberately to encourage and intensify dualism in consciousness by enhancing the capacity of the patient's ego, as observer, to control, suppress, and dominate its dualistic observed experiential realities which the patient feels are objectionable or painful to him. It is extremely questionable whether such systems can legitimately be called therapeutic.

Therefore, the only really essential therapy for the patient is that he come to learn how to convert the pathological duality of consciousness into a unitary whole, by himself. When he is able to accomplish that consistently then he no longer needs the therapist nor does he require any further therapy. He no longer disowns any of his own experiential realities. He knows how to unify and heal himself. He knows how to be his own therapist. Every successful therapeutic process should, at the outcome, always leave the patient capable of being his own therapist.

At this point the reader may be wondering why the patient, prior to coming in for therapy, does not naturally and easily achieve self-communion through his own efforts. There are two fundamental reasons why the patient makes no attempt on his own or prevents himself from establishing the self-healing, self-communion with his rejected painful feelings. In some cases the ego is convinced that the repressed feelings are more powerful than the ego's capacity to contain or control them and so it fears that the full contact of communion with the feelings will lead to the uncontrolled acting-out or overt expression of those feelings in inappropriate behavior which will lead to the ego's destruction. This may occur either from the psychological point of view in which the feelings or related behavior are interpreted as being in direct contradiction with his identified concept of self and therefore is a threat to its existence; or from the physical point of view in which he is frightened that the acting-out of those feelings will bring a returned retribution from others that could be a threat to the ego's existence, as would be especially true, for example, in the case of repressed destructive or sexual feelings. However, in fact, *self-communion with repressed feelings actually removes the cause or need for acting-out rather than facilitates acting-out.* The repressed feelings constantly push for expression into conscious awareness, not behavior, because they are obeying the basic principle of consciousness which is to restore itself to its natural condition of being a unitary whole by making conscious all that is itself. Therefore, those feelings are not really pushing for acting-out or discharge through expression into behavior, but rather they are pushing only for reintegration and complete drainage of their repressed energy which occurs once those feelings are fully acknowledged into consciousness as self, instead of being kept outside and treated as not-self and are permitted to speak for themselves to completion.

In other cases, self-communion is resisted because the ego, which is identified with the observer or controller of those painful rejected feelings equates loss of control of those feelings with total impotence of will on its part which is further equated with the extinction of the ego. From another point of view, the patient has a firm conviction that confrontation with those painful experiential realities would be more than his ego would be able to bear and would overwhelm his ego, and so he fearfully concludes that it would lead to his psychological destruction. This conviction comes about because he has learned that the closer his conscious awareness comes to having full contact with his psychological pain, the more intense is the experience of the pain, and therefore he concludes that full contact with the pain would be overwhelming and self-destructive. However, he fails to recognize and understand that proximity is not communion. Being with your pain is not the same as *being* your pain. Communion does not exist until there is not the slightest trace left of duality and separation between the pain and the observer. As ironical and paradoxical as it sounds, *communion with pain does not bring greater pain but actually yields liberation, and joy.* In fact, consciousness in communion with anything, not just with psychological pain, of course, yields peace, and joy.

It should be clear from this discussion that consciousness can never really *be* any-thing personal; it can only *know* the personal. It can only label and dualistically know or experience that particular label that it has applied to itself from a standpoint outside of it as its relative and interdependent experiencer. The instant that consciousness tries to *be* any-thing *personal,* by merging the observer or experiencer into a state of unity and thereby standing in identity with that personal experiential reality, one finds that the personal immediately dissolves, leaving consciousness in its natural Transpersonal condition which is intrinsically Peace-Love-Joy. Therefore, all psychological pain is an illusion. The only Self that is real and the only Reality that consciousness can ever *be* is Peace-Love-Joy. Whatever consciousness *knows* of itself is never real and never Itself but is only that labeled objectification or conceptual illusion which is only apparently outside of Itself. Thus, consciousness can only be what is real and can only know of itself what is unreal. The real can never become the unreal and therefore Consciousness is the Transpersonal already, and so It is no-thing that can be pursued for It is not some-thing which is outside of oneself but rather one is That already and can realize That directly when all pursuing or living in Becoming ends.

Thus, through the process of self-communion, as each rejected painful experiential reality creatively and spontaneously rises to consciousness and is totally accepted, embraced in non-duality, reunified and transcended—then in that moment is consciousness Silence. Continuing in this way until all the rejected painful experiential realities are retrieved and reunified and consciousness is no longer identified as being any relative or personalizing label, then consciousness is quiet and still to its depths and is once again in its natural condition of being a perfect Unitary Whole as the Silence and Light of pure Consciousness. Then out of that Silence of Consciousness occurs what is referred to as Transpersonal Awakening which has also been called by other names such as Self-Realization, Cosmic Consciousness, Kingdom of Heaven,

Liberation, Enlightenment, Nirvana, etc. This is the only true fulfillment for consciousness. That is Home.

In essence, Transpersonal psychotherapy is just a sophisticated form of the scriptural declarations, "to thine own self be true," or "see the truth and the truth will set you free," which I would like to paraphrase as follows: "*Be* the truth and the truth will set you free." For in being the moment to moment truth that arises in consciousness and nothing else but that, then consciousness is in unity and is liberated from the dualistic ego. If you have the direct realization that you are only one self and not two and that self is only what is or that which is your moment to moment truth that arises in consciousness, then you are *on your "way"* Home. Thus, to realize non-duality is to realize that you and the universe are one, because there is no universe until your awareness of some element of it arises in consciousness. At that moment you and that element of the universe are one because you are one or in unity with whatever arises in consciousness from moment to moment. Therefore, for example, if this moment your consciousness is confronted with a barking dog and you do not have the immediate realization that you and the barking dog are one then you have not yet Awakened from the illusion of duality. To be in non-duality is to be like a rudderless raft set adrift upon the Sea of Consciousness riding the free-flowing tides of the truth of your moment to moment spontaneous consciousness until it carries you Home; and it is with certainty that it will. Thus, when your consciousness lives in non-duality you will realize that you and the universe are one and the self-discovered realization will eventually occur that you are the all and also the One Consciousness which underlies the all. Finally will come the realization that there is only the One and being in perfect Unity with That you *are* Home.

> . . . and he who loses his way a thousand times shall have a Homecoming.
>
> Gibran

REFERENCES

Assagioli, R. *Psychosynthesis: A manual of principles and techniques.* New York: Hobbs, Dorman & Co., Inc., 1965.

Hammer, M. Quiet mind therapy. *Voices,* Spring 1971, 52-56.

Hammer, M. A therapy for loneliness. *Voices,* Spring 1972, (a) 24-29.

Hammer, M. Misconceptions of transpersonal psychotherapy. *Voices,* Fall 1972, (b) 21-26.

Maslow, A. Theory Z. *Journal of Transpersonal Psychology,* Fall 1969, 31-48.

Watts, A. *Psychotherapy east and west.* New York: Pantheon Books, 1961.

Psychotherapy as Invitation

by Sidney M. Jourard

THE INVITATION TO BECOME SICK

Psychotherapy begins when a person cannot live his life further in the ways he has, and consults with somebody who intends to help him. The fact that a person would arrive at such an impasse should provoke wonder, since all of us are gifted with intelligence that could guide us out of existential culs-de-sac. But people arrive at this point, and there are those who would be of help. How does the sufferer reach his stalemate? *I believe he chooses it.*

I agree with the existentialist thinkers (6) (19) that every man chooses his way of being in the world. But I would go further and assert that people choose their ways of being *for somebody*. A man chooses his way of being for himself, or for somebody else. His choices, naturally, yield consequences.

The way a person has chosen to exist was selected from possible alternative ways. It was selected because it seemed to be a way to fulfill or preserve *values*. These values include, for example, survival, identity, status, the love of another person, money, etc.

If we now look at some particular man's present condition, whether he be sick or well, we can ask, "Of what way of being is this condition an outcome? At whose invitation did the fellow choose this way of being and not some other? His own? His mother's? His teacher's?" And we can ask further, "What values were fulfilled, and which sacrificed, when the fellow chose and followed this way?"

Here are some examples of ways that a man might have followed: the *authentic* way, where he has been genuine in his transactions with people and true to his projects; and the *counterfeit* way, which seems to be the common, or all-American, way. And we can speak of the *involved*

Reprinted from *Disclosing Man to Himself* (Chapter 7), by Sidney M. Jourard. Princeton: D. Van Nostrand Company, 1968.

way—as in the case of one deeply committed to various projects—and the *detached, uninvolved* way. There is the *personal* way of the man who enters into dialogue with his fellows; and there is the *anonymous* way of the one who neither knows, nor is ever known by, any single human being. All these ways are possible, and each can be viewed as a response to an invitation, a response that yields consequences for well or ill.

A "neurotic" person, for example, may be seen as one who has chosen a rigid, encapsulated existence. It is safe, but it happens also to be suffocating. He chose to be this way, not only to feel safe, but also to hang on to the love of his parents or spouse. But he pays a price for his choice. Of a sexually impotent man, we may say his mother invited him by word or gesture to follow the *eunuchoid* way. He accepted the invitation, and was rewarded with his mother's approval. Some reward! Some price! But one must pay for everything in this world!

If a man's present being is the outcome of his acceptance of an invitation to *be* in some way, we can ask, "What do we know about invitation? Under what conditions is an invitation accepted or declined? Who extends the effective invitations? And who are the ones who respond to them?" We actually know a great deal about invitation, though the knowledge appears under other rubrics. We know a great deal about the psychology of suggestion, of persuasion, of hypnosis, and of leadership. Anything written under those headings seems to me to be relevant to a psychology of invitation. A good psychotherapist or a good nurse, teacher, leader, or hypnotist—even a good salesman—all these are experts at extending invitations or challenges that will be accepted. An invitation to someone carries with it the implication that the other has the power to carry it out. It is a form of the "attribution of power," as Heider (7) has written of it. The successful inviters invite others to change some aspects of their being. They invite a person to change his ways of valuing, construing, striving, behaving, or buying; and the person accepts the invitation. The therapist invites his patient to eschew phoniness and to try authenticity. The teacher invites his pupil to abandon ignorance, his present ways of thinking and believing, and to expose himself to new experiences. The leader invites or challenges his follower to carry out a mission that the follower never imagined he could accomplish. The hypnotist invites his subject to recover previously inaccessible memories, and the subject does. The nurse or doctor invites a patient to take a pill or an operation, and the patient does.

The phenomena of invitation have so powerful an effect upon man that I have wondered about the extent to which they have affected our psychological research (14). The "demand" (I would call them "invitational") characteristics of experimental settings in which psychological research is carried out have been pointed out by several workers. It is as if subjects are invited to confirm the experimenter's hypotheses, by responding in a certain way—and many do! (14) (18)

In the field of medicine, we know that certain recognized sicknesses are the result of a physician's (witting or unwitting) invitation to consider oneself weak or sick. Such conditions are designated *iatrogenic* diseases. If we speak of iatrogenic illness, is it not just as meaningful to speak of iatrogenic *wellness*? Or "mother-o-genic" wellness; or "psychologist-o-genic" wellness? Could we classify some physicians as wellness-inviters, i.e., healers, and others as sickeners, who have a knack for persuading others that they are weak, helpless, and sick? There are some people in society who have a proven flair for transmitting powerful invitations to others to regard life as pointless and hopeless and to regard themselves as weak and worthless. There may be many in society who are gifted at getting people to "give up," to yield, to give in. Goffman (4) has shown how mental hospital personnel invite or shape patients so that they will conform to current conceptions of how a madman should appear. And a visit to any mental hospital will prompt this question: "What kind of behavior and attitude are invited by the hospital buildings themselves? By the social organization that prevails there?" Laing and Esterson (10) have shown how much of the traditional psychiatric symptomatology can be explained as the outcome of invalidating and disconfirming behavior from relatives and professional people toward anyone who experiences difficulty in living. In fact, it is warranted to wonder whether hospital personnel can *take* healthy behavior when it appears in the ones called "patients," or do they rather get terrified by it when it appears and persuade the patient (invite him) to stop this nonsensical autonomy and self-expression and step into line. Do hospital personnel invite "crazy" behavior, and punish healthy behavior? In Kesey's (9) novel, *One Flew Over the Cuckoo's Nest*, patients who became bumptious were sedated or electroshocked into their appropriate social roles. If that didn't work, they were lobotomized. I don't think the story told in that novel is far from truth, at least in then existing mental hospitals.

PSYCHOTHERAPEUTIC TECHNIQUE AS SOME KIND OF INVITATION

There certainly are technical aspects of being a psychotherapist, and every major approach to psychotherapy highlights some technical way of being that the novice is obliged to rehearse until he has mastered it. The assumption is made that if you master this technique, then the people on whom you practice it will respond and commence to function fully. A virtual plethora of specialized technical approaches to the conduct of psychotherapy is described in the literature of clinical psychiatry and psychology. One of the most recent, of course, is the emphasis on conditioning techniques. We can also mention Albert Ellis' (1) type of argumentative psychotherapy (that is what I would call his therapy—he calls it "Rational-Emotive" psychotherapy). There are the interpretative work of the good psychoanalyst, and the "reflection" technique described in Carl Rogers' (17) early writings, and so on. But now let us look at techniques within the framework that I have tried to build in the early part of this article.

Whenever any new technique is presented in the literature of clinical psychology or psychiatry, something happens that is akin to what transpires in medicine when the pharmacologist produces a new tranquilizer, a new antibiotic, a new pain killer, a new "wake-upper" or a new "put-to-sleeper." A wave of enthusiasm develops among practitioners, and the new technique or the new drug is used widely, with enthusiasm and with good results; then unforeseen side effects and limits are discovered. Some of the uncritical enthusiasm and widespread application gets tempered. These comments about drugs seem exactly relevant to operant conditioning techniques, psychoanalytic techniques and client-centered techniques, and others. In each case, some pioneer has been totally committed to fostering wellness in a disturbed person. This pioneer then reached an impasse in his efforts to promote fuller functioning in his patient. The techniques and insights afforded by his past training and experiences did not help him overcome the impasse. So he wrestled with the impasse in the spirit of total commitment. In the process, he obtained a new insight or invented a new technique that worked. This state of affairs, incidentally, resembles the situation of any creative artist or investigator. Creative potentials in a person, in this case the therapist, were evoked in the context of a problem that challenged him *wholly*. The solution for this particular problem was arrived at *creatively*. The therapist, being an ambitious fellow, proceeds to publicize, to teach, and to try it out in a wide array of other problems. If he is effective in publicizing and at winning disciples, this creative person will have evolved a "school." The disciples will seek to master the technique; and after practicing it for years, they may well become highly proficient at it. If they become sufficiently practiced, they can practice the repertoire of technical behavior almost automatically while their mind and heart are elsewhere. At this point they are not at all like the pioneer who developed the technique in the spirit of total commitment. These automatic technicians remind me of a nightclub pianist who can play up to one or two hundred pieces of music without thinking; his *hands* play while *he* is involved in flirting with the female patrons or in daydreaming. This common tendency, which I think I observe pretty reliably, to try to master a technique of interpersonal relating in much the same way as you master the technique of swimming, or piano, seems to me to illustrate the all-American idolatry of "having it made," the worship of automation. It is an effort so to master an interpersonal habit that one can *impersonate a totally involved individual* while one's mind and heart are on such things as, "Does she love me?," "How is my bank account?," "Gee, she's got a good shape!"—or whatever is meaningful to the person at the time he is practicing his technique.

Here is a curious phenomenon about human transactions: whenever the other person with whom you are dealing is self-conscious or contrived, whenever he is not fully present, when his "heart is not in it," when he is doing something, with his heart elsewhere and his true purpose concealed—then you sense this inevitably; if not right away, then in due time. When the other person is impersonating sincerity, wholeness, or full presence, his performance seldom convinces for long. Even professional actors, masters at impersonating the person whose role they perform on the stage, will drop this role when they are off stage. An impersonator's true aims may not be immediately apparent in his words or actions, but they will be transmitted or disclosed somehow. All of us have a vested interest in knowing what the other person is up to. What I'm saying here is that the suave, technical, well-rehearsed psychotherapist, like the suave salesman or suave minister, is impersonating someone who he is not. He is not fully committed to the *purpose* of his profession, and the people before whom he practices his automatized techniques inevitably arrive at the point where they do not take the practitioner seriously.

Psychotherapy is not so much a science or technique as it is a way of being with another person (8). There are many reasons to be with another person and many ways to be with him. The psychotherapeutic way is the embodiment of an *intention*—the wish that the one who is Other for the therapist should experience his freedom, should be and become himself. The therapist's commitment to the value of the other's freedom, wholeness, and growth transcends his loyalty to some technique of "doing" therapy, or some theoretical orientation, e.g., psychoanalysis, client-centered therapy, or the Jungian, existentialist, or Adlerian viewpoints. The commitment to ultimate goals insures that the therapist will not become fixed on an automatized technique that reduces his patient to the status of "one of them" and which provides the therapist with a mask behind which he conceals his truer commitments. Yet this is not to say there is no place for technique in the art of psychotherapy. Technique, which must be learned from a teacher, is an *idiom* in which one expresses an initial therapeutic intent. The willingness to master techniques and to study theory is actually proof of the seriousness of purpose of the one who would become a therapist. This willingness separates the amateur from the professional.

Effective psychotherapists, who succeed in inviting sufferers to change their previous ways of being, are not technicians, though they will have mastered their techniques. How have they grown from therapeutic technicians into psychotherapists?

SOME DIMENSIONS OF GROWTH FOR PSYCHOTHERAPISTS

What is it about years of practice that makes a person a more effective therapist, if it is not increased suaveness and perfection of the techniques learned from some master? A novice psychotherapist who makes an interpretation may listen to what he has just said and wonder, "Did I say that well? Was it the right thing to say? Would my supervisor have said that?" He is chronically self-conscious. Unself-conscious mastery of beginning techniques in one's profession probably is a factor in increased effectiveness, but it certainly is not the only factor. Where, then, does a therapist grow? I shall turn to my own experience over the past ten or fifteen years for some possible answers.

Faith in the Other's Capacity for Transcendence

One change in me over the past five or ten years is the strength and basis in experience for my conviction about man's potential to transcend limits and determining forces that bear on him. I now believe there is no biological, geographical, social, economic, or psychological determiner of man's condition that he cannot transcend if he is suitably invited or challenged to do so. This conviction is scientific: it has grown out of experience and observation. Shaw (20) outlined a theory which offers promise to bring transcendence "under control." I believe there is no determiner which a man cannot get around, under, through, or over in order to pursue goals and values that have challenged him or that he has chosen to fulfill. Man's potentials for survival, for adaptation, for rehabilitation, for recovery from illness, and for growth seem barely to be scratched. Our concepts of man's limits have proven, century after century, to be too rigid. Man continually exceeds limits that science says are built into his tissue. He climbs Mt. Everest, he orbits the earth, he survives death camps, and he recovers from illnesses deemed fatal. Thus, whenever I encounter a patient who is suffering from confining and crippling effects of childhood privations and trauma and finds challenges in his present existence overpowering, rather than despair with him, and pursue all the roots of "pathology" in him, I immediately begin to wonder how it would be possible to mobilize his spirit or his capacity to transcend the present circumstances which he has let grind him down. Maybe over the years I've just become more effective at communicating my faith in their potentials to the patients themselves; or maybe I've become more effective at infecting patients with the seeds of faith in themselves. A patient will say, "You seem to have had faith in me, so I looked, and I found faith in myself." Maybe this is the factor in iatrogenic wellness—the strength of the *healer's* faith in the potentials of the sufferer to transcend the "limiting" conditions of his existence. If this is true, it raises a fascinating question: On what factors is one's faith in the *other person's* potential to transcend limiting conditions dependent? I think that question is answerable—I don't quite know how, just now; but I think as psychologists, we are duty bound to try to figure ways to measure the strength of a person's conviction *that the other fellow* has the capacity to transcend determining circumstances. It may be that bad "witches," or experts at producing iatrogenic illness, are the very ones who have either none of the faith that I am talking about, or the reverse faith. They may be absolutely convinced from their depths that people have no capacity for transcendence.

Capacity for Commitment

The second dimension of my growth as a therapist lies in increased capacity to commit myself to fostering growth or wellness in a patient. This capacity I experience as the capacity *to be there*—to be fully present to my patient, or honest enough to let him know when my thoughts are elsewhere. This capacity for commitment and full presence is experienced in the following way: I find myself accepting his pathology or growth restrictions as a *challenge,* one I continue to respond to after my present repertoire of conscious or habitual technique has been exhausted. This continued commitment in the face of failure of present techniques has resulted in innovation, in improvisation; it has elicited therapeutic creativity in me. I think that the correlate of commitment is this very increased creativity in the therapeutic encounter.

This observation prompts a digression. Something is fishy when a person practices a profession and cannot be creative in it, when he continues to practice something the same way year after year. Either the person has been brainwashed, or his creative potentials were leached from him as he received his training. Let me put it in still another way. A therapist's task is to promote wellness in another. He was trained for this task, and he begins it with a repertoire of techniques. He has learned to listen; that is very good. He has learned to make reflections of feeling and content. He has learned the art of relevant interpretation. This is his "bag of tricks," the kit of tools he utilizes in hope that they will invite a patient into growing. About 60 percent of a therapist's patients will accept his invitation to wellness, as he presents it. But what about the 40 percent of the case load that decline? It used to be that when my techniques (invitations) didn't "work," I would simply repeat them.

I would reflect feelings more vigorously and interpret more incisively. Nothing happened. I was being most noncreative. I was showing a kind of character disorder, by persisting in behavior that was not effective. I was like the auto mechanic who knew how to do only three things —tighten nuts, turn screws, and connect wires. When someone brought in a car that wouldn't run, he would turn every screw, tighten every nut, and connect every wire. The car still wouldn't work. So he would find some more screws to turn, more nuts to tighten, and more wires to connect. At the least, we would want the mechanic to try something else or to return our money. One wants responsible creativity from a practitioner.

What is it about our methods of training therapists that seems so marvelously effective in drying up trainees' courage to be resourceful and creative in the arena of their commitment? Consider the ministry. Ministers seek to move people from a hellish existence to heaven on earth, to love their brothers and to end sinning. But clergymen use few means to embody their commitment and their invitations. Maybe this is a good thing, that they seek to invite people to wholeness and goodness solely through sermons, home visits, pastoral counseling, and hospital visits. But surely there are more ways than this that could be dreamed up. I'll raise this question: Where are the creative potentials in the ministerial profession? What other ways might a minister employ to carry out his vocation—since, clearly, his present ways have not been very effective at humanizing men.

We need to examine our training to see how it prevents us from being creative in carrying out our commitments. I think our training expresses a commitment, not to healing, but to loyal membership in a cult or élite. If we were trained for commitment to fostering wellness, then we couldn't help but become creative, because the know-how built into us in our training would carry us only to the point of the first therapeutic impasse. Here, at the therapeutic impasse, is where commitment is tested: is the therapist committed to his ''school's'' techniques—or to the patient's growth? If to the latter, then he will be creative (11) and inventive; he will display and embody the intentionality of which May has written. If to the former, he will function like a cracked phonograph record, uttering the same invitation over and over, oblivious to the fact that it has been declined.

Capacity for Dialogue

A third dimension of my own growth over the past five or ten years, which I believe is related to effective psychotherapy, is growth in capacity to enter into dialogue. This entails increased ability to establish contact, and sustain an I-thou relationship of mutual unreserve, *with a broader range of humanity.* I feel I am less afraid to let myself hear, feel, and then respond honestly to a more diversified array of people than was possible for me earlier. I am less afraid to let him and me be ourselves and reveal ourselves honestly. Maybe it is just a case of my having become more whole-hearted in my invitation to terrified, self-concealing people to disclose themselves as they are. I've come to believe, as I said earlier, that people choose a mode of being as a response to others' invitations or threats. They choose schizophrenic, or hysterical, or obsessional, or depressed being—for their parents, their spouse, or their friends. Part of this sick being is phoniness itself [cf. Mowrer (12) (13)] and part of the sick being is the organism's response to a long career of inauthentic being. Now a therapist, himself a rehabilitated phony, invites the patient to try the frightening rigors of the authentic way, first with the therapist and then with others. Perhaps one grows in capacity for dialogue as a function of increased courage to be authentic with one's patient. This simple honesty functions as an invitation to him to be as he is at that moment. Certainly if one is not fully present with the patient and is not fully committed; if one is being a phony; if one is impersonating Sigmund Freud, or Carl Rogers, or Carl Whitaker and *isn't* one of these people—his effectiveness at dialogue will have been radically impaired.

A CORE STAGE IN PSYCHOTHERAPY

Successful therapeutic outcome is not a function of the techniques employed as such; rather it is an outcome of such matters as the therapist's faith in the patient's potential for fuller functioning. Faith in patients' potential may be pretty hard to hang on to. Certain patients, for example, in the back wards of state hospitals may put it to strenuous test. Here, the example set by early Christians may be relevant.—An early man of the Church replied, when asked why he believed the absurd message of Christianity: *Credo quam absurdum* ("I believe *because* it is absurd"). It may well be absurd to believe that some poor fellow has the potential to transcend a psychosis of 20 years' standing; but if you don't have some such fools in the world, nothing new is discovered.

The strength of the therapist's commitment to bringing about this transcending action on the part of the patient seems to be another factor, and the therapist's capacity for entering into dialogue seems to be the third factor beyond beginning techniques, that are involved in growing effectiveness at therapeutic work. These may also be factors in effective teaching, leadership, ministering, or anything else that involves two people, one of whom feels a responsibility to help bring about change, or a transcending state of affairs in the other.

Now let's assume that a therapist has been able to commit himself to his patient—to help this patient arrive at fuller functioning. Once this state of affairs has come into being (and it takes time to happen), the therapist and patient become a new unit. They form an I-thou "coupling." This term has a sexy sound, but it is not a sexual coupling. Nor is it without feeling, sexual or other kinds. In the limiting instance, such an I-thou unity can be depicted as a temporary linking of the receptors, central processes, and effectors of the therapist and the patient.

The approach to the ideal coupling is *gradual*, since many factors in both patient and therapist hinder its development. But let us note that when the coupling has been achieved, it is as if the patient's ego has been rendered effectively larger. Incoming information is received both by his ego and by that of his therapist. The coding of this information is likewise carried on by the new enlarged "double" ego. Decisions for action may be arrived at jointly, and the consequences of these actions are fed back, not to the patient alone, but also to the therapist. On the basis of this shared feedback, many decisions can be made and tried, with the consequence that new learning will occur in the patient. Since the therapist is committed to fuller functioning in the patient, he doesn't disengage, he doesn't undo the coupling until it becomes clear that the goal of fuller functioning is in process of being attained: the patient has improved at communication, he has increased courage, he has discovered meaningful goals, and so on. In short, he can get along in his existence without such a close coupling with his therapist.

Now let us turn to the establishment of the I-thou unity. It appears to be true that *only* within such a mutually open relationship can the therapist maximally present his therapeutic influence, at the risk, incidentally, of being demoralized or sickened by the patient. It is an open question when you get two people thus open one to the other—who is going to influence whom? I can attest that there have been therapeutic transactions where I have been sickened by the patient instead of his being ameliorated by me. When you are open, you take risks. This unity of I and thou in mutual openness, one before the other, appears to be the referent for what Fred Fiedler (2) called "the good interpersonal relationship" that he found to be a common denominator in experienced psychotherapists of different schools. This I-thou unity appears to be the medium within which brainwashing or "thought reform" goes on. It also appears to be a necessary condition for operant conditioning to occur, at least when the "reinforcement magazine" is another person. I think that it is the *sine qua non* for any kind of interpersonal influence that is not secret, where the influencer is as vulnerable and open as the one to be influenced. Any theory of therapy, any technique that embodies goodwill, is likely to be effective when the "coupling" has been attained (3). And no technique will "work" when I and thou are not thus open.

How does a relationship evolve to that point where the therapist's intent to be helpful is likely to have maximal impact on the patient? How does he arrive at the point where he will be listened to, so that his utterances and actions will be maximally experienced by the patient? I include *actions* here because nonverbal behavior is also disclosure that conveys the therapist's intent to help the patient function more fully. Let me state this again. How does the relationship between you and me evolve to the point where what I say and do will have maximal impact on you? How does it come to pass that a patient will open himself up to be known and to be influenced? This really is the nub of psychotherapy, and teaching, and love, and leadership. How do you arrive in a relationship at the point where the other person is maximally open to you and will be affected by you? I now believe that *his* openness and vulnerability to influence and to good and to harm is a concomitant of *your openness before him,* so that you are also vulnerable.

This stage of mutual vulnerability, mutual acceptability, is gradually reached. It happens sooner with some patients than with others, assuming the therapist's commitment to the patient's fuller functioning remains constant. I have an informed suspicion, one consistent with a number of lines of experimental data that we do have, that *I* am a strong determiner of how open and trusting the other fellow is going to get. I suspect that he will become as open, trusting, and vulnerable as I am willing to be with him. If I want him to be maximally open, then I have to be prepared to be maximally open. If I want him to be only half-open, then I will only get half-open. If I want him to be maximally open, but I keep myself fully closed off, peeking at him through chinks in my own armor, trying to manipulate him from a distance, then in due time he will discover that I am not in that same mode; and he will then put his armor back on and peer at me through chinks in it, and he will try to manipulate me. I believe that the psychotherapist is the leader in the therapeutic dance, and the patient follows the leader. With some of my patients this maximum, mutual openness has occurred in the first three or four sessions while with others it has taken up to 150 or 300 meetings before the patient has experienced the desired degree of trust. I suspect that when it took 301 meetings for the patient to trust me, it was because I wasn't trustworthy for 300 meetings; on the 301st meeting, I may have felt enough confidence in myself and trust in the patient that I could be open before him. Then, in that very session we experienced this maximum, mutual openness—in short, an encounter. Then, I could give a lecture to the patient, give a reflection, give an interpretation, argue, do any technical thing that seemed relevant—and it would have maximum therapeutic benefit if I happened to be wise, or it would do maximum harm if I happened just then to be a fool.

THE PSYCHOTHERAPEUTIC TOUCH

I have found that some form of physical contact with patients expedites the arrival of this mutual openness and unreserve. So far, I have only held hands with a patient, put an arm around a shoulder, or given a hug—all in the context of an unfolding dialogue. I believe we are a nation of people who are starved for physical contact. I have discussed this more fully elsewhere, but I believe the time to dispense with the touch-taboo in psychotherapy is now. Spitz's (21) and Ribble's (16) observations on the importance of mothering as a factor in optimum growth in infants are relevant here. Mothering is mediated, among other ways, by cuddling and holding. I suspect the need for such mothering is never completely lost. Harry Harlow's (5) experiments with monkeys, involving "mothers" made of wire or terry cloth, showed that physical contact with a wire mother was preferred by these little monkeys to no contact at all; and of course a nice, soft terry-cloth mother was preferred over one made of wire. Perhaps the need to feel something against his skin was the decisive factor that attracted the little monkey to a dummy mother, whether wire or terry cloth.

Physical contact, of course, is a mode of *knowing* a person, in the biblical sense. To "know" a woman, for example, certainly involves first of all her cooperation, her willingness to be known. She *lets* herself be known—that is, sexually touched and entered. More generally, and less erotically, a person lets himself be known by verbal disclosure of his experiencing; by permitting himself to be seen as he does things; and by letting another person touch him. When I ask someone, "How do you feel?," I am asking him to tell me what is going on in his experience; but I may also be asking for his permission to touch him so that I can find out what he feels like.

The most primitive mode of establishing contact with another person is to touch him—hold his hand, put an arm around his shoulder, or hug him. Words don't need to be exchanged in such a situation. Indeed, psychotherapists will often reveal their willingness to remain in contact with a patient by holding his hand when he will not or cannot communicate verbally.

The metaphor of "being turned on" describes the experience of physical contact. When part of your body is touched, you can't ignore that part of your body. It becomes "figure" in your perceptual field. You might say that that part of your body comes into being. One wonders about men or women who have never been touched or hugged, or have never been in intimate body contact with others. Could we say that their bodies have not come to life, that their bodies do not exist in the phenomenological sense? One wonders to what extent they feel that their bodies are alive. I suspect that the transformation from virginity or even preorgasmic existence to the experience of having a sexual climax is so radical as to be equivalent to a kind of rebirth. •

The metaphor of "being touched," as in the expression "Your plight touches me," is relevant here. There are many touch-associations in our language and in our everyday experience, but actual touching is hemmed in by strict social taboos.

Chiropractors touch their patients and establish lasting doctor-patient relationships, as Sulzer (22) showed. I know it is easier to talk to someone when one is in physical contact with him, so long as the meaning of the contact is mutually known. Back rubs and body massage from nurses, masseurs, barbers, and hairdressers likely all serve to make the recipients of such contact more talkative—when they are not soothed into a blissful trance. I think we shall have to learn more about physical contact and its meaning as an expression of therapeutic intent.

One of the first things that ought to be done in any state mental hospital is to train a group of masseurs in the art of coping with terrified people who are being turned on. Good, loving massages on inaccessible patients may turn them on in a way that is terrifying to them and also terrifying to the person who has just awakened them. The therapist of the future ultimately will learn from that unheeded prophet, Reich (15), and become less afraid to get into meaningful physical contact with his patient; and he will have to be able to cope therapeutically with whatever behavior and experience such contact evokes.

THE SOUND OF BADGES

Anything a therapist does or says in his relationship with a patient can be looked at as a redundant expression of a message about his *actual* commitment. Henry Winthrop has spoken of this as "acoustic badges," badges you can hear. Much of what anyone says or does has this badge function. The carrier of a fraternity pin thereby tells the viewer that he is a member of Sigma Sigma Sigma. Much of what one says in a therapy transaction, even when it appears that one is communicating many messages to the patient—that is, what actually gets across—is the single theme, "I am a psychologist, I am a psychologist." Perhaps one transmission of that message is all the patient needs. When one does repeat himself in this redundant way, he is revealing his actual commitment. This may be the desire to be seen as a member of some group of psychologists. The patient may not care. Reflections and interpretations may be experienced by the patient as expressions of the message, "I don't really care about you, I care about my fees, or my comfort, or the rightness of my theories or reflections or interpretations." Or, these same reflections and interpretations, whether awkward or apt, may be heard as repetitions of, "I want you to be healthier, I want to help you, I am trying to be helpful." If the therapist's behavior expresses a true therapeutic commitment to the patient, then the suaveness of his technique and his theory of therapy probably don't matter much. If he is genuinely committed, then anything he says and does in good faith will be seen by the patient as the expression of a man of goodwill. In the presence of a man of goodwill, patients drop their defenses. They begin to grow at that moment. When a patient experiences his therapist's sincere commitment to his well-being, he enters the core stage of trust and hope.

THE FEEL OF HEALING

I believe that trust and hope are not *contributors* to healing. Rather, they are the experienced aspect of a *total* organismic healing, or reintegration process. Trust and hope are indications that the healing or reintegration or transcendence process *has been set in motion*. Trust and hope don't cause healing. They *are* healing. We can look at healing from various perspectives. From a psychological standpoint, healing appears as a state of trust and hope. At a physiological level, it is revealed as changes in white-cell count or in some endocrinological changes. At a behavioral level, healing is manifested in growing vigor and relevance of "responding." Continued distrust and hopelessness in a patient undergoing any kind of therapy may be regarded as indications that the disintegration process is unremitting. The patient's acquiescence to determiners of his existence is persisting and may culminate in death or total withdrawal into psychosis. Anything a therapist does which invites a sick person to trust, to be self-revealing, and to have hope that a better life is possible is therapeutic. The onset of.these psychological states signifies that the healing process or desirable personality reorganization has already begun.

KEEPING THE GROWING EDGE GROWING

Now I shall speak of something neglected: opportunities to grow and to have one's growth confirmed for people in the healing, the helping, and the teaching professions. I have found them because I have needed them. I'll tell you some of the places where I found them and some of the barriers that I encountered in hunting, and trying to profit from, growth opportunities. The most valuable experience I have had beyond training, that has maintained my growing edge, is *contact with colleagues who are of goodwill* and before whom I have not been afraid to be myself; that is, be like a patient, a pupil, a teacher, or a groping, bungling, well-intentioned person trying to make sense of what he is doing and wanting to benefit from somebody else's experience. Out of informal friendships and informal workshop meetings, more formal workshops such as those held by the American Academy of Psychotherapists evolved. At Academy workshops 50 or 75 therapists spend five days and nights, *at each other*—liking one another, hating one another, reacting to one another, helping one another, experiencing one another, and sharing with one another what we do, what we don't do, why do we do it, and so on. I think therapists stultify if they don't have workshops of this sort available to them. If such are not available, then a therapist has to find someone he can trust, to tangle with, in order to avoid becoming smug, pompous, fat-bottomed and convinced that he has "the word." One of the greatest dangers of being a teacher, a psychotherapist, a nurse, a minister, or anybody else involved in trying to help others change is the delusion that one "has it made," that all-American fantasy. There is no one like a self-disclosing colleague to prod one out of such smug pomposity, and invite one back to the task.

REFERENCES

1. Ellis, A. *Reason and emotion in psychotherapy.* New York: Lyle Stuart, 1962.
2. Fiedler, F. A comparison of therapeutic relationships in psychoanalytic, nondirective and Adlerian therapy. *J. Consult. Psychol.,* 1950, *14,* 436-445.
3. Frank, J. D. *Persuasion and healing.* Baltimore: Johns Hopkins Press, 1961.
4. Goffman, E. *Asylums, Essays on the social situation of mental patients and other inmates.* New York: Doubleday, 1961.
5. Harlow, H. The nature of love. *Amer. Psychol.,* 1958, *13,* 673-685.
6. Heidegger, M. *Being and time.* London: SCM Press, 1962.
7. Heider, F. *The psychology of interpersonal relations.* New York: Wiley, 1958.
8. Hora, T. The process of existential psychotherapy. *Psychiat. Quart.,* 1960, *34,* 495-504.
9. Kesey, K. *One flew over the cuckoo's nest.* New York: Signet, 1963.
10. Laing, R. D., and Esterson, A. *Sanity, madness and the family.* London: Tavistock, 1964.
11. May, R. Intentionality, the heart of human will. *J. Humanistic Psychol.,* 1965, *5,* 202-209.
12. Mowrer, O. H. *The crisis in psychiatry and religion.* Princeton: Van Nostrand, 1961.
13. Mowrer, O. H. *The new group therapy.* Princeton: Van Nostrand, 1964.
14. Orne, M. T. The social psychology of the psychological experiment: with particular reference to demand characteristics and their implications. *Amer. Psychol.,* 1962, *17,* 776-783.
15. Reich, W. *Character analysis.* New York: Orgone Institute Press, 1949.

16. Ribble, Margaret. *The rights of infants.* New York: Columbia Univ. Press, 1943.

17. Rogers, C. *Counseling and psychotherapy.* Boston: Houghton Mifflin, 1942.

18. Rosenthal, R. The effect of the experimenter on the results of psychological research. In B. A. Maher (Ed.), *Progress in experimental personality research.* New York: Academic Press, 1964, 79-114. Also *Experimenter effects in behavioral research.* New York: Appleton-Century-Crofts, 1967.

19. Sartre, J. P. *Being and nothingness.* An essay on phenomenological ontology. London: Methuen, 1956.

20. Shaw, F. J. *Reconciliation: A theory of man transcending.* Jourard, S. M., and Overlade, D. C. (Eds.). Princeton: Van Nostrand, 1966.

21. Spitz, R. "Hospitalism," in *Psychoanalyt. Stud. Child. I.* New York: International Univ. Press, 1945.

22. Sulzer, J. Chiropractic as psychotherapy. *Psychotherapy: theory, research and practice.* 1964, 2.

The Wizard of Oz
Behind the Couch

by Sheldon Kopp

Therapist:
I am Oz, the Great and Terrible. Who are you, and why do you seek me?

Patient:
I am Dorothy, the Small and Meek. I have come to you for help. I am lost out here in this world and I want you to get me back to Kansas, where I will be safe and comfortable.

Therapist:
Why should I do this for you?

Patient:
Because you are strong and I am weak, because you are a great Wizard and I am only a helpless little girl.

Therapist:
But you were strong enough to kill the Wicked Witch of the East.

Patient:
That just happened. I could not help it.

Therapist:
Well, I will give you my answer. You have no right to expect me to send you back to Kansas unless you do something for me in return. In this country everyone must pay for everything he gets. If you wish me to use my magic power to send you home again you must do something for me first. Help me and I will help you.

Patient:
I will do anything you ask, anything. Only tell me. What must I do?

Therapist:
Kill the Wicked Witch of the West.

Patient:
No, that I cannot, will not do.

Most readers will recognize this bit of dialogue, as being more or less the way it appeared in *The Wonderful Wizard of Oz*, although I have recast it as an initial exchange between therapist and patient. It was in April 1900, that L. Frank Baum, self-appointed Royal Historian of Oz, published this first of his chronicles. He wrote it as the beginning of a series of modern wonder tales. But unlike the writers of earlier stories, he hoped to eliminate "all the horrible and blood-curdling incidents devised by their authors to point a fearsome moral to each tale."

Mr. Baum was writing, in part, to express his own dissatisfaction with Victorian ideas of building character through punishment, grave lectures, and inner struggles for self-control, sacrifice and self-denial. He visualized instead the possibility of personal growth through coming to accept ourselves, with humor if need be, and of the central role of a loving relationship in solving our problems. And, too, he believed that all of this could be accomplished only by our coming to learn that the powerful other, the authority, the Wizard to whom we look for help, is himself only another struggling human being.

The continued success of this book and of the motion picture made from it—their perpetually fresh capacity for reengaging us with delight in the adventures of their characters—is testimony to the compelling quality of his vision. In all of this I see some themes that are very much at the core of my own sort of psychotherapy. I would like, therefore, to reexamine some aspects of *The Wonderful Wizard of Oz* as a psychotherapeutic tale.

In the original story, Dorothy, the little-girl heroine of the tale, is an orphan who has come to live with foster parents, Aunt Em and Uncle Henry. Their home is dull and gray, as is everything else in the sun-baked, unyielding land of Kansas, U.S.A. Aunt Em is described as an unsmiling sober woman, thin and gaunt, who, when Dorothy first came, was so startled by the girl's laughter that it would cause her to scream and press her hand upon her heart. Uncle Henry is a man who never laughed, looked stern and solemn, and rarely spoke. It was only Dorothy's dog, Toto, and her good heart, that made her laugh and saved her from growing as gray as her surroundings. .

Early in the story, Dorothy is separated by a cyclone from her foster family, and from the world of familiarly unhappy surroundings. The storm lifts her and Toto, together with their house, and whisks them from the plains of Kansas, U.S.A., off to the fantasy-shaped, bewildering land of Oz. It is this crisis of being uprooted, flooded with fantasy, and no longer in touch with the familiar misery of home, that leads Dorothy to seek the help of the Wizard of Oz in his great palace in Emerald City. Her house, it seems, had landed on the Wicked Witch of the East and killed her. Dorothy, of course, points out that this is in no way her fault. In fact, Aunt Em had told her that there were no witches living anyway. The Good Witch of the North (a good mother at last) is of more help. She has Dorothy put on the Silver Shoes of the dead witch and refers her to the Wizard for treatment of her problems.

And so, like many patients, Dorothy seeks treatment, not out of having some perspective on her long unhappy family life, but rather in the midst of a momentary crisis that separates her from her family or from her usual ways of handling things at home. It is so often not chronic unhappiness but present confusion and situational distress that lead people to the office of the psychotherapist. All Dorothy wants is to go back home to the known safety of her unsatisfactory family life, rather than tolerate the promise of her new and unfamiliar world. *She prefers the security of misery to the misery of insecurity.*

On the way to Emerald City she meets other distressed creatures who need psychotherapy but do not know it is available until they meet Dorothy. They are, of course, the Scarecrow, the Tin Woodman, and the Cowardly Lion. The Scarecrow's problem is that he has no brains at all. Dorothy finds him perched on a stick in a cornfield, harassed by crows. He is the inadequate man, who acts foolishly. He is sure that his foolishness is no fault of his own. He simply lacks what he needs to behave competently and wisely. In the meanwhile, no one must expect too much of him, but must protect him from fire because he is stuffed with straw.

Next she comes upon the Tin Woodman standing in the woods with uplifted axe, rusted so badly that he cannot move. His problem is that though he seems very polite, he has no heart. He once was a man of flesh and blood, but was hurt so often that he gradually had all the parts of his body replaced with tin. And, alas, the heart was left out. He too is not responsible for this unfortunate state of affairs. If only someone would do something for him, he might be able really to care about people instead of merely appearing to be polite. His problem with rust requires that other people be around to oil him up, or he just won't be able to function.

The third companion startles them in the woods. It is the Cowardly Lion who menaces them with unwarranted mock ferocity, but all too quickly reveals that he is nothing but a big coward. Although he has both brains and heart and home, he lacks courage. Therefore, he cannot be expected to follow through with boldness, to risk himself or, in short, to act like a man (or rather like a lion). He roars to scare others off, but if they stay to challenge he shows his cowardice. "But how can I help it?" he pleads as he tells Dorothy that now she knows this, she must be careful not to frighten him.

Now all four know of each other's problems and set out for the therapist's office on a joint venture that you might expect to give them some sense of empathy and genuine consideration for one another. Instead, after their mutual disclosures, each mutters self-centeredly to himself.

The Scarecrow: "All the same, I shall ask for brains instead of a heart; for a fool would not know what to do with a heart if he had one."

The Tin Woodman: "I shall take the heart, for brains do not make one happy, and happiness is the best thing in the world."

The Cowardly Lion: "What they each want is certainly less important than courage."

And finally there was good sweet little Dorothy: if only she could get back home, she really didn't care whether or not the others got what they wanted. Apparently the important thing is to get one's own way.

When at last they arrive at the Palace in Emerald City, the Wizard does individual intake interviews with each of them. And as it is with new patients, each sees him very differently. He appears variously to them as a lovely winged lady on a throne, an enormous head, a ball of fire, and a most terrible monster. Each approaches him as in the dialogue that I quoted at the beginning of this piece. Each is frightened and helpless, and somehow this entitles each one of them to special help and consideration, which the Wizard absolutely must give, simply because he is adequate and strong. The Wizard, good therapist that he is, quickly comes across as a person who has his own needs. In therapy country, everyone must pay for everything he gets. That means these poor helpless patients must give something of themselves if they wish to get something for themselves.

The task that the Wizard assigns is that they must kill the Wicked Witch of the West. They would like the Wizard to destroy the bad mother for them, but no matter how great and powerful a father he seems, he cannot do for them what they must do for themselves. He cannot even tell them how to go about it. Each patient tries to cop out in his own way. Dorothy has already accidentally killed the Wicked Witch of the East, but this time she must kill willingly and not by accident or without responsibility. She is reluctant because she cannot be forceful on purpose. Scarecrow says he will not be able to help because he is a fool; Tin Woodman because he does not have heart for it; and Cowardly Lion because he is too fearful. In order to help them, however, the Wizard will not let them off the hook.

So, reluctantly, they set off to slay the Wicked Witch of the West. In the course of this adventure, they become caught up with being a part of it and with genuine concern for one another—so much so that the

Scarecrow makes wise decisions, the Tin Woodman acts out of loyalty, and the Cowardly Lion performs bravely. Eventually Dorothy is able to be happy for her friends and their achievements, even when she fears she may never achieve her own desires.

This task assigned by the Wizard is a kind of teaching by indirection. As in psychotherapy, he insists that they will get nowhere if they simply continue to bewail their fates and stubbornly to insist that because they have troubles, he must magically solve their problems (or at least be terribly sympathetic). Instead he directs their attention elsewhere.

In individual therapy we may get the patient to focus on his past history. In group therapy, we may encourage the patients' curiosity about the group process. Some of what occurs as the patient reluctantly takes on these tasks, is that he can begin to lose himself, in the sense of giving himself over to the assigned work. As this unhooks him from his willful, self-sorry demand for someone to give him relief right now, a new possibility arises! The patient can now begin to experience the therapist and the other patients as real people with selves of their own; as people who have meaning outside of himself; who can therefore be meaningful to him, and who can ultimately put him in touch with the meaning of his own life.

Once our adventurers have accomplished what they first insisted they could not possibly do—that is, the slaying of the Witch—they return to the Wizard, impatient for their rewards. They have not yet realized that they already possess them. In the course of asserting themselves at the Wizard's Palace, they reveal to themselves that he is not a Wizard at all—he is "just a common man," or worse, a humbug! When he is challenged, it turns out that he has problems of his own. Disillusioned, Dorothy tells him, "I think you are a very bad man." "Oh, no, my dear," he answers, "I'm really a very good man, though I'm a very bad Wizard, I must admit."

The Wizard then tries to help them to understand the solutions at which they have already arrived. For the Scarecrow, it was not a problem of lacking brains, but of avoiding the experiences that would yield knowledge. Now that he would risk being wrong, he could sometimes act wisely. So too with the Tin Woodman: it was not a heart he lacked, but a willingness to bear unhappiness. And, of course, the Cowardly Lion needed not courage, but the confidence to know that he could face danger even when he was terribly afraid. Then Mr. Baum, with sympathetic tolerance for human foibles, has each patient still insist that the Wizard confirm his accomplishment with some external token. In one version, the Wizard presents the Scarecrow with a Diploma, gives the

Tin Woodman a Solid Gold Watch for Loyal Service, and awards the Lion a Medal for Bravery.

As for Dorothy herself, she learns that all this time all she had to do to get home was to use the Silver Shoes she wears. She needs only knock the heels together three times and the shoes will carry her wherever she wishes to go. That is, she has learned that she has the power to go wherever she wants to go and to make changes in her life, if only she is willing to take the responsibility of recognizing and using that power.

Of course, the Wizard could have told them all this at the beginning of treatment, but they never would have believed him. How could they have accepted that they were demanding from others simple human qualities that they already possessed? The insights are too simple to be grasped, too obvious to see, and can be had only when a person stops demanding them from the powerful Wizard/Parent who is supposed to take care of him. He must give up the struggle with himself and become involved with another, and with what can be between them.

Mr. Baum revitalizes old lessons that must be learned again and again: acquiring wisdom involves risking being wrong or foolish. Being loving and tender requires a willingness to bear unhappiness. Courage is the confidence to face danger, though afraid. Gaining freedom and power requires only a willingness to recognize their existence and to face their consequences. We can find ourselves only when we are willing to risk losing ourselves to another, to the moment, to a quest, *and love is the bridge.*

But last of all, alas, there are no Wizards! And yet, as a psychotherapist, I am sometimes tempted to join the Wonderful Wizard of Oz in saying, "But how can I help being a humbug, when all these people make me do things that everybody knows can't be done?"

The Psychotherapist

In Pirsig's *Zen and the Art of Motorcycle Maintenance* (1974), Phaedrus's effort to define quality leads him on the road to madness and personal transformation. The philosophical search for what is good and beautiful, and not merely useful, seems to require a new spiritual rationality, a way of thinking and perceiving that infuses science with a sense of values and subjectivity.

Quality has been a continuing concern in psychotherapy as well. The "good" psychotherapist possesses a variety of interpersonal skills—listening, supporting, confronting, interpreting; he is familiar with a collection of techniques, a bag of tricks. He is schooled in psychological theory that explains human behavior, even if it often fails to increase human understanding.

Humanistic psychotherapy recognizes the importance of skills, techniques, and theory. Beyond these acquired or learned behaviors, however, is the person of the psychotherapist; in the psychotherapist's self resides the source of quality and effectiveness.

Some personal attributes that determine the psychotherapist's creativity are described in the papers in this section. For Quaytman, the focus is on values; the creative psychotherapist lives by life-enhancing values and clearly communicates these values to the patient. For Dumont, the focus is a broad perception of the community context in which the patient lives. Fagan sees "being present" in the psychotherapeutic relationship as a creative, effective healing force. Schutz succinctly professes the therapist's commitment to his own continued personal growth and development.

In striving for quality, desiring to be a good person, one risks narcissism and self-centeredness, and, as Colby warns, "a psychotherapist is really not God, nor even a close relative of his." For the authors in this section, the risks are well worth taking: to accept the challenge of becoming a good person is to increase the quality of the psychotherapeutic relationship—to make "goodness" possible for someone else.

REFERENCE

Pirsig, R. M. *Zen and the art of motorcycle maintenance.* New York: William Morrow, 1974.

What Makes a Creative Psychotherapist

by Wilfred Quaytman

Three months ago a woman came to see me and spoke of her reluctance to start therapy. She stated "How can I trust a therapist who probably believes in male supremacy, and will try to get me to adjust to society?"

The stimulus for writing this paper came from my first session with this woman.

In searching out which factors are important in the therapeutic relationship, emphasis has generally been placed on:

a. The motivation of the patient.
b. The severity of the patient's situation.
c. His/her faith in the therapist and the treatment method.
d. A positive transference relationship.
e. Minimal countertransference.
f. Personal qualities of the therapist (such as concern, warmth and "unconditional positive regard").

Not enough has been written about the therapist's value system as a key factor in the therapeutic relationship.

WE COMMUNICATE OUR VALUES

This is because we all have been brought up on the principle that it is essential that psychotherapists be objective, that the therapist's personal life be more or less hidden from the patient, and that therapist must guard against influencing the patient's value system or ideas. But we all know that this is impossible. We all know that, one way or another, we communicate our values to the patient. We all know that patients soon

Reprinted from the *Journal of Contemporary Psychotherapy,* Summer 1974, 6(2), 168-179. Used with permission of the author-editor, Wilfred Quaytman, Ph.D.

come to know what kind of person the therapist is, what he or she believes in, what kinds of people the therapist respects and admires. This can and does have an enormous influence over the patient.

The fact is that the psychotherapist or healer has historically always represented the society-at-large, whether he be witch-doctor, shaman or priest. They have always represented the values of the dominant majority and sought to influence people to adjust to society. The psychotherapist of today, too, stands for the values of the society-at-large in which he/she lives.

The psychotherapist represents certain values, ideas and principles of conduct with which the patient can identify or use as a model. This process occurs either through the patient's conscious choice, or "unconsciously, just as children take over behaviors and attitudes of their parents, which then become an integral part of their own personalities."

For example, some psychotherapists believe that making a lot of money is the most important goal in the world. Do you imagine that their patients will not get to know this? Some of these same therapists may like to be rich and famous. Do you think they may not encourage these qualities in their patients? Some therapists believe that their version of sexual fulfillment is the most important objective in life. Do you think that the patients will not come around to believe this too? Some male therapists believe that woman's place is in the home, and feel very threatened by competent and achieving women. Do you think that this will not affect how the therapy goes? Some therapists fear and hate non-white people. They do not invite black or Hispanic people to their homes, and strongly discourage or forbid their daughters from dating them. Do you think that their patients will not become aware of and be influenced by these attitudes?

Perhaps this is a good place to ask—what are the main values of the dominant majority in this country? An incomplete list of values would include:

1. Success as a life-goal.
2. The acquisition of wealth and property.
3. Status, prestige, fame, and notoriety.
4. Achievement.
5. Education and the acquisition of knowledge.
6. The work ethic.
7. The protection of the family.
8. Marriage as an institution, and infidelity and divorce as alternative solutions.
9. Male supremacy and the oppression of women.
10. Competition as a motivating life-force.
11. Caucasian superiority.

12. The American profit-motive, free enterprise system.
13. Some form of religious affiliation or interest.
14. War as an expression of national policy.
15. Deification of technology.
16. Neglect of poor people.
17. A system of advertising commercial products that advocates forced obsolescence, and deliberately promotes narcissism and also envy of one's neighbor's goods.
18. Mechanization of people and computerization of society's institutions.
19. Rejection of economically marginal or non-productive persons such as mentally retarded, chronic schizophrenics, physically handicapped and old people.
20. The adoration-of-youth syndrome.
21. The present democratic political, economic and social structure and institutions of the United States.
22. A class system which measures the worth of human beings in accordance with the above value system.

PRO-HUMAN AND ANTI-HUMAN VALUES

I believe that many psychotherapists uphold most of these American values. Some of these values are pro-human and constructive, and enhance human existence. Others are clearly anti-human, destructive, and diminish and alienate human beings.

If this is true, it means that many psychotherapists are consciously or unconsciously involved in a therapeutic relationship which either fosters or *passively perpetuates* anti-human and destructive values.

Furthermore, I believe it is not enough to be a *competent* therapist. A *competent* therapist helps relieve the patient's suffering, and to overcome her fears and emotional disabilities, finds more effective ways of coping with her problems, and helps her to fulfill personal goals and objectives. I repeat, it is not enough to be a *competent* therapist who relieves suffering, and helps people function better in the real world. I believe it is also necessary to deal with moral and existential conflicts in the patient.

THE PSYCHOTHERAPIST'S RESPONSIBILITY

I feel that it is also the psychotherapist's responsibility to society-at-large and to his patients to be a *creative* psychotherapist.

What makes a creative psychotherapist? Well, I have my own special definitions:

A. The creative therapist examines the American value system and tries to determine which values are anti-human and destructive and which are pro-human and enhance human life and dignity.

B. The creative therapist starts, a terribly difficult, painful and courageous soul-searching into her own values, ideas, convictions and prejudices in order to identify which are life-supporting and which diminish life.

C. The creative therapist carefully examines how she communicates her own values and ideas to the patients.

D. The creative therapist examines which values in the patient are anti-human and which are pro-human and how they affect the patient's life-functioning. A creative use of the therapist's abilities requires that he deal with these issues. I believe that a therapeutic relationship that includes a *mutual* examination of the therapist's and the patient's value system would be rewarding and indeed be creative.

This does not mean that I advocate that the therapist be judgmental or use the therapeutic hour and the patient's valuable time and money to espouse pet causes, or to go on ego trips. Not at all. What I do mean is that the creative therapist pays special attention to the extent to which the patient *passively* embraces the corruption and other toxic elements in our larger social milieu while at the same time, the therapist also pays special attention to the ways in which the patient can identify with and struggle for the healthy values in our society.

E. Moving away from corruption for a moment, another function of the creative therapist would be to make the expansion of her own life experience and knowledge an important part of her life's goals. I believe a therapist is creative if she is as ardent in advocating and risking change in herself as she is in advocating and risking change in the patient.

F. In addition, I believe that a therapist is creative to the extent that he can free himself from the rigid drama and inflexibility of official APA diagnostic categories. I am not at all suggesting that all diagnostic concepts be abandoned and replaced by here-and-now "vibrations." I do recognize the value of tentative diagnostic conceptualizations and formulations. But I feel that the psychotherapist should not be so dogmatically devoted to the medical model of pathology as to blind himself to the uniqueness of the patient, to his special individuality, to his idiosyncratic life-style, over and above the hide-bound concepts of pathology. How many therapists do you know who *automatically* label an interracial male-female relationship as pathological? How many therapists *automatically* label a societal dropout as pathological? How many therapists *automatically* label a woman as pathological who does not choose marriage as her most important life goal? How many *automatically* label non-conformity or dissent as pathological?

G. Another quality that marks the creative therapist is to be able to utilize different therapeutic approaches selectively, to be a true *eclectic,* to know how and when to be a Gestaltist or to use free association, when to interact, when to analyze a dream, when and how to confront, or when to use behavior therapy or whatever.

In conclusion, what makes a creative psychotherapist is the extent to which she can risk change, utilize diverse approaches to therapy, avoid dogma which denies a person's uniqueness, and expand her own life experience. In addition, the therapist is creative to the extent that he can divorce himself from the historical role of the psychotherapist in society and dare to question his support of the different Watergates of corruption that exist in human beings.

The Psychiatrist as Creative Artist

by Matthew P. Dumont

People who have devoted their lives to mending the broken lives of others are engaged in a mysterious process. They plumb the depths of conflicted and unhappy souls, they look for the sources of conflict and misery within the individual, in his family, his institutions, his society, his culture, and finally in the human condition itself. They assume responsibility for resolving conflicts and assuaging psychic pain. They confront the tragic absurdity of human life with the baptized ignorance of science.

We would be so much happier if we could be more like technicians and less like philosophers. We look toward basic research as shipwrecked seamen toward solid land. Yet, what are we asking of research? To tell us what the meaning of life is, to tell us why some bits of a huge, disorganized, kaleidoscopic pattern of behavior and aspiration are more important, acceptable, or modifiable than others, and to do this with a dispassionate and value-free precision? How foolish we are to think that everything that is unknown can become known in the very same way —that ecstasy, dread and ennui, ideology, sacrifice and love will become less mysterious if analyzed by the same techniques used to analyze sound, light and gravity!

Do we really have to understand everything about our work to make it meaningful? Whether in psychoanalysis or social planning, does the psychiatrist really want as precise information about his subject or the process of working with it as the biochemist or physiologist? Well, of course he does! Who would turn his back on knowledge? Yet, while the artist may not turn away from knowledge about color and its perception

Reprinted from *The Absurd Healer: Perspectives of a Community Psychiatrist* (Chapter 6), by Matthew P. Dumont, M.D. New York: Science House, 1968.

nor the musician turn away from knowledge about the physical and physiological aspects of sound transmission, he knows how really irrelevant this knowledge is to the creation of a work of art. Perhaps in some respects, at some level, or at certain times, the psychiatrist shares something with the artist. He becomes the agent of forces that he does not understand and which he does not care to understand.

The Neanderthal who drew pictures on the walls of his cave when he might better have employed himself in the hunt with his brothers was partaking of something eternal. He was capturing the soul of his prey and partaking of the elements of faith. He must have suffered as every artist does.

That divine suffering has itself been the best grist for the artist's mill. Mann's Tonio Kröger comes to mind, doomed to look at life as through a pane of glass—or perhaps a better example is Fellini's film *8½*. This film is a work of art that describes its own creation. We, the viewer, become the artist; we have no choice but to identify with the man as we see his dreams, memories, and fantasies and experience his reality. The camera is always on him or in him so that both his inner and outer world are experienced by us.

The artist is a film-maker who has taken his staff and equipment to a spa to recapture a lost inspiration or decide whether to finish his unstarted film. He awakens from a nightmare of bizarre death and judgment to confront doctors and nurses of the sanitarium and his very own Greek chorus, his co-writer who comments cynically and negatively about the meaninglessness of every event, thought, and recollection which the artist has had and has placed in his scenario. But with what incredible intensity and loving care is each experience drawn and the whole drawn together! The people seen, met, remembered are drawn with as much care and fascination as himself, his wife, his mistress, and his co-writer. Just as Rembrandt paints an old woman paring her nails with as much dignity as a duchess examining a jewel, every detail of warmth, humor, duplicity, jealousy, grief, and lust is portrayed as in itself a thing joyful to behold. After seeing the film, one can range over the film with one's memory picking out spots of exquisite perfection just as one points to a Cezanne orange or anticipates a movement of music within a favorite symphony: a dream of tearless sobbing at his father's funeral, a recollection of punishment because of boyhood sensuality and atonement before a seductively smiling madonna, an absurd mistress not loved but needed because she permits lovemaking to become a mise en scène. Such scenes are tied together into the film being made within the film being watched and the co-writer torments its creator by incessant reminders of the pointlessness of the scenes and their irrelevance to one another. But he is wrong.

Early in the story, the director attends an evening entertainment perfunctorily provided by the resort, and, after a decaying chanteuse (still fascinating despite her over-ripe voice and appearance), a mind-reading act presents itself. The shadow of a formally attired man appears on a screen. The man suddenly bursts into laughter and appears in the flesh—part clown, part mystic, part actor in his make-up—and shouts, "Maya, let's entertain these bores." He walks from table to table pulling objects from the pockets or handbags of spectators while the blindfolded seer calls them out. He holds his hands over the heads of people; she calls out their thoughts. A borderline psychotic young woman becomes hysterical at the thought that her mind with its primitive contents will be read; she is comforted and led away by her companions. Wandering behind them is our director who greets the mindreader's consort as an old friend, then asks how it is done. He says with candor and a pleased simplicity that he doesn't know, but somehow when she is in the proper frame of mind, the objects he manipulates can be seen and interpreted by her. "Will she do it for me?" asks the director. With her agent's hands over his head, the mindreader laughs and writes down three meaningless words from the childhood of the director, and we are shown the scene of their origin—a creation of maternal love and childlike charm.

The mindreader does not appear again but her agent does in the final scene, and his role becomes significant. After a crescendo of despair, frustration, and self-doubt, with fantasies of suicide and public mockery in his mind (the *paparazzi* of *La Dolce Vita* dance around him like flies), the director succumbs to the intellectual judgment of the co-writer and is about to drive off, abandoning the film, the actors, the props, everything. The co-writer drones on about how wise this decision is, when suddenly the mindreader's agent with his magic wand appears before the car. "Come," he says, "we are all ready," as if he had not heard, or was incapable of understanding, or refused to believe that the film would not be made. The director stares at him as if hypnotized, stops the car and gets out, the voice of his co-writer becoming more distant and his face no longer visible behind the reflections of sky and trees in the windshield.

The director almost mechanically walks back to the set—suddenly seeming to understand . . . what? that he does not have to understand. He must complete the film that has already been made in his own mind and in our reality because it is beautiful and moving and the actors have reproduced people who have their own life and reality, and they must not be allowed to die. The actors qua characters are brought together behind a curtain drawn by the director, and they march to his direction, now wearing white. They are all pure now (like the girl in white as an inadequate symbol of purity throughout his fantasies) because they have been cleansed of irrelevant "significance" and can now emerge as pure works of art, as abstractions uncontaminated by memory, fantasy, reality, or iconography. The march is led by the director, now holding hands with his own creations, and his final act is to place within the suddenly appearing circus ring the young actor who played his own childhood and the symbol of entertainment and magic—the clown. The fadeout is on his own child-soul piping on a bittersweet lute.

The mindreader's agent was responsible for the decision to complete the film. Why he? Because as the agent of mysterious and magical forces, he epitomizes the role of the artist. It would be absurd for this man to give up his function because he cannot understand its mechanism, just as it would be absurd for the artist not to produce his masterpiece because he cannot understand what its organization or appeal is.

Psychiatrists tease apart threads of human behavior: watch stories of grief, rage, and longing unfold before them; search for the covert behind the manifest; are confronted with paradox; scrutinize and manipulate one relationship as a paradigm of thousands of others; relate in a thousand different ways; are aware of a few and comment upon fewer facets of a whole universe of phenomena; and still insist upon being behavioral scientists. There may come a time when the analysts of behavior who want to break things down into discrete units that can be measured will be able to feed into a computer not only the words transmitted back and forth between therapist and patient, but also the intonations, the gestures, the expressions—the infinite array of metacommunications—and also the memories and associations that each communication and metacommunication brings forth to every level of consciousness in each of the two individuals. The computer may then be able to put all of this data together and come up with something resembling the truth, but of course it won't. Henri Bergson said that science takes a simple gesture and breaks it down into many still photographs, and as science becomes more advanced, the photographs increase in number and sharpness, but it can never capture the essence of the movement. That movement remains something different from the many analyzable photographs of it—interesting as those photographs are in themselves.

The therapist who recognizes love or despair or anger in his patient does not have to analyze bits of data to make that recognition. When we see a friend coming towards us, we don't stop to ask ourselves if the nose, eyes, mouth, or clothing match that of a person we think we know—we either see him as the friend or we don't.

In his ability to resort to intuitive, extrarational and immediate sources of information about his patient without the constant analysis of artificially fragmented bits of data, the psychotherapist is like the artist.

But like art, there is good and bad psychotherapy, and one of the best criteria for good art or psychotherapy is the degree of control and consistency pervading the freedom of perception and expression. In art this control may be supplied by aesthetic or iconographic considerations; in psychotherapy it is supplied by conceptual ones.

During a psychotherapeutic session the therapist may view his patient and the relationship between them in psychoanalytic terms, at other times in behaviorist terms or transactional terms; and at still other times, he may abrogate the conceptualization completely and permit himself the necessary luxury of watching the unfolding of a human drama in purely existential terms.

When I was a resident in psychiatry I had a patient who taught me that psychotherapy cannot always be guided by what is known or theorized.

A 25-year-old man entered treatment because he was unable to carry on a conversation with a woman. For two years this symptom had grown progressively more severe and incapacitating. It had begun shortly after the suicide of his young wife after one year of marriage.

He told the story of his marriage during our first interview. He had thought the relationship a happy one. There had been some conflicts with his wife about her previous dependency on her mother in the face of her new alliance with a husband, but all in all they had seemed to be compatible and sensible and capable of confronting and solving problems.

For several weeks prior to her suicide, his wife had been depressed and argumentative. On the day of her death, they arose together as usual and ate breakfast before going to their separate jobs. He usually left first while she had a second cup of coffee. On that morning as he was getting ready to leave, she asked, "Please stay a few minutes to talk with me." He responded, "All right," and sat down, but after another moment she said, "Never mind, you'd better get to work." When he returned that evening, she was dead.

He could not weep. He went through the funeral and the condolences—the whole strained, empty, uncomfortable ritual of family and friends and institutional grief feeling nothing but a numbness inside himself. He mechanically picked up the fabric of his life as a widower at 23. He was not really depressed; he slept and ate well, was not hopeless about the future, anticipated a satisfying career, and saw himself remarrying eventually. He did not look sad. Despite this there was a presence of a peculiar numbness within him at all times—as if all feelings, joy as well as grief, were locked away in some hidden chamber of his soul; and then, there was his symptom, he could not talk to women.

My supervisor and I agreed that this was a pathological grief reaction, that some source of unconscious guilt had interfered with the normal, healthy, painful, necessary process of grieving. My patient had never experienced the weeks of despair, emptiness, yearning, the burning tears that never seem to stop, that wash away the multitude of conflicted feelings that tie human souls together. Our job was to find out why. The patient and I explored his past. He had had good relationships with his parents, friends, and teachers. He was successful and competent at school and work. There had been no previous neurotic symptomatology. One overwhelmingly significant crisis in his life prior to his wife's suicide was the sudden death from heart disease of his mother ten years before. We focused on this event though the early and precipitous loss of his mother seemed to have been adequately grieved and accepted, but certainly it could have left him with a sensitivity to loss that might have fed into his present state. As this focus was sharpened, as we attempted to illuminate the bridge between the deaths ten years apart of the two most important women in his life, something happened. It happened so insidiously that it was several therapy sessions before I realized that it was happening. I found that he was becoming less spontaneous, that his memories and thoughts had become less accessible, and that I was working harder to draw them out. When I stopped drawing him out, I was confronted with a silent patient.

I tested this and said nothing for a total session, and for fifty minutes my patient said nothing. He expressed no curiosity, no dismay, no discomfort, no anger at the silence, nothing.

Armed with my supervisor's experience and advice, I interpreted the patient's silence as a resistance to therapy. We had approached an area in his psychic life that was too laden with anxiety, and his defensive reaction was to be silent. There was no response to the interpretation. When I asked him if he had any thoughts, he said he had not. His mind, he said was a blank, and so I waited.

In years past, during summers, I had swung a pickaxe, waited on tables, and carried garbage pails. In medical school I committed endless pages of information to memory. During my internship I stayed awake more than 40 hours at a time caring for seriously ill patients under impossible circumstances. But never have I found more difficult work than spending 50 minutes with a patient in psychotherapy in total, complete, absolute silence.

He never missed a session and was always on time. I, too, was always there on time, fortified with strong, black coffee to help me stay awake. After several weeks, my supervisor became a little impatient and suggested that perhaps it was time that we tell the patient to start working in therapy or leave. But I decided not to do this. Was it stubbornness in me or was I dimly, subliminally aware of some need on my patient's part for me to wait him out? Seven hours passed in silence. I kept asking myself what use this served. Expensive and urgently needed professional time was being spent. I was learning nothing about my patient, and he was learning nothing about himself. The minutes passed laboriously as if the entire weight of an individual's helplessness and despair hung on the hands of the clock. I became aware of my own impatience. It showed itself to me (and possibly to the patient) as boredom and fatigue. I also began to hypothesize deeper psychopathology in him than I had originally supposed. Was he a severe passive-aggressive personality disorder or even schizophrenic rather than merely neurotic? Then it ended, much more suddenly than it had begun.

During the eighth hour of silence, the patient heard me ask, perhaps with more warmth than he expected, "How are things going?" I said it quietly, just above a whisper. It sounded almost seductive, too seductive, I thought to myself immediately after I uttered it. He looked directly at me as he almost never did. So quickly that I remember marveling at the speed which an emotion can be transformed into a glandular secretion, his eyes became moist. He said, "I've wanted to talk so badly." The words poured out of him. He seemed to be choking his sobs back. He talked of how miserable he was during the long silence, of how he dreaded me, of how he expected me momentarily to throw back my chair in furious disgust and outraged impatience and leave him. Then, within minutes he was remembering the day of his wife's suicide, retelling it as if he were reliving it, staring at the wall opposite as if he were watching it unfold before him. It was practically the same story as he told before, but not exactly. He remembered that the night before, they had had an argument, a particularly bitter one. He remembered being annoyed with his wife's grating, conflicted dependency on her mother. He remembered thinking that he himself had lost his mother earlier than he should have and what right did his wife have to complain? His annoyance with her was not quite dissipated by sleep. And now he remembered, and winced with the remembrance, that when his wife asked him to sit and talk with her before going off to work, he had said not "All right" but "Oh, all right" with a sign of impatience, a residue of annoyance, a distinct, unmistakable metamessage of hostility to which his wife could only respond, "No, never mind. You'd better get to work." Then she killed herself.

He wept, sobs racked his body and convulsed his shoulders, and tears flowed down his face. He covered his eyes with his hands, and his fingers were white as they pressed around his eyes. In his broken, miserable and child-sobbing voice, he said, "If only . . . I had been . . . more patient . . . waited for her to talk . . . tell me how bad she felt . . . I could have comforted her . . . and . . . she'd be alive." From that hidden, locked chamber of his soul came an endless wail of guilt-ridden grief, of longing and lost love.

The silence ended, the treatment progressed; and as his grief progressed, he could take a more balanced view of his wife and her death. Eventually he could again express hostility towards her for having done such an incredibly hostile thing towards him; and eventually his grief came to an end and left him free of the painful yearning, guilt, dependency, and helplessness that is the grieving process.[1] He would never forget his wife, but he would not go on missing her so much that his life lost all meaning, hope, and integrity. Within three months his symptoms vanished. He decided to terminate his treatment shortly after becoming engaged to be married.

Later I asked myself how I could have known that the story of the subtle impatience that cut the life thread of his wife could not have been told unless my patience was strong enough to wait for it. He was unconsciously atoning for his own unconscious guilt by placing me in his position. The guilt would have been lessened had I told him to start working or leave, but the therapy would have ended with the agonizing conflict still locked in. It was not scientific fact nor rigid adherence to a process that led me to the result, it was something else, something beyond theory.

The community psychiatrist, no less than the psychotherapist, shares something with the creative artist. The forces of social change and the nature of organizational life are more complex and multifaceted than any theory can encompass. Tolstoy's General Kutozov in *War and Peace* knew about the irrational and inscrutable aspects of war. He was victorious not because he was a brilliant strategist, but because he knew how to abrogate military strategy in the face of the mysterious forces that led a cavalry charge to rally a disintegrated army to victory and that caused the defeat of an overwhelmingly superior force because of a cry of panic.

Social action no less than war requires the ability to abrogate "strategy" as well as to make use of it. Social change is an irrational mixture of rational and extrarational forces. Institutions and individuals both have complex lives, and it is rarely possible to predict with certainty what the ultimate impact on human welfare will be of any institutional change.

---

[1]One of the great psychiatric papers of all time, one which provided a quantum jump to community psychiatry, was Dr. Erich Lindemann's report on his investigations of the grieving process in the aftermath of the Coconut Grove fire in Boston. This paper, "Symptomatology and Management of Acute Grief," can be found in *The American Journal of Psychiatry*, Vol. CI, pp. 141-148.

Automation, which promised to free mankind from the burden of toil, may bring in its wake undreamed of anguish. Medical science in reducing death rates and lengthening the life expectancy may have condemned mankind to an animal-like struggle for life-space.

A great part of the effort of men to enrich themselves, to increase their freedom and to enhance the quality of their lives has resulted in the reverse. Like Sisyphus, damned to rolling his huge stone up hill, we are engaged in an absurd struggle.

The Tasks of the Therapist

by Joen Fagan

All professional persons are basically problem solvers who are employed to reduce discomfort or conflict and to increase the possibilities of certain valued outcomes for the persons who request their assistance.[1] Therapists, specifically, are engaged by persons who are dissatisfied with their own, or another's experiencing and behaving, which may include internal experiences of anxiety, discomfort, conflict, or dissatisfaction, and external behaviors that are either inadequate or insufficient for the tasks at hand or that result in difficulties with other people. The problems presented to the therapist may be central to the person and require extensive changes, or they may be peripheral and quickly solved. Not only the problems are varied, but also therapists differ widely, both in their procedures and in their effectiveness with different kinds of persons and problems. I believe that therapists and therapeutic techniques will become increasingly specialized and increasingly effective, partially as a function of research and partially as a function of rapidly growing willingness to experiment with a variety of new techniques. However, while many changes will occur, the basic tasks of the therapist will remain similar. The purpose of this article is to examine the tasks or requirements of the therapeutic endeavor under five headings: patterning, control, potency, humanness, and commitment; to indicate briefly the contributions of various approaches or "schools" to each of these; and to focus on contributions from Gestalt therapy.

Reprinted by permission of the editors and the publisher from J. Fagan, "The Tasks of the Therapist." In Fagan & Shepherd (Eds.) GESTALT THERAPY NOW. Palo Alto, California: Science and Behavior Books, 1970.

[1]While this article deals specifically with therapists, the tasks described can be modified and extrapolated to describe any professional group.

PATTERNING

The therapist is first of all a perceiver and constructor of patterns. As soon as he is informed of a symptom or a request for change, and begins listening to and observing a patient and responding to him, he begins a process that I refer to as *patterning*. While *diagnosis* is a more common term, it has the disadvantage of provoking the analogy of the medical model and implying that the purpose of the process is arriving at a specific label. A better analogy for the process of patterning is that of artistic creation, involving sometimes cognitive, sometimes perceptual and intuitive skills in interaction with the material and demands of the environment as, for example, in the creation of a mobile, in which a variety of pieces or systems are interconnected into an overall unity and balance.

As the therapist begins his contact with the patient requesting help, he has available a body of theory which is largely cognitive in nature, a background of past experience, and a number of awarenesses and personal responses derived from the ongoing interaction that have large emotional and intuitive components. From these, which may be given varying degrees of importance by a specific therapist, he begins to form an understanding of the interaction of events and systems that result in a given life style that supports a given symptom pattern. *Events* refers to the things that have happened or do happen to the patient; *systems* includes all those interlocking events that interact on a specific level of existence, such as biological systems, self-perception systems, family systems, etc. The patient is visualized as a focal point of many systems, including the cellular, historical, economic, etc. The more the therapist can specify the entire interaction, or be sensitive to the possible effects of systems he is not directly concerned with (such as the neurological), or intuit the connecting points between systems where the most strain exists, the more effective he can be in producing change. He can act on a level and at a point that promises the most positive change in symptoms or conflicts at the least cost of effort, and where the least disruptive change will occur to other systems.

An example may clarify some of the above description. A mother refers her son whose increasing stomach distress causes him frequently to stay home from school. The therapist shortly begins to accumulate information of various sorts. He learns that: the boy also has stomachaches that keep him from going to camp or from visiting relatives; the mother has few interests outside the home; the father does not like his job and also has frequent illnesses; the mother and father have intercourse very infrequently; the boy has average intelligence; the grandmother is very interested in his becoming a doctor; the other children tease him for being a sissy; his teacher is considered strict; the school system has a new superintendent who has made many changes, etc. The therapist observes that the boy waits for his mother to answer for him; that his voice is weak when he does answer; and so on through a long list of responses, observations, and experiments in which the therapist obtains some sort of assessment of the abilities of the boy and his family to respond to varying suggestions and pressures. Through these processes a picture emerges with increasing clarity. The boy, his stomach, his family, his peer group, the school, the school system, and the community come into focus with varying degrees of explicitness.

We first label our understanding of the crux of the problem and then move to intervene on one or possibly several levels, depending on our personal preference, style, and understanding. No matter how badly we do initially in spotting the interactions that are most important, there is a clear possibility that intervention on any level may sooner or later produce the changes we wish, since the systems are interlocking and a change in one system may produce changes in some or many of the other systems. (This may be paraphrased, "Everyone has a little bit of the truth.") We may start with a medical approach, choosing antispasmodics, antiemetics, or tranquilizers. We may attempt to produce primarily internal psychological changes by play therapy, hypnosis, rational-emotive procedures, or desensitization. We may attempt to set up environmental learning situations by academic coaching or by activity group therapy. We may use behavior modification by observing the ways in which the mother reinforces the boy's avoidance behavior and may work with her to change these. We may see the mother individually to help her change her perception of mothering, support her in developing outside interests, or involve her in sensitivity training. We may work with the father in exploring his frequent illnesses or in helping him to find more job satisfaction. We may select couple therapy to assist the parents in dealing with their sexual problems and developing a more satisfactory marriage. We may use family therapy to increase communication, clarify the parents' interactions with the boy, and find ways of modifying the grandmother's influence. It is also possible to arrange environmental changes, such as changing teachers or schools. We could work with the teacher or school counselor, and finally (but grandiosely) we could envision involving the school system, the community, or eventually, the country.

No matter what procedures are chosen, we will need to evaluate our results by three main criteria: how rapidly the symptom has been removed, what positive behavior has replaced it, and how little disturbance has been created in the interlocking systems. These areas of evaluation will be discussed at more length in the section on techniques that follows.

Each therapy system has its own rationale and its own ideas about personality and procedure. Techniques are designed to intervene at the place or places where the theory says the pattern can most easily be modified. All theories and techniques fail at times because no two patterns are exactly alike and the points of conflict may vary widely. However, all theories that are taken seriously have some successes since changes in any system can affect others.

The Gestalt contribution to patterning involves a de-emphasis on cognitive theory and provides extensive assistance with the therapist's own awareness. Enright[2] describes this process in detail, emphasizing the clues to underlying events and life styles that can be uncovered by awareness of the person's movements, tones, expressions, word choice, etc., and suggesting some appropriate techniques for exploration. Much of Gestalt patterning is worked out in the therapy process itself rather than by history-taking or interviewing. The meanings that result, as in dream work, are very different from the more traditional analytic interpretive approaches where certain meanings are specified in advance by theory or predicted from the patient's previous history. Of course, past events of much importance do arise from the process of exploring posture, gestures, and dreams. However, the Gestalt therapist is not interested in the historical reconstruction of the patient's life, nor in weighing the effects of various environmental forces, nor in focusing upon one specific behavior such as communication style. Rather, he is interested in a global way in the point of contact between the various systems available for observation. The interactions between a person and his body, between his words and his tone of voice, between his posture and the person he is talking to, between himself and the group he is a member of are the focal points. The Gestalt therapist does not hypothesize nor make inferences about other systems that he cannot observe, though he may ask the patient to reenact *his* perceptions of them, as in a dialogue with his father, for example. Most Gestalt procedures are designed to bear upon the point of intersection, and the nature of the other system is viewed as less important than how the patient perceives or reacts to it.

In other words, the patterning emphasis in Gestalt therapy is on the process of interaction itself, including the patient's skills in fostering and risking interaction, or blocking awareness and change. Since these are skills of importance in the intersection of any systems from the biological through the social, the Gestalt therapist sees himself as preparing the individual to interact more effectively in all aspects of life. Perls's ideas

---

[2]See Chapter 8, "An Introduction to Gestalt Techniques," and Chapter 21, "Awareness Training in the Mental Health Professions," by John B. Enright in *Gestalt Therapy Now*, Joen Fagan and Irma Lee Shepherd (Eds.). New York: Harper Colophon, 1971.

concerning a therapeutic community, which he is presently formulating, represent a possible extension of Gestalt thinking to a more extensive system.

CONTROL

No matter how clear and adequate the therapist's patterning is, he must be able immediately to exercise control or nothing else can follow. Control is defined as the therapist's being able to persuade or coerce the patient into following the procedures he has set, which may include a variety of conditions. Control is not used here with cynicism or a Svengali attitude, nor is there any implication of ignoring the value of genuine concern and liking for the patient; it simply reflects the reality that unless patients do some of the things that therapists suggest, little will happen, and that which does happen will be mostly by accident.

Whitaker (1968) makes this idea very explicit: "Therapy has to begin with a fight . . . a fight over who controls the context of therapy. . . . I want it understood that I'm in charge of what happens. I see this as the administrative battle I have to win [in Haley and Hoffman, 1968, pp. 266, 267]" (A number of other therapists have written extensively about the importance of control: Haley, 1961a, 1961b, 1963; Rosen, 1953.) Haley and Erickson often use a paradoxical double-bind, a command so phrased that there is no way of disobeying it, or disobedience involves making admissions that are extremely damaging or revealing. These not only maintain control but often contribute to a very rapid reduction in symptoms. Rosen, Bach, and others often use group pressure as a means of control. A patient may be able to meet or defeat the therapist in a fight, but his chances against eight or ten people who are aware of what he is attempting are very slim.

Part of the importance of control is that all symptoms represent indirect ways of trying to control or force others into certain patterns of behavior. The therapist has to counter being controlled by the patient's symptom pattern and also establish the conditions he needs to work. Some of the conditions will be overt behavioral requirements, such as keeping appointments, paying, bringing other family members, etc. Other conditions will be more covert or implicit, such as the willingness to give information, attempt suggestions, or produce fantasies. While the required aspects of external behavior vary from therapist to therapist, it is essential that the conditions most important to him be met to his reasonable satisfaction. It is common knowledge that patients who initially ask for special favors or conditions, such as special appointment times or reduced fees, will be more difficult to work with; and the therapist often counters by setting up stronger-than-usual controls, such as payment at each interview or the use of a consultant.

Two of the major aspects of implicit control can be examined under the concepts of motivation and rapport. Motivation is often thought of as being related to the patient's discomfort or anxiety; the higher these are, the more the patient is willing to work. However, the degree of distress can be thought of with equal validity as the willingness of the patient to relinquish control to the therapist. Some persons who are experiencing marked distress are difficult to work with because they attribute their discomfort to others via blame. Their motivation for change is high but their willingness to surrender control is low.

Rapport is usually presented somewhat ideally as the "good feeling" and amount of positive relationship between patient and therapist; more accurately it is the therapist's ability to persuade the patient, or the patient's willingness to trust the therapist's control of the situation. While liking for the therapist is probably necessary somewhere along the therapeutic process, and of value even initially, it is probably more important in the early stages for the patient to believe that the therapist knows what he's doing.

The techniques the therapist uses to gain and maintain control are often, though not necessarily, different from the ones he uses to produce personality or behavioral change. (All techniques, of course, depend heavily on the style of the individual.) The therapist must recognize, manifest, and counter the patient's efforts at taking control by his usual means, some of which will be represented by his symptoms, others more deviously. He must manage to avoid being put off, frightened, or bored by the psychotic; to keep from being had by the psychopath or enjoying him too much; and to avoid being too sympathetic or agreeing with the neurotic's formulations. He must be able to remain his own man while also becoming enough involved with the patient's life style to experience its problems and difficulties.

A special problem is presented by the patient who comes because of external coercion, such as court order, divorce threat, or parent's commands. The situation is such that the external agent has the control, and the therapist runs the risk of becoming his hireling, ostensibly agreeing that he and the patient will work hard to please this outside person. The therapist has, however, at least three main ploys to regain control: he can involve the referring agent, thus indicating that both the agent and the patient need help; he can disavow the external payoff ("It's no concern of mine whether you flunk out of school"); or he can go along by an initial identification with the person's goals to contrast with the agent's as, for example, in Schwartz's (1967) and Greenwald's (1967) offering to make their patients into better psychopaths.

External compliance with a threatened punishment has an internal parallel—the pseudocompliance and "improvement" labeled by analysts as "intellectual insight" or "transference cure" and by transactional analysts as playing "Greenhouse" or "Psychiatry" or "Gee, You're a Wonderful Therapist" (Berne, 1964). Perls's label is "bear-trapper," which describes the patient who, having learned something about the expectations of the therapist, goes through the motions of cooperation, then at a crucial moment refuses to comply with suggestions, thus catching the therapist off balance. Often the bear-trapper is a person with considerable underlying pathology who has much invested in demonstrating that he cannot be helped or changed, and that those who try do not have the power to force him. In this situation, regaining control is difficult since the patient has made it clear that efforts on the part of the therapist to control only indicate an admission of his failure. Renouncing control and admitting failure is one way of regaining it.

Another problem of control can be anticipated with the patient whose presenting symptoms include psychosis or potential psychosis, suicide, and the more severe varieties of "acting out." These are persons who in the past have effectively utilized the threat, "If you don't do what I want, then I'll . . . (kill myself, go crazy, embarrass you, etc.)." These are potent threats and can invoke fear and self-doubts, or may even blackmail the therapist into acting in ways that jeopardize his purpose and position. Suicide or homicide are the ultimate threats, and each of these may force the therapist into assuming more control than he wishes—which, of course, admits that the patient is in control. One of the most effective ways of neutralizing such threats is to make a clear contract initially. Szasz (1965a) informs patients that they will need to make arrangements with someone else if they require hospitalization; Goulding (1967) requires signed contracts from potentially suicidal patients in which they agree without reservation to make no suicide attempts while they are seeing him.

Another type of control only now beginning to be explored systematically is that offered by total environments, such as prisons and mental hospitals. For many years we attempted to deny that external control, other than gross loss of liberty and bare conformity with institution procedures, was either important or desirable. The success of behavior-modification procedures, which make many of the bare amenities of living dependent on certain patient behaviors, is forcing a reevaluation of the position that external control is not appropriate for persons who are unwilling or unable to utilize internal control. The painfully sincere and extensive study by Rogers and his associates (1967) in which competent and dedicated men attempted to modify the behavior of chronic schizophrenics by ignoring external control and attempting to assist the recovery of internal control by nondirective therapy resulted in almost complete futility. It is becoming increasingly evident that in patterning and control, chronic schizophrenics have obliterated almost all of the usual systems and procedures, and can be approached initially most effectively by very specific controls related to the immediate environment. Evidence is also accumulating to suggest that treatment of acute schizophrenic episodes may be approached most effectively by treatment of the total family (Langsley et al., 1968). The major implication of environmental control as represented by behavior modification is that it is needed to the extent to which the individual is unable or unwilling to assume internal control; to the extent to which internal control is possible, external control is insulting, inefficient, or a violation of civil liberties.

Control is most important in the beginning of therapy. The need for control decreases as cooperative control by patient and therapist increases because of greater ability to communicate in each other's language and the development of trust. However, at important points of change, the struggle for control will reemerge, usually on a more intense level, and the therapist should be prepared to fight this battle periodically.

Even initially, the attempt to maintain complete control is impossible and the appearance needs to be periodically renounced, first as a paradoxical way of maintaining control and secondly as a way of encouraging the patient's own assumption of responsibility and growth. (An excellent example of this is found in Simkin's chapter "Mary."[3]) However, the abandoning of control should be viewed as an occasional technique and not as a complete system, as in the early days of nondirective therapy, or in group situations (see, for example, Bion, 1961) where the leader refuses to assume a leadership role. The inevitable outcome is that the group, in order to fill the vacuum, engages in a struggle for leadership accompanied by considerable expression of anger. Since this is a systems effect, the leader cannot claim credit for having produced any special results, and the value to the participants is dubious. While the person whose electric supply is disrupted may be able to get along with candles and a fireplace, this demonstration of self-sufficiency is not what he is paying the power company to produce.

The Gestalt contribution to problems of control includes a number of responses and procedures. Initially the therapist encourages patient autonomy and minimizes struggles by telling the patient that if he has strong objections to complying with suggestions he can (has the

---

[3]See Chapter 13, "Mary: A Session with a Passive Patient," by James Simkin in *Gestalt Therapy Now*, Joen Fagan and Irma Lee Shepherd (Eds.). New York: Harper Colophon, 1971.

therapist's permission to) refuse, and his refusal will be honored. However, he is told that he has to state his reason for refusal. Often, as the reason is given, it can be explored for validity ("What's so terrible about being embarrassed?") and the patient will decide to continue.

Gestalt therapists ask for a clear statement from the patient concerning what he wishes to accomplish. Proceeding from this central theme keeps the emphasis on the patient's stated wishes, not the therapist's expectations. Procedures that keep in the present and make it clear that the therapist is in sensitive awareness with what is happening also decrease resistance. (When a patient begins meeting opposition from his conflicts and the discomfort that surrounds them, he may clearly resist, but this is on a very different order from resistance of control.) The patient is often asked if he would be willing to try an experiment: an acceptance carries a mild commitment to continue, while a refusal is honored if a reason is given. The patient who freezes, draws a blank, or has nothing come to mind can be asked to verbalize his refusal more specifically or to take responsibility for it by saying, "I am making my mind blank." Another procedure is to go with the resistance ("Tell me that it's no business of mine what you're thinking") and then have the fantasied therapist answer back. The value of resistance can also be approached ("What are all the good reasons for refusing me now; what does refusing do for you that is valuable for you?").

POTENCY

To justify his hire, the therapist must be able to assist the patient to move in the direction that he wishes, that is, to accelerate and provoke change in a positive direction. We are rapidly leaving the time when the therapist, in the absence of more specific knowledge, relies on "something" in the relationship that will result in "something" happening. We are approaching the time when the therapist can specify procedures that promote rapid change in a way that the patient can experience directly and others can observe clearly. For a given patient, many of the changes that do occur are a direct or by-product of the therapeutic relationship. (The therapeutic relationship is both a technique and a transcendence of techniques.) However, the therapist has need at many points of techniques, procedures, experiments, gimmicks, directions, and suggestions that can overcome inertia and promote movement. The patient who asks for specific assistance should expect to receive it.

Techniques are one of the more publicized aspects of psychotherapy; everyone knows that Freudians interpret and analyze dreams, and others hypnotize, analyze transactions, give tokens, etc. With increasing speed and accuracy, we are able to remove symptoms and change behaviors such as phobias, sexual deviations, inhibitions, etc., that only a few years ago were thought to require extended treatment. The increasing power of the therapist has resurrected two old topics that have a long history: the question of therapist authenticity versus techniques and the problem of symptom substitution.

The existentialists and neo-Rogerians (Rogers, 1951; Bugental, 1965; Carkhuff and Berenson, 1967) write powerfully of the human condition and the need for genuine relationships. However, techniques are often ignored or decried as being artificial, with the implication that authenticity cannot occur in their presence. I observed one of the most highly respected existential therapists in the country leading a group that was being observed by several hundred people and video-taped as a record of his way of working. The group, composed of student volunteers, spent over forty minutes continuing to be uncomfortably aware of the audience and verbalizing their discomfort at being observed and expected to produce. The therapist periodically shared with the group his own anxiety, selfconsciousness, and fears that nothing would happen. When, at the end of the hour, a group member finally volunteered a "problem"—that he was temporarily short of money—the group responded with great relief and vast amounts of concern and sympathy. However, neither the therapist nor the group would have had to remain "stuck" had he been willing to utilize any of a number of techniques.

Gestalt techniques appropriate to the situation would have had members of the group in turn play the part of the critical audience and the stupid, helpless child, externalize their projections, take the role of critic and criticize the audience, "ham up" their own discomfort, etc. These procedures would have allowed them to further their own growth by reducing the internalized demands of others' expectations and to reclaim and modify their disowned disapproval, while at the same time they would be reducing the audience to "ground" and then could continue with whatever needs emerged as "figure." Suffering with another when the reasons for his suffering are not genuine or allowing him to continue with discomfort when this can be reduced is hardly humane.

A second therapist on the program specialized in behavior modification in groups. His techniques invoked persons in the group into becoming involved in such obviously insincere and artificial interactions that it came as no surprise to discover that he had carefully rehearsed the group members the night before. However, there is no need to think of suffering-with or artificial techniques as representing an either-or choice; rather, they are two undesirable extremes, between which lie many combinations of the values of potency and humanness.

The problem of symptom substitution has reappeared with the advent of behavior modification, and it has apparently become important for behavior modifiers to defend their procedures and their potency against questions as to the possibility of substitution of other unwished-for behavior and lack of permanency in the behavioral changes (see, for example, Calhoon, 1968). Part of the problem concerns the rapidity of the change—the extent to which rapid change is permanent or will be replaced with equivalent symptoms. The speed with which behavior can be changed with a reasonable degree of permanence depends on whether it is central or peripherel to personality structure and to what extent it intersects with other systems that can reapply pressure to keep it in force. In other words, the combination of speed and potency of behavior change depend on the number and strength of the props that hold up a given bit of behavior. Props may be the reinforcements of other people, catastrophic expectations on the part of the patients, ignorance, unchecked assumptions, etc. Some of these may be removed easily, especially if they are discomfort-producing and if other systems are minimally affected. The question of symptom substitution must take into account three questions: whether the symptom is replaced by another on the same level, what positive goals have occurred, and to what extent other systems have been disrupted. Let us return to the example of the boy with the stomachache presented earlier and assume that he is given medical treatment of such potency that he ceases to have stomach complaints. However, he then develops acrophobia that just as effectively keeps him at home. The physician, concerned only with the physical system, states that there is no symptom substitution, that is, there are no other medical problems and therefore the problem is solved. However, the therapist, who views the boy's main problem as avoiding school, defines the phobia as symptom substitution and proceeds to treat him by behavior modification. As a result the boy attends school but cries all the time and fails his work. Another result might be that the boy's mother, finding that she can enjoy directly controlling passively resisting men, puts such pressure on her husband that a divorce occurs. While Freud apparently cured the phobia of Little Hans, his parents did divorce (Strean, 1967). Other therapists who define the problem as success at school or the mutual satisfaction of the entire family would see each of these attempts as evidences of inadequate, incomplete, or inept therapy. We can continue moving up the systems ladder by hypothesizing other possibilities: what if, because of the improvement in the entire family, they come into conflict with the authoritarian school system; or the father, by deciding to leave his job, contributes to the bankruptcy of the company he worked for?

There are no final nor even clear answers to this morass, but I can offer some suggestions:

1. It is not enough to specify the symptom to be removed; it is also necessary to describe what positive functioning is expected.

2. The most important interconnecting systems should be specified and attempts made to keep disruptions to a minimum.

3. If disruptions are inevitable, the therapist should specify his value choice.

The three points above need amplification and the detailing of underlying assumptions. One is that, with very few exceptions, symptoms represent a positive as well as a negative force. Most symptoms, be they medical, individual, or social, even though painful, disturbing, and time consuming, are indicative of intersections that need to be repaired lest greater damage occur. In trying to change symptoms, we must always look to the larger system to note whether the symptom is justified. (It is possible that the school system could become so destructive that to force children's attendance would be to contribute to much more serious problems than would arise from nonattendance.) Symptoms may also have positive value, such as holding a couple together.

With our powerful Western technology we change and redo large parts of our physical environment without any appreciation of the values that we are negating and without any provisions for replacing their loss. As a result we are constantly being faced with land erosion, floods, air pollution, drops in water-tables, etc. Similarly, in therapy we are creating a technology that lets us change personality faster than we know how to solidify it or provide for the fragments left behind. If we attempt to specify what is healthy in a symptom pattern, then we will know more clearly what to leave alone.

It is also important to specify the replacement behavior for symptomatic difficulties, even though this is presently somewhat utopian. Of what value is it to remove a snake phobia—what does this contribute to living in a positive sense? Or, if we remove overt homosexual behavior, is asexuality adequate, or ability to have intercourse with randomly chosen females? Or do we aim toward the formation of a sustained, personally satisfying heterosexual involvement? Most therapists would prefer to avoid the specification of positive goals, since this involves them in clear value choices and since achievement may be embarrassingly short of the goals. It is also true that most patients request the removal of symptoms rather than specifying replacement behavior, and their goals usually change during the treatment process as additional possibilities become available. However, the therapist who does not consider the question of goals in their broader aspect becomes a mere technician, or a flunky of the values of the culture and its institutional systems.

Finally, and also ideally, if we have done our jobs thoroughly, we have not markedly disrupted any other system. This is a complicated issue, and only some of the parameters can be suggested here. It is, of course, true that growth and change are both disruptive of systems. The child will leave home in the process of growing up; changes in other systems will make an institutional administrative arrangement inadequate, causing different and expanded procedures and organization, and perhaps another kind of discomfort. We therefore have to decide whether the disruption of a system is inevitable or whether it is destructive, that is, whether it creates wounds that require extensive energy to heal, energy that could be better used for expanded growth. This question is one for Solomon; however, the therapist, even with his much more limited resources, should still have at least an awareness of his role as a system disrupter. A denial of this effect ("The only thing I do is to change a person's specific behavior") can be regarded as gross myopia. For example, consider a therapist whose patients are primarily dissatisfied housewives. In his work with them, he fosters their becoming appropriately more demanding and assertive. However, the end result is frequent marital problems and divorces, as the husbands reject their wives' demands or use them as excuses for affairs, etc. Much of this could be avoided if the therapist were willing to see couples jointly (or could modify his strong rescue needs). If the goal is to make a person less dependent, then the immediate question can be raised, less dependent upon whom? It follows that the "whom" may have some responses of his own that will likely lead to strains in the family system. If the therapist is aware of these strains, he can take steps to anticipate and deal with them.

Sometimes disruption cannot be avoided. If we are able to "decraze" a late-adolescent schizophrenic whose family refuses to be changed, then one or both parents may show psychotic symptoms themselves. (At times, one measure of change is the disruption of interrelated systems or the extent of the pressures they employ to force return to earlier states.) There are times when systems may well need to be abandoned: when the student should drop out of school or the worker quit his job. The therapist no longer has the luxury of avoiding the problem by decreeing that no decisions be made during therapy (life moves too quickly for this), nor can he ignore the fact that changes resulting from therapy inevitably create decision situations. Helping the patient with deciding in a given situation whether to run, fight, or compromise requires a full measure of the therapist's humanness. In general, I would prefer to maintain rather than to disrupt systems. However, this implies degrees of wisdom and power that are not yet consistently available.

When leaving a system is inevitable, the therapist can assist the patient with the reduction of unfinished business by having him in the therapy session confront, in directly spoken fantasy, the person(s) with his resentments, appreciations, regrets, and good-bys.

Finally, the therapist can predict for the patient as early as possible that system disruption may occur, allowing him to anticipate and have increased choice in the outcome. While the choice of end goals is basically the patient's, the therapist has the responsibility of anticipating and reminding the patient of as many choices as possible. There are unfortunately many conditions that reduce the number of options, and with a given patient, quite limited goals are often inevitable, given limited resources and rigid systems. The therapist should be able to accept these while being aware of further possibilities.

One of the major contributions of Gestalt therapy is the power of its techniques, which make possible the very rapid reaching of deep emotional levels. It should be noted that having access to potent techniques presents a temptation to overuse them, and the therapist needs to be aware that he has other tasks of importance.

HUMANNESS

The therapist's contribution to the therapeutic process as a person and the importance of the genuineness and depth of the therapeutic relationship have been emphasized by a large number of therapists. Humanness, as it is used here, includes a variety of involvements: the therapist's concern for and caring about his patient on a personal and emotional level; his willingness to share himself and bring to the patient his own direct emotional responses and/or pertinent accounts of his own experiences; his ability to recognize in the patient gropings toward deepened authenticity, which need support and recognition; and his continued openness to his own growth, which serves as a model for the patient.

Some patients' needs are peripheral and can be adequately attended to by therapists with only brief or minimal involvement. But many—if not most—people were raised by families who, even while doing the best they could, taught them less about being human than they need to know. If a patient's problems stem from inadequate rearing, then the teaching of more adequate behavior is basically a process of rearing. This requires adequate humanness in the therapist who assumes the parenting role, since he will serve extensively as a model and will have to make many value-laden decisions. This does not rule out briefer therapeutic contacts. There is a trend among some therapists who assume long-range responsibility to suggest or arrange for patients at certain stages such adjunct experiences as sensitivity training, art therapy, structural reintegration, or marathons. There is also an increasing emphasis among some behavior modifiers to consider their assignment unfinished until more adequate behavior is substituted for the symptom that is removed.

In raising children, it is the subtle learnings, attitudes, and non-verbal messages that are perhaps the most important. As the father teaches his son to fix the sled, or the mother shops for clothes with her daughter, they communicate perceptions of the child as stupid or bright, pleasant or unpleasant, likable or disgusting, and demonstrate attitudes such as interest, endurance, and enjoyment. Factual knowledge and routine bits of information are most efficiently taught by teaching machines or their equivalents, but not tolerance or curiosity, nor the value of "wasting" time.

Patients inevitably put therapists in a parental position, that is, they see them as having the secrets of living and test them in many ways to see if they will be adequate models. I tell patients, "Basically what we are doing here is seeing if I, as I am now, could have grown up in your family as you present it to me in your person, and remain sane." The patient in rapidly alternating ways involves me with his problems to see if I can respond more adequately than his parents could, and presents me with his parent's problems to see if I can find better ways of dealing with them than he was able to. For those patients for whom therapy is and becomes a central and intense experience, external living crises become relatively less important, and reenactments of growing-up crises occupy increasing attention. They progress backward through time and present their unsolved problems in a roughly reverse temporal order. Most often the final decision to accept me totally as parent comes as the result of a crisis, often following a minor mistake I made at the same time the patient is beginning to come to grips with core problems. (A somewhat limited example is given in Fagan, 1968.) The crisis is unexpected in that I can never anticipate its presentation; in retrospect it becomes apparent that the patient sets up a situation in which I am put to the test that his parents failed most badly. The crisis clearly measures my understanding of the patient's patterning, my ability to control, my potency, but most of all my humanness, since a response is unavoidable and usually must be immediate and genuine, drawing on resources that lie far below the level of techniques. I do not always pass the test. Sometimes when I do not, the patient tries again later; sometimes he gives up and adopts lesser goals; sometimes he turns to other sources of help. When I have passed, I know immediately since the patient in an unmistakable way becomes my infant and our feelings toward each other involve a kind of adoration (for example, Searles, 1965, Chap. 21). We work our way back up through developmental milestones of childhood and adolescence until the patient is as well regrown as my own resources as a parent allow. [Other descriptions of this process are given by Whitaker and Malone (1953) as the *core phase,* and by Carkhuff and Berenson (1967) as the *downward and upward stages* of therapy.] It is of course true that many therapists do not and/or cannot involve their patients to this extent, and many patients ask for assistance of a much more limited nature. However, deep personal regrowth is still experienced by those involved as either patients or therapists as the crux of therapy.

On a less intense and involved level, but still important, are those crises of living on which the therapist must respond to the patient more from this humanness than from his knowledge or techniques. These would include a severe illness, a child killed, an important goal having become unattainable, a deep rejection. Before or after dealing with those aspects that are correctable, there exists the need for bearing those parts that can only be borne. The therapist needs to know from inside himself when his presence is the most important contribution he can make to the healing process, and when his response as one human being to another is more important than any therapeutic busywork.

The events of the past few years—the civil rights struggles, student rebellions, experimental college movements, hippie communities, and the explosive growth of sensitivity training and group experiences —bespeak a level of hunger for new ways of experiencing, relating, learning, governing, etc., but they also are contributing to the development of a number of people whose experimentations are producing new levels and patterns of authenticity. If therapists fall too far behind in their own growth, they will be out of touch with an increasing proportion of the population.

The making of oneself into a whole and genuine person is probably the most difficult and painful aspect of becoming a therapist, but, for many, it is also the most valuable and important part. Many therapists who see authenticity as a primary task of the therapist fear those who, having stopped short in their own struggles with growing, substitute increased emphasis on control and potency, with a corresponding lack of regard for questions of value associated with the ability to produce personality change. The question of who controls the controllers becomes more acute as control over behavior becomes more possible. In the name of mental health, many horribly inhumane and degrading things have been done to people (Szasz, 1965b) and will no doubt continue to be done. Those who are certain of the good that they do are more to be feared than those who are more willing to admit and struggle with their own personal limitations, to share their doubts, and to express their values.

The contributions of Gestalt therapy to the humanness of the therapist come primarily in the workshop setting, which offers therapists direct experience with their own inauthenticities and avoidances. The emphasis on eperiencing rather than computing, and the fostering of here-and-now awareness, pleasure, excitement, deep emotional involvement, and direct interaction seem especially designed for therapists, many of whom tend toward obsessive and depressive styles. Experiencing and observing ways in which authenticity can be distinguished from its many imitations is a valuable contribution.

Gestalt theory confronts therapists as directly as patients with reminders of the values and pleasures of living that can get pushed aside by our occupational hazards of overemphasis on work, responsibility, accomplishment, and study. Finally, in work with patients, Gestalt techniques offer a variety of ways of allowing them a rapid, deep, and authentic experience with themselves which provides an increased knowledge of what is possible as well as allowing a quick and direct "knowing" on the part of the therapist.

COMMITMENT

A number of major and minor commitments are necessary to the therapy process. The therapist commits himself to a vocation with its attendant demands for continued growth of his own understanding and ability. He also commits himself to individual patients in his work with them. Finally, he commits himself to contributing to the field as a whole by his research, writing, training of students, etc.

Commitment, or the continuing involvement and acceptance of assumed responsibilities, requires high levels of interest and energy. Interests may be maintained in a variety of ways. There are many problems that have large cognitive components, including understanding patients and constructing patterns. There is the broader task of theory addition and construction, or the long-term satisfaction of a research program. Also involving are the deep satisfaction of seeing the growth of patients, the challenge and excitement of devising new procedures and techniques, and the steady increments of the therapist's person and powers. However, no therapist can avoid boredom, depression, and doubts related to the therapeutic process and his own procedures, either for brief moments or for extended periods. If the therapist's techniques are mechanical and boring, involving him only passively or superficially, or if the interaction required creates too much anxiety, then the therapist will either be spurred to less directly central areas such as research or, unfortunately, training.

Gestalt therapy places most emphasis on the therapist's commitment to himself in terms of enhancing his involvement and excitement in the day-to-day tasks. It also provides or suggests ways for the therapist to assist himself in exploring his own boredom and doubts when they occur. In these respects it enhances both therapist and patient interest and offers ways of getting both "unstuck" when faced with the inevitable impasses.

Some final thoughts: The five tasks described in this paper will vary in their relative importance in response to many factors; the context surrounding therapy, specific requirements and limitations, the types of problems presented, and the time sequence or stage of therapy. At times the therapist will experience conflicts between two of the tasks, for example, between control and humanness. As the emphasis shifts from task to task, to some extent the image of the therapist shifts, in a way that, with much magnification, parallels the popular stereotypes of the therapist as the mind reader who knows all, as the hypnotist who can control persons against their will, as the magician who has a collection of magic tricks, as the loving Big Daddy or Mommie, and as the faithful, patient family retainer.

In summary, many requirements are made of the therapist as he sets out to assist another person. These have been discussed under five headings: patterning, control, potency, humanness, and commitment. The therapist's response to these involves him as a complete person, including his intellectual knowledge and cognitive abilities, his interpersonal effectiveness, his emotional awareness and personal sensitivity, his values and interests, and his experience in living. Certainly one of the continued challenges and fascinations of therapy is the variety of demands that it places on the therapist and its ability to require and evoke from him an involvement and utilization of all his resources.

REFERENCES

Berne, E. *Games people play.* New York: Grove Press, 1964.

Bion, W. R. *Experience in groups, and other papers.* New York: Basic Books, 1961.

Bugental, J. F. T. *The search for authenticity: An existential-analytic approach to psychotherapy.* New York: Holt, Rinehart & Winston, 1965.

Calhoon, D. D. Symptom substitution and the behavioral therapies: A reappraisal. *Psychological Bulletin,* 1968, *69,* 149-156.

Carkhuff, R. R., & Berenson, B. G. *Beyond counseling and therapy.* New York: Holt, Rinehart & Winston, 1967.

Fagan, J. Message from mother. *Psychotherapy: Theory, Research and Practice,* 1968, *5,* 21-23.

Goulding, R. Introductory lectures in transactional analysis. Atlanta, Ga., 1967.

Greenwald, H. Treatment of the psychopath. *Voices,* 1967, *3*(1), 50-61.

Haley, J. The art of psychoanalysis. In S. I. Hayakawa (Ed.), *Our language and our world.* New York: Harper & Brothers, 1959.

Haley, J. Control in brief psychotherapy. *Archives of General Psychiatry,* 1961, *4,* 139-153. (a)

Haley, J. Control in psychotherapy with schizophrenics. *Archives of General Psychiatry,* 1961, *5,* 340-353. (b)

Haley, J. *Strategies of psychotherapy.* New York: Grune & Stratton, 1963.

Haley, J. & Hoffman, L. *Techniques of family therapy.* New York: Basic Books, 1968.

Langsley, D. G., Pittman, F. S., Machotka, P., & Flomenhaft, K. Family crisis therapy —results and implications. *Family Process,* 1968, *7,* 145-158.

Rogers, C. R. *Client centered therapy.* Boston: Houghton Mifflin, 1951.

Rogers, C. R. (Ed.) *The therapeutic relationship and its impact: A study of psychotherapy with schizophrenics.* Madison, Wisc.: University of Wisconsin Press, 1967.

Rosen, J. N. *Direct analysis: Selected papers.* New York: Grune & Stratton, 1953.

Schwartz, L. J. Treatment of the adolescent psychopath—theory and case report. *Psychotherapy: Theory, Research and Practice,* 1967, *4,* 133-137.

Searles, H. F. *Collected papers on schizophrenia and related subjects.* New York: International Universities Press, 1965.

Strean, H. S. A family therapist looks at "Little Hans." *Family Process,* 1967, *6,* 227-234.

Szasz, T. S. *The ethics of psychoanalysis: The theory and method of autonomous psychotherapy.* New York: Basic Books, 1965. (a)

Szasz, T. S. *Psychiatric justice.* New York: Macmillan, 1965. (b)

Truax, C. B., & Carkhuff, R. R. *Toward effective counseling and psychotherapy: Training and practice.* Chicago: Aldine, 1967.

Whitaker, C. A., & Malone, T. P. *The roots of psychotherapy.* New York: Blakiston, 1953.

My Philosophy of Psychotherapy

by William Schutz

1. What is your approach to psychotherapy?

My goal as a psychotherapist is to help create conditions which make it easier for you, the patient, to be honest with yourself, aware of yourself and others, to take responsibility for yourself, and to realize that your life is your choice. I am not concerned with the specific content of the life you choose unless you are bothered by it, unless you want my opinion as a person, or unless I want to react to it. I am concerned with helping you to achieve clarity, to not deceive yourself, to be in touch with how you are feeling. I relate to you in whatever way it takes to achieve these aims. I am available. I am as honest and open as I am capable of being. I share my feelings, I suggest, urge, withdraw—whatever I feel like doing, because I have made clear that you are responsible for yourself, and that includes dealing with me.

2. Has your approach to psychotherapy undergone any basic change since you first started?

I've changed. I came out of the traditional psychoanalytically oriented therapy tradition. I was cool, I interpreted, I was aloof, I took responsibility for all patients. Now I act the way I feel, and take whatever responsibility I feel like taking, usually based on what I think will be most effective and on how I feel at the moment. As I become more comfortable about my reputation, fear less the censure of my colleagues, reduce my need to be dazzling, have less need to be needed, and so on, the more I am willing to let group members take responsibility for themselves.

Reprinted from *Journal of Contemporary Psychotherapy,* 1974, 6(2), 412-416. Used by permission of author and publisher.

I've also changed in that I believe in honesty more thoroughly. I change as I begin to *really* understand the things I think I believe. Honesty does indeed lead to energy and freedom. The more I can let everyone know anything about me, the more free I feel.

I've changed in that originally I didn't understand how central the body is in human growth. I was militantly a *social* scientist rather than a *biological* scientist, while a graduate student. I didn't understand that there is no important distinction between body and mind, and that the body is a golden road to self-understanding. For this realization, I'm indebted especially to Alex Lowen, Ida Rolf and Moshe Feldenkrais.

3. What is your evaluation of the present state of the practice of psychotherapy?

I don't really know the present state of psychotherapy. From my position I don't have an overview. The methods that I think are promising seem far more widely used now than ten years ago. These new methods—body oriented, non-verbal, fantasy, eastern, mystical—are influencing traditional methods in what seem to me to be valuable ways.

4. What role should psychotherapy play in society-at-large?

I look upon the way I do psychotherapy as continuous with the way I live. Psychotherapy is a procedure for realizing a person's full potential. So is life. The encounter principles of honesty, responsibility and awareness apply equally to psychotherapy and to everyday living. The Encounter Culture is an attempt to make this application. It is an alternative to the Watergate ethic.

5. Would you attempt a prediction about the future role of psychotherapy as a profession?

My predictions are primarily either wishes or fears that I meet by anticipating the worst.

My wish for the future is that psychotherapy becomes absorbed into a larger quest for human evolution. The rehabilitation role of therapy will give way to prior strengthening, to joy maintenance. Techniques now available and to be developed will help people to achieve awareness and control over their own functioning. Biofeedback, meditation, sensory awareness, Feldenkrais and fantasy are now leading in that direction. Once control is achieved, we can choose for ourselves whether we want to be ill, or have mystical experiences, or whatever.

Psychotherapy will exist to remove blocks to achieving this state. The more successful it is, the more unnecessary it becomes.

6. How do you feel about being a psychotherapist?

I've found being a therapist an excellent way to work on my own personal growth. Because of the therapeutic method I've adopted, I become a better therapist primarily by working out my own problems. The freer I am, the more I can allow others to enter into difficult personal and interpersonal areas.

Periodically I tire of doing therapy, due to the repetition, my fear of disappointing, and probably other reasons I'm not aware of. I never really wanted to be a therapist. I began as a researcher and teacher. Being a therapist evolved as it became clear that I would learn about people better that way. I'm not basically a healer, I have never had a continuous practice, nor do I want to. I enjoy being a therapist more as I learn how to allocate a place for it in my life. It helps me to understand my fundamental quest: what's it all about?

The Patient

as Collaborator

The person who comes for help to a humanistic psychotherapist is still likely to be called a "patient," although that label carries the connotation of a passive recipient who undergoes treatment. The patient is a person prior to his acceptance of the patient role, as Whitaker and Malone remind us in their article: a person who accepts a role so that, paradoxically, he can become a more fully functioning and real human being. The process of transfomation—moving from being "just me" to someone fully human and perhaps beyond that—is detailed in the selections by Rogers and Maslow.

Personhood via psychotherapy is not available to everyone. The charge against psychoanalysis—that it is a middle-class treatment for middle-class persons with middle-class hangups—can be made against the newer psychotherapies as well. Humanistic psychotherapy has accomplished no significant breakthroughs for the patient who is poor, unmotivated, or chronically schizophrenic.

In his review of the research literature, Enrico Jones explores the results of psychotherapy with the poor. He concludes that the class-related biases of mental health professionals may be as important in producing negative therapeutic results as any personality characteristics of lower-class patients, and that the expectation gap between psychotherapist and patient has yet to be bridged by the newer therapies.

Jones's review is not an indictment of humanistic psychotherapy, but it provides a challenge to those who consider psychotherapy as a way to fulfill human potential: some way must be found to allow those who are handicapped by social conditions and cultural biases to collaborate in their own growth processes.

The Patient as a Person

by Carl A. Whitaker and Thomas P. Malone

THE PEARL

Said one oyster to a neighboring oyster, "I have a very great pain within me. It is heavy and round and I am in distress."

And the other oyster replied with haughty complacence, "Praise be to the heavens and to the sea, I have no pain within me. I am well and whole both within and without."

At that moment a crab was passing by and heard the two oysters, and he said to the one who was well and whole both within and without, "Yes, you are well and whole; but the pain that your neighbor bears is a pearl of exceeding beauty."

Gibran[1]

The general public has accepted for years the quip that to the psychiatrist every person is a patient. Although we deny this publicly, the accusation comes very near to the truth. It has many implications. Among ourselves, we recognize that a person sees in others only what he has seen in himself. It may be then that the psychiatrist sees others as patients since he so frequently faces his own patient facet. This appraisal may provide us with a more honest basis for our orientation in psychotherapy. As we will see further on, the therapist sees himself as a person only after he has been a patient. From this we recognize that all persons have similar potentialities and that, therefore, all persons are *potentially* patients. We must, however, differentiate between these potential patients and the actual patient who comes into the office for treatment.

Reprinted from *The Roots of Psychotherapy,* by Carl A. Whitaker and Thomas P. Malone. Blakiston Press, 1953. Used with permission of the authors.

[1]From Kahlil Gibran,"The Wanderer: His Parables and His Sayings." Copyright © Alfred A. Knopf, Inc. Used with permission.

THE GENESIS OF A PATIENT

Psychotherapy can be utilized in two fundamental ways: It can provide help for the patient in need of psychiatric treatment for very specific symptoms, and it can help the socially adequate and fairly mature individual to become more creative than formerly and, in general, to develop more of his capacity to function as a well-integrated adult. Accordingly, psychotherapy may help the "sick" individual, or it may actualize the potential capacities of the average "normal" person. Potential patients fall, roughly speaking, into three groups: those who come with pathology grossly apparent to the outside world (society), those whose pathology becomes obvious only in the interviews, and those whose pathology is discernible only to the patients themselves. The mere fact that the individual has gross pathology, however, does not mean that he becomes automatically a patient. Many people continue to operate on a compensated level and repeatedly deny all offers of help. In this group, even those who obviously should be patients are not. As a matter of fact, one of the growth experiences of the young therapist evolves from his effort to convert a sick person into a *patient*. In his enthusiasm as a professional person, the young therapist will often respond in a professional manner to a bit of pathology revealed in a social setting. He thereby shows little recognition of the importance of the patient's initiative in bringing his problem to a therapist, or the importance of isolating his "therapeutic role" from the realities of ordinary social living. Thus, the young therapist may respond to the depression of a friend while at a cocktail party. Such an approach often succeeds in freezing the depressed friend and making him more anxious. The next day, the therapist may realize he has lost a friend, or be startled by the distant reaction of his erstwhile friend and "patient." Furthermore, even a patient who comes to the office with gross pathology may reject his offer of help in the same way. Both these individuals could be patients and could benefit from therapy, *but they do not accept their patient status.* What does this mean?

Previously, we discussed the implication that psychopathology represents, in one sense, a request for therapy. This request may be consistently and aggressively denied consciously and may be detectable only on a symbolic level. A patient, then, is simply defined as a person who asks for help from the psychotherapist. An individual may be able to ask for help from one therapist and not from another. Even when the patient asks for help, there remains the problem of the therapist's "hearing" him. Some therapists can hear a request for help even when expressed in the obtuse symbolic language of the schizophrenic, whereas others seem to have difficulty unless the patient demands help more directly.

One schizophrenic patient, who had rather rigid paranoid feelings, kept demanding in the initial interviews, "I want to get out of here. Please let me out of here. I've got to get out of here so that I can lead a normal life." Superficially, she was talking about leaving the interview room. On a symbolic level, she was speaking of getting out of her schizophrenic isolation and, in this sense, symbolically begging for help. Even with this request, she still was not a patient. She was not a patient until the therapists not only theoretically knew, but more important, subjectively felt, that she was asking for their help. With the concurrence of her need felt in both herself and the therapists, she became a patient.

Patient status, in general, involves acceptance on the part of both parties of a felt need. Patient status has, therefore, two ingredients. First, the concept "patient" as used here becomes a biological concept. It implies the existence of a discrepancy between the individual's current effectiveness in his living and his biological potential. This deletes from the concept of "patient" the cultural relativity which has caused psychiatrists so much concern in the past. One culture may satisfy certain needs more fully than others or accept one type of personal deficiency more readily than another. However, the objective basis of the individual being a patient is precisely the difference between what he is and what he could be. The second ingredient of patient status is a subjective acceptance of his need, and its presentation, whether consciously or unconsciously, to another person in order to obtain help with it. Finally, the therapist must accept that need as something with which he can struggle. Only when these objective and subjective ingredients occur together can it be said that this person has become a patient.

Patient status, then, is defined by the therapeutic process itself. It does not antecede it, nor does it exist apart from therapy. It is not equivalent to pathology. An individual may have gross pathology and not be a patient, or have minimal pathology and be a patient. In the case of the deteriorated schizophrenic previously discussed, she became a patient when the therapist developed the capacity to recognize her need so that it became meaningful to him personally, and consequently provoked some emotional response in him. As this developed, she demanded, with increasing urgency, the rights of her patient status.

The above dynamics appear most openly in collaborative therapy. The authors frequently qualify their acceptance of a patient with the understanding that his parent or spouse obtain therapy simultaneously. This poses a difficult task since these individuals see themselves as normal in comparison with the "real" patient and have no conviction of their own need. The problem has additional facets since, just as frequently, the therapist to these latter individuals has little advance conviction of their need. The initial struggle in this therapy, thus, seeks to achieve a bilateral, felt acceptance of their need on the part of both patient and therapist. The relative's acceptance of his patient status usually follows the therapist's recognition of his emotional involvement in it. We have belabored this point to give force to our conviction that the process of psychotherapy is bilateral, even to the extent of insisting that the therapist's reaction may constitute the determining factor in bringing about patient status in an individual. From here on, we are going to discuss, primarily, the patient's dynamics despite the artificiality of such an abstraction.

BARRIERS TO PATIENT STATUS

The patient's decision to see a therapist is no easy one. What brings the patient to the therapist? The pressures which force him to take this step must be fairly urgent ones. He has essential barriers to overcome. The first, and probably most important of these, evidences his unwillingness to upset his own neurotic equilibrium. This compromise, even though it limits his gratifications in life, also satisfies him in certain ways. For example, it provides him with some kind of protection and enables him to live on a fairly safe, though sterile, level. He senses that therapy may cause him to reverse the defensive compromises of a lifetime. The fact that he lacks much appreciation of the possibility of achieving a more adequate level of living makes it all the more difficult for him to seek treatment. Sometimes the patient comes to the therapist because he wishes, not so much to grow, as to repair those self-therapeutizing patterns through which he has obtained certain "subsistence level" gratifications, and which, for various reasons, are now breaking down. For example, one overt homosexual wanted to make sure that he would not fall in love. Yet, despite all this, the patient's coming to the therapist, in the face of years of compromise living, implies a deep recognition of the tremendous power of the long-suppressed growth impulse in himself as an individual. To see the almost unprovoked stirrings of the need to grow in the deteriorated schizophrenic forces one to respect the dominant role of this urge in the hierarchy of living impulses.

The person who comes to a therapist defies, in a sense, many of his own cultural values. This constitutes a serious deterrent. For example, in seeking therapy, he tacitly blames his culture for its failure to provide him with adequate "growth nutrition," i.e., with therapy. Thus, the very act of coming to the therapist points up many of the deficiencies of the community within which he lives. More particularly, he implicates those members of the community who live in close association with him. One wonders, therefore, just how much of the hostility which our culture expresses against psychiatry, and against psychotherapy, reflects some latent recognition of the fact that the need of its members to seek therapy constitutes a reflection upon the community in which they live.

Be that as it may, the patient comes only because something powerful in him overcomes both a lifetime of compromise living and the cultural pressures enforcing submission to the parents and parent substitutes. The patient must also overcome the anxiety mobilized by the recognition that his auto-therapeutic functions have failed. Indeed, he has to reject the culture and its therapeutic function in order to isolate himself from the culture by coming to the professional therapist. Lastly, he must reject an earlier therapeutic relationship to some individual (social therapist) within the culture, e.g., the referring physician. Even the individual who has not been referred has usually struggled for satisfaction of his emotional needs with some other individual or group in his community at some time in the past.

THE SOCIAL THERAPIST

Patients seldom, if ever, come to a professional therapist without having first experienced some growth in a previous therapeutic relationship. Social therapists often help patients therapeutically, though their relationship may not be a professional one. Everyone in the community functions at one time or another as a therapist to the needs of others. We call this process "social therapy." They usually are not conscious of the process of therapy and, as therapists, have marked limitations. Nevertheless, in their relationship with a specific person, they frequently provide a modicum of gratification. This measure often gives the patient a first glimpse of the possibility of growth through therapy. In this sense, we are convinced that most, if not all, patients are referred from social to professional therapists. What happened to the patient prior to his first interview with the professional therapist represents what we call the "pre-interview phase of therapy." This implies that an increase in the number and adequacy of social therapists in any community might be a partial answer to the problems of preventive psychiatry.

Many difficulties beset the transfer of the patient from a social to a professional therapist. An almost inevitable hostility develops toward the social therapist, resulting from his failure to be completely effective. Part of this hostility toward the social therapist represents transference of infantile feelings of rejection. Whatever its source, these feelings are transferred onto the professional therapist to whom the patient responds, early in their relationship, much as the patient had responded to his social therapist. We frequently hear such remarks as, "You sound just like my husband," or "I don't see why my doctor sent me to you." This last illustration contains the core of another difficulty. Patients develop deep transference to their social therapists, e.g., referring internist which, later on, hinders the development of a deep relationship to the professional therapist.

The therapist must "work through" his own response to this hostility and his competition with the social therapist before the relationship can go beyond the point of the previous rejection. This "working through" on the part of the therapist brings to the patient, at the outset, some indication of the limitations and immaturities of the therapist. Acceptance of these by the patient expands the initial professional relationship into a more personal one. In a sense, it implies a recognition by the patient that the therapist has a fantasy life of his own, which will inevitably play a part in the development of his own fantasy life.

CULTURE: THE LAST BARRIER

As mentioned above, the patient's fantasy of therapy includes the fear that therapy is possible only in defiance of the culture. In order to conform to his culture, the patient has had to develop a façade of maturity. He has denied repeatedly those deeper needs which he felt were antagonistic to cultural demands. Now, confronted with an opportunity to express his childlike needs, the patient must first break through his pseudo-adult pattern. In doing so, he fears that the therapist will respond to his needs as his culture has done, i.e., by denying these infantile needs. Were this to happen, he might then be unable to re-establish his protective façade. Furthermore, he intuits that the therapist will offer him such satisfactions that he will become a helpless child and might be held forever dependent. Patients frequently say, "I'm afraid that if I really let myself become a little baby, I'll never grow up (again), and you wouldn't take care of me." This wish opposes the hostile, aggressive demand that the culture (or therapist) take care of him. The ambivalence of dependence and assertion of adequacy characterizes the initial period of psychotherapy.

The patient turns to the therapist as a possible escape from the struggle within himself. His concept of the therapist reflects a cultural stereotype which includes some of the following characteristics: the therapist has all the magic which the child ascribes to the parent, i.e., in his presence the patient will suddenly and miraculously be cured. In this sense, the physician becomes the witch doctor of our culture. In his fantasy, the patient depends on this omnipotent parent to share his burden and to carry the onus of his disease. The therapist also engenders hate, as someone who deprives the patient of part of his individuality. The unique needs of each individual patient mold his interpretation of the cultural stereotype. Its specific characteristics are determined by the constellation of that individual's "intra-psychic family." When the intra-psychic family of the patient comes to include in this manner also the doctor-therapist, the process of therapy, as an intra-psychic phenomenon, begins. Conversely, and in much the same manner, the patient is, in turn, an introject, and so becomes part of the intra-psychic dynamics of the therapist. This means that the process is a bilateral one. The patient's stereotype of the therapist fuses with the members of his own intra-psychic family. In this sense, the doctor may be anybody —God, teacher, the devil, the nurse, or society. The individual patient's projections are numberless.

These cultural barriers to the patient's obtaining psychotherapy find their most direct expression in the patient's family. The family has a deep sense of guilt since the patient's sickness attests to their failure to mature him adequately. They have further difficulty in bringing him to the therapist, since often the emotional homeostasis (economy) of the family centers around the patient. They sense that if the patient changes, they too must change. For example, the "martyred" wife of the alcoholic patient not only fulfills a mother role, but satisfies her own neurotic needs by keeping her husband dependent. Therefore, if the alcoholic husband comes for therapy, this disrupts her compensatory neurotic patterns by breaking up the dovetailing of two previously complementary neuroses. Often the resentment, guilt, and neurotic dependence of the family expresses itself as a fatalism about the patient being able to recover. They say to the patient, "We want to give you whatever is necessary for you to get well," but beneath this is the fatalism and resentment engendered by their own failure to have given him what would have kept him well. When the patient comes to the therapist, much of the family's ambivalence falls upon the therapist, and the patient now has to adjust to the added problem of their feelings about the therapist.

In spite of the projections of the patient and the cultural barriers, the therapist must maintain himself as a person in his own right, so as to be able to alter the make-up of the patient's intra-psychic family. Antagonism between the patient and the culture (particularly the family) presents the therapist with many administrative and personal problems. A psychiatrist often accumulates hostility toward the family of the patient. He senses how the family rejects the patient, and he resents this. This resentment in turn increases the family's antagonism toward him. Ordinarily, neither the family nor the therapist can openly express their resentment since each feels bound by the culture. Should the therapist express his personal feelings to the family, he frees himself for a more adequate relationship to the patient but endangers his professional status with them.

This may only become a problem after therapy has begun and the patient begins to get well. For example, the father of an adolescent schizophrenic, recovering at last as a result of intensive therapy, decides suddenly that the treatment has failed and withdraws the patient from therapy. The patient's recovery apparently provokes guilt and anxiety in the parent, which he resolves by this withdrawal. Not only does the patient's therapy upset the family by removing the patient from *them* and thereby changing the family's dynamics, but often in removing the pre-psychotic from the family, one deprives the latter of its most functional therapist member. A portion of the family's aggression toward the professional therapist originates in these same dynamics.

Confronted with such uncertainties, the patient brings to therapy all the mechanisms at his command in order to protect himself from further rejection. These protective mechanisms, when manifested in therapy, are thought of as resistances.

Resistances also have a very specific therapeutic function. They do not simply provide the patient with protection from anxiety but, on a deeper level, they also protect him from this new parent whose feelings and capacities he presumes but must discover for himself. Resistances thus occupy a central place in the beginning phase of therapy, and require a bilateral relationship for their resolution. If one looks at resistance from this point of view, one notes at once that the therapist, too, frequently brings to the initial interview a good number of his own resistances, and uses them in the same manner. In both persons, resistances function to provide protection against rejection by the other person. A new rejection would be more painful than the mere recall or re-enactment of past rejections, because of the additive effects of the repetition compulsion.

Of course, many of the patient's resistances are derived from his recognition of the therapist's inadequacies. The patient constantly searches for the real potential in the therapist. Once he discovers it, he may force the therapist to function at his fullest capacity. We have all seen patients whose resistances disappeared rapidly. This rapid movement derives from the more or less complete personal involvement of the therapist and from his readiness to give to the patient that which is more than implicit in his professional role. We would even suggest that the ideal therapist would encounter no resistance whatsoever.

At the outset of treatment, the patient means little to the therapist, except as a representative of all previous patients, and in a reality sense, a professional responsibility. He may also perceive the patient as a symbol of the culture. Finally, of course, the therapist has unconscious motivations which facilitate the transition to personal involvement with the patient.

The growth impulse provides the positive motivational factor which enables the patient to struggle in order to get beyond the above barriers. This is identical with those biological forces operative in the structure and function of the body itself which impel the growth of the total organism. Certain internal tension systems may bind the patient's energy in such a manner that very little free energy remains available, yet the power used in the therapeutic process, to a large extent, derives from the patient himself. The implications of this for the conduct of the therapeutic relationship are many and pervasive, but not different in general character from similar implications which are obvious to the biologist or the physiologist on the basis of his understanding of the body's function, and especially, of its reparative function. We have already, in some detail, taken up the implications of this finding for the therapeutic process, although we did not discuss its pertinence to the understanding of the problem of psychopathology. The self-reparative capacities of the patient can be brought to bear in the therapy by utilizing the free energy components of the patient's personality to the limit. Indeed, in order to free further quanta of energy, the patient must find even greater access to his own unconscious energies. This means that he does more in therapy than just learn how to use his already available energy more constructively. Since the neurotic binding of this energy has been brought about by the pressures of the culture, this bound energy must be liberated on a level more primitive than a cultural one. The therapist can, and does, use forces available within the individual in order to release this bound energy. The therapist may then become concerned because of some doubt of the patient's capacity to reorient himself in terms of reality, and his undervaluation of the capacity of the culture to reintegrate the patient into its framework. In general, psychiatry tends to *underestimate* the constructive capacity of the human being. This reflects a general medical bias, since many physicians also *underestimate* the physiological potential of the human body, even though they have scientific proof of the capacity of tissue to continue to function despite seemingly insuperable difficulties.

CONCLUSION

We have followed the patient from his initial impulse to seek therapy, which he derived from his social therapist, into the process of therapy with a professional therapist. Once in that process, the patient can only be seen within the bilateral relationship. This makes it difficult to discuss him as a separate person. His limited separateness as an individual in the central therapeutic process may be compared to the limited autonomy of the nursing infant as a person. The infant can be understood fully only within the framework of his relationship to the mother. Here we will simply "pick up" the patient as he leaves the process of therapy. Assuming an adequate therapy, certain minimal changes have taken place.

This, at once, raises a controversial question which has been bandied about in psychiatry for many years: What is a cured patient? Let's ignore the superficial conception of treatment as consisting of the alleviation of symptoms. We agree with those who say that successful therapy may not always require a complete redirection of the dynamics of the person's energy. This concept can perhaps be best expressed negatively. Patients do not enter therapy with a large infantile segment in their makeup and emerge from it as adults. Neither has the child finished his growth when, as an adolescent, he leaves home. Restructuring of the personality does not always occur in therapy, and perhaps not even growth itself, but rather, therapy means an overcoming of the inertia in the all-but-static growth process. The patient does not leave the therapist "mature." He leaves "different," in that he has gained access to those processes within himself and within society through which he can become mature. Further, he leaves with the understanding that he must struggle time and time again in his lifelong effort to achieve more and more maturity. The experience of relating himself to another human being on a primitive level has taught him to go beyond the existing limits of his personality and to become involved in a deep and emotionally satisfactory symbiosis. He can now give expression to more of his needs, be they infantile, adolescent, or adult, and can accept the response to and gratification of these needs and feelings with less guilt, shame, or sense of debt than before. He has found that he can emerge intact and with a new sense of his own worth and a deeper sense of his own integrity from such an experience. He has also discovered a greater sense of the integrity of others. The actual and specific content and framework of this therapeutic experience assumes less and less importance. He has gained the capacity to demand, obtain, and participate in a new experience. Therapy has gone beneath the cultural encrustation, and has biologically unshackled certain bound energy systems in the individual. The original function of these systems was the repair of the organism in its totality. The patient now brings this new capacity to bear upon his whole life experience. Most, if not all, of his specific conflicts and their genetic basis he then works through subsequent to professional therapy, and with individuals other than professional therapists. Therapy provides the patient with access to the whole gamut of therapeutic possibilities ordinarily available within every group and which the culture of each group has developed through many centuries. In short, the patient gets access to other human beings and, incidentally, enters the community as an adequate social therapist, no longer so concerned with himself that he cannot get and give therapy to others in a social setting.

What It Means
to Become a Person

by Carl R. Rogers

This chapter was first given as a talk to a meeting at Oberlin College in 1954. I was trying to pull together in more completely organized form, some of the conceptions of therapy which had been growing in me. I have revised it slightly.

As is customary with me, I was trying to keep my thinking close to the grass roots of actual experience in therapeutic interviews, so I drew heavily upon recorded interviews as the source of the generalizations which I make.

In my work at the Counseling Center of the University of Chicago, I have the opportunity of working with people who present a wide variety of personal problems. There is the student concerned about failing in college; the housewife disturbed about her marriage; the individual who feels he is teetering on the edge of a complete breakdown or psychosis; the responsible professional man who spends much of his time in sexual fantasies and functions inefficiently in his work; the brilliant student, at the top of his class, who is paralyzed by the conviction that he is hopelessly and helplessly inadequate; the parent who is distressed by his child's behavior; the popular girl who finds herself unaccountably overtaken by sharp spells of black depression; the woman who fears that life and love are passing her by, and that her good graduate record is a poor recompense; the man who has become convinced that powerful or sinister forces are plotting against him—I could go on and on with the many different and unique problems which people bring to us. They run the gamut of life's experiences. Yet there is no satisfaction in giving this type of catalog, for, as counselor, I know that the problem as stated in the first interview will not be the problem as seen in the second or third hour, and by the tenth interview it will be a still different problem or series of problems.

I have however come to believe that in spite of this bewildering horizontal multiplicity, and the layer upon layer of vertical complexity, there is perhaps only one problem. As I follow the experience of many clients in the therapeutic relationship which we endeavor to create for them, it seems to me that each one is raising the same question. Below the level of the problem situation about which the individual is complaining—behind the trouble with studies, or wife, or employer, or with his own uncontrollable or bizarre behavior, or with his frightening feelings, lies one central search. It seems to me that at bottom each person is asking, "Who am I, *really*? How can I get in touch with this real self, underlying all my surface behavior? How can I become myself?"

THE PROCESS OF BECOMING

Getting Behind the Mask

Let me try to explain what I mean when I say that it appears that the goal the individual most wishes to achieve, the end which he knowingly and unknowingly pursues, is to become himself.

When a person comes to me, troubled by his unique combination of difficulties, I have found it most worth while to try to create a relationship with him in which he is safe and free. It is my purpose to understand the way he feels in his own inner world, to accept him as he is, to create an atmosphere of freedom in which he can move in his thinking and feeling and being, in any direction he desires. How does he use this freedom?

It is my experience that he uses it to become more and more himself. He begins to drop the false fronts, or the masks, or the roles, with which he has faced life. He appears to be trying to discover something more basic, something more truly himself. At first he lays aside masks which he is to some degree aware of using. One young woman student describes in a counseling interview one of the masks she has been using, and how uncertain she is whether underneath this appeasing, ingratiating front there is any real self with convictions.

> I was thinking about this business of standards. I somehow developed a sort of knack, I guess, of—well—habit—of trying to make people feel at ease around me, or to make things go along smoothly. There always had to be some appeaser around, being sorta the oil that soothed the waters. At a small meeting, or a little party, or something—I could help things go along nicely and appear to be having a good time. And sometimes I'd surprise myself by arguing against what I really thought when I saw that the person in charge would be quite unhappy about it if I didn't. In other words I just wasn't ever—I mean, I didn't find myself ever being set and definite about things. Now the reason why I did it probably was I'd been

doing it around home so much. I just didn't stand up for my own convictions, until I don't know whether I have any convictions to stand up for. I haven't been really honestly being myself, or actually knowing what my real self is, and I've been just playing a sort of false role.

You can, in this excerpt, see her examining the mask she has been using, recognizing her dissatisfaction with it, and wondering how to get to the real self underneath, if such a self exists.

In this attempt to discover his own self, the client typically uses the relationship to explore, to examine the various aspects of his own experience, to recognize and face up to the deep contradictions which he often discovers. He learns how much of his behavior, even how much of the feeling he experiences, is not real, is not something which flows from the genuine reactions of his organism, but is a façade, a front, behind which he has been hiding. He discovers how much of his life is guided by what he thinks he *should* be, not by what he is. Often he discovers that he exists only in response to the demands of others, that he seems to have no self of his own, that he is only trying to think, and feel, and behave in the way that others believe he *ought* to think, and feel and behave.

In this connection I have been astonished to find how accurately the Danish philosopher, Søren Kierkegaard, pictured the dilemma of the individual more than a century ago, with keen psychological insight. He points out that the most common despair is to be in despair at not choosing, or willing, to be oneself; but that the deepest form of despair is to choose "to be another than himself." On the other hand "to will to be that self which one truly is, is indeed the opposite of despair," and this choice is the deepest responsibility of man. As I read some of his writings I almost feel that he must have listened in on the statements made by our clients as they search and explore for the reality of self—often a painful and troubling search.

This exploration becomes even more disturbing when they find themselves involved in removing the false faces which they had not known were false faces. They begin to engage in the frightening task of exploring the turbulent and sometimes violent feelings within themselves. To remove a mask which you had thought was part of your real self can be a deeply disturbing experience, yet when there is freedom to think and feel and be, the individual moves toward such a goal. A few statements from a person who had completed a series of psychotherapeutic interviews, will illustrate this. She uses many metaphors as she tells how she struggled to get to the core of herself.

As I look at it now, I was peeling off layer after layer of defenses. I'd build them up, try them, and then discard them when you remained the same. I didn't know what was at the bottom and I was very much afraid to find out, but I *had* to keep on trying. At first I felt there was nothing within me—just a great emptiness where I needed and wanted a solid core. Then I began to feel that I was facing a solid brick wall, too high to get over and too thick to go through. One day the wall became translucent, rather than solid. After this, the wall seemed to disappear but beyond it I discovered a dam holding back violent, churning waters. I felt as if I were holding back the force of these waters and if I opened even a tiny hole I and all about me would be destroyed in the ensuing torrent of feelings represented by the water. Finally I could stand the strain no longer and I let go. All I did, actually, was to succumb to complete and utter self pity, then hate, then love. After this experience, I felt as if I had leaped a brink and was safely on the other side, though still tottering a bit on the edge. I don't know what I was searching for or where I was going, but I felt then as I have always felt whenever I really lived, that I was moving forward.

I believe this represents rather well the feelings of many an individual that if the false front, the wall, the dam, is not maintained, then everything will be swept away in the violence of the feelings that he discovers pent-up in his private world. Yet it also illustrates the compelling necessity which the individual feels to search for and become himself. It also begins to indicate the way in which the individual determines the reality in himself—that when he fully experiences the feelings which at an organic level he *is*, as this client experienced her self-pity, hatred, and love, then he feels an assurance that he is being a part of his real self.

The Experiencing of Feeling

I would like to say something more about this experiencing of feeling. It is really the discovery of unknown elements of self. The phenomenon I am trying to describe is something which I think is quite difficult to get across in any meaningful way. In our daily lives there are a thousand and one reasons for not letting ourselves experience our attitudes fully, reasons from our past and from the present, reasons that reside within the social situation. It seems too dangerous, too potentially damaging, to experience them freely and fully. But in the safety and freedom of the therapeutic relationship, they can be experienced fully, clear to the limit of what they are. They can be and are experienced in a fashion that I like to think of as a "pure culture," so that for the moment the person *is* his fear, or he *is* his anger, or he *is* his tenderness, or whatever.

Perhaps again I can clarify this by giving an example from a client which will indicate and convey something of what I mean. A young man, a graduate student who is deep in therapy, has been puzzling over a vague feeling which he senses in himself. He gradually identifies it as a frightened feeling of some kind, a fear of failing, a fear of not getting his Ph.D. Then comes a long pause. From this point on we will let the recorded interview speak for itself.

Client: I was kinda letting it seep through. But I also tied it in with you and with my relationship with you. And that's one thing I feel about it is kind of a fear of it going away; or that's another thing—it's so hard to get hold of—there's kind of two pulling feelings about it. Or two "me's" somehow. One is the scared one that wants to hold on to things, and that one I guess I can feel pretty clearly right now. You know, I kinda need things to hold on to—and I feel kinda scared.

Therapist: M-hm. That's something you can feel right this minute, and have been feeling and perhaps *are* feeling in regard to our relationship, too.

C: Won't you let me *have* this, because, you know, I kinda *need* it. I can be so lonely and scared without it.

T: M-hm, m-hm. Let me hang on to this because I'd be terribly scared if I didn't. Let me *hold* on to it. *(Pause)*

C: It's kinda the same thing—*Won't* you let me have my thesis or my Ph.D. so then . . . 'Cause I kinda *need* that little world. I mean. . . .

T: In both instances it's kind of a pleading thing too, isn't it? Let me *have* this because I need it *badly.* I'd be awfully frightened without it. *(Long pause.)*

C: I get a sense of . . . I can't somehow get much further . . . It's this kind of *pleading* little boy, somehow, even . . . What's this gesture of begging? *(Putting his hands together as if in prayer)* Isn't it funny? 'Cause that . . .

T: You put your hands in sort of a supplication.

C: Ya, that's right! Won't you *do* this for me, kinda . . . Oh, that's *terrible!* Who, me, *beg*?

Perhaps this excerpt will convey a bit of the thing I have been talking about, the experiencing of a feeling all the way to the limit. Here he is, for a moment, experiencing himself as nothing but a pleading little boy, supplicating, begging, dependent. At that moment he is nothing but his pleadingness, all the way through. To be sure he almost immediately backs away from this experiencing by saying "Who, me, *beg*?" but it has left its mark. As he says a moment later, "It's such a wondrous thing to have these new things come out of me. It amazes me so much each time, and then again there's that same feeling, kind of feeling scared that I've so much of this that I'm keeping back or something." He realizes that this has bubbled through, and that for the moment he *is* his dependency, in a way which astonishes him.

It is not only dependency that is experienced in this all-out kind of fashion. It may be hurt, or sorrow, or jealousy, or destructive anger, or deep desire, or confidence and pride, or sensitive tenderness, or outgoing love. It may be any of the emotions of which man is capable.

What I have gradually learned from experiences such as this, is that the individual in such a moment, is coming to *be* what he *is*. When a person has, throughout therapy, experienced in this fashion all the emotions which organismically arise in him, and has experienced them in this knowing and open manner, then he has experienced *himself*, in all the richness that exists within himself. He has become what he is.

The Discovery of Self in Experience

Let us pursue a bit further this question of what it means to become one's self. It is a most perplexing question and again I will try to take from a statement by a client, written between interviews, a suggestion of an answer. She tells how the various façades by which she has been living have somehow crumpled and collapsed, bringing a feeling of confusion, but also a feeling of relief. She continues:

> You know, it seems as if all the energy that went into holding the arbitrary pattern together was quite unnecessary—a waste. You think you have to make the pattern yourself; but there are so many pieces, and it's so hard to see where they fit. Sometimes you put them in the wrong place, and the more pieces mis-fitted, the more effort it takes to hold them in place, until at last you are so tired that even that awful confusion is better than holding on any longer. Then you discover that left to themselves the jumbled pieces fall quite naturally into their own places, and a living pattern emerges without any effort at all on your part. Your job is just to discover it, and in the course of that, you will find yourself and your own place. You must even let your own experience tell you its own meaning; the minute *you* tell it what it means, you are at war with yourself.

Let me see if I can take her poetic expression and translate it into the meaning it has for me. I believe she is saying that to be herself means to find the pattern, the underlying order, which exists in the ceaselessly changing flow of her experience. Rather than to try to hold her experience into the form of a mask, or to make it be a form or structure that it is not, being herself means to discover the unity and harmony which exists in her own actual feelings and reactions. It means that the real self is something which is comfortably discovered in one's experiences, not something imposed upon it.

Through giving excerpts from the statements of these clients, I have been trying to suggest what happens in the warmth and understanding of a facilitating relationship with a therapist. It seems that gradually, painfully, the individual explores what is behind the masks he presents to the world, and even behind the masks with which he has been deceiving himself. Deeply and often vividly he experiences the various elements of himself which have been hidden within. Thus to an increasing degree he becomes himself—not a façade of conformity to others, not a cynical denial of all feeling—nor a front of intellectual rationality, but a living, breathing, feeling, fluctuating process—in short, he becomes a person.

THE PERSON WHO EMERGES

I imagine that some of you are asking, "But what *kind* of a person does he become? It isn't enough to say that he drops the façades. What kind of person lies underneath?" Since one of the most obvious facts is that each individual tends to become a separate and distinct and unique person, the answer is not easy. However I would like to point out some of the characteristic trends which I see. No one person would fully exemplify these characteristics, no one person fully achieves the description I will give, but I do see certain generalizations which can be drawn, based upon living a therapeutic relationship with many clients.

Openness to Experience

First of all I would say that in this process the individual becomes more open to his experience. This is a phrase which has come to have a great deal of meaning to me. It is the opposite of defensiveness. Psychological research has shown that if the evidence of our senses runs contrary to our picture of self, then that evidence is distorted. In other words we cannot see all that our senses report, but only the things which fit the picture we have.

Now in a safe relationship of the sort I have described, this defensiveness or rigidity, tends to be replaced by an increasing openness to experience. The individual becomes more openly aware of his own feelings and attitudes as they exist in him at an organic level, in the way I tried to describe. He also becomes more aware of reality as it exists outside of himself, instead of perceiving it in preconceived categories. He sees that not all trees are green, not all men are stern fathers, not all women are rejecting, not all failure experiences prove that he is no good, and the like. He is able to take in the evidence in a new situation, *as it is,* rather than distorting it to fit a pattern which he already holds. As you might expect, this increasing ability to be open to experience makes him far more realistic in dealing with new people, new situations, new problems. It means that his beliefs are not rigid, that he can tolerate ambiguity. He can receive much conflicting evidence without forcing closure upon the situation. This openness of awareness to what exists at *this moment* in *oneself* and in *the situation* is, I believe, an important element in the description of the person who emerges from therapy.

Perhaps I can give this concept a more vivid meaning if I illustrate it from a recorded interview. A young professional man reports in the 48th interview the way in which he has become more open to some of his bodily sensations, as well as other feelings.

C: It doesn't seem to me that it would be possible for anybody to relate all the changes that you feel. But I certainly have felt recently that I have more respect for, more objectivity toward my physical makeup. I mean I don't expect too much of myself. This is how it works out: It feels to me that in the past I used to fight a certain tiredness that I felt after supper. Well, now I feel pretty sure that I really *am* tired—that I am not making myself tired —that I am just physiologically lower. It seemed that I was just constantly criticizing my tiredness.

T: So you can let yourself *be* tired, instead of feeling along with it a kind of criticism of it.

C: Yes, that I shouldn't be tired or something. And it seems in a way to be pretty profound that I can just not fight this tiredness, and along with it goes a real feeling of *I've* got to slow down, too, so that being tired isn't such an awful thing. I think I can also kind of pick up a thread here of why I should be that way in the way my father is and the way he looks at some of these things. For instance, say that I was sick, and I would report this, and it would seem that overtly he would want to do something about it but he would also communicate, "Oh, my gosh, more trouble." You know, something like that.

T: As though there were something quite annoying really about being physically ill.

C: Yeah, I'm sure that my father has the same disrespect for his own physiology that I have had. Now last summer I twisted my back, I wrenched it, I heard it snap and everything. There was real pain there all the time at first, real sharp. And I had the doctor look at it and he said it wasn't serious, it should heal by itself as long as I didn't bend too much. Well this was months ago—and I have been noticing recently that—hell, this is a real pain and it's still there—and it's not my fault.

T: It doesn't prove something bad about you—

C: No—and one of the reasons I seem to get more tired than I should maybe is because of this constant strain, and so—I have already made an appointment with one of the doctors at the hospital that he would look at it and take an X ray or something. In a way I guess you could say that I am just more accurately sensitive—or objectively sensitive to this kind of thing. . . . And this is really a profound change as I say, and of course my relationship with my wife and the two children is—well, you just wouldn't recognize it if you could see me inside—as you have—I mean—there just doesn't seem to be anything more wonderful than really and genuinely —really *feeling* love for your own children and at the same time receiving it. I don't know how to put this. We have such an increased respect—both of us—for Judy and we've noticed just—as we participated in this—we have noticed such a tremendous change in her—it seems to be a pretty deep kind of thing.

T: It seems to me you are saying that you can listen more accurately to yourself. If your body says it's tired, you listen to it and believe it, instead of criticizing it; if it's in pain, you can listen to that; if the feeling is really loving your wife or children, you can *feel* that, and it seems to show up in the differences in them too.

Here, in a relatively minor but symbolically important excerpt, can be seen much of what I have been trying to say about openness to experience. Formerly he could not freely feel pain or illness, because being ill meant being unacceptable. Neither could he feel tenderness and love for his child, because such feelings meant being weak, and he had to maintain his façade of being strong. But now he can be genuinely open to the experiences of his organism—he can be tired when he is tired, he can feel pain when his organism is in pain, he can freely experience the love he feels for his daughter, and he can also feel and express annoyance toward her, as he goes on to say in the next portion of the interview. He can fully live the experiences of his total organism, rather than shutting them out of awareness.

Trust in One's Organism

A second characteristic of the persons who emerge from therapy is difficult to describe. It seems that the person increasingly discovers that his own organism is trustworthy, that it is a suitable instrument for discovering the most satisfying behavior in each immediate situation.

If this seems strange, let me try to state it more fully. Perhaps it will help to understand my description if you think of the individual as faced with some existential choice: "Shall I go home to my family during vacation, or strike out on my own?" "Shall I drink this third cocktail which is being offered?" "Is this the person whom I would like to have as my partner in love and in life?" Thinking of such situations, what seems to be true of the person who emerges from the therapeutic process? To the extent that this person is open to all of his experience, he has access to all of the available data in the situation, on which to base his behavior. He has knowledge of his own feelings and impulses, which are often complex and contradictory. He is freely able to sense the social demands, from the relatively rigid social "laws" to the desires of friends and family. He has access to his memories of similar situations, and the consequences of different behaviors in those situations. He has a relatively accurate perception of this external situation in all of its complexity. He is better able to permit his total organism, his conscious thought participating, to consider, weigh and balance each stimulus, need, and demand, and its relative weight and intensity. Out of this complex weighing and balancing he is able to discover that course of action which seems to come closest to satisfying all his needs in the situation, long-range as well as immediate needs.

In such a weighing and balancing of all of the components of a given life choice, his organism would not by any means be infallible. Mistaken choices might be made. But because he tends to be open to his experience, there is a greater and more immediate awareness of unsatisfying consequences, a quicker correction of choices which are in error.

It may help to realize that in most of us the defects which interfere with this weighing and balancing are that we include things that are not a part of our experience, and exclude elements which are. Thus an individual may persist in the concept that "I can handle liquor," when openness to his past experience would indicate that this is scarcely correct. Or a young woman may see only the good qualities of her prospective mate, where an openness to experience would indicate that he possesses faults as well.

In general then, it appears to be true that when a client is open to his experience, he comes to find his organism more trustworthy. He feels less fear of the emotional reactions which he has. There is a gradual growth of trust in, and even affection for the complex, rich, varied assortment of feelings and tendencies which exist in him at the organic level. Consciousness, instead of being the watchman over a dangerous and unpredictable lot of impulses, of which few can be permitted to see the light of day, becomes the comfortable inhabitant of a society of impulses and feelings and thoughts, which are discovered to be very satisfactorily self-governing when not fearfully guarded.

An Internal Locus of Evaluation

Another trend which is evident in this process of becoming a person relates to the source or locus of choices and decisions, or evaluative judgments. The individual increasingly comes to feel that this locus of evaluation lies within himself. Less and less does he look to others for approval or disapproval; for standards to live by; for decisions and choices. He recognizes that it rests within himself to choose; that the only question which matters is, "Am I living in a way which is deeply satisfying to me, and which truly expresses me?" This I think is perhaps *the* most important question for the creative individual.

Perhaps it will help if I give an illustration. I would like to give a brief portion of a recorded interview with a young woman, a graduate student, who had come for counseling help. She was initially very much disturbed about many problems, and had been contemplating suicide. During the interview one of the feelings she discovered was her great desire to be dependent, just to let someone else take over the direction of her life. She was very critical of those who had not given her enough guidance. She talked about one after another of her professors, feeling bitterly that none of them had taught her anything with deep meaning. Gradually she began to realize that part of the difficulty was the fact that she had taken no initiative in *participating* in these classes. Then comes the portion I wish to quote.

I think you will find that this excerpt gives you some indication of what it means in experience to accept the locus of evaluation as being within oneself. Here then is the quotation from one of the later interviews with this young woman as she has begun to realize that perhaps she is partly responsible for the deficiencies in her own education.

> *C:* Well now, I wonder if I've been going around doing that, getting smatterings of things, and not getting hold, not really getting down to things.
>
> *T:* Maybe you've been getting just spoonfuls here and there rather than really digging in somewhere rather deeply.
>
> *C:* M-hm. That's why I say—(*slowly and very thoughtfully*) well, with that sort of a foundation, well, it's really up to *me*. I mean, it seems to be really apparent to me that I *can't depend on someone else* to give me an education. (*Very softly*) I'll really have to get it myself.
>
> *T:* It really begins to come home—there's only one person that can educate you—a realization that perhaps nobody else *can give* you an education.
>
> *C:* M-hm. (*Long pause—while she sits thinking*) I have all the symptoms of fright. (*Laughs softly*)
>
> *T:* Fright? That this is a scary thing, is that what you mean?
>
> *C:* M-hm. (*Very long pause—obviously struggling with feelings in herself*).
>
> *T:* Do you want to say any more about what you mean by that? That it really does give you the symptoms of fright?
>
> *C:* (*Laughs*) I, uh—I don't know whether I quite know. I mean—well it really seems like I'm cut loose (*pause*), and it seems that I'm very—I don't know—in a vulnerable position, but I, uh, I brought this up and it, uh, somehow it almost came out without my saying it. It seems to be—it's something I let out.
>
> *T:* Hardly a part of you.
>
> *C:* Well, I felt surprised.
>
> *T:* As though, "Well for goodness sake, did I say that?" (*Both chuckle.*)
>
> *C:* Really, I don't think I've had that feeling before. I've—uh, well, this really feels like I'm saying something that, uh, *is* a part of me really. (*Pause*) Or, uh, (*quite perplexed*) it feels like I sort of have, uh, I don't know. I have a feeling of *strength,* and yet, I have a feeling of—realizing it's so sort of fearful, of fright.
>
> *T:* That is, do you mean that saying something of that sort gives you at the same time a feeling of, of strength in saying it, and yet at the same time a frightened feeling of *what* you have said, is that it?
>
> *C:* M-hm. I am feeling that. For instance, I'm feeling it internally now—a sort of surging up, or force or outlet. As if that's something really big and strong. And yet, uh, well at first it was almost a physical feeling of just being out alone, and sort of cut off from a—a support I had been carrying around.

T: You feel that it's something deep and strong, and surging forth, and at the same time, you just feel as though you'd cut yourself loose from any support when you say it.

C: M-hm. Maybe that's—I don't know—it's a disturbance of a kind of pattern I've been carrying around, I think.

T: It sort of shakes a rather significant pattern, jars it loose.

C: M-hm. (*Pause, then cautiously, but with conviction*) I, I think—I don't know, but I have the feeling that then I am going to begin to *do* more things that I know I should do. . . . There are so many things that I need to do. It seems in so many avenues of my living I have to work out new ways of behavior, but—maybe—I can see myself doing a little better in some things.

I hope that this illustration gives some sense of the strength which is experienced in being a unique person, responsible for oneself, and also the uneasiness that accompanies this assumption of responsibility. To recognize that "I am the one who chooses" and "I am the one who determines the value of an experience for me" is both an invigorating and a frightening realization.

Willingness to be a Process

I should like to point out one final characteristic of these individuals as they strive to discover and become themselves. It is that the individual seems to become more content to be a *process* rather than a *product.* When he enters the therapeutic relationship, the client is likely to wish to achieve some fixed state: he wants to reach the point where his problems are solved, or where he is effective in his work, or where his marriage is satisfactory. He tends, in the freedom of the therapeutic relationship to drop such fixed goals, and to accept a more satisfying realization that he is not a fixed entity, but a process of becoming.

One client, at the conclusion of therapy, says in rather puzzled fashion, "I haven't finished the job of integrating and reorganizing myself, but that's only confusing, not discouraging, now that I realize this is a continuing process. . . . It's exciting, sometimes upsetting, but deeply encouraging to feel yourself in action, apparently knowing where you are going even though you don't always consciously know where that is." One can see here both the expression of trust in the organism, which I have mentioned, and also the realization of self as a process. Here is a personal description of what it seems like to accept oneself as a stream of becoming, not a finished product. It means that a person is a fluid process, not a fixed and static entity; a flowing river of change, not a block of solid material; a continually changing constellation of potentialities, not a fixed quantity of traits.

Here is another statement of this same element of fluidity or existential living, "This whole train of experiencing, and the meanings that I have thus far discovered in it, seem to have launched me on a process which is both fascinating and at times a little frightening. It seems to mean letting my experiences carry me on, in a direction which appears to be forward, towards goals that I can but dimly define, as I try to understand at least the current meaning of that experience. The sensation is that of floating with a complex stream of experience, with the fascinating possibility of trying to comprehend its ever-changing complexity."

CONCLUSION

I have tried to tell you what has seemed to occur in the lives of people with whom I have had the privilege of being in a relationship as they struggled toward becoming themselves. I have endeavored to describe, as accurately as I can, the meanings which seem to be involved in this process of becoming a person. I am sure that this process is *not* one that occurs only in therapy. I am sure that I do not see it clearly or completely, since I keep changing my comprehension and understanding of it. I hope you will accept it as a current and tentative picture, not as something final.

One reason for stressing the tentative nature of what I have said is that I wish to make it clear that I am *not* saying, "This is what you should become; here is the goal for you." Rather, I am saying that these are some of the meanings I see in the experiences that my clients and I have shared. Perhaps this picture of the experience of others may illuminate or give more meaning to some of your own experience.

I have pointed out that each individual appears to be asking a double question: "Who am I?" and "How may I become myself?" I have stated that in a favorable psychological climate a process of becoming takes place; that here the individual drops one after another of the defensive masks with which he has faced life; that he experiences fully the hidden aspects of himself; that he discovers in these experiences the stranger who has been living behind these masks, the stranger who is himself. I have tried to give my picture of the characteristic attributes of the person who emerges; a person who is more open to all of the elements of his organic experience; a person who is developing a trust in his own organism as an instrument of sensitive living; a person who accepts the locus of evaluation as residing within himself; a person who is learning to live in his life as a participant in a fluid, ongoing process, in which he is continually discovering new aspects of himself in the flow of his experience. These are some of the elements which seem to me to be involved in becoming a person.

Self-Actualization and Beyond

by Abraham H. Maslow

In this article, I plan to discuss ideas that are in midstream rather than ready for formulation into a final version. I find that with my students and with other people with whom I share these ideas, the notion of self-actualization gets to be almost like a Rorschach ink blot. It frequently tells me more about the person using it than about reality. What I would like to do now is to explore some aspects of the nature of self-actualization, not as a grand abstraction, but in terms of the operational meaning of the self-actualizing process. What does self-actualization mean in moment-to-moment terms? What does it mean on Tuesday at four o'clock?

The Beginnings of Self-Actualization Studies

My investigations on self-actualization were not planned to be research and did not start out as research. They started out as the effort of a young intellectual to try to understand two of his teachers whom he loved, adored, and admired and who were very, very wonderful people. It was a kind of high-IQ devotion. I could not be content simply to adore, but sought to understand why these two people were so different from the run-of-the-mill people in the world. These two people were Ruth Benedict and Max Wertheimer. They were my teachers after I came with a Ph.D. from the West to New York City, and they were most remarkable human beings. My training in psychology equipped me not at all for understanding them. It was as if they were not quite people but something more than people. My own investigation began as a prescientific or nonscientific activity. I made descriptions and notes on Max

From CHALLENGES OF HUMANISTIC PSYCHOLOGY by J. F. T. Bugental. Copyright © 1967 by McGraw-Hill, Inc. Used with permission of McGraw-Hill Book Company.

Wertheimer, and I made notes on Ruth Benedict. When I tried to under-stand them, think about them, and write about them in my journal and my notes, I realized in one wonderful moment that their two patterns could be generalized. I was talking about a kind of person, not about two noncomparable individuals. There was wonderful excitement in that. I tried to see whether this pattern could be found elsewhere, and I did find it elsewhere, in one person after another.

By ordinary standards of laboratory research, that is of rigorous and controlled research, this simply was not research at all. My generaliza-tions grew out of *my* selection of certain kinds of people. Obviously, other judges are needed. So far, one man has selected perhaps two dozen people whom he liked or admired very much and thought were wonderful people and then tried to figure them out and found that he was able to describe a syndrome—the kind of pattern that seemed to fit all of them. These were people only from Western cultures, people selected with all kinds of built-in biases. Unreliable as it is, that was the only operational definition of self-actualizing people as I described them in my first publication on the subject.

After I published the results of my investigations, there appeared perhaps six, eight, or ten other lines of evidence that supported the find-ings, not by replication, but by approaches from different angles. Carl Rogers's findings (1961, etc.) and those of his students add up to corrob-oration for the whole syndrome. Bugental (1965, pp. 266-275) has of-fered confirmatory evidence from psychotherapy. Some of the new work with LSD,[1] some of the studies on the effects of therapy (good therapy, that is), some test results—in fact everything I know adds up to corroborative support, though not replicated support, for that study. I personally feel very confident about its major conclusions. I cannot con-ceive of any research that would make major changes in the pattern, though I am sure there will be minor changes. I have made some of those myself. But my confidence in my rightness is not a scientific datum. If you question the kind of data I have from my researches with monkeys and dogs, you are bringing my competence into doubt or call-ing me a liar, and I have a right to object. If you question my findings on self-actualizing people (Maslow, 1954, pp. 203-205; Maslow, 1962), you may reasonably do so because you don't know very much about the man who selected the people on whom all the conclusions are based. The conclusions are in the realm of prescience, but the affirmations are set forth in a form that can be put to test. In that sense, they are scientific.

The people I selected for my investigation were older people, peo-ple who had lived much of their lives out and were visibly successful.

---

[1]See, for example, Chapter 16 [Robert Mogar, Editor], in J. F. T. Bugental, *Challenges of Humanistic Psychology*. New York: McGraw-Hill, 1967.

We do not yet know about the applicability of the findings to young people. We do not know what self-actualization means in other cultures, although studies of self-actualization in China and in India are now in process. We do not know what the findings of these new studies will be, but of one thing I have no doubt: When you select out for careful study very fine and healthy people, strong people, creative people, saintly people, sagacious people—in fact, exactly the kind of people that I picked out—then you get a different view of mankind. You are asking how tall can people grow, what can a human being become? These are the Olympic gold-medal winners—the best we have. The fact that somebody can run 100 yards in less than ten seconds means that potentially any baby that is born into the world is, in theory, capable of doing so too. In that sense, any baby that is born into the world can in principle reach the heights that actually exist and can be described.

Intrinsic and Extrinsic Learning

When you look at mankind this way, your thinking about psychology and psychiatry changes radically. For example, 99 percent of what has been written on so-called learning theory is simply irrelevant to a grown human being. "Learning theory" does not apply to a human being growing as tall as he can. Most of the literature on learning theory deals with what I call "extrinsic learning," to distinguish it from "intrinsic learning." Extrinsic learning means collecting acquisitions to yourself like keys in your pocket or coins that you pick up. Extrinsic learning is adding another association or another craft. The process of learning to be the best human being you can be is another business altogether. The far goals for adult education and any other education, are the processes, the ways in which we can help people to become all they are capable of becoming. This I call intrinsic learning, and I am confining my remarks here entirely to it. That is the way self-actualizing people learn. To help the client achieve such intrinsic learning is the far goal of counseling.

These things I *know* with certainty. There are other things that I feel very confident about—"my smell tells me," so to speak. Yet I have even fewer objective data on these points than I had on those discussed above. Self-actualization is hard enough to define. How much harder it is to answer the question: Beyond self-actualization, what? Or, if you will: Beyond authenticity, what? Just being honest is, after all, not sufficient in all this. What else can we say of self-actualizing people?

B-Values

Self-actualizing people are without one single exception, involved in a cause outside their own skin, in something outside of themselves. They are devoted, working at something, something which is very precious to them—some calling or vocation in the old sense, the priestly sense. They are working at something which fate has called them to somehow and which they work at and which they love, so that the work-joy dichotomy in them disappears. One devotes his life to the law, another to justice, another to beauty or truth. All, in one way or another, devote their lives to the search for what I have called (1962) the "being" values ("B," for short), the ultimate values which are intrinsic, which cannot be reduced to anything more ultimate. There are about fourteen of these B-values, including the truth and beauty and goodness of the ancients and perfection, simplicity, comprehensiveness, and several more. These B-values are described in the appendix to my book *Religions, Values and Peak Experiences* (1964). They are the values of being.

Meta-Needs and Meta-Pathologies

The existence of these B-values adds a whole set of complications to the structure of self-actualization. These B-values behave like needs. I have called them *meta-needs*. Their deprivation breeds certain kinds of pathologies which have not yet been adequately described but which I call *meta-pathologies*—the sicknesses of the soul which come, for example, from living among liars all the time and not trusting anyone. Just as we need counselors to help people with the simpler problems of unmet needs, so we may need *meta-counselors* to help with the soul-sicknesses that grow from the unfulfilled meta-needs. In certain definable and empirical ways, it is necessary for man to live in beauty rather than ugliness, as it is necessary for him to have food for an aching belly or rest for a weary body. In fact, I would go so far as to claim that these B-values are the meaning of life for most people, but many people don't even recognize that they have these meta-needs. Part of our job as counselors may be to make them aware of these needs in themselves, just as the classical psychoanalyst made his patients aware of their instinctoid basic needs. Ultimately, perhaps, we shall come to think of ourselves as philosophical or religious counselors.

We try to help our counselees move and grow toward self-actualization. These people are often all wrapped up in value problems. Many are youngsters who are, in principle, very wonderful people, though in actuality they often seem to be little more than snotty kids. Nevertheless, I assume (in the face of all behavioral evidence sometimes) that they are, in the classical sense, idealistic. I assume that they are looking for values and that they would love to have something to devote themselves to, to be patriotic about, to worship, adore, love. These youngsters are making choices from moment to moment of going forward or retrogressing, moving away from or moving toward self-actualization. As counselors, or as meta-counselors, what can we tell them about becoming more fully themselves?

BEHAVIORS LEADING TO SELF-ACTUALIZATION

What does one do when he self-actualizes? Does he grit his teeth and squeeze? What does self-actualization mean in terms of actual behavior, actual procedure? I shall describe eight ways in which one self-actualizes.

First, self-actualization means experiencing fully, vividly, selflessly, with full concentration and total absorption. It means experiencing without the self-consciousness of the adolescent. At this moment of experiencing, the person is wholly and fully human. This is a self-actualization moment. This is a moment when the self is actualizing itself. As individuals, we all experience such moments occasionally. As counselors, we can help clients to experience them more often. We can encourage them to become totally absorbed in something and to forget their poses and their defenses and their shyness—to go at it whole hog. From the outside, we can see that this can be a very sweet moment. In those youngsters who are trying to be very tough and cynical and sophisticated, we can see the recovery of some of the guilelessness of childhood; some of the innocence and sweetness of the face can come back as they devote themselves fully to a moment and throw themselves fully into the experiencing of it. The key word for this is "selflessly," and our youngsters suffer from too little selflessness and too much self-consciousness, self-awareness.

Second, let us think of life as a process of choices, one after another. At each point there is a progression choice and a regression choice. There may be a movement toward defense, toward safety, toward being afraid; but over on the other side, there is the growth choice. To make the growth choice instead of the fear choice a dozen times a day is to move a dozen times a day toward self-actualization. Self-actualization is an ongoing process; it means making each of the many single choices about whether to lie or be honest, whether to steal or not to steal at a particular point, and it means to make each of these choices as a growth choice. This is movement toward self-actualization.

Third, to talk of self-actualization implies that there is a self to be actualized. A human being is not a *tabula rasa*, not a lump of clay or plastocene. He is something which is already there, at least a "cartilaginous" structure of some kind. A human being is, at minimum, his temperament, his biochemical balances, and so on. There is a self, and what I have sometimes referred to as "listening to the impulse voices" means letting the self emerge. Most of us, most of the time (and especially does this apply to children, young people), listen not to ourselves but to Mommy's introjected voice or Daddy's voice or to the voice of the Establishment, of the Elders, of authority, or of tradition.

As a simple first step toward self-actualization, I sometimes suggest to my students that when they are given a glass of wine and asked how they like it, they try a different way of responding. First, I suggest that they *not* look at the label on the bottle. Thus they will not use it to get any cue about whether or not they *should* like it. Next, I recommend that they close their eyes if possible and that they "make a hush." Now they are ready to look within themselves and try to shut out the noise of the world so that they may savor the wine on their tongues and look to the "Supreme Court" inside themselves. Then, and only then, they may come out and say, "I like it" or "I don't like it." A statement so arrived at is different from the usual kind of phoniness that we all indulge in. At a party recently, I caught myself looking at the label on a bottle and assuring my hostess that she had indeed selected a very good Scotch. But then I stopped myself: What was I saying? I know little about Scotches. All I knew was what the advertisements said. I had no idea whether this one was good or not; yet this is the kind of thing we all do. Refusing to do it is part of the ongoing process of actualizing oneself. Does *your* belly hurt? Or does it feel good? Does this taste good on *your* tongue? Do *you* like lettuce?

Fourth, when in doubt, be honest rather than not. I am covered by that phrase "when in doubt," so that we need not argue too much about diplomacy. Frequently, when we are in doubt we are not honest. Our clients are not honest much of the time. They are playing games and posing. They do not take easily to the suggestion to be honest. Looking within oneself for many of the answers implies taking responsibility. That is in itself a great step toward actualization. This matter of responsibility has been little studied. It doesn't turn up in our textbooks, for who can investigate responsibility in white rats? Yet it is an almost tangible part of psychotherapy. In psychotherapy, one can see it, can feel it, can know the moment of responsibility. Then there is a clear knowing of what it feels like. This is one of the great steps. Each time one takes responsibility, this is an actualizing of the self.

Fifth, we have talked so far of experiencing without self-awareness, of making the growth choice rather than the fear choice, of listening to the impulse voices, and of being honest and taking responsibility. All these are steps toward self-actualization, and all of them guarantee better life choices. A person who does each of these little things each time the choice point comes will find that they add up to better choices about what is constitutionally right for him. He comes to know what his destiny is, who his wife or husband will be, what his mission in life will be. One cannot choose wisely for a life unless he dares to listen to himself, *his own self,* at each moment in life, and to say calmly, "No, I don't like such and such."

The art world, in my opinion, has been captured by a small group of opinion and taste makers about whom I feel suspicious. That is an *ad hominem* judgment, but it seems fair enough for people who set themselves up as able to say, "You like what I like or else you are a fool." We must teach people to listen to their own tastes. Most people don't do it. When standing in a gallery before a puzzling painting, one rarely hears "That is a puzzling painting." We had a dance program at Brandeis not too long ago—a weird thing altogether, with electronic music, tapes, and people doing surrealistic and Dada things. When the lights went up everybody looked stunned, and nobody knew what to say. In that kind of situation most people will make some smart chatter instead of saying, "I would like to think about this." Making an honest statement involves daring to be different, unpopular, nonconformist. If we cannot teach our clients, young or old, about being prepared to be unpopular, we might just as well give up right now. To be courageous rather than afraid is another version of the same thing.

Sixth, self-actualization is not only an end state but also the process of actualizing one's potentialities at any time, in any amount. It is, for example, a matter of becoming smarter by studying if one is an intelligent person. Self-actualization means using one's intelligence. It does not mean doing some far-out thing necessarily, but it may mean going through an arduous and demanding period of preparation in order to realize one's possibilities. Self-actualization can consist of finger exercises at a piano keyboard. Self-actualization means working to do well the thing that one wants to do. To become a second-rate physician is not a good path to self-actualization. One wants to be first-rate or as good as he can be.

Seventh, peak experiences (Maslow, 1962; Maslow, 1964) are transient moments of self-actualization. They are moments of ecstasy which cannot be bought, cannot be guaranteed, cannot even be sought. One must be, as C. S. Lewis wrote, "surprised by joy." But one can set up the conditions so that peak experiences are more likely, or he can perversely set up the conditions so that they are less likely. Breaking up an illusion, getting rid of a false notion, learning what one is not good at, learning what his potentialities are *not*—these are also part of discovering what one is in fact.

Practically everyone does have peak experiences, but not everyone knows it. Some people wave these small mystical experiences aside.

Helping people to recognize these little moments of ecstasy[2] when they happen is one of the jobs of the counselor or meta-counselor. Yet, how does one's psyche, with nothing external in the world to point at—there is no blackboard there—look into another person's secret psyche and then try to communicate? We have to work out a new way of communication. I have tried one. It is described in another appendix in that same book (*Religions, Values and Peak Experiences*) under the title "Rhapsodic Communications." I think that kind of communication may be more of a model for teaching, and counseling, for helping adults to become as fully developed as they can be, than the kind we are used to when we see teachers writing on the board. If I love Beethoven and I hear something in a quartet that you don't, how do I teach you to hear? The noises are there, obviously. But I hear something very, very beautiful, and you look blank. You hear the sounds. How do I get you to hear the beauty? That is more our problem in teaching than making you learn the ABC's or demonstrating arithmetic on the board or pointing to a dissection of a frog. These latter things are external to both people; one has a pointer, and both can look at the same time. This kind of teaching is easy; the other kind is much harder, but it is part of our job as counselors. It is meta-counseling.

Eighth, finding out who one is, what he is, what he likes, what he doesn't like, what is good for him and what bad, where he is going and what his mission is—opening oneself up to himself—means the exposure of psychopathology. It means identifying defenses, and after defenses have been identified, it means finding the courage to give them up. This is painful because defenses are erected against something which is unpleasant. But giving up the defenses is worthwhile. If the psychoanalytic literature has taught us nothing else, it has taught us that repression is not a good way of solving problems.

Desacralizing

Let me talk about one defense mechanism that is not mentioned in the psychology textbooks, though it is a very important defense mechanism to the snotty and yet idealistic youngster of today. It is the defense mechanism of *desacralizing*. These youngsters mistrust the possibility of values and virtues. They feel swindled or thwarted in their lives. Most of them have, in fact, dopey parents whom they don't respect very much, parents who are quite confused themselves about values and who, frequently, are simply terrified of their children and

---

[2]See Chapter 14, by Herbert Otto [Editor], in J. F. T. Bugental, *Challenges of Humanistic Psychology.* New York: McGraw-Hill, 1967.

never punish them or stop them from doing things that are wrong. So you have a situation where the youngsters simply despise their elders —often for good and sufficient reason. Such youngsters have learned to make a big generalization: They won't listen to anybody who is grown up, especially if the grown-up uses the same words which they've heard from the hypocritical mouth. They have heard their fathers talk about being honest or brave or bold, and they have seen their fathers being the opposite of all these things.

The youngsters have learned to reduce the person to the concrete object and to refuse to see what he might be or to refuse to see him in his symbolic values or to refuse to see him or her eternally. Our kids have desacralized sex, for example. Sex is nothing; it is a natural thing, and they have made it so natural that it has lost its poetic qualities in many instances, which means that it has lost practically everything. Self-actualization means giving up this defense mechanism and learning or being taught to resacralize.[3]

Resacralizing

Resacralizing means being willing, once again, to see a person "under the aspect of eternity," as Spinoza says, or to see him in the medieval Christian unitive perception, that is, being able to see the sacred, the eternal, the symbolic. It is to see Woman with a capital "W" and everything which that implies, even when one looks at a particular woman. Another example: One goes to medical school and dissects a brain. Certainly something is lost if the medical student isn't awed but, without the unitive perception, sees the brain only as one concrete thing. Open to resacralization, one sees a brain as a sacred object also, sees its symbolic value, sees it as a figure of speech, sees it in its poetic aspects.

Resacralization often means an awful lot of corny talk—"very square," the kids would say. Nevertheless, for the counselor, especially for the counselor of older people, where these philosophical questions about religion and the meaning of life come up, this is a most important way of helping the person to move toward self-actualization. The youngsters may say that it is square, and the logical positivists may say that it is meaningless, but for the person who seeks our help in this process, it is obviously very meaningful and very important, and we had better answer him, or we're not doing what it is our job to do.

Put all these points together, and we see that self-actualization is not a matter of one great moment. It is not true that on Thursday at four

---

[3]I have had to make up these words because the English language is rotten for good people. It has no decent vocabulary for the virtues. Even the nice words get all smeared up. "Love," for instance.

o'clock the trumpet blows and one steps into the pantheon forever and altogether. Self-actualization is a matter of degree, of little accessions accumulated one by one. Too often our clients are inclined to wait for some kind of inspiration to strike so that they can say, "At 3:23 on this Thursday I become self-actualized!" People selected as self-actualizing subjects, people who fit the criteria, go about it in these little ways: They listen to their own voices; they take responsibility; they are honest; and they work hard. They find out who they are and what they are, not only in terms of their mission in life, but also in terms of the way their feet hurt when they wear such and such a pair of shoes and whether they do or do not like eggplant or stay up all night if they drink too much beer. All this is what the real self means. They find their own biological natures, their congenital natures, which are irreversible or difficult to change.

THE THERAPEUTIC ATTITUDE

These are the things people do as they move toward self-actualization. Who, then, is a counselor? How can he help the people who come to him to make this movement in the direction of growth?

Seeking a Model

I have used the words "therapy," "psychotherapy," and "patient." Actually, I hate all these words, and I hate the medical model that they imply because the medical model suggests that the person who comes to the counselor is a sick person, beset by disease and illness, seeking a cure. Actually, of course, we hope that the counselor will be the one who helps to foster the self-actualization of people, rather than the one who helps to cure a disease.

The helping model has to give way, too; it just doesn't fit. It makes us think of the counselor as the person or the professional who knows and reaches down from his privileged position above to the poor jerks below who don't know and have to be helped in some way. Nor is the counselor to be a teacher, in the usual sense, because what teachers have specialized in and gotten to be very good at is the "extrinsic learning" I described above. The process of growing into the best human being one can be is, instead, intrinsic learning, as we saw.

The existential therapists have wrestled with this question of models, and I can recommend Bugental's book, *The Search for Authenticity* (1965), for a discussion of the matter. Bugental suggests that we call counseling or therapy "ontogogy," which means trying to help people to grow to their fullest possible height. Perhaps that's a better word than the one I once suggested, a word derived from a German author, "psychogogy," which means the education of the psyche. Whatever the word we use, I think that the concept we will eventually have to come to is one that Alfred Adler suggested a long, long time ago when he spoke of the "older brother." The older brother is the loving person who takes responsibility, just as one does for his young, kid brother. Of course, the older brother knows more; he's lived longer, but he is not qualitatively different, and he is not in another realm of discourse. The wise and loving older brother tries to improve the younger, and he tries to make him better than he is, in the younger's own style. See how different this is from the "teaching somebody who doesn't know nothin'" model!

Counseling is not concerned with training or with molding or with teaching in the ordinary sense of telling people what to do and how to do it. It is not concerned with propaganda. It is a Taoistic uncovering and *then* helping. Taoistic means the noninterfering, the "letting be." Taoism is not a laissez-faire philosophy or a philosophy of neglect or of refusal to help or care. As a kind of model of this process we might think of a therapist who, if he is a decent therapist and also a decent human being, would never dream of imposing himself upon his patients or propagandizing in any way or of trying to make a patient into an imitation of himself.

What the good clinical therapist does is to help his particular client to unfold, to break through the defenses against his own self-knowledge, to recover himself, and to get to know himself. Ideally, the therapist's rather abstract frame of reference, the textbooks he has read, the schools that he has gone to, his beliefs about the world—these should never be perceptible to the patient. Respectful of the inner nature, the being, the essence of this "younger brother," he would recognize that the best way for him to lead a good life is to be more fully himself. The people we call "sick" are the people who are not themselves, the people who have built up all sorts of neurotic defenses against being human. Just as it makes no difference to the rosebush whether the gardener is Italian or French or Swedish, so it should make no difference to the younger brother how his helper learned to be a helper. What the helper has to give is certain services that are independent of his being Swedish or Catholic or Mohammedan or Freudian or whatever he is.

These basic concepts include, imply, and are completely in accord with the basic concepts of Freudian and other systems of psychodynamics. It is a Freudian principle that unconscious aspects of the self are repressed and that the finding of the true self requires the uncovering of these unconscious aspects. Implicit is a belief that truth heals much. Learning to break through one's repressions, to know one's self, to hear the impulse voices, to uncover the triumphant nature, to reach knowledge, insight, and the truth—these are the requirements.

Lawrence Kubie (1953-1954), in "The Forgotten Man in Education," some time ago made the point that one, ultimate goal of education is to help the person become a human being, as fully human as he can possibly be.

Especially with adults we are not in a position in which we have nothing to work with. We already have a start; we already have capacities, talents, directions, missions, callings. The job is, if we are to take this model seriously, to help them to be more perfectly what they already are, to be more full, more actualizing, more realizing in fact what they are in potentiality.

REFERENCES

Bugental, J. F. T. *The search for authenticity.* New York: Holt, Rinehart and Winston, 1965.

Kubie, L. The forgotten man in education. *Harvard Alumni Bulletin,* 1953-1954, *56,* 349-353.

Maslow, A. H. *Motivation and personality.* New York: Harper & Row, 1954.

Maslow, A. H. *Toward a psychology of being.* Princeton, N.J.: Van Nostrand, 1962.

Maslow, A. H. *Religions, values and peak experiences.* Columbus, Ohio: Ohio State Univer. Press, 1964.

Rogers, C. R. *On becoming a person.* Boston: Houghton Mifflin, 1961.

Social Class and Psychotherapy: A Critical Review of Research

by Enrico Jones

A good deal has been written about the implications of an individual's social class background for the outcome of psychotherapy. Points of view are varied and sometimes conflicting. Clinical lore holds that psychotherapy, which requires of the client, among other things, the capacity for introspection, the ability to articulate feelings and ideas freely, and a certain amount of psychological-mindedness, is a more appropriate treatment for people from middle-class backgrounds, who supposedly possess these characteristics to the requisite degree, than for those of lower social class backgrounds, who allegedly do not. Freud (1905), in a statement which reflects the class consciousness and elitest mentality of his society and era as well as his perception of the prerequisites of successful psychoanalysis, claimed that ". . . those patients who do not possess a reasonable degree of education and a fairly reliable character should be refused . . ." (p. 263), and rejoiced in the fact that ". . . precisely the most valuable and most highly developed persons are best suited for this procedure" (p. 264). Garfield (1971), after a comprehensive review of the research literature on client variables in psychotherapy, concludes that at least, traditional dynamic, long-term psychotherapies are generally ineffective with clients of low socioeconomic status. In contrast, Riessman and Scribner (1965) argue that such a conclusion is based on a selective emphasis on certain characteristics which such persons supposedly do not possess and a disregard for qualities which may indicate a positive potential for psychotherapy—e.g., a tendency not to isolate or intellectualize. They suggest that those from lower-class backgrounds may be far better therapy prospects than is generally realized.

Reprinted by special permission of The William Alanson White Psychiatric Foundation, Inc. From *Psychiatry*, November 1974, 37, 307-320. Copyright © The William Alanson White Psychiatric Foundation.

This discussion will attempt, through a careful exploration of the pertinent research literature, to bring together the empirical evidence bearing upon the relationship of social class factors to psychotherapy, and thereby to probe the myth that lower-class persons are generally not suitable for—i.e., do not want, or will not continue in—individual, insight-oriented psychotherapy. The question of what characteristics render an individual amenable to psychotherapy and whether or not these are class related is but one aspect of a complicated relationship between social factors and mental health care that involves social-psychological as well as clinical issues. Other, equally important aspects of this relationship will be addressed: contingencies which govern the entry of the lower-class person into psychotherapy, the expectations that the lower-class person has of psychotherapy in comparison to those of the person from a middle-class background, and therapists' attitudes toward lower-class clients. Futhermore, if it is indeed true that traditional psychotherapies are significantly less effective with lower-class clients than with middle-class clients, the question arises as to what are the alterations or innovations that could be developed and implemented in order to increase the effectiveness of mental health care for lower-class clients.

SOCIAL CLASS AND ENTRY INTO PSYCHOTHERAPY

Who Is Accepted for Treatment?

Several studies have considered who is selected for treatment by clinical personnel from among those who seek it. All of these studies were conducted in low-cost clinics where fees were generally set according to the client's income, so that cost of treatment need not be considered a contributing variable. Schaffer and Myers (1954) found that higher status patients were more readily accepted into treatment in their study of a psychiatric outpatient clinic in a major teaching hospital. Utilizing Hollingshead's Social Index Scale (Hollingshead and Redlich, 1958) they determined that 64% of class II and 55% of class III patients were accepted for individual psychotherapy, while only 34% of class IV and 3% of class V patients were accepted. Moreover, when therapists were ranked according to their status position within the clinic, the senior staff generally treated patients from classes II and III, while the majority of the residents' cases were from classes III and IV, and medical students treated persons primarily from classes IV and V. A later study (Cole et al., 1962) corroborated the finding that the higher a prospective client's social status, the more likely it is he will be accepted for treatment. However, they failed to replicate the relationship between the rank of the therapist and the social class of his patients in regard to psychiatrists and medical students; but they did find that the clients of the psychiatric social workers in this clinic, who worked with the patients' spouses, were primarily from the lowest two social classes. Similar findings are reported in a study by Brill and Storrow (1960), who found a significant relationship between social class and a patient's acceptance for treatment, but no significant relationship between a patient's social class and the training and experience of the therapist.

A wider-ranging study by Rosenthal and Frank (1958) examined all those patients who were referred for psychotherapy from a variety of sources at the Henry Phipps Clinic (Johns Hopkins Hospital) during a three-year period. They found a significant relationship between referral for psychotherapy and such variables as age, race, education, income, and diagnosis; thus psychiatrists refer significantly more white than black patients, the better educated, the younger, and those in the upper rather than the lower income range. Bailey et al. (1959) reported similar findings in their study of a Veterans Administration Clinic. They too found that assignment of patients to psychotherapy was related to high socioeconomic status while assignment to the psychosomatic clinic occurred more frequently with those of low socioeconomic status. Finally, Hollingshead and Redlich, in their epic research, reported that higher status patients disproportionately received psychotherapy while lower-class patients were more often treated with "direct, authoritative, compulsory" methods, such as electroshock, tranquilizers, and confinement.

The preponderance of evidence clearly indicates that a person's social class figures importantly in whether or not he will be offered treatment, and possibly determines his therapists' level of training and experience if he is fortunate enough to be accepted. The obvious question is, then, why this is true. Hollingshead and Redlich suggest that psychiatrists tend to select "good" patients, that is, those who possess social and intellectual standards similar to their own. Rosenthal and Frank similarly conclude that "psychiatrists consider as good candidates for psychotherapy those patients with whom they can more easily communicate and who share their value systems" (p. 333). Phrased less kindly, this selection process is the expression of an ugly class bias or, as Davis (1938) aphoristically described it, the manifestation of the "invidious, discriminatory aspect of social life" in the mental health field. The bias of mental health professionals against accepting clients of low social status as patients is further delineated by Brill and Storrow, who found that during the initial intake interview interviewers tended ". . . to react less positively to the lower class patient and to see him as less treatable for psychotherapy than his upper class counterpart" (p. 343).

It could be argued, of course, that therapists' evaluation of lower-class clients as not "good" patients may not simply be related to their difficulty in accepting the lower-class value system or in communicating and empathizing with the lower-class client; instead, their evaluation might be related to specific personality characteristics of lower-class clients that make them less amenable to psychotherapy than upper-class clients. This issue is considered later in detail.

Social Class and Diagnosis

It is instructive to take up the matter of diagnosis and psychological test evaluation in relation to social class factors. A number of investigators, including Rosenthal and Frank and Bailey et al., have discovered significant relationships between severity of diagnosis and acceptance for treatment, suggesting that clinicians view the sicker patient as a poorer treatment risk. This supposition seems to be borne out in Luborsky et al.'s (1971) review of a host of studies, all of which indicate that the more serious diagnoses (involving "schizophrenia," "psychotic trends," or "psychosis") are associated with less improvement in psychotherapy.) Furthermore, and more germane to this discussion, there is evidence that diagnosis, particularly by psychological test evaluation, may be subject to the influence of the examiner's bias in such a way that lower class persons tend to be diagnosed as more severely ill.

Recent investigations have considered the examiner's influence upon the subject during the process of diagnostic evaluation, especially with projective techniques (Mehlman, 1952; Miller, 1953). Haase (1964) specifically investigated the role of socioeconomic class factors in examiner bias. He hypothesized that examiners' awareness of clients' social status would result in relatively favorable Rorschach evaluations of middle class clients and unfavorable evaluations for lower class clients. Eight Rorschach protocols were constructed in four matched pairs, so that each pair was identical for all the important scoring determinants and ratios, and similar in content. Social histories of the eight alleged patients were also constructed, so that the four pairs were identical in every respect except for the income and occupation of the family head. Occupation and corresponding incomes were assigned so as to place four of the histories in the lower class and their matching histories in the middle class. Seventy-five clinical psychologists were asked to judge four protocols with their attached middle class histories, and the twins of each of the four Rorschachs with a lower class history attached. The results demonstrated a clear bias detrimental to the lower class in relation to each of three criteria: prediagnostic impression, diagnostic scores and prognostic scores. Furthermore, there was a statistically significant tendency for psychologists to prefer a diagnosis of character disorder or psychosis for the lower class client as opposed to one of normal or neurotic for the middle-class client. Interestingly, there was no evidence of relationships between the psychologist's judgmental bias and his own class origin, level of experience, or theoretical orientations, or with the type of clientele he usually treated.

Although in practice diagnostic evaluations are invariably carried out in face-to-face contact rather than through the blind scoring of diagnostic protocols, Haase's findings that lower-class clients are likely to be diagnosed as more disturbed not only provide additional information as to why prospective lower-class clients (who are often seen as character disorders or psychotics) are less frequently accepted for treatment than middle-class clients, but also lend additional weight to the notion that mental health professionals have discriminatory class biases toward lower-class patients. Indeed, if bias effects emerge when diagnoses are based upon psychological tests, which are generally considered technical and more or less objective, their influence upon decisions based solely upon clinical impressions, as most are, may well be stronger. These considerations force us to raise a question about Hollingshead and Redlich's well-known finding that psychotic disorders are almost three times more prevalent in the lower strata than in the upper classes, especially in the light of Schaffer and Myers' finding that the class distribution of psychotics and neurotics among those who applied for treatment at a low-cost psychiatric outpatient clinic was similar.

It might perhaps be argued that the bias in diagnostic evaluation which Haase discovered is not the result of prejudice, but that the judgment of lower-class protocols as more pathological reflects a basic assumption that "class membership—attainment and maintenance of middle class standing—in and of itself is a criterion determining better prognosis and less pathology" (Haase, p. 245). Indeed, a good deal of research would seem to indirectly support this point of view. For instance, Luborsky et al. conclude in their exhaustive compendium of research on the factors which influence the outcome of psychotherapy that persons with higher social achievements are better suited for psychotherapy because ". . . people who can achieve in spheres requiring social skills should also do so in psychotherapy" (p. 151). They cite several studies which have found positive relationships between socioeconomic, occupational, and educational achievements and successful outcome of psychotherapy; they further note that the combination of these achievements into single comprehensive measures of social competence has successfully predicted improvement in psychotherapy.

There is, however, a curious circularity to this line of reasoning. As the above review and discussion indicate, lower-class clients are less likely to be seen as "good" patients, are diagnosed less hopefully, tend to evoke less positive responses on the part of therapists, and, probably as a result of these factors as well as others, are less likely to be accepted for treatment than their middle-class counterparts; it should come as no surprise that when they are treated they are less likely to improve. What we have here sounds suspiciously like a self-fulfilling prophecy. Yet very few clinicians would be willing to explicitly and openly take the position that "attainment and maintenance of middle class standing in and of itself is a criterion determining better prognosis and less pathology."

Considering social class attainment as *itself* an index of health, pathology, or personality competence would, of course, suppose an open society in which individuals could move readily from their class of origin to the limit of their personal ability. The assumption of an open-class society, as Davis has pointed out in his classic statement, is an illusory ethic deeply embedded in the mental hygiene movement *qua* social movement, and is a fundamental determinant of notions about what constitutes "normal" behavior. The implications of this survey of the literature thus far corroborate Davis' claim that the content of mental hygiene is predominantly middle class and that there is an implicit assumption among professionals in the field that the lower class cannot totally assimilate the ways of thinking and behaving that alone insure against untreatable pathology or, once a person is maladjusted, permit a cure. This contention is supported by Cole et al.'s (1962) empirical finding that middle-class persons are significantly more likely to be rated as "socially improved" than lower-class persons upon discharge from treatment.

Who Rejects Treatment?

Not only are lower-class clients less likely to be accepted for treatment, but also they are less likely to accept it if offered. Rosenthal and Frank found that patients of lower educational and income levels more often refused psychotherapy when it became available; Yamamoto and Goin (1966) discovered a significant correlation between lower socioeconomic status and failure of a client to keep his initial appointment. Gibby et al. (1953) reported that significantly more blacks than whites refused therapy after an initial diagnostic interview. Thus, while mental health professionals tend to reject patients of the lower classes for psychotherapy, the rejection seems to be mutual.

SOCIAL CLASS AND CONTINUATION IN PSYCHOTHERAPY

Who Stays in Treatment?

Since mental health workers and lower-class clients seem to reject each other, one would hypothesize that once a lower-class client entered treatment, he would be more likely to drop out and to drop out after a shorter period than the client of higher socioeconomic status; and, indeed, the research literature bears out this supposition. Rosenthal and Frank reported that only 30% of the black patients, as compared to 60% of the whites, has six or more hours of therapy, and that only 33% of the patients with less than eighth-grade education has six or more hours, in contrast to about 66% with nine or more years of education. The researchers conclude that the characteristics of patients which led psychiatrists to refer them—i.e., race,[1] education, and income—also predisposed them to remain in treatment. Schaffer and Myers also found significant correlations between class status and duration of contact with a psychiatric outpatient clinic. They reported that of those patients who came only once, 75% were from classes IV and V, while 74% of those who maintained contact for more than 25 weeks were from classes II and III. A more methodologically sophisticated examination of the relationship between class position and duration of treatment was done by Imber et al. (1955); their study controlled for the likelihood, noted above, that lower-class patients will be treated by inexperienced therapists. Therapists were matched in experience and level of training (they were required to be beyond a minimum level in both) and were assigned patients rather than being allowed to select them. Both therapists and patients were under administrative pressure to remain in psychotherapeutic contact for at least six months. The results showed that 43% of lower-class patients had no more than four psychotherapy interviews, whereas only 11% of middle-class patients dropped therapy by the end of the fourth interview.

Comparable findings about the relationship of social class status to continuation of psychotherapy are reported in a host of studies (Cole et al., 1962; Bailey et al., 1959; Auld and Myers, 1954; Gibby et al., 1954; Rubinstein and Lorr, 1956; Sullivan et al., 1958). A careful search through the literature disclosed only two studies which failed to find a strong association between social class and continuation in psychotherapy (Overall and Aronson, 1964; Lorr et al., 1958). The

---

[1]Although this discussion is concerned primarily with a definition in terms of economic class, any discussion of non-middle-class culture in America must consider race as well as economics.

weight of the data, then, clearly indicates that there is a correlation between class and continuation in therapy.

Class, Length of Treatment, and Outcome

Generally speaking, clinicians believe that the longer the treatment continues, the more favorable the outcome of psychotherapy. This notion derives from a particular conceptual model of psychotherapy, viz., that therapy is necessarily a prolonged relationship and in order for it to be successful the patient should achieve insight into the connection between his complaints and his past and present interpersonal problems. There is some research that seems to support this position. Lorr et al. (1962) and Bailey et al. (1959) both report modest findings that support the idea that the longer the treatment, the better the outcome. Luborsky et al. note in their review that 20 out of 22 studies of time-unlimited treatment have found that longer treatment is associated with positive outcome. However, they suggest several alternative interpretations to the seemingly obvious conclusion that more therapy is better than less: patients who are getting what they need stay in treatment longer, and those who are not drop out sooner; moreover, therapists may overestimate positive change in patients who are in treatment longer, or insist that some minimum number of sessions is needed before real change can occur (p. 154). The latter interpretation is supported by studies indicating that therapists' ratings of improvement tend to be correlated positively with the length of treatment (Seeman, 1954; Standal and van der Veen, 1957); such findings are undoubtedly related to the "insight" model of therapy most clinicans follow.

While most of the literature suggests a positive relationship between duration of therapy and outcome, detailed evaluations of outcome for early terminators have not been extensively carried out. The few studies that have examined this issue have found that the relationship between successful outcome and length of treatment is not a linear one. Cartwright (1955) obtained counselors' ratings of success in client-centered psychotherapy for 78 clients. He found that his sample fell into two groups of improved patients. One group was composed of successful short-term clients, the other, successful long-term clients. Within each group the number of interviews and the success rating were positively related. However, Cartwright also found a "failure zone," ranging around 17.5 interviews, and identified it as the period when potential long-term clients dropped out of therapy. In short, Cartwright found a curvilinear relationship between duration and success. Taylor (1956) found the same curvilinear relationship when he plotted successful outcome ratings against duration of therapy for 309 cases treated at a psychoanalytically oriented clinic; Rosenthal and Frank similarly discovered that in general improved cases had either between 1 and 5 or between 11 and 20 treatment sessions.

Cartwright hypothesized that brief successful cases and longer successful cases differ in the kinds of problems presented by the client. He suggested that short-term clients had mainly situational problems, while long-term clients had more enduring personality diffculties, and that the "failure zone" should be assigned to the beginning of long-term therapy rather than to the end of short-term therapy.

Unfortunately, none of the studies included socioeconomic status as an independent variable; nevertheless, these data are of special interest in the light of the information concerning the high rate of early termination among lower-class clients. If it is assumed, as it generally is, that length of treatment is directly related to positive outcome, it could be reasonably concluded that psychotherapy is a vain venture for the lower-class client, and that he derives very little benefit from it. Either he discovers it is not what he needs and drops out, or, as Heine and Trossman (1960) suggest, he terminates prematurely in compliance with the therapist's implicit, covert rejection of him as being relatively unsuited for treatment. On the strength of Cartwright's, Taylor's, and Rosenthal and Frank's findings, an alternate interpretation can now be considered: Could it be that lower-class clients frequently come to treatment primarily with situational problems which are effectively resolved by short-term therapy? Thereafter, the lower-class client may not have the time, inclination, or motivation to explore "deeper" personality problems, and he terminates therapy satisfied that his difficulties are alleviated. In other words, it is likely that lower-class clients often have significant reality problems which they do not have sufficient practical information to solve, so that brief contact with a therapist can be helpful. This is certainly a reasonable conjecture in view of the rediscovery by community psychology of the relationship of psychological health to the social and environmental exigencies of housing, employment, and child rearing—all problems that particularly affect members of low income communities. Thus even though lower-class clients tend to drop out of therapy, or are pushed out by negative attitudes of therapists, it is nevertheless possible that they can, and do, derive real benefit from brief psychotherapeutic contact.

SOCIAL CLASS AND SUITABILITY FOR PSYCHOTHERAPY

Who Is Suitable for Therapy?

People from different social strata may well differ in many psychosocial and personality respects, but are these differences relevant for predicting failure in psychotherapy? Is there dependable evidence that suitability depends on *any* particular personal qualities, whether or not class related? While a great deal of the information derived from research in psychotherapy is tentative and conflicting, this is particularly true of studies concerning the relationship of personality variables to outcome. To make matters more difficult for present purposes, none of these psychological attributes have been systematically studied in relation to social class. Furthermore, as Garfield (1971) notes, it is difficult to evaluate outcome research—and hence the relationship of personality variables to outcome—because of the variations among studies in "outcome criteria, the relative significance of these criteria, variations in the type of therapy offered, variations in the training and competence of the therapists studied, and differences in the kinds of client samples treated" (p. 285). Still another complication is that many studies do not differentiate between length of treatment and outcome, and, as was suggested previously, the relationship between these factors is at best ambiguous. For example, Taulbee (1958) investigated the relationship of personality variables to continuation in therapy. He found that the following pretherapy client characteristics were related to continuation in therapy: minimal defensiveness, persistence, an introspective attitude, feelings of inadequacy and inferiority, strong dependency needs, emotional responsiveness, and feelings of depression and anxiety. He further claims, without explaining the basis for his conclusion, that ". . . there is evidence . . . that these personality variables are associated with improvement as well as with continuation in therapy" (p. 87).

Client characteristics associated with positive outcome in psychotherapy in a number of studies include motivation, intelligence, capability of experiencing deeply and immediately, and high level of dysphoric affect (Luborsky, 1971; Garfield, 1971; Rogers et al., 1967). In a sophisticated study, specifically designed to examine the relationship of class membership to distress levels of neurotic symptomatology, Derogatis et al. (1971) found that lower status patients were significantly more depressed and generally manifested substantially higher distress levels than upper-class patients. Among the remaining variables associated with successful outcome, only IQ might be expected to be positively correlated with indices of social class. However, the current heightened awareness of the discriminatory bias of IQ tests against both ethnic and lower-class subcultures renders an evaluation of the relationship of intelligence to social class and psychotherapy problematic. Moreover, clinicians have long been aware that performance on intelligence tests —that is to say, IQ—is at least in part a measure of psychological health (Allison et al., 1968). Thus the fact that clients with higher intelligence tend to have more positive outcomes in psychotherapy may simply be a restatement of a common finding of outcome research: the healthier the patient is to begin with, the better the outcome; the sicker he is to begin with, the poorer the outcome.

The fact that motivation should be associated with positive outcome seems at first glance to be eminently reasonable and quite straightforward. Upon closer examination, however, the relation of motivation to outcome and social class is less than clear-cut, particularly since clients' motivation for psychotherapy is typically measured through interviewer or therapist ratings. Raskin (1961) designed a study to clarify the meaning of motivation to enter psychotherapy or, more precisely, to identify the variables therapists associate with this concept. He found that education, occupational level, awareness of psychological difficulties, type of treatment expected, and therapist liking of the patient were all significantly correlated with therapist rating of motivation for psychotherapy. It becomes apparent, then, that therapists' notions of motivation for therapy are embedded in the same complex of values, assumptions, and predilections which govern their selection of clients for treatment.

A careful perusal of the literature yielded very little evidence that suitability for psychotherapy depended on any class-related personality characteristics. One of the few such investigations is that of Brill and Storrow, who attempted to evaluate "psychological-mindedness" in relation to social class. Through analysis of data collected at an intake interview, the researchers found that lower social class was significantly related to lower "estimated" intelligence, to a tendency to see the presenting problem as physical rather than emotional, to a desire for symptomatic relief only rather than "overall help," to lack of understanding of the psychotherapeutic process, and to a lack of desire for psychotherapy. They also reported that the interviewer tended to react less positively to the lower-class client and saw him as less treatable by psychotherapy than the middle-class client. This study seems to validate the assumption that lower-class clients are frequently not suitable candidates for psychotherapy and to support middle-class therapists' stereotypes of lower-class clients. However, the study suffers from the same circular thinking noted earlier. Evaluations were determined by intake interview ratings which may have been made by the therapists; and no checks on the reliability of evaluations are reported, which suggests that only one interviewer rated each client. This type of research method is egregiously vulnerable to the subjectivity, misperceptions, and biases of the raters; and in the context of what is known about therapists' attitudes toward lower-class clients, the findings of this study may represent a manifestation of the self-fulfilling prophecy phenomenon alluded to earlier.

Another set of findings relevant to this discussion is that of the Wisconsin Project (Rogers et al., 1967) concerning the importance of the "core" conditions of therapists' empathy, warmth, and congruence with the patient in client-centered therapy. The researchers found that, among other variables, high socioeconomic status and high verbal intelligence in clients were positively correlated with rated therapist empathy and patient-perceived congruence, as well as with positive indices of process and outcome in psychotherapy, suggesting that the client's social class background influences the nature of the therapeutic relationship in important ways. As Rogers et al. remark,

> In those cases where the patient enters therapy with a fair degree of expressive capacity and/or motivation for self-exploration, the therapist's corresponding involvement may be enhanced. . . . The more responsive the patient, the more likely it will be that the therapist can communicate the genuineness of his concern, for, and interest in, the patient as a person. On the other hand, patients lacking these capacities will generally fail to evoke similar therapist involvement. That is, the unmotivated, defensive and reluctant patient from a different (lower) socioeconomic background may not provide the therapist sufficient opportunity to deepen the relationship, and may thus severely limit the therapist's ability to communicate and function effectively. [pp. 308–309]

Though serious questions have been raised about the generalizability of the importance of the core therapist conditions to nonclient-centered therapy (Bergin and Jasper, 1969; Garfield and Bergin, 1971), these findings probably reflect something which occurs across theoretical orientations and modes of therapy—i.e., therapists find it difficult to empathize and communicate with lower-class clients. The above quotation is noteworthy, too, in that it places the blame for unsuccessful treatment squarely on the client and fails to consider the therapist's values, his unfamiliarity with lower-class life-styles and *Weltanschauung,* and his inability to speak the lower-class client's language. Although such deficiencies in the therapist are at least half the problem, the guilt is seen rather as lying with the lower-class client, who simply does not bring the characteristics with him that are presumed to be necessary for the development of a therapeutic relationship. This assumption is a curious role reversal of responsibility for mental health relationships.

Others have arrived at a more balanced view. Rosenthal and Frank remark that therapists prefer as patients those who they believe will maintain a prolonged therapeutic relationship, who typically are those whose socioeconomic and educational levels are most similar to their own. They found that these criteria generally do identify patients who will continue therapy for longer periods of time (those who get along comfortably with their therapists) but are not directly associated with improvement in therapy. Garfield and Affleck (1961) similarly found that the therapist's liking of the patient, interest in taking the patient into treatment, and good prognostic ratings of the patient—implying a conviction that a good therapeutic relationship can be developed—are all highly correlated with each other, but none was predictive of duration of therapy nor of positive outcome. It seems, then, that therapists have definite notions about the kinds of clients who are good therapy risks, and related preferences about what kind of client they like to work with. No doubt these ideas also relate to therapists' theoretical conceptions about psychotherapy as well as to the class-related biases and assumptions about lower-class clients noted earlier. However, none of the suppositions about the personal characteristics that make a client amenable to psychotherapy, whether or not they are related to social class, have been convincingly validated in an empirical fashion.

Class and Expectations About Therapy

The only class-linked client characteristic that does seem associated with the psychotherapeutic process and outcome—that is, the relationship has substantial empirical support—is the client's expectations about psychotherapy. An interesting study designed to investigate the relationship between initial client expectations and continuation in therapy (outcome was not studied) was that carried out by Heine and Trosman. They devised a questionnaire to discover how a patient viewed his anticipated therapeutic experience. They asked for the patient's reasons for seeking therapy, his expectations as to what kind of help he would receive, and his views on how this help would be given. Through a less formal but similar inquiry they delineated therapists' modal expectations about therapy. Neither the presenting complaint nor the client's stated opinion regarding the potential efficacy of therapy bore any relationship to continuance in therapy. However, the *mutuality of expectations* about therapy between patient and therapist was significantly associated with duration. The modal expectations for their sample of therapists included: (1) the patient should desire a relationship in which he has an opportunity to talk freely about himself and his discomforts; (2) the patient should see the relationship as instrumental to the relief of discomfort, rather than expecting discomfort to be relieved by an impersonal manipulation on the part of the therapist alone; (3) the patient should therefore perceive himself, in some degree, as responsible for the outcome.

The researchers suggest that two situations are created: When the patient's ideas about therapy are congruent with the therapist's, the former is rewarded with the therapist's interest and attention, but when the patient holds another set of expectations—e.g., he will receive medicine—he is, in effect, rejected. Although their study did not include social class as an independent variable, Heine and Trosman conclude that expectations about therapy are probably related to social class, and that incongruent patient-therapist expectations may contribute to the well-documented phenomenon of early termination among lower-class clients.

The similar study by Overall and Aronson directly investigated expectations about psychotherapy in patients of lower socioeconomic class. Forty lower-class clients were given questionnaires regarding their expectations before their initial interviews; after the interview they were given another questionnaire concerning their reactions to what actually occurred in the interview. The results indicated that the lower-class patients expected the therapists to assume an active, medical role in the interview, that the actual conduct of the therapists during the interview was less active and medically oriented than the clients expected, and that the degree of discrepancy between client expectations and their perception of what actually occurred in the interview was significantly and positively related to whether the client returned for treatment. In order to explain their results, the researchers invoke Heine and Trosman's chain of circumstances: to the extent that the lower-class client's expectations are congruent or incongruent with those of the therapist he is accepted or rejected by the therapist; the client perceives the therapist's attitude; this perception influences his decision to return or continue treatment. However, another possible interpretation of these results is, quite simply, that those who felt they were getting what they wanted, returned; those who didn't, did not return.

Another investigation concerning class-related expectations about psychotherapy was conducted by Goin et al. (1965). This study improves upon Heine and Trosman's and Overall and Aronson's in measuring outcome as well as duration, and in gauging the nature of client expectations in a more subtly differentiated manner. The study was carried out at the Psychiatric Clinic of the Los Angeles County General Hospital, where the overwhelming majority of clients were from classes IV and V and 20% were black. The researchers hypothesized that most lower-class patients would expect help in the form of active advice, reassurance, and support in a few sessions, rather than from treatment centered around the long-term development of introspection and self-understanding. The patients' reactions were observed as they were given treatment congruent or incongruent with their expectations.

Of these lower-class clients, 52% indicated their wish to solve their problems by talking about their feelings and past life—i.e., they wanted insight therapy; 48% wanted active help, either in the form of advice (34%) or medication (14%). The majority (60%) expected their needs to be met in 10 or fewer treatment sessions; only 20% expected more than 25 sessions. There was no relationship between expected duration of treatment and type of treatment desired. Those clients who expected advice and received it did not stay in treatment longer than those who expected advice and did not get it. However, 72% of those who expected advice and received it reported that they had improved, while only 57% of those who expected advice and did not receive it reported improvement. The fact that patients whose expectations about therapy were incongruent with the nature of the treatment did not terminate earlier than those whose expectations were congruent contradicts Overall and Aronson's findings with respect to duration. However, there is indirect support for Overall and Aronson's results in the fact that more clients whose expectations were met reported better outcomes than those whose expectations were not.

Thus, Goin et al. discovered that lower-class clients frequently know what they want and feel their problem is alleviated when they get it. This finding also fits the supposition discussed earlier that lower-class clients often have significant reality problems but lack adequate information to solve or cope with them, and that therapists are most helpful when they take a problem-solving approach to treatment. But perhaps the most interesting finding of this study is that 52% of these lower-class clients wanted insight therapy. Although there is no direct evidence that the expectations about therapy of a middle-class population would be any different, Goin et al. explicitly comment that they were surprised by this finding and attribute this unexpected sophistication about psychotherapy to the "popularization of mental health concepts through comic strip characters and television serials"! It seems that the myth that lower-class patients do not want and cannot benefit from individual psychotherapy is beset by contradictory evidence from two different directions: lower-class patients sometimes want, and often benefit from, a brief, problem-solving orientation; and they frequently want insight-oriented therapy, even though they may subsequently receive little benefit from it for reasons that are more a function of therapists' attitudes than of their own "unsuitability" for treatment.

IMPLICATIONS OF RESEARCH FINDINGS FOR PSYCHOTHERAPY WITH LOWER-CLASS CLIENTS

The research literature indicates that persons from lower socioeconomic class backgrounds are less frequently accepted for treatment, are more likely to be assigned to inexperienced therapists, and continue in therapy for a briefer period of time than their middle-class counterparts. All of this is undoubtedly in part related to the fact that therapists clearly prefer clients who are intelligent, verbal, educated, and introspective.

They consider lower-class clients to be undesirable or lacking in the requisite attributes of candidates for psychotherapy. There is, however, no clear-cut evidence that the characteristics which supposedly make a person a good risk for psychotherapy are, in fact, associated with positive outcome (though they are related to continuation in therapy). Moreover, there is no reliable evidence that lower-class clients do not possess the characteristics which clinical wisdom considers necessary for a person to be amenable to psychotherapeutic influence. Indeed, a growing number of clinicians and researchers are expressing the conviction that lower-class patients are more psychologically-minded (Goin et al., 1965) and verbally expressive (Riessman, 1964; Gould, 1967), and are generally better therapy risks (Riessman and Scribner, 1965), than is commonly assumed, and moreover, that they may sometimes get what they need from therapy despite the generally negative attitudes of mental health workers. It must be noted that mental health professionals are not alone in revealing class-related biases. Numerous instances of like distortions detrimental to the lower class in other areas of psychological evaluation and in assumptions underlying research hypotheses have now been documented (for examples see Haase, 1964; Lorr et al., 1958).

The Patient

It is also undoubtedly true that some clients are less suitable for psychotherapy, and it is quite possible that a greater proportion of such patients are from lower socioeconomic class backgrounds than from middle-class backgrounds. Nevertheless, the characteristics which make these people less suitable for psychotherapy remain yet to be explicitly defined. If it is true that sometimes lower-class patients are unsuitable, then the issue of how to increase the efficacy of treatment with such clients must be addressed. This review of the literature indicates that education and expectations about psychotherapy, two variables apparently relevant to duration and outcome of therapy, distinguish lower-class from middle-class patients.

Could the lower-class client's expectations about therapy be changed in order to make him a better therapy risk? Such an effort was carried out by Hoehn-Saric et al. (1964). The investigators developed a "Role Induction Interview" designed to educate the client about psychotherapy so that his expectations would be more congruent with his therapeutic experience. The Role Induction Interview involved: (1) a general exposition of psychotherapy; (2) the expected behavior of patient and therapist; (3) preparation for certain phenomena in therapy, such as resistance; and (4) indication that improvement should not be expected before four months of treatment. The patients who received this interview significantly exceeded a control group of patients on criteria of both process and outcome. Truax and Carkhuff (1967) found in a similar study that exposing prospective clients to a 30-minute tape recording of "good" therapy behavior had a positive effect on the outcome of their therapy. It seems, then, that it is possible to modify one of the empirically validated characteristics that render some lower-class clients less amenable to psychotherapy.

The Technique

Rather than focusing on patient deficiencies, another point of view can be assumed—that psychotherapy as practiced is inadequate for this type of client. It has been suggested that the *principles* of mental health are middle class in content (Davis, 1938); others have argued that the *practice* of therapy, with its emphasis on verbal behavior and its future orientation, is middle class as well (Gould, 1967) and hence less adapted to the values and style of lower-class patients. Several researchers and clinicians have suggested changes in technique. Gould advises informality, nonverbal contact, flexibility in scheduling, role-playing, education, guidance, and a generally more directive approach in therapy with lower-class clients. Baum and Felzer (1964) and Overall and Aronson (1964) similarly suggest a more active role on the part of the therapist working with the lower-class client, especially in the initial interviews when the client's expectations about therapy and how it works should be expressly addressed. Riessman and Scribner (1965) argue that in the treatment of lower-class clients the insight model of therapy should be scrapped in favor of different modes of therapy including role-playing, group therapy, and family therapy. However, such techniques still do not take account of the lower-class clients' wishes and expectations; and it is not altogether clear that a number of middle-class clients might not benefit with like alterations in techniques.

The Therapist

Another possibility for increasing the efficacy of therapy with lower-class clients is to institute some form of matching procedure. The issue of therapist-client match and its effect on therapy is a complex one. While Mendelsohn and Geller (1965) report a curvilinear relationship between patient-therapist personality similarity and outcome, most studies indicate that greater patient-therapist similarity is associated with better outcome (Luborsky et al., 1971). The implications of these findings for treatment of lower-class clients were clarified in a small study by Carkhuff and Pierce (1967). In this study, the researchers trained four lay counselors, two white and two black; one counselor in each pair was from a middle-class background, the other from a lower-class background. Each of the counselors was assigned 16 clients who were distributed equally among the four classifications represented by the counselors. Taped segments of the interviews were rated according to depth of self-exploration in interpersonal process, a variable which has been associated with positive outcome in psychotherapy (Truax and Carkhuff, 1964). Congruent race and social class of patient and therapist were found to be significantly related to patient depth of self-exploration, as were the interaction between patient and therapist variables. Carkhuff and Pierce conclude that "the patients most similar to the race and social class of the counselor involved tended to explore themselves most, while patients most dissimilar tended to explore themselves least" (p. 634). Similarly, the research literature on A-B therapist types has very tentatively suggested that B-type therapists (briefly described, those who tend to have mechanical-technical interests) are more effective than A-type therapists (those who do not have such interests) in working with lower-class clients (McNair et al., 1962; Carson, 1967). Thus, although the evidence is uncertain, therapy with lower-class clients might be enhanced by judicious pairing of client and therapist.

A final possibility for increasing the effectiveness of therapy with lower-class clients lies in changing, or more carefully selecting, those therapists who work with such clients. It seems just as important to increase the effectiveness of therapists in treating the lower-class person as to discover means for rendering such clients more suitable for therapy. The small number of studies that address themselves to this issue again bears testimony to the one-sidedness of the thinking of clinicians and researchers about who is responsible for the success or failure of treatment. A small minority of workers in the field have at least considered this issue. Rogers et al. (1967) comment that the therapist must be particularly skillful and sensitive if he is to involve the reluctant client, or a client from a lower socioeconomic class background; if he is remote or superficial, he may dampen the client's initial enthusiasm. A study conducted by Baum et al. (1966) found that therapists who were more secure, clinically experienced, and task oriented, and who had undergone personal therapy themselves, established better relationships with lower-class clients and had a lower dropout rate with such patients than other therapists. In a similar vein, Hughes (1972) found that white therapists who had undergone personal therapy had better outcomes in therapy with nonwhite clients than therapists who had not.

More research about how therapists can become more effective with lower-class clients is obviously needed. It must be stated, though, that if some lower-class clients are unsuitable for psychotherapy, many therapists are themselves unsuited for working with lower-class clients.

REFERENCES

Allison, J., et al. *The Interpretation of Psychological Tests;* Harper & Row, 1968.

Auld, F., Jr., and Myers, J. K. "Contributions to a Theory for Selecting Psychotherapy Patients," *J. Clin. Psychology* (1954) 10:56-60.

Bailey, M. A., et al. "A Study of Factors Related to Length of Stay in Psychotherapy," *J. Clin. Psychology* (1959) 15:442-444.

Baum, O. E., and Felzer, S. B. "Activity in Initial Interviews with Lower Class Patients," *Arch. General Psychiatry* (1964) 10:345-353.

Baum, O. E., et al. "Psychotherapy, Dropouts, and Lower Socioeconomic Patients," *Amer. J. Orthopsychiatry* (1966) 36:629-635.

Bergin, A., and Jasper, L. "Correlates of Empathy in Psychotherapy: A Replication," *J. Abnormal Psychology* (1969) 74:477-481.

Brill, N. Q., and Storrow, H. A. "Social Class and Psychiatric Treatment," *Arch. General Psychiatry* (1960) 3:340-344.

Carkhuff, R. R., and Pierce, R. "Differential Effects of Therapist Race and Social Class upon Patient Depth of Self-exploration in the Initial Clinical Interview," *J. Consulting Psychology* (1967) 31:632-634.

Carson, R. C. "A and B Therapist 'Types': A Possible Critical Variable in Psychotherapy," *J. Nervous and Mental Disease* (1967) 144:47-54.

Cartwright, D. S. "Success in Psychotherapy as a Function of Certain Actuarial Variables," *J. Consulting Psychology* (1955) 19:357-363.

Cole, N. J., et al. "Some Relationships Between Social Class and the Practice of Dynamic Psychotherapy," *Amer. J. Psychiatry* (1962) 118:1004-1012.

Davis, K. "Mental Hygiene and the Class Structure," *Psychiatry* (1938) 1:55-65.

Derogatis, L. R., et al. "Social Class and Race as Mediator Variables in Neurotic Symptomatology," *Arch. General Psychiatry* (1971) 25:31-40.

Freud, S. "On Psychotherapy (1905)," *Standard Edition of the Complete Psychological Works,* Vol. 7; Hogarth, 1953.

Garfield, S. "Research on Client Variables in Psychotherapy," in A. Bergin and S. Garfield (Eds.), *Handbook of Psychotherapy and Behavior Change;* Wiley, 1971.

Garfield, S. L., and Affleck, D. C. "Therapists' Judgments Concerning Patients Considered for Psychotherapy," *J. Consulting Psychology* (1961) 25:505-509.

Garfield, S., and Bergin, A. "Therapeutic Conditions and Outcome," *J. Abnormal Psychology* (1971) 77:108-114.

Gibby, R. G., et al. "Prediction of Duration of Therapy from the Rorschach Test," *J. Consulting Psychology* (1953) 17:348-354.

Goin, M. K., et al. "Therapy Congruent with Class-linked Expectations," *Arch. General Psychiatry* (1965) 13:133-137.

Gould, R. E. "Dr. Strangeclass: Or How I Stopped Worrying About the Theory and Began Treating the Blue-collar Worker," *Amer. J. Orthopsychiatry* (1967) 37:78-86.

Haase, W. "The Role of Socio-economic Class in Examiner Bias," in F. Riessman et al. (Eds.), *Mental Health of the Poor;* Free Press, 1964.

Heine, R. W., and Trosman, H. "Initial Expectations of the Doctor-Patient Interaction as a Factor in Continuance in Psychotherapy," *Psychiatry* (1960) 23:275-278.

Hoehn-Saric, R., et al. "Systematic Preparation of Patients for Psychotherapy, I. Effects on Therapy Behavior and Outcome," *J. Psychiatric Research* (1964) 2:267-281.

Hollingshead, A. B., and Redlich, F. C. *Social Class and Mental Illness;* Wiley, 1958.

Hughes, R. "The Effects of Sex, Age, Race and Social History of Therapist and Client on Psychotherapy Outcome," unpublished doctoral dissertation, Univ. of Calif., Berkeley, 1972.

Imber, S. D., et al. "Social Class and Duration of Psychotherapy," *J. Clin. Psychology* (1955) 11:281-284.

Lorr, M., et al. "The Prediction of Length of Stay in Psychotherapy," *J. Consulting Psychology* (1958) 22:321-327.

Lorr, M., et al. "Frequency of Treatment and Change in Psychotherapy," *J. Abnormal and Social Psychology* (1962) 64:281-292.

Luborsky, L., et al. "Factors Influencing the Outcome to Psychotherapy," *Psychol. Bull.* (1971) 75:145-185.

McNair, D. M., et al. "Therapist 'Type' and Patient Response to Psychotherapy," *J. Consulting Psychology* (1962) 26:425-429.

Mehlman, B. "The Reliability of Psychiatric Diagnosis," *J. Abnormal and Social Psychology* (1952) 47:577-578.

Mendelsohn, G. A., and Geller, M. H. "Structure of Client Attitudes Toward Counseling and Their Relation to Client-Counselor Similarity," *J. Consulting Psychology* (1965) 29:63-72.

Miller, D. "Prediction of Behavior by Means of the Rorschach Test," *J. Abnormal and Social Psychology* (1953) 48:367-375.

Overall, B., and Aronson, H. "Expectations of Psychotherapy in Lower Socio-economic Class Patients," in F. Riessman et al. (Eds.), *Mental Health of the Poor;* Free Press, 1964.

Raskin, A. "Factors Therapists Associate with Motivation to Enter Psychotherapy," *J. Clin. Psychology* (1961) 17:62-65.

Riessman, F. "Are the Deprived Non-verbal?," in F. Riessman et al. (Eds.), *Mental Health of the Poor;* Free Press, 1964.

Riessman, F., and Scribner, S. "The Under-Utilization of Mental Health Services by Workers and Low Income Groups: Causes and Cures," *Amer. J. Psychiatry* (1965) 121:798-801.

Rogers, C. R., et al. (Eds.), *The Therapeutic Relationship and Its Impact;* Univ. of Wis. Press, 1967.

Rosenthal, D., and Frank, J. D. "The Fate of Psychiatric Clinic Outpatients Assigned to Psychotherapy," *J. Nervous and Mental Disease* (1958) 127:330-343.

Rubinstein, E., and Lorr, M. "A Comparison of Terminators and Remainers in Outpatient Psychotherapy," *J. Clin. Psychology* (1956) 12:345-349.

Schaffer, L., and Myers, J. K. "Psychotherapy and Social Stratification: An Empirical Study of Practice in a Psychiatric Outpatient Clinic," *Psychiatry* (1954) 17:83-93.

Seeman, J. "Counselor-Judgments of Therapeutic Process and Outcome," in Rogers, C. R., and Dymond, R. F. (Eds.), *Psychotherapy and Personality Change;* Univ. of Chicago Press, 1954.

Standal, S. W., and Van Der Veen, F. "Length of Therapy in Relation to Counselor Estimates of Personal Integration and Other Case Variables," *J. Consulting Psychology* (1957) 21:1-9.

Sullivan, P. L., et al. "Factors in Length of Stay and Progress in Psychotherapy," *J. Consulting Psychology* (1958) 22:1-9.

Taulbee, E. S. "Relationship Between Certain Personality Variables and Continuation in Psychotherapy," *J. Consulting Psychology* (1958) 22:83-89.

Taylor, J. W. "Relationship of Success and Length in Psychotherapy," *J. Consulting Psychology* (1956) 20:332.

Truax, C. B., and Carkhuff, R. R. "Significant Developments In Psychotherapy Research," in L. E. Abt and B. F. Reiss (Eds.), *Progress in Clinical Psychology*, Vol. 6; Grune & Stratton, 1964.

Truax, C. B., and Carkhuff, R. R. *Toward Effective Counseling and Psychotherapy;* Aldine, 1967.

Yamamoto, J., and Goin, M. K. "Social Class Factors Relevant for Psychiatric Treatment," *J. Nervous and Mental Disease* (1966) 142:332-339.

Creative Approaches

When psychotherapy is redefined, new approaches follow. New theories allow a fresh vision of what happens in the therapeutic session, and the therapist is no longer the "doctor" who "cures," but a teacher, tour guide, catalyst, coach, or midwife who is there to stimulate and witness personality change.

The papers presented in this section are representative of the hundreds of new approaches that are available in current therapeutic practice. Like many of the new techniques, most of the approaches described here originated outside the consulting room; in fact, it is characteristic of humanistic psychotherapy to borrow perspectives from other fields and to synthesize them into the therapeutic work. What works in theater, dance, or children's games can also work, or so it seems, in the therapeutic relationship.

Elsa First reviews techniques of family therapy that have emerged from the double-bind hypothesis of schizophrenia. Many family therapists view themselves as anthropologists consulting to very small tribes, outsiders who can view the distorted communication system and intervene to correct it. Elsa First finds that family therapy solves problems that older approaches were not aware of, but that the results of family therapy are, as yet, unconvincing.

Anthony describes his therapeutic approach, in which he serves as a Zen master to provide patients with problem situations that cannot be resolved by logical thinking and conventional social rules. In Zen Transactional Therapy, the therapist is a provocative, teasing teacher prompting the student/patient to achieve enlightenment.

Fantasy has been a diagnostic tool in traditional psychotherapy; the paper by Purinton, Healy, and Whitney exemplifies its therapeutic use. Guided fantasy is presented as a structured experience that provides a creative way for a patient to experience and communicate his inner life.

Techniques that promote contact and immediacy are part of the contribution of Gestalt therapy. Tobin details a method of dealing with the common "hanging-on" reaction in psychotherapy. Saying good-bye to the past aids the patient to close down unfinished business so that it is possible for him to focus on the present.

In rediscovering the body, psychotherapists are learning what actors and dancers have always known: the moving body is the center of human experience. Psychotherapy, as Alperson defines it, involves reestablishing connections between body and mind, and movement therapy helps to integrate the flow of energy between sensory, kinesthetic, and symbolic levels.

The New Wave in Psychiatry

by Elsa First

Some psychiatric patients (most notably, young adult schizophrenics) seem unable to get better because of the pressures their families exert on them. This common clinical observation gave rise, some fifteen years ago, to attempts to treat families as a whole. The number of clinicians treating families has since multiplied (there were several thousand at the last government count, with training programs at a dozen major city teaching hospitals), and they would describe themselves as the Family Therapy movement. There are two main schools within family therapy. One derives from psychoanalysis, and is interested in how the inner lives of family members interlock. The other school, more controversial though increasingly influential, is interested in families as "systems." The instructions of a systems-minded supervisor to a beginning family therapist might run like this:

Assemble the family in one room. Ask them to pick out one of their problems and to try to negotiate a solution. Sit back and follow the structure of their conversation—the form, not the content—the sequences of "transactions" that take place. A transaction might take the form of people blaming each other, or of a child raising his demands

Reprinted with permission from *The New York Review of Books*. Copyright © 1975 Nyrev, Inc. The above article is a review of (a) *Techniques of Family Therapy* by Jay Haley and Lynn Hoffmann. Basic Books, 480 pp., $14.00; $4.95 (paper); (b) *Change: Principles of Problem Formation and Problem Resolution* by Paul Watzlawick, John Weakland, and Richard Fisch. Norton, 172 pp., $7.95; (c) *Families and Family Therapy* by Salvador Minuchin. Harvard University Press, 320 pp., $10.00; and (d) films available from the Philadelphia Child Guidance Clinic: *I Think It's Me–Difference Display as a Contextual Event, A Family With a Little Fire,* and *The Open Door: A Structural Approach to a Family with an Anorectic Child.*

each time the parents are about to agree, or of one person "invalidating" another's perceptions. See what you can learn about the family by watching the patterns of their communication. Ask yourself: What alliances are formed in this family, and when? Why do their arguments never reach "closure" and what keeps happening to prevent a resolution? Where does the child's "symptom" (for example, withdrawal or provocative courting of danger) appear in this sequence of transactions?

Making observations of this kind is clearly a persuasive experience, especially as it soon becomes apparent that every unhappy family does indeed have certain sequences of "transactions" which seem to recur automatically. It is doubtful whether a young psychiatrist or social worker who tries this experiment could ever think about the problems of therapy exactly as he did before. However, to carry it out, a different sort of attention from that of a psychoanalyst is required. The psychoanalyst, deliberately using his own empathy as a tool, pays close attention to the emotional "content" of what people say. While it is true that he observes the style of communication in order to detect "defenses," he asks himself a rather different question: What form of relationship is this patient trying to re-create with me? Family therapy shifts the emphasis to the family as a whole and to the transactions within it as they take place in the present.

Many in the family therapy movement prefer to think of themselves as anthropologist-consultants to very small tribes in distress rather than as doctors who cure individual "cases" of psychological illness. Their new style of thinking was shaped by the work of the anthropologist Gregory Bateson[1] and in fact all the books under review derive in part from the Palo Alto research group that, under Bateson's leadership in the mid-Fifties, produced the "double-bind theory of schizophrenia." This hypothesis has since become (to borrow Auden's words on Freud's death) a whole climate of opinion, not least through its influence on R. D. Laing.

Jay Haley, family movement spokesman, was a member of the Palo Alto group, as were John Weakland and the late Don Jackson, who appears in the book by Haley and Hoffman, and to whom *Change* is dedicated. Salvador Minuchin's style of therapy was shaped by his work with Oriental immigrant families in Israel and with the families of black and Puerto Rican delinquent boys at the Wiltwyck School; but he has also been much influenced by Haley, whom he invited to join the

---

[1]See Gregory Bateson, *Steps to an Ecology of Mind* (Chandler, 1972; Ballantine, paper).

Philadelphia Child Guidance Clinic.[2] These books thus offer an opportunity to re-examine double-bind theory and some therapeutic techniques that have emerged from it during the last twenty years.

What the double-bind hypothesis did was to translate the relationship between the schizophrenia-producing mother and her child into communications theory. The hypothesis starts from the observation that the talk of schizophrenics leaves out—or leaves ambiguous—the signals or "meta-messages" which tell us whether a message is serious or playful, real or imaginary, ironic or direct, literal or metaphoric. As Haley first suggested, schizophrenics cannot distinguish among different kinds of logical discourse; he and Bateson drew on Whitehead and Russell's demonstration that confusion of "logical types" creates paradox. Why do schizophrenics apparently refuse all relationships by refusing to qualify their own messages? What could such schizophrenic communication be an adaptation to? It was, as Bateson put it, a response to a mother who continually puts her child in a paradoxical bind by a) giving him mutually contradictory messages, while b) implicitly forbidding him to recognize or point out what she is doing. If he could blame her he would be out of the bind; but such children sacrifice themselves in order to maintain the fiction that their parent's "mystifications" (as Laing later called them) make sense.

Bateson specified what sort of mother this was: one who is made anxious and hostile by closeness to her child but finds it intolerable to acknowledge this. When the child approaches she withdraws, but when the child then moves away she becomes pseudo-affectionate and accuses him of being unloving. Such phenomena are readily observable, and Bateson's description of them was simple and elegant.

Psychoanalysis doesn't contradict the double-bind hypothesis. Bateson's work meant that there were now two ways of describing the same phenomena. You could talk in psychoanalytic language about a highly ambivalent mother who projected her own hostility, an infant who lacked experiences of mutuality and so developed a weak ego, etc., or you could talk about the same behavior as a "dysfunctional

---

[2]Another major influence on the Palo Alto group was the imaginative work of Milton H. Erickson, the doyen of medical hypnotism, who wrote the foreword to *Change*. Erickson advised Bateson and Mead on their work on trance in Bali. From his work comes the understanding that trance can be seen not just as an inner state but as a form of relationship, and that inducing trances typically proceeds by double-bind communications. See also Jay Haley, *Uncommon Therapy* (Norton, 1973; Ballantine, 1974, paper), which is about Erickson's work.

relationship" which shows itself in disturbed communication. But if you do the latter, the emphasis shifts from past to present, from inner dynamics to communication, from pathology to a peculiar adaptation. Haley, in his *Strategies of Psychotherapy,* published in 1963, spelled out one version of the implications of double-bind theory. Unfortunately, Haley's notoriously sardonic style has made it nearly impossible for anyone educated in psychoanalysis to give him attention.

Every communication, Haley wrote, functions both as a report and a command; and as a command each communication can be seen as redefining the nature of the relationship one is having with the partner. If I discuss the weather I may be defining our relationship as one in which we will only talk about conventional matters. If you then ask me why I am talking about the weather, you have redefined our relationship as more intimate. (Try observing this. It can be unnerving.) Every relationship (marriage, therapy) can be seen, Haley says, as an implicit power struggle over who defines the nature of the relationship. In the above example, if it is a psychoanalyst who asks why I talk about the weather, he has thereby taken control of the context: my pleasantries are now something to be examined. All symptoms of "disturbance," according to Haley, should be looked at as strategies that control relationships that cannot be controlled by other means. (Part of the strategy is the claim that the symptom is involuntary.)

Haley also suggested that we look at all situations in which one person sets out to change another, whether by hypnosis, religious conversion, psychoanalysis, behavior therapy, family therapy, or whatever, and ask what formal characteristics they have in common. He found that they all contained "benign" double-binds, i.e., they make it impossible for the patient to re-create the kinds of relationships he has formed in the past.

Minuchin, Haley, and their colleagues command our attention, moreover, because they represent one of the first concerted attempts to apply systems-theory concepts to the practice of psychotherapy. Their defenders say they are trying to give us a grammar of situations rather than a grammar of individual motives. As such, their work appeals to the loyalty of those who sympathize with Bateson's plea that we need to think "ecologically," in terms of patterns and relationships, rather than in linear fashion, in terms of cause and effect, individual vs. environment, etc. (Minuchin, for example, calls himself a "context-oriented" therapist, in contrast to those who are "individually oriented.") Their clinical methods, however, can strike outsiders as unpleasantly manipulative and authoritarian. And their style suggests that something of Bateson's vision has been lost in translation.

"Family therapy is best defined as what a number of family therapists are doing," write Haley and Hoffman in the introduction to their book, which combines interviews with noted family therapists and transcripts of representative sessions. "To learn what it is they do, one must watch them at work and inquire about their actions. . . . From such queries we learn what a therapist's beliefs are about his work. If these be rationalizations, that is what all clinical writing is." This calculated ingenuousness and mistrust of explanatory concepts are characteristic of Haley, but they also reflect the state of the art. When C. Christian Beels and Andrew Ferber, who are more ecumenical teachers of family therapy, set out to survey their field, they too watched therapists at work through one-way screens, studied video tapes, and interviewed colleagues. Their report[3] sounded a similar note:

> It was pointless to try to abstract "the technique" from these many approaches, since the personal stamp of the therapist was so clearly the first thing we had to understand. . . . We avoided the evaluation of theory because we believed that in many cases the theory advanced was a rationalization for the practice. . . .

Indeed, at first view all that the various forms of family therapy may seem to have in common is that the whole family is usually in the clinic or the consulting room at once, and that the setting is somehow public; the tape recorders, video cameras, and one-way screens suggest an audience. Therapists may have co-therapists, and the one - way screen may harbor behind it a supervisor, armed with a microphone that he may use to intervene. The therapist himself may disappear behind the screen, emerging like a *deus ex machina* when the plot gets to thick.

Family therapy, like some family quarrels, needs witnesses, to keep track. The watchers often prefer to be watched too, to guard against their being drawn in to take sides in a way that would perpetuate the family's patterns. Family members, also, may be taken behind the screen, to show them how the family gets on without them (for example, to show an intrusive grandmother that her daughter can cope with the children). The invisible drama of the transference has been replaced by what has been described as a kind of Brechtian theater. The therapist functions as stage director, and some (Minuchin is one) double as actors too.

Despite their shyness of concepts, the systems-theory therapists, as I'll call them, do have some. Following Don Jackson, they try to look at families as systems that are kept together, or kept within certain limits of behavior, by homeostatic mechanisms which continually re-establish

---

[3]"What Family Therapists Do," in *The Book of Family Therapy,* edited by Andrew Ferber, Marilyn Mendelsohn, and Augustus Napier (Aronson, 1972; Houghton Mifflin, 1973, paper).

the status quo. (Examples might be: whenever this wife shows a certain degree of resentment, her husband deprecates himself; whenever these parents quarrel, their child diverts them by becoming troublesome; whenever another child shows a certain degree of independence, his mother labels it as dangerous or disturbed.) They are not interested in the history or causes of a symptom, but in how it serves to regulate present behavior.

"The identified patient's symptoms can be assumed to be a system-maintaining or a system-maintained device," Minuchin asserts. He allows that a symptom may arise because of the individual's "particular life circumstances," but he believes it then always gets "supported" by the system. This is a useful assumption for opening one's eyes to such phenomena, and a difficult one to falsify in any given instance. (The authors of *Change*, however, lose my confidence when they reveal their cavalier assumption that the origin of most symptoms is essentially trivial, e.g., that a phobia about going out to shop starts from an accidental fit of dizziness at a department store door.)

In contrast to psychoanalysts, and to the more psychoanalytic family therapists, the systems-theory therapists place little reliance on insight as an agent of change. "I believe that insight is a by-product of change," Carl Whitaker said in an interview. "You have to go past it to see what it is." Moreover they assume, arguing from cybernetics, that if one family member does try to change, the rest of the "system" will respond so as to minimize or eliminate that change. So they feel they have to interfere actively in the pattern of the family's functioning in order to make it possible for something new to happen. "In order to transform the system, the therapist has to intervene so as to unbalance the system," says Minuchin, who may do so by taking sides, in various tacit but obvious ways. (Scholastic attention is given to how and when Minuchin changes his seat.) Don Jackson says, "You don't really point it [the system] out, you disturb it first. Otherwise they'll never see it. . ." because each person will simply blame the other for starting the system in the first place.

The family therapists may have the family "enact" new ways of behaving in the session. (Example: having the children sit with their backs turned while their parents get on with a quarrel.) They may assign homework "tasks" (shutting a bedroom door two hours daily, so as to establish privacy). They may deliberately stage a crisis (as Minuchin does when he tells the parents of an anorectic girl to try to force her to eat) or they may give instructions that will exacerbate the situation. Don Jackson, asked how he might try to produce insight, if he ever wanted to, replied, "I would tell them to treat [this] daughter the way they are already treating her, and let *them* discover how they're treating her. In other words, try to produce a 'runaway' in the system. That would produce more 'insight' than just telling them what I think they're doing. . . . Prescribing the symptom is more likely to produce insight than telling people how the mind works."

But while systems-theory therapists don't value insight, they do use all manner of persuasion to convert the family to their way of seeing its communications as strategies. They will, for example, ask each person what he or she could do that would upset or please the others. Their initial sessions seem to be devoted to propagandizing the family, more or less skillfully, into the view that it is the whole family that is "hurting," as Virginia Satir, in *Techniques of Family Therapy,* puts it.

In *Families and Family Therapy,* Mr. Smith, an anxious and paranoid-seeming middle-aged husband, is on the verge of returning to a mental hospital:

> *Smith:* I think it's my problem. I'm the one who has the problem.
>
> *Minuchin:* Don't be so sure. Never be sure.
>
> *Smith:* Well, it seems to be. I'm the one that was in the hospital and everything. . . . I don't know if it's caused by anybody, but I'm the one that has the problem.
>
> *Minuchin:* Mm. If . . . let's follow your line of thinking. If it would be caused by somebody or something outside of yourself, what would you say the problem is?

But Smith continues deferring to his wife's complaints. And when Minuchin mentions the wife's bad temper, Smith shows more anxiety: "Are we on television?" Finally, Minuchin himself has to bring up the fact, known from a previous psychiatrist, that the wife is frigid. Smith acknowledges that his "condition" could relate to this; the wife "accepts the label of sick" and Smith is told he needs to help his wife overcome her difficulty. The hospital is avoided; marital therapy with sex counseling ensues.

The film made of this session is entitled *I Think It's Me–Difference Display as a Contextual Event.* This last phrase is so splendid a flourish of systems rhetoric that it seems almost self-parody. Family therapists value "difference" since it is difference that makes the world go round, as everyone knows who remembers Bateson's lovely definition of "information" as "a difference that makes a difference." But the difference referred to here is simply Mr. Smith's tendency to behave in a bizarre way under stress, particularly the tic-like scrabbling of his hand on his chair; the camera zooms in on this to show that it occurs whenever Mrs. Smith implies he is sick, and subsides whenever Minuchin redefines him as normal by making a point of how much he, Minuchin, resembles Smith.

In his treatment sessions, Salvador Minuchin comes across as a show-man; he loves to play the expert or the duffer, whichever he thinks will work. He seems canny, cheerfully domineering, anti-intellectual, and genuinely sympathetic toward poor families. According to Minuchin, every unhappy family is unhappy in one of two ways: they are either too "enmeshed" or too "disengaged." The cure is to "restructure," by put-ting "boundaries" around "subsystems," and his book is full of dia-grams, which look a bit like football plays, and which he uses to point out where the realignments should take place. The psychoanalytic family therapists I've talked with feel he deserves credit for trying to present a comprehensive theory in a field which had none.

He has recently received much attention for his research project in which young adolescents suffering from anorexia—rejection of food —are treated by family therapy. Anorexia can be fatal; it is difficult to handle. It astonishes many that it should be amenable to family treat-ment. Does Minuchin's success imply that even so grave and seemingly "psychotic" a disturbance is best described as merely a "contextual event"?

What follows is Minuchin's typical procedure in treating an anorec-tic patient, abstracted from several transcripts and video tapes. We see the family in the hospital where the emaciated daughter has continued to lose weight. Lunch is brought in for everyone. Minuchin tells each parent in turn to try to get the daughter to eat. This part is usually agonizing to watch: the parents are awful, the girl stubborn and desper-ate. The parents always fail, and Minuchin calls a halt once the scene reaches some appalling if ludicrous climax, such as the enraged father trying to stuff a hot dog down his daughter's throat. You have failed, he tells the parents. And you will always fail so long as you fight your battles through the girl, and undercut each other's efforts, as you just did. You must learn to work together if she is to live.

Minuchin then tells the girl that she has been fighting for her inde-pendence in a family where the only remaining opportunity to rebel was in not eating. She has won; she has humiliated and defeated her parents in front of the doctor. And as she gets stronger, she will be able to do battle in other matters. Meanwhile, of course, she must eat, but now she is offered a choice, chicken or hamburger? and so on down the menu. By the end of the session she is unobtrusively eating, and is discharged within a week.

Minuchin may continue to take charge of the girl's eating, perhaps by having her phone him whenever she wants to eat anything (paradox-ical tactics). Meanwhile the parents are encouraged to apply "behavior modification": the girl must stay in bed unless she gains her weekly quota. Since anorectics are hyperactive, this is strong punishment. Family therapy will continue, and will also deal with the "behavior problems" some ex-anorectics develop.

It is an ingenious therapy: half ritual drama, half behaviorism. As Sir William Gull said in the nineteenth century, when he named the syndrome *anorexia nervosa,* "The treatment required is obviously that . . . the patients should be fed at regular intervals, and surrounded by persons who would have moral control over them. . ." It is clear that Minuchin mobilizes the parents to exert a degree of "moral control." It is interesting also that ritual drama works. The staged crisis is at least a temporary exorcism of the girl's negativity, and Minuchin construes it for her as a rite of passage: she has "defeated" her parents. I do not think it necessarily proves anything new about the supposed causes of anorexia, or that anorexia isn't part of a larger disturbance of personality which may later persist as struggle with "internal" parents. But the scene does make powerfully visible the hidden binds the parents have been imposing on the girl.

We learn much about the ethos of family therapists by watching one of their most favored and most fascinating techniques, which is called "relabeling" or "reframing." They consider it to be highly effective. As Haley himself might have observed, one of the first things which gurus, shamans, and psychotherapists do when they set out to change someone is to convey to them that the world is not what it seems, and that their habitual categories may not apply. Magical feats will serve to do this, and so will interpretations of the unconscious, and so too, the family therapists believe, will "relabeling."

Relabeling has distinguished ancestry in Bateson's application of the "Theory of Logical Types" to the study of communication. Every message is qualified by the label given to it by the "meta-message." The significance of anything changes according to what class or set you assign it to—reward or punishment, praise or blame, the playful or the earnest, etc. Change the context and you can modify the facts, or everybody's attitude to the facts. The relabelers are engaged, so they believe, in changing the context. They hope that this will free everybody to behave differently in the next context.

Thus in family therapy patients are to be relabeled as normal; symptoms are to be relabeled as rational tactics; and wherever possible what looks negative is to be relabeled as positive. (Probably the boldest example of this was the husband who had chased his wife with an axe, and was told he .was trying to get close to her.) Candide was clearly a talented relabeler, and so too was Tom Sawyer, whose "reframing" of the task of whitewashing a fence is quoted as exemplary by the authors of *Change*. Here are some examples of relabeling in practice:

1. The family of an anorectic is asked, "How long have you had this fasting problem?"

2. A young schizophrenic, barely managing to survive as a failing student, is brought to the therapist by his mother, who claims he is headed for another breakdown. The boy complains that his parents dole him a weekly allowance on the basis of how "sick" or "good" he seems. Watzlawick et al. write, "In the presence of the mother it was pointed out to the son that he had every right to defend himself by threatening to cause a far greater expenditure by suffering another psychotic break. The therapist then made some concrete suggestions as to how the son should behave in order to give the impression of impending doom —these suggestions being mostly reformulations of the somewhat weird behavior the son was engaging in anyway."

This is relabeling the symptom as a voluntary tactic. Result: the mother felt free to get angry at the son; she settled an adequate allowance on him so that he could "sink or swim"; the son saved up and got a car, becoming more independent.

3. In *Techniques of Family Therapy*, two cold upper-class parents —collusive in their attitude that all-things-must-be-bright-and-beautiful—are confronted with their college-age daughter, who has just had an acute schizophrenic episode. The mother, who plays the martyr, starts to cry.

> *Father:* I certainly am [sighs] sorry to see, ah, Mrs. Starbuck hurt by, ah, things that Sue was saying.
> *Sue:* Oh, I don't mean to hurt her. . . .
> *Therapist (Don Jackson):* I wonder that she was crying necessarily because she was hurt. Has that been established? . . . [To mother] . . . Because you responded to your daughter with I think a rather touching closeness, I don't think it was just a hurt. . . .

Jackson explains his technique: "This is simply taking the motivation that has been labeled in a negative way and labeling it in a positive way. . . . If they have been defining what they are doing in one way for many many years, and if I can suddenly define it another way, it shocks them a little out of believing that they're always right. . . ."

4. A session in Minuchin's book (and in the film *A Family With a Little Fire*) is an act of relabeling from start to finish: A hard-working black mother of four, more relieved than sorry that her ex-husband no longer visits the family, comes to the clinic because her seven-year-old daughter has, for the second time, set fire to the mother's bed. The therapist, Braulio Montalvo, praises the children for their competence in putting out the fire. He notes silently that the mother tends to use as a

scapegoat the fire-setting child, Mandy, who had been the father's favorite. Mandy hides behind a book, whereupon the mother reprimands her. Montalvo deliberately misunderstands, and asks Mandy to read aloud: "She was reading O.K." Prescription: Mother is to spend ten minutes a day teaching Mandy to light matches safely. Also her teacher is to encourage her good reading. Throughout, Montalvo is reassuringly low-key. Fire-setting doesn't recur.

Throughout this session the fire has, by implication, been "labeled" an accident. Because of the taboo on interpretation, particularly of anything negative, no one told Mandy that it was natural she missed her father, or explored whether she blamed her mother for his disappearance. Perhaps the mother did get the message to appreciate Mandy more. But perhaps what also happened was that the clinic provided Mandy with an authority figure, Montalvo, who said she wasn't so bad after all, just as her father used to do. Psychoanalysts used to call this a "transference cure"; they still could.

The interpretations psychoanalysts make, of course, are also a form of relabeling. They too relabel the patient's irrationality as understandable and acceptably human. Reflection on this raises provocative questions. Doesn't all therapy provide a change of context? Does all anxiety signal loss of context? I am dubious about some family therapists not because they relabel but because they do so in so facile and Pollyannaish a way.

Another contribution of Bateson's, although it is no longer acknowledged as such and seems to have been somewhat oversimplified, has to do with the notion of complementarity. During his work in Bali with Margaret Mead, Bateson became interested in what kept cultures together or drove them apart (he called these latter factors "schismogenic"). He described two basic forms of relationship between groups in a culture as symmetrical and complementary. In a symmetrical relation the same behavior is exchanged; more of it in A is answered by more of it in B. Examples would be boasting, or ritual gift exchanges, or commercial rivalry. Such relations tend to be ones of rising competition, as in armament races.

In complementary relations, opposite and mutually dependent behaviors are exchanged, e.g., nurturance/dependency; exhibition/spectatorship; dominance/submission. Complementary relations may tend to increase cohesion. However, bateson also saw from the beginning that complementary relations could become increasingly polarized if they lead "to a progressive unilateral distortion of the personalities of the members of both groups, which results in mutual hostility." Family therapists look for ways to change symmetrical relations into complementary ones, and often seem to sentimentalize the "complementary."

Therapist (Carl Whitaker): Come on, Dad. Do you solve the problem of Mom coming on so strong by sort of being nice and quiet?

Mr.Dodds: Yes, I think we are quite opposite in personality. She is, like you say, quite fiery.

Whitaker: Do you appreciate that? Do you like it?

Mr. Dodds: Yes, I guess in a way it's good.

Whitaker: I sort of feel like that's the way we marry. I married a wife with fire because I was kind of soft and easy.

Minuchin's commentary: "The therapist makes an interpretation of complementarity. . . . Again the terms emphasize positives: the mother is strong, the father is nice. Another therapist, more concerned with pathology, might call her controlling and him passive."

What about the clinical success of the family therapists? They seem to be good at doing certain things: at getting very disturbed adolescents some freedom from very disturbing families; at teaching families how to manage a symptom (such as asthma—another Philadelphia project) without reacting to it in ways that make it worse; and at keeping schizophrenics out of hospitals. Beyond that, it is hard to judge their work because they publish only the early sessions, not later stages of treatment which may go on for two years. Nor do some of them worry much over the number of families who walk out after one meeting. They happen to work mainly with a lower-middle- and working-class clinic population, and their faith in the power of genial persuasion may reflect their clients' diffidence toward professionals.

Minuchin's underlying assumption, which he states humanely, is that most people cannot change very much. Haley has always inveighed against the kinds of questions psychoanalysts ask about whether deeper changes in personality take place. He believes we can tell only whether behavior has changed. Watzlawick et al. believe that most contemporary therapy creates more problems than it cures by implying "utopian" goals of personality change, and that it is cruel to view a symptom as just the "tip of an iceberg." The art of therapy, in their eyes, is to define a problem as narrowly and pragmatically as possible, and then to deal with it.

The authors of *Change* take a conservative political position; they find most social welfare programs "utopian" too. They are, however, training probation officers in the use of paradoxical techniques, e.g., to gain the trust of the probationers in their charge, the officers are advised to say, "You should never fully trust me or tell me everything."

Jay Haley once remarked in *Families and Family Therapy* that he suspected the essence of therapeutic technique was in the "mixture of forcing people to behave differently but phrasing it in such a way that they can't resist because you're on their side." The authors of *Change* have much in common with Haley, and even include one of his old examples of such technique (suggesting a dearth of canonical anecdotes in Palo Alto). The example: If a frigid wife is, according to psychiatric theory, hostile to her husband, then she should be told that she is trying to protect him from the full force of her sexuality. Because of her hostility, she will decide to stop protecting him.

Young family therapists are gratefully reading *Change* because it tells them how to look at situations of conflict as feedback systems. Moreover, it spells out the mysteries of their tradition: elementary set theory, the theory of logical types, the notion of logical paradox (double-binds). *Change* is deliberately and provocatively obnoxious, but its clumsiness is, I suppose, inadvertent. Important ideas reappear in it as snappy formulas. (Bateson shows that cybernetics implies a new notion of what constitutes an explanation: Cybernetic explanation is a-causal, because it deals with form, not substance, relationships, not things. Watzlawick, Weakland, and Fisch just tell you to ask "What is happening?" rather than "Why?") *Change* uses the cybernetic definition of change to rationalize an exceedingly manipulative approach to patients—an approach which is more properly justified by cynicism, not cybernetics.

As I trace it, this notion of change first appears, innocently enough, in Bateson's thoughts about a porpoise: the experimenters were trying to teach the porpoise to produce new behavior. Each time it did something new accidentally, they would reward it. The porpoise would begin each show by displaying its latest "new" trick, but it wouldn't get a reward unless it did something still newer, by chance. The porpoise grew understandably moody. But finally it caught on: it went into a state of creative agitation, and at its next performance produced four pieces of behavior never before observed in the species. It had learned to learn.

This corresponds with the cybernetic notion of change. There is "first order" change: this is merely substituting one item of data (or behavior) for another. Then there is second order change: this is a change in the kind of operation that is carried out—"a change in its [the computer's] *way* of behaving." Second order change means a shift to a "meta-level" of programming.

Change was written to expound the rationale that implicitly had been guiding the authors' eight years of "problem solving" at their Brief Therapy Center in Palo Alto. What they'd been doing, it seems, is looking at situations and asking: What in this could be seen as an analogy to a logical paradox—or to a closed positive feedback circuit (where A = go to B, and B = go to A)? What could they then suggest that would resolve the problem at a meta-level? Their examples are uninspiring: a teenager stays out late; his parents become more restrictive; conflict mounts. Moral: The attempted countermeasure is often part of the problem. Solution: Tell the parents to play helpless and unconcerned; the teenager will become responsible.

The problem solvers have, they confess, only one problem, which is how to get people to do what they tell them to do. For this too there is a strategy, which they devised especially for those patients who are just too "cautious," for example, to "risk" looking for a job or a mate. They call it the "Devil's Pact." We have a plan, they say, which is likely to succeed, but you will probably think it is too absurd or inconvenient or risky, and turn it down. Therefore we will not tell you what it is unless you promise in advance to do it. Go home and decide: if you don't agree, don't come back.

Well, yes, of course. The issue in all therapy is how to produce commitment or willingness to change, how to create what psychoanalysis calls the "therapeutic alliance." I do not mean to condone their use of this ultimate little gimmick when I point out that it could also be seen as a coarse version of a formula which is found in many therapeutic contracts. The formula is, roughly: I will ask you to do something which requires that you surrender your ordinary rationality for a while and so trust in me or in something larger which I may represent. The psychoanalyst's rule that the patient at least try to free-associate also fits this formula, as do some tasks set by shamans and gurus to beginners.

Accepting the irrational task, letting go of one's usual means of controlling the world, is, of course, already a first step in changing—and it also establishes one's commitment to the therapist and the therapy. And yes, Watzlawick, Weakland, and Fisch's "Pact" might impel a certain kind of patient to "put himself blindly into the hands of another person," as they themselves describe it. And for some this might represent a small but significant step toward change. The offer of the "Pact" might drive some others to suicide, but this too could be edifyingly discussed as an example of "second order change."

The epistemology of cybernetics, Bateson has informed us, is anti-Aristotelian. Cybernetics, in his view, suggests that we are all prisoners of seeing things in pairs of opposites. The way out of conflict (or "oscillation," in computer terms) is to realize that we are neither one nor the other pole, neither A nor B, but something which contains both. This is what Bateson's extraordinary analysis of Alcoholics Anonymous as a therapy is all about. The alcoholic must "surrender" (to God, in the AA scheme) and stop pitting his "sober" self against his "drunken" one, i.e., he must acknowledge that both his sober ego and his drunken irrationality are part of a larger system.

Bateson proposed the AA procedure as a typical example of therapeutic change. Similarly, to venture an example suggested by this model: a schizoid person could be seen as oscillating between the need to be special and a sense of being worthless; the more he needs to be special, the more worthless he will feel, and vice versa. Therefore to change he will need to stop seeing the world in terms of special vs. worthless. The authors of *Change* are also in effect proposing that we use this model in looking at situations of conflict, both outer and inner. But their notions of inner conflict are decidedly sketchy. And their raffish problem-solving is not, I think, what Bateson meant at all.

The systems therapists announce they are working with a new paradigm, or model of thinking, one which, they are the first to tell us, is discontinuous with the psychoanalytic one. When one paradigm arises to rival another, as Thomas Kuhn has suggested, there may be a longish interregnum, during which people will decide their allegiance on all sorts of grounds. They may prefer the cultural style of the adherents of the new paradigm. Many family therapists, for example, consider themselves less "elitist" than psychoanalysts (partly because they deliberately put themselves on an equal footing with patients by revealing their own personalities, instead of remaining a blank screen for transference. Meanwhile, without acknowledging that it is the patient's transference which has invested them with authority, they use that authority). If the new paradigm solves problems which the old one failed to solve, that often convinces people that it is the only one that makes sense. These books do not assure me that the solutions of family therapy are as yet so convincing.

Zen Transactional Therapy

by Robert M. Anthony

Everyone possesses a human-relations model that includes rules for conduct at home, work, and everyday social situations. These rules reflect the attitudes and beliefs a person has about these settings. They also demonstrate explicit or implicit goals relating to every area of human behavior, such as intimacy, influencing others toward change, protecting the ego, degree of equality between others and self, what is humorous and what is not, etc.

A model is ultimately sociotherapeutic if it abides by the following guidelines:

1. The user of the model does not take himself or the model seriously, no matter how important he or it may seem. A corollary rule would instruct the user to laugh at himself or others whenever he or they take the model seriously. Seriousness here is defined as an automatic emotional investment in the model, which causes the user to neurotically hold onto it in the presence of new information, to equate the loss of the model with a loss of esteem or threat to personal integrity, or to act destructively with others in order to perpetuate the model. A humorous concern for others means that when one enjoys himself more, he has more concern for others.

2. The user of the model holds the personal worth of users of different models on a par with his own, and he commits himself to their personal growth as well as to his own.

3. The user of the model recognizes that his choice of that particular model was based on a value judgment; he does not punish others who violate the principles of his model or use other models. Included in this guideline is the recognition that those who derive legal sanction from their position in a society's power structure frequently exact retribution and revenge upon those who do not accept the power structure's model. A corollary would state that if force is used in the application of a particular human-relations model, it is always to be used gently and is never to inflict harm to the resistor of that model. Such benign coercion

should always have the dual aim of increasing the resistor's response repertoire in his everyday life and of preventing him from inflicting harm on others.

4. The model ultimately has application to all spheres of living: interpersonal, social, economic, and political.

If he adhered to these four guidelines, the user of any model would be constructive in his everyday human transactions. He would be able to laugh at himself and the model, to treat the users of other models with the same equality and dignity with which he treats the users of his model, to stimulate the personal development of all others regardless of their particular model, and to apply his model everywhere.

ORIGIN AND DEVELOPMENT OF THE HUMAN-RELATIONS MODEL

The therapeutic model of personal and social change presented here arose out of dissatisfaction with my inability—and that of others—to stimulate pervasive, mutually experienced, responsible human intimacy. I was amazed and disturbed that those with the titles "psychiatrist," "psychologist," or "social worker" were unable to demonstrate in their everyday lives how one came to develop such a necessary human condition as intimacy. Even more disconcerting was the discovery that most of these professionals lived different lives at home, at work, and in social settings—and that these compartmentalizations of behavior were considered desirable. This all seemed absurd. I felt that the foundation of all human conduct should be that of a loving and responsible intimacy.

The graduate schools I attended provided little knowledge of this foundation; they mainly taught one to compete with other students, get the job done, and acquire the appropriate professional role. I was essentially programmed to become an effective therapist product who kept a correct, safe emotional distance from others, especially clients and colleagues.

The first psychotherapeutic skills I learned as a graduate student were psychoanalytic techniques and behavior modification. These skills proved to be inadequate in developing the intimacy between myself and clients that I felt was necessary to avoid a continuously destructive society. I had not yet become existentially aware that each theory of psychotherapy is intricately tied to a theory of personality. And that, more importantly, most of these theories ultimately rested upon a model of man as an encapsulated entity, in need of ego defenses, and with little ability to change his basic emotional make-up.

The deficiencies of such models became poignantly apparent when I came across the writings of Alan Watts on Eastern thought, especially

Zen Buddhism. I was then primed for the Zen Buddhist concept of the insulated ego as scum of the sea of experience and awareness. The societal destructiveness of our Western world was revealed to me through reading about the agonizing efforts of Zen students to solve Zen koans and their desire to live disciplined lives in order to obtain freedom from the linear influences of their prior, conventional lives. I became sensitive to the continuous and serious efforts of individuals in our society to reduce tension in order to conserve their identities and to insure their separateness from others.

Particularly striking in these readings was the description of the merriment and humor that Zen masters incorporated in dealing with their students. I found this ingredient significantly absent when professional psychologists taught others, whether students or colleagues.

My forays into Zen thought helped me to begin constructing a model of therapeutic change, but it was only after I discovered the interpersonal gaming systems described by Jay Haley, Eric Berne, and Timothy Leary that my system began to resemble an integrated conceptual framework. The idea of an everyday gaming world of human relationships seemed so simple, and yet to me, so marvelous: if man existed in a gaming arena, his potential for constructive freedom and intimacy increased immeasurably.

I also began to discover, both in clinical practice and in growth relationships outside of therapy, *that to be in emotional need of others was to be destructive to them.* I found that when we need people we become parasitic, that when a person is the object of needfulness he is reduced to a thing, a consumable product, to be ultimately discarded if a better thing comes along. I became aware that the probability of constructiveness with others increased as one *preferred* them, that is, did not *need* them. I also discovered, however, that the transition from a needful to a preferential relationship with others is difficult and is hampered by the constant lure of a totally encapsulated and satisfying dependency.

Recognizing the preference-for-others principle enabled me to construct a parsimonious, basic model of constructive human conduct, a model that could be used consistently and constantly. I set out to teach my clients to become "sociotherps"—human beings who manipulate themselves and others for mutual enhancement.

There are five major principles of the model presented here; together they are called Zen Transactional Therapy (ZTT). The first action principle emphasizes the importance of having an identity that is inclusive of all persons and things all the time. The next four action principles help to incur and sustain the attitudes, thoughts, and feelings of such an identity, as well as to promote constructive actions toward the people and things that make up this identity. Thus, the second action principle encourages one to be tension-explorative in all areas of life. The third action principle encourages the user of the model to play humorously with life, especially when he is striving for constructive social ends. The fourth action principle encourages the recognition and acceptance of all of life as being made up of transactional games, with a person always being affected by the ones he plays. The fifth action principle directs the user of the model to act *preferentially* (non-needfully) with others and with himself at all times, so that *no one* is treated as an object.

I. THE INFINITE IDENTITY PRINCIPLE: CORPORATE AND CORE (VERSUS INSULAR) IDENTITY

All that a person becomes derives from his senses. Whatever he experiences, conceives, reflects on, anticipates, imagines, or acts on is located within the brain, which influences the rest of the bodily processes. Given this process, if a person's family, society, and cultural environment teach him to compartmentalize his everyday experiences into rigid units of "I" versus "others," *and* to defend the encapsulated integrity of the "I" from the experiential thrusts of the "others," he exists in a destructive, paradoxical state. He expends excessive and unnecessary internal energy constructing internal barriers in a delusional exercise of self-conflict.

Personal identity consists of all that is inside and outside the body, including the external physical world, and incorporates all that has been, is now, and exists as potential for the future. Identities may be referred to as "corporate" and "core." Core identity includes physical and genetic makeup and all those thoughts, feelings, actions, and accumulated experiences (i.e., cultural, family, educational) *that a person brings to any present situation.* Core identity also includes the attitude, conviction, and inner feeling that all that has existed, exists, or will exist in time and space is oneself. Corporate identity extends to those experiences and events *that are occurring at this moment in and outside one's immediate presence, or will occur in all future time and space.* One's total identity includes himself and all other people and things—past, present, and future.

This identity concept contrasts with the popular conviction in Western (and some Eastern) civilizations that one's identity is separate and distinct from all other identities—that all are locked in separate, self-contained bodies. One major characteristic of this insular-identity conviction is the feeling or fear of being utterly alone—even though one may be with friends and loved ones. Because Western people are so thoroughly trained to insulate themselves from others, they have consequently developed deep feelings of loneliness. These entrenched feelings of loneliness in turn substantiate the conviction of an "insular" self, and the vicious cycle continues. (It is popularly accepted in Western societies, for example, that the worst punishment that can be inflicted on a person is to be kept physically isolated from others.)

For persons from Western civilizations to develop a feeling or conviction of a core and corporate identity, they must be willing to lovingly experience the loneliness necessary to bring them into a total experiential relationship with others and with the world about them. The loneliness will pass, and its extinction will contribute to the dissolving of the insular identity (with its internal defenses) and the acceptance of the "other" as its vital own.

The recognition of ultimate, infinite identity is the beginning of maturity. Just as a bulb incorporates the potential for the blossoming flower, so did our primitive ancestors incorporate the seed for a potentially consummate and vastly differentiated, yet integrated human. People can deviate temporarily from their ultimate union with themselves, but even given such deviation, there is an inner stability that exerts its influence to get humans back on the appropriate path toward unity.

Because the core-corporate concept is all-inclusive, every person uses his experiences to become his own theoretician. This contrasts distinctly with the Western World's popular concept of an absolute or universal morality of "goods" and "evils" laid down by a separate and all-powerful God-figure. Within the core-corporate concept, morality does not come from outside people, because there are no such dichotomies as "inside" and "outside." Rather, rules for constructive living derive from people's unified but diverse experiences.

The "I-create-myself" orientation involves an openness to all experiences, whether positive and illuminating or abhorent and distasteful. This does not mean that one acts destructively toward others or toward oneself. For Western peoples, however, accustomed to an insulated, dichotomous view of themselves and the world, this does require an acceptance, a willingness to painfully imagine and feel all that they have learned would make them "evil," "guilty," and "sinful." The purpose of such a course is to develop an open attitude toward all that is happening in the world as part of oneself. Only at this point can one choose to be consummately constructive with others.

The corporate-core concept recognizes that there must be an illusion of choice, because we are influenced by the past, culture, and environment, and cannot completely free ourselves of them. However, one can free himself of the feeling of entrapment in the controversy of free choice versus determinism, and act as if a choice does exist. Further, if one does not act as if he has complete choice, but becomes concerned about his self-constructed problem, he will permit self-concern to prevent him from being with others. The spontaneity of action precludes constant introspection.

One must discipline oneself, however, to ad lib life. A part of this discipline involves learning to become constantly aware of one's surroundings, without attaching word labels in the process. To develop this awareness, one must gently push words aside, or not hold on to them when they interfere with perception. Looking with awareness, yet without words, is a difficult discipline for anyone.

II. THE TENSION-EXPLORATION PRINCIPLE: PREFERENCE TO ENHANCE (VERSUS A NEED TO PROTECT) OTHERS AND ONESELF

Our society teaches us that anxiety, frustration, and emotional pain are negative feelings to be quickly avoided, it thereby cheats us of the chance to become free and know joy. As a result, we are conditioned to act in a prescribed, safe, familiar manner. In Zen Transactional Therapy, the only constant is change—change occurring in the mercurial, fleeting moments of the "here and now." In playing ZTT, we are saying that one can tolerate experiential pain when the desired end is personal growth. We do not need so many defenses against emotional pain. Yet, most of us are used to reacting reflexively with others—gravitating toward emotions that are positive and avoiding those that are negative.

The quality that distinguishes a human is his ability to choose among different ways of acting with others—no matter what his first impulse is. Thus, it is possible to experience frustration, anger, sexuality, and to feel these things greatly, and yet not act them out. In fact, one must experience negative feelings up to one's limit of tolerance so that they can be extinguished.

Unless negative emotions can be experienced without the usual avoidance reactions, they will never go away. Positive emotions too, should be felt intensively, without the necessity of acting them out. (There is no need to fear that sexual feelings, too, will diminish and disappear forever, because one's glands are continuously producing hormones.) The intent is to become *human*, to learn to choose among possible actions, no matter what one's feelings may be. Without such choice, our behavior would be like that of the lower animals: a series of conditioned reactions, with choices dependently tied to innate drives, emotions, and instincts. The antithesis of this behavior is to explore anxiety and to continuously explore new intellectual, interpersonal, and kinesthetic realms.

Because increasing tension can be physically stressful, we must be aware of our own health and the health of others when initiating these explorations. Adding maximal amounts of tension to existent poor health can only accelerate its decline. Yet, tension cannot be continuously ignored or avoided without physical harm. Tensions of any kind will have adverse effects on the body if they are rejected or continuously suppressed. Tensions so treated can produce physiological symptoms, e.g., ulcers, tension headaches, backaches. Only when tensions are acknowledged as one's own, and not drained off by avoidance, do they diminish and ultimately disappear. Whether one decides to increase tension gradually or all at once is a matter of personal choice and is influenced by a number of factors: state of physical health, private or institutional setting, tolerance level for tension, or degree of motivation for personal development.

The continuous exploration of inner conflicts or "hangups" will eventually lead to virtual elimination of all such stresses. This will not be the case, however, for new experiences. Although the constant facing of stress will, in time, lead to its extinction, future learning situations will produce new stresses—necessitating further confrontation. Yet, it is only through new experiences (especially interpersonal ones) that one becomes more universal in one's being.

Unless people are tension-producing with others, they are being tension-reductive; personal transactions are seldom neutral. *Every interpersonal situation is potentially growth-producing.* The path of least interpersonal friction is the path of least enrichment. Within Western societies every interpersonal style, from the "normal" to the psychotic, is a defensive one and is aimed at tension and anxiety reduction. The hallucinations, bizarre mannerisms, and "craziness" of the psychotic are but extremes of the already caricature-like behavior of the "normal," who avoid tension by the socially acceptable means of being "nice" and "pleasant" with others. The almost ludicrous need to be liked and to protect the insular self produces the variety in acceptable styles found in our society—styles that at first glance seem the epitome of emotional and mental health.

If we are to become appropriate in our enhancement of tension and experiential enrichment of others, we must learn to look out from and through ourselves to perceive others. Instead of continuously focusing on our own anxieties, frustrations, emotions, desires, and needs, we must learn to look through them—that is, to socio-inspect others. This constructive socio-inspection, however, must be carried out with a loving attitude toward one's own feelings, conflicts, and needs. For example, if I were experiencing tension as a result of anger or hostility toward someone, I would try to treat my tension as if it were a beloved part of me, as if it were one of my children interrupting a conversation with a friend. I would not allow it to disrupt my seeing and relating to this person, but would feel it intensely while focusing my attention and awareness on the other person.

Socio-inspection is one of the key elements of the ZTT approach. It is mainly through focusing outside oneself that the pathways for new sensory, informational experiences are kept open. If one is constantly introspective and dwells only on previous experiences, one, in effect, shuts out sensory contact with the world.

There are those who focus on the outside world not for the purpose of allowing change, but for defensive avoidance of themselves—to block new experiences and awareness of their own emotional tensions and pains. Before such a person can appropriately play Zen Transactional Therapy, he must first learn to recognize his avoidances, and then be instructed in the currently available body-and-feeling-awareness therapies (e.g., primal therapy, Gestalt therapy, sensory relaxation, bio-energetics, meditation) in order to reintegrate his mind with his bodily sensations. When he is tuned in to his feelings, he is then ready for constructive socio-inspection, which is aimed at unifying his core experiences with those of his corporate ones.

Our Western societies are destructive mainly because of their self-protective philosophies; these encourage continuous introspection and self-avoiding socio-inspection, rather than constructive socio-inspection, and thus establish rigid life styles of tension avoidance. This avoidance is always linked to an attitude of seriousness, an attitude that contrasts with the third key principle of Zen Transactional Therapy.

III. LIFE IS HUMOROUS PLAY (ESPECIALLY WITH THE SERIOUS PARTS)

Life can have constructive meaning only when we recognize that we are at humorous play—in whatever we do. When a person takes himself seriously, he does not see himself at play and becomes destructive with others (his corporate selves), usually in the name of some noble cause or truth. Unless humor is used continuously—especially when the self is taken seriously—the consequences will be physical and interpersonal destructiveness. Most people in our society seem to have the idea that if they are serious enough, they will make it through life without dying. We are therefore not to rock the emotional boat—especially with waves of laughter. We are to stay experientially safe; and this is a serious business, a *deadly* serious business.

The amount of punishment and sadism in our society is directly proportional to the extent of self-protection against emotional pain. This self-protection also incurs various masochistic games, e.g., suicide, self-belittlement, self-accusation, for our society gives little positive support or instruction in self-love and, especially, its verbal expression. Masochistic games allow people to protect their insular selves from change by preventing unfamiliar and unknown tensions and inse-curities.

Most people react negatively when another laughs at them as they are, taking themselves seriously; they consider this humor absurd, child-ish, phony, insensitive, hostile, defensive, evasive, or crazy. They equate protection from anxiety (and great seriousness) with caring, and anyone who promotes anxiety is considered bestial.

Humor, one of the most important aspects of Zen Transactional Therapy, is a tool to stimulate people to play themselves. There are three types of humor:

1. Purposeful humor, for the deliberate manipulation of others;

2. Spontaneous, reactive humor, used to manipulate others;

3. Spontaneous, reactive humor, *not* involving the manipulations of others.

Such humor may function in a number of situations and for a number of purposes:

1. To shock someone loose from his automatic responses, so that he can consider alternative ways of acting (e.g., presenting a caricature of an over-solicitous life style).

2. To elevate tensions by giving an unexpected response (e.g., laughing when someone automatically performs social amenities).

3. To illustrate the absurdity of avoidance (e.g., humorously directing the attention of a group to a person who has just stated, "I just want to observe what is going on.").

4. To free someone from being caught up in serious introspection (e.g., by whimsically assuming the pose of Rodin's "The Thinker" when someone tries to dispel negative feelings by intellectualizing).

5. To spontaneously share joyous relief after someone has worked through an anxiety (e.g., when an inhibited person in a new group gives impressions of the others and, to his surprise, discovers that he is not rejected).

6. To spontaneously recognize a situational absurdity (e.g., when a person states that what he is and how he behaves is preset and unchangeable).

7. To spontaneously express one's own freedom to play and flow with life (thereby indicating that care and concern do not have to incorporate heavy, morose experiences).

8. To demonstrate that one can act humorously even though feeling angry, frustrated, or depressed.

To clarify this last statement: our society praises the "real person" who can coordinate his actions, thinking, and feelings, and convey them to another. This means of relating, however, often leads to emotional "dumping" (of such feelings as anger, depression, frustration, sexuality), when the other person is merely an innocent stimulus.

Paradoxically, this same society teaches us that genuineness is a fickle quality, jumping about from our actions, to our thoughts, to our feelings—never securely tied to any one. For example: a "hero" is regarded as "real" because of his heroic actions, despite any fearful ("cowardly") feelings. On the other hand, a person will often be described as "phony" if at a social gathering he acts pleasant when he feels bitter and hostile.

In contrast, Zen Transactional Therapy ascribes genuineness to all three spheres of functioning and, in fact, considers "genuineness" unimportant. What is important is that one be constructive with oneself and others. It matters little if one is constructive by acting in accordance with his feelings and thoughts or if one is constructive by acting *differently* from what he is feeling or thinking.

Actions strengthen or diminish emotions, feelings, or tensions. By behaving coordinately with one's feelings, one strengthens them; if a person acts seriously when he feels serious, he will strengthen serious feelings. On the other hand, if he withholds actions or behaves in a manner contrary to that stimulated by his feelings, but allows himself to experience these feelings fully, they will eventually disappear. An important consideration here is that one's attitudes be supportive of one's actions, whether to strengthen or extinguish feelings, and that one be committed to changing the destructive aspects of himself.

ZTT laughter is not the laughter of sadism, but of appropriateness. Humor is not used to inflict pain, nor to encourage mental self-flagellation, but only to *expose* suffering for what it is: an ally in the self-conspiracy to prevent change and the reunion of core and corporate experiences.

The use of language in ZTT frequently is indirect and designed to carry many possible meanings. Language is manipulated playfully as a tool, using gestures, facial expressions, and intonation to convey different meanings. In our society, however, words are often used to put experiences into categories alien or allied to the individual. Thus, positive emotions and feelings are labeled "good" and are accepted as part of the person's insular identity. Negative feelings and reactions, e.g., anger, on the other hand, are labeled "bad" and are considered unacceptable to one's insular view of himself.

One can either use language as a servant, or be its slave. The playful manipulation of language is one of the most useful ways of bringing about the ultimate reunion of mankind with itself. This ability to manipulate language brings us to the fourth major aspect of Zen Transactional Therapy.

IV. THE GAMING PRINCIPLE: A TRANSACTIONAL (VERSUS AN INTERACTIONAL) VIEW OF INTERPERSONAL GROWTH

Many persons in Western society believe that every act they perform toward or with others influences only the others and has no personal effect on themselves. This is the "push button," interactional view of dealing with others. Given this attitude, one can inflict physical pain, even death on others, for whatever cause or "truth," and yet feel unsullied by one's actions. This viewpoint is usually incorporated within a philosophy of insular identity, and therefore the killing, mutilating, or impoverishment of others is seen as distinct and separate from the insulated self.

The philosophy and interpersonal therapy of Zen Transactional Therapy incorporates a transactional view of one's relatedness to others. That is, there is a reciprocal effect to every action committed with or toward others. My actions affect not only others but myself as well. If I kill others, I become a killer. If I demean others, I become mean. If I enhance others through anxiety stimulation, I enhance myself also. I become what I do. Thus, in ZTT, all that I do with others I do to enhance myself.

In ZTT, interpersonal relationships are lawful, just as the physical universe is lawful. Most insular people will readily accept a lawful physical universe and the sciences of physics and chemistry. However, when those same people view interpersonal relationships, they have great difficulty accepting their lawfulness. They will accept some aspects of psychology, anthropology, and sociology as long as these have little bearing on the serious and sacred parts of their lives. But lawfulness in human transactions ceases when one deals with these sacred areas and thus prevents one from being aware that he is always manipulating others for either destructive or constructive purposes.

All life is made up of games. A person is always involved in interpersonal games; he is always manipulating for goals such as knowledge, affection, dependency, power, sex, self-actualization, or acceptance. These goals are met by interacting with others on an emotional level, expressed by language and gestures. The latter are directed at others, often without awareness, as rewards or punishments depending on whether others help or hinder attainment of one's goals.

There are a number of good books on this subject of interpersonal gaming. From the ZTT view, most games are either tension-explorative or tension-reducing.

Since we are always playing games, we need to become aware of the use of games if we are to become free to choose among them. If we accept this, we can learn to take charge of our lives, and not merely react to others. To take charge means to be able to act differently from the way we are "made" to feel by others.

The ZTT therapist deals with the games. He disciplines himself not to take any of them seriously, not even the life-death game. He recognizes that interpersonal gaming stops only at death, and even then there is the funeral game.

When two people are bantering, A may suddenly say to B, "That isn't a laughing matter." He has thereby initiated a game. The rules demand that B become serious in demeanor and language. A has already penalized B, because the admonition was accompanied by a slight frown, a negative shake of the head, and a disapproving tone. These nonverbal cues convey that A is annoyed, and this annoyance is purposeful. Although he may not be aware of it, A's aim is to force B to play the expected serious role. If the latter's attitude toward tension is that it is destructive, he will quickly become serious and will even convey, with nonverbal cues, a slight apology. A will then reward this by changing the penalizing cues to those of approval. His tension and anger cues will diminish, and B's internal tension will also be reduced. After this serious communication has ended, A may further reward B by smiling as he leaves, and saying, "See you later" or "Been nice talking to you," thus implying that he is forgiving and will not reject B in the future.

Such conspiring for tension reduction is destructive and cheats both persons of an opportunity to experience anxiety without letting it control the situation. If one's attitude toward anxiety is an embracing one, he would experience the increased tension without acting to reduce it. He would, in all likelihood, continue to laugh at the other's seriousness, while verbally trying to help him recognize his attempt to make another person behave as he wants them to. If, however, one felt that another person was going to hit him, he would initially play a serious role, pointing out the destructive behavior, thus reducing tension to the point where it need not be destructively acted out. He would then try to have the other person stay with his destructive feelings until they went away. At that point he would begin playing humorously, hopeful that the other person would be ready to laugh with him.

Like the Zen master, the ZTT "master" provides students with problem situations in which logical thinking and the usual conventional, social rules do not apply. The only acceptable solutions are those to which the student experientially (intuitively) comes himself. That is, he must risk himself without the aid of his previous reasoning, social and cultural props. Only when the student stands alone is it possible for him to experience a here-and-now awareness of his unification with the world around him.

The major differences between the Zen master and the ZTT "master" are those of game(s) selection and arena. Both play what to the student appear to be nonsensical word games (paradoxes). Both also act humorously or seriously, depending on which is appropriate to stimulate awareness change in the student. Both direct the student to rise above such relative concepts as right and wrong, good and bad, love and hate, etc. The Zen master, however, most often plays his games within a circumscribed, situational ritual, with roles strictly defined for and consciously accepted by both the student and himself. And a significant part of the Zen master's teaching (gaming) armamentarium include meditation and the parable, riddle, or koan. The ZTT "master," on the other hand, plays his games everywhere, within and without formal settings. Also, he plays ZTT with everyone, whether they define themselves as students or not. Furthermore, the ZTT "master" focuses heavily on intra- and interpersonal games (as bridges to ZTT enlightenment). Paradoxical, interpersonal games with the student are considered especially important.

Becoming aware that one is gaming is not easy to do. We are taught to be genuine, to be "real," without consciously manipulating ("playing games") with ourselves or others. Yet we are also taught that there are legitimate games such as mild teasing, quipping, or joke telling. Moreover, there are strictures against overlapping our "real" and game-playing behaviors. If such an overlap does occur (for example, a defendant in court purposely making fun of the judge), the transgressor is viewed by others as an object for attack, pity, or psychiatric help.

Our society requires that we see each other as incapable of manipulation except, paradoxically, when we are not being "real." Being "real" requires that we indicate that we are not playing, that we express every feeling directly, whether negative or positive, and that we accept as very serious the guilt of not being "real" when it is expected of us.

A "real" person would not have any difficulty accepting the premise that anxiety is the bridge to the immediacy of experience. He would, however, have great difficulty accepting a humorous appreciation of that anxiety and an interpersonal gaming view of involvement and evolvement with others.

The possibility of developing a new kind of human being by giving him the capability of purposefully acting and thinking contrary to his habitual feelings may seem absurd. The ZTT therapist, however, approaches himself and others as artistic media—to be constructively manipulated. Manipulation of others is most therapeutic when we "use" them needlessly; that is, without dependence on the person or the outcome of the manipulation. This brings us to the fifth major aspect of Zen Transactional Therapy.

V. PREFERENTIAL RELATEDNESS TO (VERSUS NEED FOR) OTHERS

Acting preferentially with others is the hardest work there is, yet it is necessary in order to achieve core-corporate unity. Ordinarily we expect others to fulfill our needs, and we become frustrated, angry, and irritated when these needs are not fulfilled. A person's makeup includes a number of needs, both innate and learned. And unlike animals, he can selectively and consciously choose how to satisfy those needs. Basic survival requirements such as breathing, eliminating, eating, and drinking are vital to his existence, and delay in fulfilling these requirements can quickly result in serious debilitation or death. Yet, if one feels that life and death are not serious affairs, one is not likely to be destructive in satisfying his survival needs at the expense of others. Further, having equal concern for both oneself *and* others can lead to the willingness to give up one's life for these others so that their basic needs can be satisfied. An example of this behavior can be drawn from wartime experiences in which parents gave food necessary for their own nourishment to their children instead. In a sense, the parent acts as if the child were a part of his corporate identity, and thus must be kept alive, even at the expense of the parent's core self.

With needs less immediate or not necessary for purposes of survival, one is able to deal with them as preferences when interacting with others. This means that he can exert control over these needs to the extent that when they are not satisfied in any one situation, he will not feel a frustrating sense of loss. Examples of these needs are: being adequate or important, giving and receiving affection, intimacy, dependency, sex, status, power and control over others, self development, possession of loved ones, etc. Whatever the particular need, a person's needful relationship with others always incorporates a needful relationship within himself. Such needfulness develops both conscious and unconscious expectations of how others and oneself *should* behave in order for one to feel contented or satisfied. Such expectations are always coercive.

How does one go about turning needs into preferences? To begin with, *these needs must be identified as they occur.* One way of accomplishing this is to be aware that all needful relationships have emotional consequences, such as:

1. Feelings of loss, emptiness, loneliness, depression, despair, or anger without the desired other person or the attainment of desired goals. An example of the former is when a needed person rejects us, dies, or leaves us for another person. An example of the latter is when we need recognition, status, power, or economic security.

2. Envy or jealousy of others.

3. Guilt, self-hate, or shame over actions committed or omitted in everyday living.

4. Hostility, anger, frustration, or irritation at other people, things, or events that do not conform to expectations.

5. Happiness or joy over another's loss or misfortune.

6. Happiness, joy, or sensual and sexual feelings, for which there is a compulsive longing for their possession or perpetuation.

These emotional reactions can indicate that unfulfilled nonsurvival needs are both stimuli and coercion toward action. And when one coerces oneself and others to fulfill such needs, one behaves promiscuously, treating oneself and others as objects, with little or no probability of experiential evolvement.

Once non-survival needs are identified by their emotional reactions, *the next step is to feel them in all their intensity until they disappear* instead of temporarily reducing (avoiding or being distracted from) them through such behaviors as arguing; blaming; screaming; drinking alcohol; compulsive working, eating, socializing, or sexual activity; taking drugs; or obsessive thinking or fantasizing.

Non-survival needs always scream out for satisfaction; they will stimulate rationalization to the extent that it will seem appropriate to gratify them immediately. But if we are to treat others unpromiscuously, we must commit ourselves to experiencing these needs—and their associated emotions—intensively in order to extinguish them. These emotions will continually flare up, but will eventually burn out if not fueled by gratification. With the extinction of each need, preferential relationships with others become more likely. That is, one can be with others, and if they do not act as one would wish, one can walk away and go on to something else without feeling hurt or loss.

During the elimination of any need there will be frequent feelings of loss and emptiness. This experiential impasse, however, must be negotiated in order to develop preferential living. These feelings will eventually be replaced with a buoyancy and joy that will create a feeling of contact (core-corporate union) with the rest of the world. Intense needs generate tunnel vision. They are willing to admit only a narrow range of sensations or stimuli; all else is relegated to insignificance. And when this occurs, when these needs are not fulfilled, the individual can feel that life is not worth living. On the other hand, when needs have been transformed into preferences, one can sample from life's experiences as if they were on an infinite banquet table.

Because most of us operate needfully with others, one should begin relationships in the following manner: accept no actions of intimacy, love, sex (while still experiencing and acknowledging the feelings) with another person until both persons can truthfully say, "I will always work to see that my needs do not interfere with my 'seeing' you," or "When I don't need you, I can really love you." One should really be concerned when someone says, "I need you, I really love you," for at this moment, if one accepts *that* kind of "love," one can ultimately expect a needfully destructive relationship.

The most difficulty arises in selling the attitude of, "I don't need you, I love you" to those newly and needfully in love because at that point they usually see each other as completely satisfying each others' needs. They feel no need of anyone else but themselves. This "non-need," however, is not growth-producing; rather, it is an experiential shutting out of everyone else and a process of mutual leeching from each other.

Zen Transactional Therapy is at once *both* a selfish and an altruistic system, contrasting sharply, for example, with those produced by the Christian and Jewish (insular identity) theologies. The Judeo-Christian position presumes that when an insular "I" is altruistic, it is not selfish, for its altruistic behavior is seen as affecting only the other insular "I's" and not itself. Yet, since the altruistic, insular person obtains positive feelings about doing good and is often venerated by others, he can easily be viewed as doing this good selfishly—though he seldom would admit it. Insular selfishness has a different conceptual twist from insular altruism, and is not always judged as destructive by those who are acceptant of the insular rules of living. Active selfishness (e.g., hoarding) is usually seen as bad (needful?) and as adversely affecting both the perpetrator and his victim. Occasionally though, insular selfishness may be evaluated as having no adverse effect on others, as, for example, when an insular person decides to become a recluse. Because everyone is encapsulated within his own "I," he can sometimes be seen as "doing his own thing" independently of others and with no transactional effect on them.

In the Zen Transactional Therapy view, however, this absence of effect is an illusion. When persons avoid tension-seeking, experiential growth, and ultimate experiential reunion with others, they are contributing to the impoverishment and destruction of both themselves and others—by omission.

The statements above indicate the Zen Transactional Therapy view of a constructive society. They also express a prophecy for the future of mankind: that the next evolution of man will not be so much biological as social and interpersonal. Children in their early childhood and preadolescent years would be taught to experience every feeling, from anger to sensuality, and would find socially constructive ways of verbalizing and expressing them. During a child's formative years, adults would deal with destructive behavior mainly by ignoring it or by impersonally restraining the child. Experimental and clinical behavioral psychology has established that when adults show little or no emotion when children react negatively, the negative reactions diminish or disappear altogether. Without antagonistic, emotionally-laden reactions by others, the negative behavior of children is not sustained—because it no longer works.

In the later preadolescent and early adolescent stages of the child's development, adults would begin to introduce the techniques and attitudes of Zen Transactional Therapy. Children would begin to learn the use of humorous play with their own and others' feelings and behavior. They would also begin learning to act differently from the reflexive dictates of their own feelings.

In the later adolescent and adult years, the completion of their social development would take place. The major focus would, of course, be on learning how to play continuously with their feelings. This play would entail experiencing negative feelings to extinction, while focusing on others and behaving constructively with them. At these stages, behavior would not reflect negative feelings, although they would be openly accepted and felt. In addition, the adolescent and adult would continue to learn how to make "aware" choices with positive feelings, so that they would not be coercive to themselves or others. At this level of social development, there would be a population of "sociotherps" acting constructively and having positive feelings toward their corporate selves.

Layers of Self—
A Group Fantasy Technique

by Michael Purinton, Jim Healy, and Bill Whitney

The purpose of this article is to acquaint the reader with an original fantasy exercise based on the self theories of Rouke (1968) and Perls (1970). Both theories state that each person is composed of many different ego layers and that beneath these ego layers is a true inner self. The fantasy exercise is designed to lead each person on a trip through his superficial outer layers and his negative inner layers until finally he gets in touch with his unique inner self. Following the fantasy exercise, each person is encouraged to create a drawing of the unique ego layers he experienced during the fantasy exercise.

LAYERS OF SELF

The self of any individual is uniquely composed of many different layers. One way of understanding the layers of self is to view the individual as an onion—a series of skins or layers, one inside the other. The outer layers are more superficial and are more easily seen by others. The inner layers are more private and spiritual.

Rouke (1968) diagrammed the self as being composed of three layers:

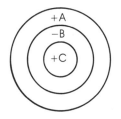

+A   Positive but false self
−B   Negative but false self
+C   Source of dignity and humility

Reprinted from *Psychotherapy: Theory, Research and Practice*, 1974, 11(1), 83-86. Used with permission of authors and publisher.

The outer layer (+A) is superficially positive. This outer layer contains the images, or facades a person presents to the world. These images are positive and "good" and are designed to gain respect and approval from other people. In general, these outermost layers contain the many ways a person habitually views himself positively. This defensive layer (+A) is superficially positive and is not real.

The second layer (−B) is the negative self-concept and is hidden from other people. The second layer may include feelings of being weak and worthless, feelings of anger and hate, or feelings of loneliness and sadness. However, these images of self are inaccurate also. Most people avoid this level of self, as living with these negative feelings and self images is uncomfortable.

In avoiding the second layer of self (−B), the third layer of self (+C) is also avoided. The third layer is the true inner core of the self. This inner core of self contains a person's unique ego-layers—a person's source of dignity, humility and spirituality. These are the layers beyond the manipulative roles and feelings that characterize day-to-day interactions. These layers are often described in terms of energy and color, of form and movement, and of serenity and calmness. This core is the center of self.

The analogy of the onion describes these layers of self appropriately. The outer layer must be peeled off or penetrated in order to arrive at the second layer; the second layer must be peeled off or penetrated in order to arrive at the inner layer. As long as one layer is being avoided or is impenetrable, the inner core will remain an unknown mystery.

Perls (1970) uses a similar although more complex model to describe the layers of self. He sees man using his energy to maintain five outer layers which prevent the authentic self from emerging. Perls' model of man is diagrammed:

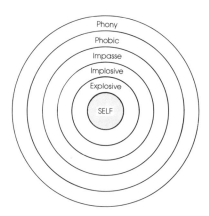

The outermost layer is the phony layer. Perls calls this the Eric Berne layer where we play games and play roles. In this layer we behave "as if" we were intelligent, as if we were important, as if we were something other than what we are. These "as if" games are all designed to manipulate other people for support, attention, or recognition.

If we become aware of the phony layer and try to be more genuine and honest, we encounter pain, hurt, sadness or despair. The fear of being all these negative emotions is the second layer, the phobic layer. In this layer are all the objections to being what we are. We invest a lot of energy in this layer in an attempt to protect ourselves from being overwhelmed by a flood of negative emotions.

The phobic layer has to be penetrated in order to arrive at the impasse layer. Within the impasse there is the feeling of not being alive, a feeling of deadness. At this point we feel we are nothing; we have no energy, no life force. The impasse represents a stuck point in that all personal energy is directed towards maintaining the status quo.

If the impasse layer is penetrated, the implosive layer then emerges. Within the implosive layer are all the energies necessary for living. At this point the life energies are frozen and invested unused. If a person has a want or a desire and does not act on this want, his energy is then bottled up and held inside. The turning inward of energy and holding it in is the implosive layer.

The externalizing of personal energy from the implosive layer outward takes place in the explosive layer. At this point a person literally explodes into life; he blossoms into authenticity. There are essentially four types of explosion: explosion into joy, explosion into grief, explosion into orgasm, and, explosion into anger. Sometimes these explosions are very mild. The reaction depends on the amount of energy a person has invested in the implosive layer.

The explosion of energy outward allows the authentic self to emerge. Perls (1970) characterizes the authentic self as a mature person who is self-supporting. A mature person is capable of experiencing and sustaining all types of emotional experiences and deals with these experiences in the "here and now" of the situation. The mature person utilizes his own resources rather than manipulating the environment for support.

Perls' model of self contains a "dynamic quality" which is lacking in the model of self presented by Rouke. Perls (1970) states that no one can stay in touch with his inner core more than a small percentage of the time, rather within each person there is a rhythm of moving inward to contact the inner core and then moving outward again. Rouke's model is more static. Rouke seems to imply that ideally a person would rid himself of his outer layers and live in the nirvana of his inner core.

LAYERS OF SELF IN A GROUP

Each member of a group has a unique composition of his layers of self. At any given point in the life of a group, the members may be observed revealing some level of themselves to the group. The depth of the members' self-disclosures may range from a superficial level to a deeper, more intimate level. The layers of self fantasy offers one strategy to help each group member get more deeply in touch with his personal layers of self and enables each person to share his unique composition of his layers of self with the group.

LAYERS OF SELF FANTASY

1. Explanation (Necessary before Fantasy)

One way of understanding yourself is as an onion—a series of different selves one inside the other. The outer ones are more superficial and more easily seen by others; the inner ones are more private and more profound. Each person's layers and sequencing of layers are unique, but there are some generalizations that can be made about the patterns of layering. In general, the outer-most layers are the habitual ways you view yourself positively, ways you are "good." These are ways you get respect and approval from people you want to impress and ways you get love from those whose love you want. Near the end of the successive positive layers begin negative ones: fears and angers and sadnesses. They may include feelings of being weak, wishes to be taken care of, resentments about mistakes that authority makes, and angers about the imperfections of the world. They may also include sexual fears and frustrations. They are likely to include some loneliness. The layers in this second band include most of your negative feelings and self-images. Most people try to avoid these layers of self. In fact, most people have some fears or sadnesses which they feel could swallow them up—such as fear of death, or going crazy (or losing control) or being alone and loved by no one. Beneath your negative layers of self are your unique ego layers, your private sources of dignity and humility. These are the layers beyond the roles and feelings which you were taught as a child. As long as you are avoiding part of the negative band, it is difficult to push beyond the negative to get in touch with these unique ego layers. These last layers are often very metaphorical —described in terms of energy, color, form, movement, or quietness. Some find that they can get beyond the ego layers to fundamental essences beyond the ego.

2. Transition

Now I want you to explore your layers of self through a fantasy trip. It is important to get comfortable and relax, but not to fall asleep. You can sit back in your chair or you can lie down. . . . Close your eyes and attend to your body. Notice places in your body where there is tension or aching. Wherever you find a tension, tighten it much tighter—hold it very, very tight—and then relax. Enjoy the relaxation and then look for another tension. Tighten it, hold it, relax and enjoy the relaxation. If you are not aware of tension, just try to deepen your relaxation. Continue until you feel quite relaxed. Then begin focusing on your breathing. Focus on the way you breathe out. Try to breathe out more fully, more deeply and even a little more slowly. Let the breath come in automatically. Give your breath out a sound—a hum or AOM or whatever feels like you. Let's see if the group can begin to breathe together—one slow, deep breathing out together.

3. Fantasy

Now I'd like you to picture yourself on a moonlit night at the edge of some giant, magic woods. . . . These old woods seem warm and inviting and exciting. . . . As you walk along the edge you discover a secret path leading deep into the woods. . . . You feel surprised and lucky to have discovered it. . . . Without much hesitation you decide to follow the path. . . . It's too much of a special chance to pass up. . . . The full moon lights the path well. . . . You follow it as it winds deeper and deeper into the woods. . . .

Take your time and pay attention to your senses . . . notice what your woods look like and smell like. . . . The bright moon allows you to see quite a lot of your surrounding. . . . Touch one of the trees by the side of your secret path. . . . Take some time and take pleasure in your trip. . . . The path leads to a cave at the base of a mountain—a cave inhabited by some special magical guides. You feel attracted to the cave and walk toward it. . . . Inside you can see some flickering lights. . . . You enter the mouth of the cave. . . . You find yourself in a fairly large room lit by candles on the walls. . . . At the far side is a stone staircase spiraling upward, into the depths of the mountain. . . . The stairs are wide and well lit by more candles. . . . You begin climbing. . . . The stairway twists around and around upward. . . .

Eventually you reach the room of a wise and caring sorceress. . . . She is there to conjure images for you—images of your superficial selves, selves which probably seek approval, esteem, love and admiration from others. . . . She will conjure these images for you slowly. . . . Each time she produces an image for you of a progressively deeper level of yourself as an approval seeker, you will go over that image for a while—taking it in in great detail and remembering it well, before nodding to her and letting her know that you are ready for her to conjure a different image. . . . Stay with this for a while now. . . .

After a while you will have received all of the images from her that she feels you are ready for at this time. . . . There is one image which is very important for you to see which she did not show you, because she felt you were not ready. . . . That image exists inside a room next door. . . . You can see the door to that room. . . . Approach it slowly. . . . Know that on the other side of that door is an image of a 'phoney' role you play to get attention and approval from others. : . . It is an important image to confront someday. . . . You can choose to open the door or not. . . . Those who want to will open the door, experience this room and then return. . . . Those who choose to keep the door closed should reflect on the images given by the sorceress. . . .

Now it is time to leave this room. . . . On the far side of the room is a winding stairway going down and around. . . . Follow it. . . . Attend to the feelings in your body as you walk down. . . . Notice what the stairway is like, the walls, the sounds, the smells. . . .

Eventually you reach a giant door. Spend some time taking in this door. . . . It won't open easily for you, but you will be able to open it. . . . Now you enter a faintly lit room. In the middle is a very old and wise magician who is going to put you in touch with your negative selves —your negative self-images. He has a special loving and caring way which will put you very profoundly in touch with these self-images. Experience them deeply. . . . Remember them. . . . Notice how lovingly he puts you in touch with these deeper and deeper layers of yourself. . . . Take time and explore yourself. . . .

As a final caring gesture, he points the way to a narrow stairway down to the deepest part of the cave. Thank him and start down. . . . Experience yourself moving closer and closer to the last door. . . . Open it. . . . Now you are entering a very soft quiet room. . . . As you enter, you feel a sense of personal strength entering you. . . . Something about the room enhances the power of whoever enters. . . . You sit in the middle of a soft carpet in this, the deepest part of the cave. . . . As your personal strength grows, you find yourself able to get in touch with the progressively deeper layers of yourself until finally you experience your ultimate essence. Take time, experience each level deeply; Remember them well. . . .

Now it's time to leave this room and move out of the cave. . . . You follow a tunnel which is a shortcut back. . . . Just before you reach the entrance room, the cave widens into a small room. . . . In the dim light of the room you can make out the forms of all of the selves you have encountered. . . . They have important things to say to each other. . . . It is important for you to pause here and let each of these selves speak to the others. . . .

When this conversation is over, say goodbye to the fantasy and come back to this room. Spend a minute turning into the here-and-now, experience the colors, the people, your own body. . . .

Now make a record of the selves you encountered.

RECREATING THE IMAGES

Following the fantasy, each person is provided with a large piece of newsprint and a box of crayons and is asked to draw the images of his layers of self as vividly as he saw them during the fantasy trip. The drawing provides a vehicle for each person to get more deeply in touch with his layers of self, to integrate the images he experienced into his awareness, and to share the many facets of himself with the group.

The layers of self fantasy is a powerful technique for helping group members work through their superficial outer layers, their negative inner layers and get in touch with their inner core. The drawing of the layers of self offers a creative way for each member to experience himself and the sharing of these drawings with the group brings a feeling of intimacy and oneness to the group.

REFERENCES

Perls, F. S. Four lectures. In J. Fagan & I. L. Shepherd (Eds.), *Gestalt therapy now.* New York: Harper & Row, 1970.

Rouke, F. The who am I technique. In G. Taylor (Ed.), *The verbal "who am I" technique in psychotherapy.* New York: Psychosynthesis Research Foundation, 1968.

Saying Goodbye
In Gestalt Therapy

by Stephan A. Tobin

I find that most patients have failed to say goodbye and finish some relationship that terminated in death, divorce, ending of a love affair, or in some other way. This "hanging-on" reaction occurs with missing persons who were of strong emotional significance to the patient. The relationship does not have to have been filled with love. In fact, *most* such relationships were characterized by much fighting and resentment rather than by love.

The adaptive reaction to the loss of a loved person is a fairly long period of grief followed by renewed interest in living people and things. The adaptive reaction to the loss of a hated person presumably would be relief. The hanging-on reaction is to inhibit the emotions triggered by the loss and to keep the person present in fantasy.

In this paper I shall discuss the causes of the hanging-on reaction, the symptomatic results in the hanger-on, Gestalt therapy techniques I use in working with patients to say goodbye, and a sample of such work.

CAUSES OF THE HANGING-ON REACTION

One cause of the hanging-on reaction is the presence of much unfinished business between the two persons long before the relationship terminates. By "unfinished business" I mean the inhibition of an emotion that was experienced at one or more times during the relationship. A simple example would be the employee who feels angry towards his boss but, because he is frightened of being fired, decides not to express

Reprinted from *Psychotherapy: Theory, Research and Practice*, 1971, 8(2), 150-155. Used with permission of author and publisher.

his feelings. Until he expresses his anger in some way, he is left with the physical tension that results from the impasse between the physical excitation of the anger and the inhibiting force that suppresses the emotion. He may try to deal with this unfinished situation in indirect ways, e.g., by having fantasies about telling his boss off or about the death of his boss in an accident, or by taking it out on his wife and children when he goes home that night. No matter what he does, he is tense and anxious and has a nagging feeling of not having done something he should have done. Until he finds some *direct* way of finishing the business of his anger towards his boss, he will be unable to relax or involve himself fully with any person or in any activity. In addition, his relationship with his boss will be strained.

This is, of course, a minor situation that probably wouldn't cause much difficulty. Most of the people I see in therapy have accumulated many unfinished situations of great emotional intensity. For example, one man as a child was continually humiliated and rendered helpless by his father. To express his rage toward his father would have meant his own destruction. Today he continually attempts to finish this situation by provoking authority figures into attacking him and then attacking back.[1]

How do people stop themselves from finishing situations? First, most of them are unaware of their bodies and, since all feelings are located in the body, they are unaware of their feelings. This lack of awareness makes it impossible for them to finish emotional situations. Even if they do become aware of their emotions, they are apt to suppress them; their minds tell them they shouldn't be angry, shouldn't express love, shouldn't feel sad. So they turn off the messages their bodies give them and the emotional excitement then turns into physical pain, tension, and anxiety.

A second way people stop themselves from finishing situations is by placing great value on some of the secondary gains they get from hanging on. If the present is unexciting or if they feel incapable of getting involved with other people, they can relieve their loneliness by thinking about past relationships. While one might imagine that these past situations are pleasurable, more often than not they are negative. Hanging-on to resentment, for example, can be used to enable one to

---

[1]The Freudians have discussed such neurotic behavior and have coined the term "repetition compulsion" to describe it. They have not, however, dealt with the physical changes that take place. In addition, Freudian therapy, with its stress on thinking and its endless why-because games reinforces hanging-on to the past rather than encouraging letting go of it. Behaviorism, on the other hand, while working towards the elimination of outmoded response tendencies, does not give the client tools he can use to prevent future hanging-on reactions.

feel self-righteous or self-pitying, characterological ways of being many people are willing to settle for. Resentment can also be used as an excuse for not getting close to the object of one's resentment.

For example, a woman in a therapy group talked continually about what an awful mother she had. Whenever anyone else spoke of his mother, she would very dramatically start to recount the "terrible" things her mother had done to her. When I asked her to imagine her mother in the room and to talk to her, she would blame her mother for ruining her life. She would not, of course, ever confront her mother directly with her resentment; her excuse was that she didn't want to hurt her mother and, "It wouldn't do any good anyway." Her real reason for not confronting her was that she didn't really think she had the resources to change her existence and her mother served as a ready excuse for her failures in life. Another benefit of her game was that she could project all her own undesired traits on her mother; when I pointed out that she resembled her description of her mother in many ways, she would shudder and plead with me not to say that because she hated her mother so much.

While her complaints to the group afforded her some expression of resentment, the situation was still incomplete for her. She still harbored resentment and hatred which appeared even when she was not speaking of her mother in her tone of voice, her posture, and her gestures.

Self-righteousness, which is a particularly prevalent side-benefit of hanging-on, is common in those patients who evaluate every conflict between themselves and others in a good-bad, right-wrong fashion. They think that the only way to resolve a conflict is for one person to admit that he is guilty or bad or stupid. Since admitting to these judgments is humiliating and degrading, many people hang on to their resentments hoping that the other will see the light and humiliate himself by admitting he was wrong.

So we see that even before termination of the relationship, there is a great deal of unfinished business. Matters become more complicated when one of the persons leaves and the relationship is ended.

HANGING-ON AFTER TERMINATION OF THE RELATIONSHIP

The unfinished business can be between a parent and child, between spouses, between lovers, between friends, or between any other two people who have had an intense, long-standing relationship. There is much unfinished business within the relationship while it lasts; when the relationship ends—through death, divorce, one person moving away from the other, etc.—the relationship itself becomes unfinished. The individual is still carrying around much accumulated unexpressed emotion: old resentments, frustrations, hurts, guilts, and even unexpressed love and appreciation. The presence of these unexpressed emotions makes it difficult for him to finish the relationship simply because the other person is no longer around to hear them. One of the ways it can be done is for the person to express his feelings in fantasy to the one who is gone. I find, however, that few of my patients have done this. There are a number of reasons why they have not.

First of all, some of the ways in which people prevent themselves from finishing things discussed in the previous section are also used to prevent themselves from finishing the relationship and saying goodbye. Many patients have been unaware of what they felt at the end of a relationship. For example, a young man in a workshop I ran was almost completely unaware of the intense guilt and grief he felt about his sick pet cat whom he had had to have destroyed.

People also get much secondary gain from not letting go. The woman who is fearful about attempting new relationships with men can use her attachment to her dead husband as an excuse for not getting involved.

Many Americans have simply lost the ability to let go of dead relationships because of their distaste for intense emotion of any kind, particularly when a death has occurred. The mourning process, which is recognized as natural and necessary in other parts of the world, frequently does not occur in the United States. The Kennedy wives, e.g., were praised for their lack of public emotion after their husbands were assassinated. In contrast, the widow of Tom Mboya, the African politician, was shown in a national magazine attempting to throw herself on her husband's grave.

Another example of this inability to do what is necessary to finish dead relationships is the individual who has been jilted. Instead of venting his feelings of hurt and anger, he is apt to keep them to himself so as not to give his jilter any "satisfaction" for rejecting him. The adaptive reaction to divorce would be for each person to express his lingering restments and to go his separate way; instead, most divorced people continue hanging-on in a kind of guerrilla war, particulary when complicated alimony and child settlement agreements are legally enforced.

Another reason for my patients' inability to say goodbye is their unwillingness to experience the pain they would feel if they did let go. Probably as a reaction to American Puritanism, which taught people that life was supposed to involve nothing but pain, we have become a nation of people who believe it's wrong to feel any pain at all. As soon as most people feel anxious, they take tranquilizers or smoke pot; as soon as they come into conflict with others, they try to end the conflicts as quickly as possible by either avoiding the others or by trying to overpower or manipulate them and "win." Rather than letting go of dead relationships, most people avoid the emptiness and loneliness by "keeping busy," by finding a new relationship as quickly as possible, or by pretending that the dead person is still around.

Finally, many people avoid saying goodbye because they feel that letting go, particularly of the dead, is a dishonor to them. Most of my patients no longer believe in a life hereafter, and they often feel that the only kind of immortality possible is to be remembered by the living. They don't realize that, had they really had a meaningful relationship with the person when he was still around, had they really said "hello," they would have been continually enriched and changed through the relationship (Friedman, 1970). The lost person then would *really* have become part of the one who is left and live on in a much more meaningful way—as a part of that person's being—instead of as an introjected lump of dead matter that comes between the person and his world.

RESULTS OF HANGING-ON

Physical symptoms are one result of hanging-on. Some patients have identified parts of their bodies as representatives of the persons who are gone. Two women I saw in therapy kept their mothers present in the form of ulcers. Another example is a young woman with whom I worked in a weekend workshop who had chronically cold hands, maintained an attitude of contemptuous aloofness towards others, and literally would not touch others. Her mother had died when she was three and she became aware during our work together that her cold hands were both links with her cold, dead mother and also symbolized her mother. When she was able to say goodbye to her mother, her hands suddenly warmed up and she was able to make meaningful contact with others for the first time in her life.

Other people identify their whole beings with dead people and appear to be walking zombies: their voices and faces are expressionless, their movements are controlled and mechanical, and they report feeling physically numb.

Secondly, those who have refused to say goodbye usually exhibit emotional symptoms. For example, those who have identified with dead people are emotionally dead. I am not referring to depressed persons; these people feel neither depression nor anything else. There are also, however, many persons who, because of incompletion of the mourning process, become chronically depressed in an attenuated way. They are gloomy, apathetic, and have little real interest in life. They have been depressed for such a long time that they frequently are even unaware of their depression.

Another emotional result of the hanging-on reaction is a whiny, self-pitying attitude towards oneself, and a blaming, complaining attitude towards the person who has gone. The whiner often uses the lost person as an excuse for his inadequacies: "If my father had loved me more, my life wouldn't be such a mess now." The obverse of the whiner is the person who blames himself rather than the dead person and feels guilty: "If I had been nicer to my father before he died, he would have been happier and I would be better off now. Now there's no way I can make it up to him."

A third symptom is an inability to form close relationships. One who is continually fantasizing about the past or is having relationships with people who are gone, has little time for those still around. He does not see or hear or feel in the present.

I have found that the more a person is able to finish things in a relationship, the more authentic that relationship is. What happens, however, in most intimate relationships is that, after a while, there are so many unexpressed resentments and disappointments that the people in the relationship cease really seeing or hearing each other or feeling *in the present*. In contrast, those people who can say "goodbye" when they part temporarily are better able to get fully involved with each other in a fresh, meaningful, realistic way when they next meet.

Thus, in a very important sense, saying goodbye to the dead parent or the divorced spouse is an identical process to expressing feelings to another person and to letting him go during a temporary absence.

WORKING WITH PATIENTS ON SAYING GOODBYE

The first step in helping the patient who is hanging-on to say goodbye is *to make him aware of hanging-on* and of how he is doing this. Usually something the patient says or does in group or individual therapy makes me suspect that he is in conflict about some unfinished business. Sometimes it is a dream in which the dead person appears, sometimes a gesture (e.g., a few patients have looked up when speaking and I found out they were looking up at "heaven"), sometimes the patient appears so lifeless that I have a hunch he has identified with a dead person.

I then ask the patient if he has some unfinished business with someone who is gone and, if the answer is affirmative, I ask him if he wants to say goodbye. Most patients at this point will say that they do; if they openly state they do not wish to let go, I will just work with them long enough to get them aware of their objections to saying goodbye. If they still insist, after finding out their objections, that they don't want to let go and are in no conflict about this, I stop at this point. If a patient does wish to work on saying goodbye, I then proceed to the next stage.

WORKING THROUGH THE UNFINISHED BUSINESS

The second step is, I first take an empty chair and place it in front of the patient and ask him to imagine the dead person sitting in it. I next ask him what he experiences as he imagines the dead person there. Whatever the emotion or thought expressed, I ask the patient to say that directly to the dead person. Frequently, e.g., patients experience resentment at not having been "loved enough," or guilt about not having been kinder to the dead person before he died. After he has said what he wants to, I ask him to switch chairs and become the dead person. Frequently the patient will spontaneously say something; if he does not, I again ask him what he is experiencing, this time as the dead person. When he replies, I ask him to say to himself sitting in the other chair. The dead person as imagined by the client may feel anger for the lack of kindness in the patient towards himself. The dead person may become defensive at the resentment expressed by the patient, and give excuses for the lack of love. After the dead person has had his say, I ask the patient to switch back to playing himself in the first chair, and he is asked to reply to the fantasied dead one. When the patient gets into the two roles completely, I ask him to let himself switch back and forth as he finds himself changing roles.

In almost every case there is much emotion expressed—anger, hurt, resentment, love, etc. When the patient seems to have no more unfinished business, I ask him if he feels ready to say goodbye. Frequently patients say they are ready to say goodbye but are unable to do so when I ask them to say it directly to the imagined dead love-object. At other times they say goodbye but it just doesn't sound convincing. In either case, I help them to become aware that they are not ready to let the dead go, either because of a fear they won't be able to find living people to relate to, or because they have more unfinished business. I do not push or encourage the patient as long as he is willing to take responsibility for his hanging-on.

If the patient is ready to terminate the relationship, however, there is usually some explosion of emotion. Usually the patient completes the mourning process and cries; occasionally, however, the emotion is one of great relief and joy at the dead weight that has been eliminated. When this kind of work occurs in a group, it tends to be a very moving experience for me and all the other people present. Typically, feelings of greater group closeness, warmth, and a kind of profound, religious love of all of life are expressed by all the people participating as observers of this work.

I have done no systematic study of the follow-up effects, but my impression is that the results are long-lasting: little or no thinking about the dead person, a feeling of more energy, and increased interest in life and other people.

CLINICAL EXAMPLE

The following is a re-creation of some work I did with a woman in a weekend workshop with whom I had had no previous contact. The woman, whom I shall call "Mrs. R.," was a married housewife in her mid-thirties. She spoke in a very mechanical way, sounding like a child who was reciting a poem she had been forced to memorize but didn't understand. In her relationship with her husband and children she played the part of a masochistic martyr, controlling them by showing how much they made her "suffer." Our work on her saying goodbye to her dead mother started during a dream in which her mother appeared. While working on the dream, her voice and demeanor suddenly changed; she began to cry and sounded whiny and complaining. I asked her if she had some unfinished business with her mother and she said:

> *Mrs. R:* Well . . . if only she had loved me, things would be different. But she didn't and . . . and I've never had any real mother love (crying).
> *S (Steve Tobin):* Put your mother in that chair and say that to her.
> *Mrs. R:* If only she had cared for me, I'd be much better today'.
> *S:* I want you to say this to her, not to me. Can you imagine her sitting there in front of you?
> *Mrs. R:* Yes, I see her as she looked when she was still alive. Mother, if you had only loved me. Why couldn't you ever tell me you loved me? Why did you always criticize me? (almost a wail, more tears)
> *S:* Now switch over to the other chair and play your mother. (She moves over to the other chair and doesn't say anything.)
> *S:* What do you experience as your mother?
> *Mrs. R:* I-I-I don't know . . . I don't know what she would say.
> *S:* Of course you don't know. She's not around any more. You're playing the part of you that is your mother. Just say whatever you experience there.
> *Mrs. R:* Oh, I see. Well, I don't know what to say to her.
> *S:* Say *that* to her.
> *Mrs. R M* (Mrs. R as Mother): I don't know what to say to you. I *never* knew what to say to you. I really did love you, you know that. Look at all the things I did for you, and you never appreciated it. (voice sounds defensive and whiny)
> *S:* Now switch back and reply as yourself.
> *Mrs. R S* (Mrs. R as Self): Loved me! All you ever did was criticize me. Nothing I ever did was good enough! (voice beginning to sound more whiny). When I got married to J. you disapproved, you were always coming over and telling me what I was doing wrong with the kids. Oh, you never came right out and said anything, but you were always making snide remarks or saying, "Now, dear, wouldn't it be a good idea to put another blanket on the baby." You made my life *miserable*; I was always worrying about you criticizing me. And now I'm having all this trouble with J. (breaks down and starts to cry.)
> *S:* Did you hear your voice?

Mrs. R S: Yes.

S: What did you hear in it?

Mrs. R S: Well, I guess I sounded kind of complaining, like I'm feeling sor—like I'm feeling mad.

S: You sounded more like feeling self-pity. Try this on for size: say to your mother, "Look what you've done to me. It's all your fault."

Mrs. R S: Look what you've done. Everything's your fault.

S: Now let yourself switch back and forth as you find yourself changing roles.

Mrs. R M: Come on, stop blaming me for everything. You are always complaining about something. If you had been better—if you had been a *decent* daughter, I wouldn't have had to criticize you so much.

Mrs. R S: Oh, oh, (under her breath) Damn. (She's swinging her right leg slightly.)

S: Notice your leg.

Mrs. R S: I-I'm shaking it.

S: Exaggerate that, shaking it harder.

Mrs. R S: (shakes leg harder, it begins to look like a kick)

S: Can you imagine doing that to your mother?

Mrs. R S: No, but I-I-I-I'm sure feeling pissed at her.

S: Say this to her.

Mrs. R S: I feel pissed off at you! I hate you!

S: Say that louder.

Mrs. R S: I hate you! (volume higher, but still some holding back)

S: Louder!

Mrs. R S: I HATE YOU, YOU GODDAMNED BITCH. (She sticks her leg out and kicks the chair over.)

S: Now switch back.

Mrs. R M: (voice sounds much weaker now) I-I guess I didn't show you much love. I really felt it, but I was unhappy and bitter. You know all I had to go through with your father and brother. You were the only one I could talk to. I'm sorry . . . I wanted you to be happy . . . I wanted so much for you.

Mrs. R S: You sure did! . . . I know you did love me, Mother, I know you were unhappy (voice much softer now, but sounding real, not whiny or mechanical). I guess I did some things that were ba—wrong, too. I was always trying to keep you off my back.

Mrs. R M: Yes, you were pretty sarcastic to me, too. And that hurt.

Mrs. R S: I wish you had told me. I didn't think you were hurt at all.

Mrs. R M: Well, that's all over now.

Mrs. R S: Yeah, it is. I guess there's no use blaming you. You're not around any more.

S: Can you forgive your mother now?

Mrs. R S: Mother, I forgive you . . . I really do forgive you. (starts crying again, but not in the whiny way of before. She sounds genuinely grieving and cries for a couple of minutes.)

S: Now switch back.

Mrs. R M: I forgive you too, dear. You have to go on now. You can't keep blaming me forever. I made my mistakes but you have your own family and you're doing okay.

S: Do you feel ready to say goodbye now?

Mrs. R S: Yes. I-I think so (starts to sob). Goodbye, Mother, goodbye. (breaks down, cries for a few minutes)

S: What do you experience now?

Mrs R: I feel better. I feel . . . kind of relieved, like a weight is off my back. I feel calm.

S: Now that you've said goodbye to her, to this dead person, can you go around and say hello to the live people here, to the group?

Mrs. R: Yes, I'd like that.

(She goes around the room, greets people, touches some, embraces others. Many in the group are tearful. When she reaches her husband, she starts crying again, and tells him she loves him, and they embrace.)

REFERENCES

Friedman, L. F. *Personal Communication*, 1970.

Carrying Experiencing Forward Through Authentic Body Movement

by Erma Dosamantes Alperson

Movement Therapy is a process therapy that is concerned with how an individual transforms an ongoing flow of energy to overt body movement to imagery to verbalization. Movement Therapy differs from most verbal therapies, in that at the outset it places the person in direct contact with her implicit bodily-felt experiencing rather than in verbalization. It appears to facilitate the integration of two modes of experiencing: the intuitive-preverbal with the rational-verbal.

Personality change is promoted when a person is able to make contact with a bodily-felt level of experiencing which is implicit (knowable only by the person herself) and is able to verbalize or make explicit, at least some portion of it (Gendlin, 1971).

> . . . A body sense of a problem or situation is pre-verbal and pre-conceptual . . . it is not equivalent to any one verbal or conceptual pattern. To attend to it or speak from it is a further living and therefore a further structuring, a carrying forward [Gendlin, 1969, p. 8].

Unsuccessful psychotherapy clients are characterized by a tendency to "intellectualize" and "externalize" their problems (Gendlin et al., 1968). The former implies that while the person may have a cognitive understanding of her difficulties, she lacks an emotional involvement with them; the latter refers to the fact that the person disclaims herself as the source of her problems and places all responsibility for them onto some external source (e.g. other people, the system). This externalizing attitude effectively prevents the person from experiencing herself as the source of her own experiential body process.

All contemporary verbal psychotherapies concerned with individual growth and behavioral change suffer to one degree or another

---

Reprinted from *Psychotherapy: Theory, Research and Practice*, 1974, *11*(3), 211-214. Used with permission of author and publisher.

from a fragmenting approach to the totality of a person's experiencing. By adopting the role of an observer looking at her experience rather than that of its potential creator, the individual is likely to end up by objectifying her experience and that of others. Furthermore, the very language that verbal therapies depend on to communicate, often serves to further alienate the person from her own experiential body process (Chace, 1953). According to Gunther (1968), verbalizing and analyzing our experience leads us to filter out the uniqueness of each evolving event; we learn to see the world from a series of expectations, leaving little room for surprise at the unexpected or unknown. When we distance ourselves from our own experiential body process, we literally cut ourselves off from the kinesthetic and sensory input on which we rely to know our various feeling reactions toward ourselves and the world (Fisher, 1963; Laing, 1965).

This body-sense dissociation, however, is not peculiar to only those persons we usually consider to be most regressed. Wallen (1970) lists at least three ways that most of us use to prevent ourselves from having fuller contact with our bodily-felt level of experiencing: (a) a person may have poor perceptual contact with her world or with her own body (such an individual may not be aware what her various body parts are doing at any given moment in time); (b) the person may block the open expression of an urgent need (the person who is aware of needing affection but is nevertheless unable to reach out to others); (c) the person may "repress" some unacceptable reaction (the individual who blocks a reaction of anger). Gestaltists such as Wallen, accept Reich's view of repression as a motor phenomenon. They claim that when a need arises, there is a muscular response; this response may be inhibited by the contraction of antagonistic muscles which prevent the original impulse from being fully expressed. Repression is effective when this contraction becomes chronic and habitual.

It is obvious from the examples cited above, that therapists need to find more effective means of facilitating their clients' awareness of their experiential body process. A growing recognition of this need, is evident in the work of some psychotherapists (Reich, 1949; Gendlin, 1962; Lowen, 1967; Perls, 1969). These approaches share in common the notion that to make contact with one's felt-level experiencing, involves experiencing one's self from an "inside-looking-out" perspective (Rugg, 1963, p. 76). This perspective involves placing oneself at the center of one's experiencing process. This attitude enables the person to engage and become involved in a process, self-discovering what her experience is as it unfolds in her immediate awareness and as she risks herself in action in the world. The earliest example of contacting this source of her own experiencing is through her body (Schilder, 1935).

If my body is the physical reality of "me," in motion, it reveals me in a visible and obvious way to myself and to others. Our bodies in motion confirm or betray our verbal communications (Reich, 1949; Lowen, 1967). When our movements and words are in harmony, we experience ourselves as "together" or congruent; when they contradict each other, we experience ourselves as dissociated from our bodies. Hunt (1966) claims that the moving body is the center of man's experience. How we move not only reveals what has been conceptualized and been by us, but our movements themselves are capable of generating feelings, which are then transformed into images, precepts, memories and concepts (James, 1905; Bull, 1951).

MOVEMENT THERAPY

Movement therapy concerns itself with the latter process of transformation, i.e. how we transform an ongoing continuous flow of energy and incipient body movement to felt-body movement to imagery to verbal symbols. Movement therapists concerned with this transformation process believe that it is possible for a therapist sensitized to a range of human movement experience to actually *see* the ways in which a person blocks the expression of her needs; to see what it costs the person to give up old movement patterns and explore new ones; to see how experienced blocks in the person's movement process may be worked through and integrated by her.

Early movement therapy sessions are guided by the therapist; through a variety of structured movement tasks the person is encouraged to explore the range of her movement responses and increase her sensitivity to her body as an instrument for experiential feedback. An early movement session might include the following structured movement tasks:

(1) *Exploration of one's external environment.* The person is encouraged to explore the space around her; as she moves, she is asked to attend to the speed of her walk, the length of her stride; the amount of energy she expends as she moves and the amount of space she covers. If the movement session occurs in the context of a group, the person may be asked to notice others' usage of space, time and energy and be aware of the differences and similarities from her own.

(2) *Exploration of one's internal environment.* The client may be asked to get quiet and focus her attention inwardly to her own internal space and allow whatever sensations, feelings, images, and thoughts that emerge, to flow naturally without clinging to them or evaluating them in any way.

With time, the movement therapy sessions proceed to make greater usage of the person's own imaginative responses. As the client's movement repertoire gains in range and becomes more differentiated, the degree of external structure offered by the therapist is decreased and the person increasingly self-directs her own movement experience. The function of the therapist changes from that of a guider to that of an observer whose function it is to see that the movement process proceeds unimpeded. The therapist intercedes only when the client encounters a block in her movement.

At the conclusion of each movement session (which generally runs for two hours), the therapist solicits whatever verbal comments the individual cares to make to her movement experience. In this way, connections with feelings, images, memories or ongoing events get made by the person herself in relation to her own movement experience.

Involvement with the movement therapy process begins when the person can attend quietly to an inward impulse, experienced as a sensation, when she allows this impulse to flow naturally outward, without evaluating or consciously willing its expression. This process results in felt-movement. Whitehouse (see reference), a pioneer in the movement therapy field, believed that felt-movement which placed the person in contact with herself, could not be willed or "put on like a dress or coat" but had to be discovered in the body and be allowed to happen [p. 5]. Lowen (1970) refers to this kind of movement outward as an "e-motion." He believes that this kind of movement is an impulse "which in its movement through the organism is perceived as a feeling. . . . Depending upon its aim and goal, we describe the feeling as love, anger, fear, etc. [p. 2]."

The felt-movement process appears to be characterized by two distinctive phases. The early phase involves facilitating the person's reactivity to internal and external stimuli as well as helping the individual release residual muscular tension. During the first phase the person becomes aware of the relation between her own energy levels and varying feeling states. In addition, during the first phase, the person begins to explore new, non-characteristic movement patterns. By the end of the first phase, the person is capable of moving freely (i.e. without necessity to evaluate or censor her movement) and with feeling (with involvement).

Moving freely and with involvement (authentic movement), allows the person to make contact with experienced tensions and blocks. These are experienced as disruptive of the flow of the felt-movement process. During the second phase, the individual experiences periods of "being stuck." Her movement begins to meet with some resistance; this resistance is experienced as stemming from within herself and the person responds by causing a disruption in her own movement process. The person finds herself at a choice-point; she can choose to stop and remain stuck at the point of impasse, or she can decide to continue despite some discomfort, to confront through movement her experience of being blocked. A synthesis of felt-movement (as explored through process-oriented movement therapy) and verbalization (of the kind that speaks directly from the person's own ongoing subjective experience) can promote perceptual and behavioral change.

The following is an account of a non-psychotic person moving through an experience of "being stuck." This account demonstrates how an authentic movement process can connect with images (these appear to be visual representations of the problem the person is working through) and how the "meaning" of this experience attains further clarification and closure through subsequent verbalization.

> Deidre had been involved in movement therapy for several weeks, attending sessions twice weekly. This day, she moved as though all parts of her body were glued to the floor. This pattern was repeated several times. After a short while, she opened her eyes and verbalized that she "felt stuck and could go no further." The movement therapist suggested that she stay with these feelings but explore them in movement. Deidre began to move again, following the same pattern she had been moving in prior to the disruption; soon, however, her movements became exploratory; she extended a foot around her periphery as though marking a circle about herself. At the end of the movement session, she recalled that during this part of the session, she had had a spontaneous image of a cave and that as she moved to explore this cave through movement, she felt the cave's rough, grainy exterior and its deep, dark and ominous interior. Although frightened, she continued to explore her imaginary cave until she finally reached its bottom—a deep, dark pool of water; almost instantaneously, the pool of water was transformed into an ocean; she found herself in the center of it; swimming endlessly. Finally exhausted she crawled onto the shore. To her amazement what she had anticipated would be an inhospitable setting turned out to be different. The sand turned into a dark, rich and fertile soil. She stood up and began to explore her surroundings through movement. As she moved, she became aware of a rich verdant jungle about her. She imagined sun rays caressing her body; she felt warm and very much alive. Her movements became expansive and joyous. At the end of her journey, she just sat and wept. In reflecting back on her moving experience at the end of the session, Deidre mentioned that she felt as though she had discovered a new source of creation deep within herself. A week later she volunteered the comment that whatever she did (e.g. writing a paper) felt "effortless" and that over-all she was less evaluative of herself.

The above illustration demonstrates how making contact with one's experiential body process through an authentic movement experience is a "carrying forward" (Gendlin, 1969) of experiencing; that when conceptualization stems directly from such a felt-movement experience, past unresolved concerns may achieve resolution and fresh new meanings can be created by the person out of her experience.

REFERENCES

Bull, N. *The attitude theory of emotion.* New York: Coolidge Foundation Publishers, 1951.

Chace, M. Dance as an adjunctive therapy with hospitalized patients. *Bulletin of the Menninger Clinic,* 1953, *17,* 219-225.

Fisher, S. A further appraisal of the body boundary concept. *Journal of Consulting Psychology,* 1963, *27,* 62-74.

Gendlin, E. T. *Experiencing and the creation of meaning.* New York: Free Press of Glencoe, 1962.

Gendlin, E. T., Beebe III, J., Cassens, J., Klein, M., & Oberlander, M. Focusing ability in psychotherapy, personality and creativity. In J. M. Shlien (Ed.), *Research in Psychotherapy.* Vol. III. Washington: American Psychological Association, 1968.

Gendlin, E. T. Focusing. *Psychotherapy: Theory, Research and Practice, 1969, 6*(1), 4-15.

Gendlin, E. T. A theory of personality change. In A. Mahrer & L. Pearson (Eds.), *Creative developments in psychotherapy.* Cleveland: Case Western Reserve University, 1971.

Gunther, B. Sensory awakening and relaxation. In H. A. Otto & J. Mann (Eds.), *Ways of Growth.* New York: Viking Press, 1968.

Hunt, V. The biological organization of man to move. *Developmental Conference on Dance,* 1966, 51-63.

James, W. *The principles of psychology;* Vol. II. New York: Holt, 1905.

Laing, R. D. *The divided self.* Baltimore: Pelican Books, 1965.

Lowen, A. *The betrayal of the body.* New York: Macmillan, 1967.

Lowen, A. The body in therapy. *American Dance Therapy Association Proceedings,* 1970, 1-9.

Perls, F. S. *Gestalt therapy verbatim.* Lafayette, Ca.: Real People Press, 1969.

Reich, W. *Character analysis.* New York: Farrar, Strauss and Giroux, 1949.

Rugg, H. *Imagination.* New York: Harper and Row, 1963.

Schilder, P. *The image and appearance of the human body.* London: Keagan, Paul, Trench, Trubner, 1935.

Wallen, R. Gestalt therapy and gestalt psychology. In J. Fagan & I. Shepherd (Eds.), *Gestalt therapy now.* Palo Alto: Science and Behavior Books, 1970.

Whitehouse, M. *Physical movement and personality.* Typed manuscript, undated.

Group Approaches

Humanistic psychotherapy is mainly a public psychotherapy. Providing therapy in groups and workshops has not only popularized creative methods, it has also provided the sharpest distinctions between traditional and newer methods. The papers in this section provide a sample of the voluminous group literature, samples that illustrate the broad range of issues involved.

Teicher and his associates provide a balanced view of the distinction between group psychotherapy and the intense- or encounter-group experience. They see validity in both approaches and urge the assimilation of encounter techniques into mental health practice.

Horwitz discusses ways in which the group psychotherapist can capitalize on the powerful forces operating in the group. In many traditional approaches to group psychotherapy, the focus is on the individual while the group dynamics are ignored. Group-centered interventions flow from the perception of the group as a new organism, and raise a different set of theoretical and practical concerns.

Banet presents a theory of therapy-group development based on the ancient Chinese scripture, the *I Ching*. He proposes a cyclic model of change, and incorporates group phenomena into a series of dialectic movements over time. He attempts to provide a conceptual structure for events occurring in the psychotherapeutic group.

Despite the flurry of group activity, group work remains a frontier for humanistic psychotherapy. These papers present provocative discussions of enduring issues.

Group Psychotherapy and the Intense Group Experience: A Preliminary Rationale for Encounter as a Therapeutic Agent in the Mental Health Field

by Arthur Teicher, Laura de Freitas, and Adele Osherson

In the last decade, both lay and professional journals have been flooded by articles on intense group experiences such as encounter, sensitivity, body awareness, and marathons.[1] These articles may be categorized in the following ways: (1) those that zealously present the intense group experience, extolling it as a panacea, in polemics that attempt to convert the "uninitiated and unbelieving" (Bach, 1966; Burton, 1969; Mintz, 1967; Rogers, 1969; Stoller, 1968); (2) those that straddle issues and attempt to force the intense group experience into the framework and rationale of group psychotherapy, using it as a substitute (Rabin, 1971; Rachman, 1969-70); (3) those that level serious charges against it, label it fraudulent, or enumerate the damage it does or that is inherent in it (Kuehn and Crinella, 1969; Rosenbaum, 1969-70; Spotnitz, 1968; Strean, 1971-72; Yalom and Lieberman, 1971). The basic premise common to most of these articles is the assumption, explicit or implicit, that encounter group experience is a new form of therapy, an "innovation" which expands, improves, or remedies the inadequacies of traditional group psychotherapy.

Reprinted from *International Journal of Group Psychotherapy*, 1974, 24, 159-173.

[1]Although labeled differently, these groups have enough in common to be viewed as a phenomenon and will be referred to here as "the intense group experience" or "encounter."

This paper is not predicated on the assumption that encounter is a form of therapy, and consequently it takes no position in the controversy for or against encounter as a substitute for group psychotherapy. Encounter is a new and unique phenomenon in its own right and merits an objective evaluation. In addition to an examination of the intense group experience, this paper will attempt to fulfill the following purposes: (1) to determine that population which can best be benefited by participation; (2) to clarify the differences between the intense group experience and group psychotherapy; (3) to ascertain the relationship between the intense group experience and group psychotherapy as social, psychological, and therapeutic phenomena; (4) to differentiate between sociocultural deficiencies and psychopathological states; (5) to develop a rationale consonant with the functions and natural qualities of the intense group experience which will fit it into its place within the mental health field.

I

An examination of the literature on the intense group experience indicates that there is general agreement on the following points: First, a wide range of individuals are attracted to such experiences for many and varied reasons (Bach, 1966; Rachman, 1969-70; Stoller, 1968). Second, there is little concern given to the selection of participants. The very nature of the intense group experience as now practiced militates against screening (Back, 1972). Third, the emergence of the intense group experience is related to sociocultural deficiencies (Back, 1972; Toffler, 1970). These deficiencies appear in an urbanized society that is highly sophisticated and mobile, secularized, and oriented toward industrialization and automation. Such a society can readily foster alienation, impersonalization and dispair in some segments of the population. The proponents of the intense group experience, on viewing these sociocultural conditions, seem to have arrived at two conclusions: that these human social responses (alienation, impersonalization, and despair) are pathological because such symptoms are also found in states of psychopathology, and that the present instruments of psychotherapy are inadequate because they do not meet the needs of a drastically changing environment.

Conclusions can also be drawn that relate more closely to the data on group experiences and sociocultural changes, namely: that we are dealing with two basic human conditions rather than one, and that these two different conditions can best be treated in two different ways by two different instruments. One set of conditions may be labeled *sociocultural deficiency states*, the other *psychopathological states*. Those authors who contend that these two states are the same are skillfully agile in extract-ing similarities out of widely disparate entities; they fallaciously assume identity where only parallels exist. The parallels drawn are elaborate (Rachman, 1969-70), but there are fundamental differences both in the nature of these two states and in the instruments required to correct them. It is the assumption of this paper that each generic condition has its own etiology, its own frame of reference, and must run its own course within the modality most applicable and appropriate for it.

II

The intense group experience is an interpersonal activity in which group action is the sole end and feedback is of primary concern. It is generally a short-term phenomenon, with time limits varying from four to forty-eight hours. Accepted social norms are either disdained or abandoned, and standards of behavior are established which create a strong emo-tional impact on the participants. Back (1972) describes these standards as follows: ". . . .frankness substitutes for tact, self-expression for man-ners, nonverbal techniques for language, and immediacy for responsibil-ity" (p. 31). In an informal setting that attempts to induce trust in the leader and other participants, the methods employed stress contact, both physical and verbal, to produce an emotional atmosphere which invites self-exposure.

Focus and activity vary from group to group, depending upon the orientation of the leader. Most leaders interact as fellow members, ab-rogating all responsibility for group action or subsequent results. Perls (1969) states openly, "Sir, if you want to go crazy, commit suicide, improve, get turned on, or get an experience that would change your life, that is up to you. You came here out of your own free will" (p. 75).

Change itself is the primary purpose of the intense group experi-ence. It is "a change whose direction is not necessarily determined" (Back, 1972, p. 31) beyond the pursuit of happiness or "joy" (Schutz, 1967). Despite the use of scientific language, encounter denigrates scien-tific methodology and ignores the principles of human behavior. It is an experience of induced excitement which makes its own rules and grop-ingly attempts, with little success, to find new ways of relating within a supposedly different social environment. This "different" environment is never clearly stated; anything which displeases is attacked, but no thought is given to the creation of a viable alternative. As presently practiced, encounter is basically an anti-establishment and anti-therapy activity, offering destruction of the old without construction of the new; the "new" environment is usually nothing more than the rubble of the old.

III

In order to delineate the population for which the intense group experience is appropriate, it is necessary to address ourselves to the differences between bona-fide states of psychopathology and states of sociocultural deficiencies.

Although psychopathology can be defined in many ways, there are some general rubrics describing this state which hold constant without violating the idea of normality as a relative concept. A pathological condition is rooted in a history of lifelong difficulties: internalized rages and frustrations, blocked emotions, and specific areas of incompetence, dating back in time in terms of *personal deprivations*. A clinical examination of the patient's life-style dynamics demonstrates how personal deprivations are interwoven with biocharacterological development,[2] creating powerful compulsive drives that override volition and the conscious use of choice in making life decisions. There is a lack of integration of the various components of the psyche due to trauma or maldevelopment; consequently, maladaptive functioning may be seen as the end-product of pathological growth processes. Usually, personal deprivations arise out of intense sibling rivalry, lack of appropriate family feelings, and conflicts with maternal or paternal figures, either in perceived or actual struggles involving injustices or power clashes. *Personal deprivations* are often accompanied by somatic distress which has clinical antecedents in emotionally distorted, traumatic life experiences of an idiosyncratic, individualized nature.

When a human being is blocked by pathological factors in the growth sequence which leads to individuation, self-rootedness, and the establishment of an identity, there follows a burgeoning of attitudes and character traits that result in ego-alien experiences, such as depression, phobias, and depersonalization. These are generally accompanied by compulsive, recurrent behavior contrary to the person's intentions. Such symptom reactions are often experienced by the individual as feelings of being "lonely," "alienated," and "in despair." Patterned modes of perception and cognition continue to support this pathological process, guaranteeing experiences that lead to further distortions of reality and increasing loss of autonomy, characteristics solely of pathology (Shapiro, 1965). An example of this process is the inability of the very young child to master the loss of a relationship to a loved object (the mother, or surrogate). The resultant pathology manifests itself in repression, denials, and an arrest of the mourning process. The denial of

---

[2]The thinking in this paper regarding biocharacterological development follows psychoanalytic constructs of personality development and their deviation into pathology (Freud, Sullivan, Jung, Adler).

234 Creative Psychotherapy

reality creates a painful discordance in the child; he projects the cause of his pain onto the external world and then proceeds to act on it. These and other pathological mechanisms result from the operation of internal processes that interfere with adaptive behavior. Such identity distortion and psychic pathology requires the intervention of psychotherapy.

The definition of psychopathology presented above has been, in essence, person- or organism-oriented. In contrast, the sociocultural deficiency state requires a definition that is essentially environment-oriented because it is rooted in actual intake deprivation.[3] In this state, distress is experienced when the individual is confronted with real environmental insufficiencies. Reality distress arises in a rapidly changing society in which the loss of spiritual convictions, an eclipse in transcendental values, a decline in morality, and a breakdown in traditional belief systems have not been replaced by unifying and synthesizing social forces that nurture individual development. Loneliness caused by environmental lack (as opposed to the loneliness of pathological alienation) can be seen in the adolescent who, raised within value systems which are verbalized but not acted upon, experiences the adult world as hypocritical and bewildering. In frustration and anger, he turns against established society, often violently. Feeling duped and deceived, he searches avidly for a sustaining belief in the hope that it will provide gratification which, in turn, will stem depersonalization.

Suffering from such external deficits, an adolescent may *also* experience himself as "lonely," "alienated," and "in despair," but his feelings are not the product of a pathological condition. Rather, his state of need is the consequence of a real and observable lack in the external world; it does not result from unconscious conflicts or the pathological disguising of sources of pain. The disruption in functioning of the socioculturally deprived individual is based on a reality impoverishment and is not to be confused with a state of psychopathology. To illustrate by way of analogy, an individual starving in a blockaded country, cut off from his source of food supply, will lose weight. This weight loss is patently different from that accompanying such physical illnesses as cancer or tuberculosis. Confusing one with the other overlooks fundamental differences in causation which must be fully grasped in order to arrive at an appropriate remedy. The remedy for weight loss due to starvation is food; for illness it is medical treatment. Starvation is this illustration obviously does not reflect psychopathology induced by unconscious forces that create inner stress. It is a deficiency state reflecting an experienced social deprivation.

---

[3]It is conceivable that extended deprivation might, at a critical point, result in a breakdown of health-preserving processes, but this possibility requires further study on its own merits.

The question may now arise as to why some adolescents, or adults for that matter, experience sociocultural deprivations more sharply than others. Many people assume that the adolescent who reacts explosively and destructively has "succumbed" to deprivation and that his responses are therefore pathological. We believe that this *non sequitur* is an illogical conclusion. To return to our previous analogy, if the starving citizenry of a beseiged city are driven by hunger to attack a storehouse containing food, one cannot label their behavior as pathological. Such a response could just as readily be seen as a form of problem-solving. Pathology would be illustrated if one were to feed the citizens and they still remained starved enough to attack the storehouse; then one might assume an inability in the organism to absorb and utilitze food to stave off hunger. It is our belief that each organism has its own threshold for determining at what point the absorption of the stimulus is a threat to its intactness.[4] Related to this threshold are defenses that determine the manner in which an organism will respond. These defenses trigger behavioral responses which are labeled "withdrawal," "fight," "flight," or "collaboration." The response of the organism to ecological conditions does not imply pathology. Pathology, in our definition, refers to defectiveness in the organism which leads to malfunctioning or inappropriateness of response within the framework of these definitions. It is possible for any individual to suffer from either a pathological state or sociocultural deprivations, or from both simultaneously.

A large contributor to the malaise stemming from this deprivation is the lessening sphere of religious influences and institutions. It is our assumption that man is essentially a spiritual being; that any attempt to block this expression also serves to dehumanize him. Primitive peoples handled life crises through rites of passage which are lost to us today and may be sorely missed by many in our culture. While such rites had as their central figure an individual making a transition from one life stage to another, other purposes were served; besides cushioning the individual against shock in the face of change, they provided an opportunity for group participation and contact, and were a binding force for all. At present there is no evidence that modern man has relinquished his need for spiritual expression, ritualized or otherwise, within a community setting.

The tendency in our culture to avoid direct experience and to blunt affect (Siller, 1969) has further intensified an impoverished social environment. This repressive tendency frustrates the deep human hunger for community, for contact and engagement, and for interdependent living, especially in the young (Slater, 1970). These frustrated yearnings,

---

[4]Allergic reactions may be perceived in the same way, i.e., as safety measures within the body's coping system.

exacerbated by external dangers such as nuclear threat, social unrest, and involvement in a poorly understood war, create a sense of despair regarding both the present and the future. Again, this is social deprivation, *not* psychopathology.

There is an urgent need for solace and comfort when religious institutions and the family unit provide little guidance in coping with stultifying life experiences. Confronted by this unmet need, more and more individuals who feel the loss of once-cherished beliefs and habits blindly seek surrogate systems to give them relief, often in the form of instant gratification. But individuals whose discomfort and resentment arise from realistic cultural deficiencies must not be confused with those who require the repair of, or remedy for, personality malfunctioning. Only a differential diagnosis will reveal whether the person's complaint is psychopathological or a reflection of actual reality deprivation. Such diagnosis can then lead to appropriate action; referral either to psychotherapy for the correction of a damaged psyche due to internal conflicts or to an intense group experience for the nourishment which can compensate for external social deficits (Teicher, 1972). The cornerstone of skilled and ethical practice rests on the correct assessment of the individual and his condition (Small, 1972).

IV

The intense group experience can provide reality replenishment for those suffering from sociocultural deficits because the encounter group can be a microcosm that reduces social estrangement and ameliorates the distress caused by environmental lack. Administered systematically to the appropriate population, encounter methods would provide human contact for those who fail to find it in interpersonal living. They offer an opportunity for communication to socially isolated individuals in a highly mobile and impersonalized urban society that gives rise to boredom, distrust of intimacy, and a lack of social competence. In the encounter group there can be rapport with others who have endured the same type of loneliness and are hungry for personalized social experiences. This is exemplified in the case of strangers on a train confiding in each other to an unusual degree, implicity assuming that they will never meet again. In the same way, participation in an intense group experience serves to offset the inner emptiness, dehumanization, and despair of the "socially starved" without the long-term investment that calls for responsible involvement.

Those suffering from psychopathology require a different kind of program. Their need is for corrective treatment, that is, psychotherapy.

The goal of therapy is not the replenishment of a social hunger but the remediation of an illness through the restoration of psychic processes which have become impaired or have not developed adequately. Psychotherapy is a time-consuming, complex activity that involves the intellective, emotional, conative, and cognitive apparatus of the individual (Demarest and Teicher, 1954). Its aim is the resolution and reduction of conflicts in a life style that has already ravaged the individual despite the fact that he resides in "the midst of plenty." Persons with a history of psychopathology cannot integrate new behavior in a short-term intensive group experience. In group psychotherapy relearning is accomplished in small, graduated steps under the control and responsibility of the therapist; defenses are worked through and time is allowed for cognitive restructuring of emotional experiences. The techniques employed allow the patient to perceive his impact on others and theirs on him. In comprehending the distortions and irrationality of his unconscious motivational system, and in seeing their manifestations in conscious behavior, he can resolve the conflict and reorder his own system of hierarchical values. The goal of group psychotherapy is individuation within a social context. Once psychic processes are rehabilitated, the individual is then able to sustain and fulfill himself by utilizing what is available in both his inner and outer environment.

If the encounter phenomenon and group psychotherapy are totally unlike entities, applicable to distinctly different conditions, is there a relationship between the two? We believe there is. The relationship between the two phenomena can be established if each is viewed in its natural perspective within the mental health field. This field consists of two main types of activity, mental hygiene and mental and emotional treatment. In spite of their surface similarity, these two aspects of the field are sharply distinctive. Mental and emotional *treatment* deals primarily with the amelioration, care, and cure of psychopathological conditions that have already manifested themselves. On the other hand, mental *hygiene* is a prophylaxis. It addresses itself to the prevention of pathology and the maintenance of a healthy psychological state. To clarify this point, let us use an analogy in the field of dentistry. Proper diet and care of the teeth, such as brushing and cleaning, constitute dental hygiene. Dental treatment, however, requires a completely different set of complex skills. One can use the intense group experience as a mental hygiene activity, a preventive practice which provides a proper or adequate "psychological diet" for those who are malnourished by their sociocultural environment. The appropriate use of this "diet" can buttress psychological health and may possibly prevent deterioration leading to pathology. For a *psychopathological state,* a different set of operations is required; a treatment program, either group or individual psychotherapy, or some form of organic intervention.

To develop a systematic rationale for the intense group experience that will place it in the mental health field as an ameliorative agent, the differences between the intense group experience and group psychotherapy must be thoroughly demarcated, enunciated, and understood, to prevent confusion and overlap for both the patient and the practitioner. This paper is in complete agreement with Carl Rogers (1970) that encounter is ". . . .the most rapidly spreading *social* invention of the century, and probably the most potent. . . ." (p. 1). It is a unique innovation, a form of human interaction spontaneously generated to fill a new and urgent social need. We recognize its contributions in that context alone. The intense group experience is *not* to be confused with group therapy or any other treatment program.

To recapitulate the differences: Encounter generally has no specific goals—because goals at present are dependent on the leader and change with different leaders—while therapy has both short- and long-range aims beyond the immediate experience. Once it is incorporated into the mental hygiene scheme, the encounter experience will have the specific goals of nurturance and gratification. Group action then will serve to feed the actual sociocultural deprivations of the participants. These specific goals will enable encounter hygienists to develop standard procedures which will then be open to assessment and evaluation. This will allow encounter to become a grounded discipline within the mental health field, as is the case with group therapy. Therapy as a discipline has a theoretical basis for the understanding of human behavior and the correction of its impairment and malfunctioning. Until now, encounter has not only lacked but shunned any theoretical basis for conceptualizing human behavior, and therefore the activities that stem from it cannot be considered reparative, let alone a substitute for therapy. This lack of theory does not permit any understanding of psychic health beyond the recognition of pain. No basis is provided for formulating what constitutes an "out-of-order" condition in the organism or how to repair it. As in spontaneous remission, any reparative results in participants are accidental rather than the outcome of procedural practices.

The intense group experience is an unformalized, nonprocedural activity designed to provide ongoing experiences of a ventilating and nurturing nature; it encourages the generation and expression of feelings that eventuate in physical, social, or emotional engagement within a permissive social setting. As such, it fulfills the requirements of a prophylaxis and can be a powerful prophylactic agent in maintaining the mental health necessary for contented and productive human functioning.

V

If the intense group experience is to serve its proper function, it must not create further problems for its participants by trespassing in areas with which it cannot deal. Concerned professionals are becoming more and more aware of the ethical and moral issues involved in the untrammeled growth of encounter groups which make claims they are unable to fulfill. *The present pressing need for ethical controls in encounter groups cannot be overstated.* The requirements are the same as for clinical practice: responsibility for oneself and the patient. A rationale specifically devised for encounter experience as a prophylaxis is now a necessity. Consideration must be given to the following points:

Screening of participants. Despite the pressure of popular demand, the unwary and naive must be protected. One of the prime dangers in confusing hygienic and therapeutic needs is that of unwitting damage being done to vulnerable individuals; those who suffer the restrictions of emotional illness often seek out intense group experiences in the hope of making empathic contact with others. While viewing reality in terms of phenomenological experiencing is of hygienic benefit for those suffering societal lacks, it is worse than fruitless for those individuals with a therapeutic need that has been bypassed.[5] When such a need is present, any direct attempt to elicit emotionally laden responses may expose the individual to experiences beyond his tolerance. Since there is a risk of psychological decompensation, any person wishing to participate in an intense group experience which deals with data generally considered to be private and personal should be screened and diagnosed by the group leader(s) in one or more individual interviews. As a result of such diagnostic assessment the leader(s) should then accept only those persons where there is relative certainty that subsequent emotional pressures in the group situation will not result in personal disorganization.

Professionalism of the leaders. In order to meet social exigencies and to offset the damage that has been incurred by "free-wheeling attitudes, it would be advisable that standards be adopted for those who would lead encounter experiences as prophylactic devices. (1) Any persons offering any form of encounter or intense group experience to the general public in acceptance of a fee are practitioners in the field of mental health. Obviously, as practitioners, they would be expected to adhere to the ethics of professional practice in any one of the mental health disciplines. Belonging to a mental health discipline would indicate a firm

---

[5]In the review of the literature at the beginning of this paper, reference was made to authors who offer evidence that persons suffering from certain pathological conditions do not belong in encounter groups (Kuehn and Crinella, 1969), and further, that others have been damaged by it (Yalom and Lieberman, 1971).

scientific grounding which would enable them to recognize both the intrapersonal patterns of participants and the methods required to utilize phenomenological experiencing. (2) In order to be in touch with their feelings and to recognize their countertransferential behavior, leaders should be urged to undergo personal psychotherapy and the confronting of their own problems. (3) As with all professional services, it is recommended that announcements of encounters adhere to standards of good taste and include only a brief description of the experiences to be expected. However, as the Goodman Report (1972) emphasizes, such announcements should be more specific when participants are expected to engage in behavior beyond the limit of usual social communication (e.g., when explicitly designed inducements toward psychological regression are to be used). (4) We also agree with Goodman that provision should be made for a leader or a reasonable substitute to be available for post-group supportive sessions with any participant(s) who might require follow-up. Since encounter experiences are of short duration and contact with encounter leaders is haphazard, this is a necessity.

Goals. In order to function as hygienic agent, encounter methods should be structured to include the following: (1) The exploration of personal relationships in an instructive manner. Any psychological or physical coercive pressure should be viewed as dehumanizing. (2) A task-oriented purpose. Ideally, confrontation and mutual interchange should trigger each participant's social processes, so that eventually he can leave the encounter group and maintain himself elsewhere. Unless this goal is kept in mind, encounter devolves into either a pointless (albeit gratifying) repeated activity or, worse, a cult in which those with unrealistic expectations become dependent upon a charismatic leader whom they see as promising deliverance (Yalom and Lieberman, 1971).

VI

In summary, this paper is an attempt to depict the distinctive difference between two phenomena: intense group experiences and group psychotherapy. It has also endeavored to distinguish between the two populations which, in the opinion of the authors, each can serve best. When these two human activities are practiced ambiguously, without discrimination, they are not only harmful to the participants but do an injustice to the activity itself. This paper attempts to present a preliminary systematic rationale for the use of each of these group instruments with the appropriate population. This rationale accomplishes the following: (1) it encompasses both activities within the framework of the mental health field, one as a prophylactic and preventive measure, the other as a treatment program; (2) it provides a place for differential diagnoses so that the appropriate instrument may be selected for the individual who can most benefit by its application; (3) if, after a short period of exposure to the intense group experience, a more malignant condition is uncovered (which the diagnostic assessment did not reveal), the group leader and participating member have more potently corrective procedures readily available to them, since both are incorporated within the mental health field instead of being rival or conflicting activities; (4) the tenets and responsibilities of the clearly enunciated discipline of mental health provides the participating individual with the protection and safeguards that an unsupervised intense group experience does not now offer. Screening, assessment, diagnosis, and the leader's responsibility for his professional activities eliminate abusive or degrading practices. This can only be accomplished when standards of systematic and integrated training replace the diffuse and impulse-dominated exposures which the loosely-knit encounter movement currently accepts as sufficient leadership training.

In this paper we have dealt with fundamental principles, not sporadic uses of technique. A group therapist who includes procedures from the intense group experience in his therapeutic armamentarium is not of necessity conducting an encounter experience. The encounter technique is an audiovisual aid that is as valid as any other tool (i.e., analogy or paradigmatic device) which reduces the obstructive nature of verbal communication for those whose obsessive defenses preclude affective integration of the human response. Encounter "games" can help to concretize an idea or an emotion and aid in working through a conceptualization in an emotionally meaningful experiential manner. Such games can help to demonstrate latent qualities in those who are not skilled in perceiving them through conventional methods. They offer the opportunity for immediate application of a concept or principle without subjecting it to attrition or the resistance of delay. However, it is not one or two techniques which make up a rational or philosophical basis for the practice of a total activity. This holds true for *both* activities. Just as catharsis does not make the intense group experience a treatment program, so "touching" does not make treatment an encounter experience.

Only by incorporating encounter into the mental health field will the scientific jargon currently used in the intense group experience become subject to the close scrutiny of scientific philosophy, scientific self-assessment, and evaluation, allowing claims for "innovations" and "innovative techniques" to be judged in objective terms rather than by the excited testimonials of an emotionally aroused public.

REFERENCES

Adler, A. (1927), *The Theory and Practice of Individual Psychology*. New York: Humanities Press, 1951.

Bach, G. R. (1966), The Marathon Group: Intensive Practice of Intimate Interaction. *Psychol. Rep.*, 18:995-1005.

Back, K. W. (1972), *Beyond Words*. New York: Russell-Sage.

Burton, A. (1969), *Encounter: The Theory and Practice of Encounter Groups*. San Francisco: Jossey-Bass.

Demarest, E. W. and Teicher, A. (1954), Transference in Group Psychotherapy: Its Uses by Co-Therapists of Opposite Sexes. *Psychiat.*, 17:187-202.

Freud, S. (1916-17), Introductory Lectures on Psycho-analysis. *Standard Edition*, 15 & 16. London: Hogarth Press, 1963.

Goodman, M. (1972), Ethical Guidelines for Encounter Group Leadership. (A committee report for the New Jersey State Psychological Association.)

Jung, C. G. (1959), *Basic Writings of C. G. Jung*. New York: Random House.

Kuehn, J. L. and Crinella, F. M. (1969), Sensitivity Training: Interpersonal "Overkill" and Other Problems. *Amer. J. Psychiat.*, 126:840-844.

Mintz, E. E. (1967), Time-Extended Marathon Groups. *Psychother: Theory, Res. & Prac.*, 4(2).

Perls, F. S. (1969), *Gestalt Therapy Verbatim*. California: Real People Press.

Rabin, H. M. (1971), Any Answers to the Compelling Arguments against Encounters and Marathons? *Psychother. Bull.*, 4:16-19.

Rachman, A. W. (1969-70), Marathon Group Psychotherapy: Its Origins, Significance and Direction. *J. Group. Psychoanal. & Proc.*, 2:57-74.

Rogers, C. R. (1969), The Group Comes of Age. *Psychol. Today*, 3:27-31, 58-61.

Rogers, C. R. (1970), *Carl Rogers on Encounter Groups*. New York: Harper & Row.

Rosenbaum, M. (1969-70), The Responsibility of the Group Psychotherapy Practitioner for a Therapeutic Rationale. *J. Group. Psychoanal. & Proc.*, 2:5-15.

Schutz, W. C. (1967), *Joy*. New York: Grove Press.

Shapiro, D. (1965), *Neurotic Styles*. New York: Basic Books.

Siller, J. (1969), Psychological Situation of the Disabled with Spinal Cord Injuries. *Rehabil. Lit.*, 30:290-296.

Slater, P. (1970), *The Pursuit of Loneliness*. Boston: Beacon Press.

Small, L. (1972), The Uncommon Importance of Psychodiagnosis. *Profess. Psychol.*, 3:111-119.

Spotnitz, H. (1968), Discussion of Stoller's Accelerated Interaction. *This Journal*, 18:236-239.

Stoller, F. H. (1968), Accelerated Interaction: A Time-Limited Approach Based on the Brief, Intensive Group. *This Journal*, 18:220-235.

Strean, H. S. (1971-72), Social Change and the Proliferation of Regressive Therapies. *Psychoanal. Rev.*, 58:581-594.

Sullivan, H. S. (1953), *The Interpersonal Theory of Psychiatry*. New York: Norton.

Teicher, A. (1972), The Role of Group Process in the Study of Personality Development. *J. Group. Proc.* 4:7-19.

Toffler, A. (1970), *Future Shock*. New York: Random House.

Yalom, I. D., and Lieberman, M. A. (1971), A Study of Encounter Group Casualties. *Arch. Gen. Psychiat.* 25:16-30.

Group-Centered Interventions in Therapy Groups

by Leonard Horwitz[1]

Currently the great controversy in the group field is that between the therapist who uses existentialist methods, encounter techniques, marathons, and nonverbal methods versus the traditional, psychoanalytically oriented group approach. A less visible, but nonetheless significant split among the "traditionalists" is that between those group therapists who focus upon the group as a whole as opposed to those who decry the idea of the therapy group functioning as an entity. Some of the latter (Wolf and Schwartz, 1962) have vigorously attacked the proponents of the group-as-a-whole approach as failing in their responsibilities to the patient who, they believed, was being deprived of his autonomy as an individual.

Although a few writers have attempted to come to grips with this problem, the issue has largely lain dormant in the group psychotherapy literature. Also, there have been no programs until now devoted to this subject sponsored by the American Group Psychotherapy Association. Some panels have dealt with the problem of why the group therapists and group dynamicists have not been able to influence each other more effectively and have been concerned with the inability of the therapist to make use of such considerations as group cohesion, norm-setting, decision-making, and so forth. But basically the argument addressed in this paper is not that between the social scientist who studies small groups as opposed to the psychotherapist. Rather, I am attempting to contrast two divergent approaches to analytic group psychotherapy

"Group-Centered Interventions in Therapy Groups," by Leonard Horwitz is reprinted from *Comparative Group Studies*, Vol. 2, No. 3 (Aug. 1971), pp. 311-331, by permission of the Publisher, Sage Publications, Inc.

[1]The author gratefully acknowledges the helpful suggestions of the Menninger Foundation Group Study Group and in particular the detailed comments of Doctors Ramon Ganzarain, Francisco Gomez, and Paulina Kernberg.

—those which emphasize groupwide interpretations and those emphasizing individual interventions.

It would be interesting to speculate about why debates between these two divergent points of view have been so rare. It may be partly because the group-as-a-whole approach is in the main a British ideology, having been propounded by Bion, Ezriel, and, to some extent, Foulkes. The American versions of this viewpoint have been expressed in writings of Whitaker and Lieberman (1964) and to some degree by Arsenian et al. (1962). But the major current in America has been predominantly in opposition to group-centered work with therapy groups and the advocates of the group-centered approach have been unusually silent on this matter.[2] The author and his colleagues at the Menninger Foundation have been practicing a group-centered approach for several years and appreciate this opportunity to engage in a dialogue on this topic.

The wide discrepancy between these two schools of thought may be illustrated by quotations from the individuals who best represent the two polar positions. Bion (1959) writes that the therapist's greatest pitfall is that of attempting to do individual therapy in the group. Despite the individual patient's pressure for attention to his complaints, the therapist makes his greatest contribution to helping the patient with his neurosis by directing his attention to his characteristics as a group member and to the emotionally laden "basic assumptions" which grip the group. Bion (1959: 81) warns quite pointedly: "if the psychiatrist can manage boldly to use the group instead of spending his time more or less unconsciously apologizing for its presence, he will find that the immediate difficulties produced are more than neutralized by the advantages of the proper use of the medium."

On the other hand, Slavson (1964: 64) writes:

> the therapeutic process, by its very nature, is antagonistic to group formation and group dynamics. Reinforcement of feelings and intensification that periodically set in, should they be permitted to run their course, do result in specific dynamics. In analytic therapy groups, however, this is prevented by the intervention of the therapist and by his and other members' interpretations, thus dissipating the building up of group patterns and group effort. By their very nature, therapeutic groups favor interpersonal *interaction*, rather than group patterns.

Before discussing the tenets of the group-centered position, let us examine the points of agreement, the common ground between the two

---

[2] A move to present this point of view to American group therapists was made recently by Heath and Bacal (1968) who described the rationale and method of group psychotherapy practiced at the Tavistock Clinic. The fact that such an article needed to be written, over twenty years after the method was introduced in England, indicates how unreceptive American practitioners have been to this point of view.

points of view. Of course, it is just as incorrect to regard all of the group-centered writers as a monolithic whole as it would be to describe the individual-centered theorist as holding identical points of view. But practically all analytical group therapists, group or individually centered, probably subscribe to these propositions:

(1) The goal or objective of both therapists is to treat, help, or cure the individual patient; the therapist who attends to the group as a whole is using this technique in order to effect changes ultimately in individuals, not in his group.

(2) Both schools attempt to provide the patient with insight into the unconscious basis of his symptoms or behavior by interpreting transference and resistance; group-centered therapists attempt to do this by addressing themselves mainly to the group transference.

(3) The interaction and interstimulation in the group situation provides an excellent medium in which to elicit characteristic responses. These here-and-now responses are used by all therapists for the interpretation of infantile wishes and associated character defenses.

(4) Groups may react in unison or in concert, particularly in response to an affectively loaded event. Bion believes this unitary response is always present; Slavson believes it is occasional.

THE GROUP-CENTERED POSITION

What constitutes the group-as-a-whole view of a therapy group? The position has been attributed to Bion as chief architect, and espoused in various forms by Ezriel, Foulkes, and Whitaker and Lieberman. While these writers have prominent differences in their views about the nature and handling of groups, they all emphasize a wholeness and unitary functioning in group sessions. This unified conception consists mainly of the idea that members of a group come under the influence of a *shared emotion;* that is, at any given moment they share a common wish or drive which cannot be expressed openly or freely because of the unacceptability of these impulses and the fear of untoward consequences. Bion (1959) calls this underlying wish the "basic assumption" life; Ezriel (1952) describes the conflict as the "common group tension"; and Whitaker and Lieberman (1964) have labeled it the "group focal conflict."

This shared fantasy or wish dominates a given segment, or session, or series of sessions and becomes the organizing theme around which the contributions of patients may be understood. When the therapist begins to understand the underlying theme of a session, he is able to fit most, if not all, of the otherwise disparate pieces into place, in jigsaw puzzle fashion. Bion emphasizes three basic assumptions (dependence, fight-flight, and pairing) while the others do not attempt to confine the thematic content solely to these categories.

As in individual treatment, the shared fantasy or wish is rarely experienced as a conscious wish and is usually expressed in the form of a metaphor. A group wish that is frequently observed is the attempt to find a messianic leader, one whose omnipotence will nurture, protect, and magically cure the patient. Its manifestations and forms of expression are multivaried, depending on the composition of the group and its styles of communication. But the essential point for this discussion is the fact that all the members of the group are struggling with the same wish at the same time. They experience it in different ways, depending on the differing intensity of impulses and on the defensive makeup characteristic of each individual. Under the pressure of dependence, some individuals may find these wishes ego-syntonic and even justified; others may feel them so distasteful as to employ reaction formations and assume a counterdependent stance, characteristic of the adolescent rebellion; still others, with a low tolerance for angry feelings, may find it necessary to bottle up such impulses and retreat into silence and minimal participation. In other words, individual reactions will carry the stamp of characterological formations typical of each member. The group-centered approach, as described by Sutherland (1952) and Ezriel (1952), consists of interpreting both the group conflict as well as each individual's modes of coping with it.

As mentioned earlier, the proponents of the group-centered approach do not share identical views on this property of groups. Bion and Ezriel, for example, believe that the principle of unitary functioning applies at all times in a group's life. Whitaker and Lieberman, on the other hand, emphasize that shared conflicts predominate only during certain periods and are followed by the group's arriving at an enabling solution. Foulkes does not espouse the view that patients are always simultaneously concerned with a group issue. If we may be permitted to extend his metaphor of the therapist as the conductor, sometimes the entire group may be playing a symphony while at other times it may play a concerto; i.e., group accompaniment to one of its soloists. He mentioned in a recent article (1968) that his group at one meeting excluded him and acted as though his presence was neither wanted nor needed. In the next meeting the group was filled with guilt over having "killed" the therapist. But these groupwide reactions do not occur invariably and without exception, according to Foulkes. He may at times focus upon reactions of individuals but he tries to remain constantly cognizant of the effect of these personally oriented interventions upon the group. He tends to address patients who represent a group theme and attempts to focus upon such persons as examples of a group problem, conflict, or feeling. He prefers such interventions over those with an individualistic focus.

Thus, the purest group-centered approach is that adopted by Bion and Ezriel, both associated with the Tavistock Clinic. They not only believe that group members share common conflicts, but they are potentially under the influence of such tensions at any and all moments of the group's life. Like other clinical material, the manifest content must be translated into its underlying meanings.

PROBLEM OF EVIDENCE

What evidence is there to support this principle of unitary functioning? Unfortunately we are not in a position to cite experimental evidence on this subject. It would be most difficult to devise a crucial experiment to test the validity of the "unitary hypothesis." The presence or absence of a theme cannot be assessed directly from the primary data, like a recording or transcript of a therapy session. The fascination and frustration of clinical work derives from the inference-making process which a trained clinician must apply to his data before he can extract therapeutically useful interventions. As Rapaport (1960) once put it, since the canons of clinical inference are not well established, there is always the danger in clinical research of verifying a hypothesis by "smuggling" it in with one's inferences.

Without adequate formal research on this matter, we must turn to other kinds of evidence on this question. We are unable to use the observation of workers who find, or fail to find, a shared theme in their groups. However puzzling, we must observe the unusual phenomenon of patients with English accents addressing themselves to group themes while their American counterparts (with a few notable exceptions) seem to speak with a more ruggedly individualistic voice.

An important theoretical consideration bearing on this question is that derived from social systems theory, basic to many current group and community approaches. Donne's famous line that "the bell tolls for thee" poetically observes that a social unit as a whole affects every component part of the system and conversely a change in one part leads to a change in the configuration of the whole. Family therapists have long observed that when the "sick" member of a family unit is removed, another candidate for that position is sometimes sought out to serve the function previously filled by the missing member. If the sick member was a child, he may have served the need in the family to be the cement in a shaky marriage, or he may have gratified an exaggerated need of the couple to find an object to nurture and infantilize, and so forth. Such dynamisms have been frequently observed in therapy groups. Scapegoating, for example, involves a collusion between an angry group and a masochistic member to vent its hostility against a target which is more available than the original and primary one. Arsenian et al. (1962) have used the term "billet" to describe the necessary functions in a group which one or more members must fill for the group to survive: cohesion, dispersion, and ambivalence. A similar line of thinking is expressed by Redl (1963) in his concept of "role suction," a process by which a member is pressed into service by the group to express the group's wishes. The member's behavior in this instance may be understood and explained as much by the group's pressure as by his own personal needs.

A second argument in behalf of the holistic point of view is the fact that human beings, however unique, are basically similar in their emotional lives. They share a physical constitution and developmental history which dispose them to shared psychological needs and dispositions. Bion's three basic assumptions—fight-flight, pairing, and dependence—subsume three major human drives, i.e., aggression, sexuality, and the wish to return to the earlier state of infantile dependence. These common features of human emotional life are the substratum on which a holistic conception is built. The similarities among group members make it possible for them to react with shared fantasies.

But it is still necessary to offer some explanation, a mechanism whereby the members at any given moment are caught up in the same emotional problem. Redl's "contagion" effect (1963), so dramatically observed in mobs, offers at best a limited explanation. Unquestionably the contagion effect operates in small groups and has been described by several authors. Anthony (1968: 296) has referred to the panic reaction which engulfs a group when "in a setting of fearfulness and rage . . . the group loses confidence in itself and in its own identity and feels abandoned by the therapist. He compares this reaction to a transference neurosis in psychoanalysis. Foulkes and Anthony (1965) describe a "resonance" effect in which unconscious wishes in one member arouse similar feelings in other members.

Freud's (1922) study of large groups offers an insight into the dynamics of "contagion." He believed that a leader, such as the commander of an army, becomes an idealized figure who comes to occupy a central role in the ego-ideal of the entire organization. This shared identification with the leader, according to Freud, results in a libidinal bond being established among the members. Redl (1942) attempted to broaden this explanation by introducing two additional mechanisms. One is the "guilt assuaging effect of the initiatory act" in which an individual feels free of his responsiblity for his unacceptable behavior because someone else did it first, very commonly observed in children. The other explanation is the infectiousness of the unconflicted person on the conflicted one, in which anxiety-reduction occurs when a conflicted individual finds another who has resolved this conflict and experiences some relief by the association and relationship with the other person.

Perhaps it is some form of contagion to which Ezriel alludes when he describes the process by which a common group tension arises. When a remark made by one member, usually at the beginning of the session, "clicks" or resonates with the dominant unconscious fantasies of other members, it leads to a series of interrelated contributions based on the shared common fantasy aroused in the group. Usually, the fantasy is based on a common reaction to the therapist who is the dominant tranference figure in the group.

The explanatory concept offered by Bion (1959: 116) is that of "valency . . . the individual's readiness to enter into combination with the group in making and acting on the basic assumption . . . the capacity for spontaneous instinctive cooperation in the basic assumptions." This capacity is present in all individuals to a greater or lesser degree and operates automatically and unconsciously. He calls such participation "instantaneous, inevitable and instinctive."

Many instances of the group acting as a unit may be adduced to illustrate this phenomenon but obviously more is required. All group therapists, depending on their orientation, observe it in operation, at least on rare occasions, and some see it frequently. The group-centered therapists, however, observe this phenomenon throughout the life of the group. But we are faced with a lack of adequate substantiation for one point of view or the other.

Lacking clear and decisive evidence, this writer would like to suggest that *the group-centered point of view is a valuable working hypothesis for a group therapist.* Someone sagely observed that therapists find what they look for in a group. There is no question that the individually oriented group therapist can, by his interventions, fractionate the group so that whatever the members share tends to go underground or get dissipated. By the same token, the group-centered approach will lead to a magnification and enhancement of the shared feelings, wishes, and fears of the group members. For the present, therefore, a therapist's choice between the two alternative methods should be based upon which seems to offer the greatest therapeutic yield.

ADVANTAGES OF GROUP-CENTERED APPROACH

The first advantage of the group-centered approach is that it helps to reduce the problem of which individual will receive the focus of the group's and the therapist's attention. Insofar as the therapist interprets shared emotions and shared fantasies, he is implicitly inviting all of the members to participate. In the individually centered approach, a member's contribution is seen as primarily his own individual problem and tends to be dealt with as such. Of course, others may join in with similar experiences. But the tendency will be for the group and the therapist to focus upon one or possibly two people at a time, rather than search for and uncover the common elements that are being shared by all. Moreover, all therapists tend to be vulnerable to the pitfall of the "squeaky wheel getting the grease." In the group-centered approach, an individual's contribution or interaction with other members is always understood by the therapist as a piece of the whole. The therapist is thus helped to avoid the ever-present hazard in the group of favoring one patient over the others with his interest and attention.

A second problem which the therapist circumvents is the likelihood of misunderstanding by failing to view an individual's behavior as embedded in the context of the whole group. When a group member is heard as the spokesman for a group point of view, his behavior is often understood quite differently than when he is seen independently of the group. For example, a group member began a session by referring to his recent preoccupation with inferiority feelings. He launched into a rather long-winded recitation of the history of such experiences, how his parents contributed to these feelings, and how unsuccessful his efforts had been to overcome them. The group listened half-heartedly but kept the speaker going by occasional questions. When the therapist finally intervened and addressed himself to the entire group for some clarification of what was motivating this group pattern, a most interesting shared fantasy began to emerge. They all had developed a feeling in the group that nothing good could possibly emerge from their group experience as long as they were unable to have the therapist's attention all to themselves. Hence, an unconscious compact had developed in which they would give one member at a time a full session in which they could get all of the group's time and in essence wait their turn. The group's shared fantasy of the need to defend themselves against competitive feelings, the latent content, was much more significant than the one member's manifest preoccupation.

A third advantage is one which has been observed by therapists of all persuasions and is often described as a special advantage of the group situation. It is the supportive effect of a patient perceiving that his anxieties, weaknesses, and conflicts are also present in other group members. He becomes reassured that his feelings of alienation and isolation from others because of unacceptable wishes and thoughts is unwarranted, that his frailties are indeed a part of the human condition. Such group experiences provide support to the individual to participate more freely in disclosing hidden aspects of himself which in turn usually produces an enhancement of the patient's self-esteem. This effect is not found exclusively in group-centered groups, of course, but is probably heightened in a setting where commonalities among patients are constantly being sought out and uncovered.

In addition to the support experienced in sharing anxieties or conflicts and its benefit to self-esteem, there is also a facilitating effect upon expression and self-disclosure in a group because of a phenomenon which is best described as the "protection of the group theme." As the patient begins to appreciate that his wishes and fantasies are almost always shared in some degree by the others in the group, the anxiety associated with their expression is dampened. Childish dependent wishes, present in all of us, may be voiced with less guilt, fear of punishment, and threat to self-esteem. The common fear among neurotic people that certain behavior or fantasy life must be concealed lest their unattractive, even "depraved," condition be known, becomes a decreasingly inhibiting factor as the group begins to appreciate the commonalities of their inner lives. Thus, the "protection of the group theme" encourages and facilitates the expression of thoughts and feelings essential for the therapeutic process.

A most important corollary of this phenomenon is the intensification of a therapeutically useful regression where the group-as-a-whole technique is used. Any factor which contributes to the expression and uncovering of preconscious and unconscious material stimulates the experience and verbalization of genetically earlier, more immature fantasies and modes of reaction. These then emerge as transference reactions for the therapist to interpret and thus contribute to the patient's greater understanding of less accessible parts of himself. These regressive reactions in the transference are useful therapeutically when they are "in the service of the ego," when they are controlled and reversible, and when the patient's observing ego is capable of stepping back and taking distance from his experiencing ego.

There is an interesting split between therapists on the issue of the "dilution" of transference. Some, like Slavson (1964), assert that the presence of other group members contributes to making the group a more realistic situation than a one-to-one setting and therefore leads to a lessening of transference distortions. According to this view, the more regressive layers of the transference are not elicited in a group situation. Bion (1959), in contrast, describes the deepest levels of experience occurring in his groups. He refers to "psychotic anxieties" being elicited, perhaps an ill-chosen term for early, primitive fantasies and mechanisms like splitting, projection, and introjection (Ganzarain, 1960). According to this view, the regressive aspects of the transference may be as deep and as intense as any expressive psychotherapy, if not more so. My colleagues and I, using a modified Bion approach, have been impressed with the speed and intensity of regression in our groups, even in our training groups for psychiatric residents (Horwitz, 1967).

The discrepancy in these views may be explained, I believe, by the methods which the two schools employ. The group-centered approach exploits group dynamic processes to the fullest; the "individualist" approach attempts to snuff them out whenever they appear. When a patient becomes involved in a group emotion, the group-centered therapist views this as a desirable occurrence which he will be able to exploit therapeutically. The intensified emotions, in the individual and the group, highlight for each individual some aspect of his own impulse-defense configurations. Thus, the patient who shares dependence wishes with others in the group will often experience more intense strivings than he would if this problem were being dealt with on an individual basis.[3] Such heightened emotions bring out individual defenses with greater sharpness. In other words, the group phenomena are seen as working in concert with the individual's reactions and produce behavior which will often appear with great clarity. The proponents of the individually centered approach believe, on the other hand, that group phenomena must be "nipped in the bud" lest they obscure the individual's idiosyncratic and unique reactions. But by neutralizing, fragmenting, and fractionating these group reactions, they are undoubtedly reducing the therapeutically desirable regressive impact of the group. Anthony (1968: 290) described the effect in this way: "Wolf's psychoanalysis of groups could theoretically lead to greater depth, but in my opinion, his reluctance to use the dynamics of the group in conjunction with his approach would interfere with this." In contrast, says Anthony, Ezriel's method "adds to a deepening of the process, since both factors, individual and group, are harnessed to the same yoke and therefore pull the process further."

DIFFERENCES IN THERAPEUTIC STRATEGIES

This fundamental discrepancy in the two approaches leads to a number of important differences in therapeutic strategy. The perennial problem of indications and contraindications for group psychotherapy is largely embedded in the larger question of what kind of group one is conducting. Freedman and Sweet (1954), for example, have written a thoughtful

---

[3]Two factors giving rise to this effect have already been mentioned: contagion and protection of the group theme. A third is the aim-inhibition existing in group settings: the presence of others reduces the possibility of the gratification in reality of instinctual impulses within the session itself. Scheidlinger (1968) enumerates a number of other forces favoring regression in groups.

and well-reasoned article in which they contend that a specific indication for a group is the patient classified as borderline personality and base this conclusion on the dilution of transference and the reality-oriented nature of the groups they conduct. They reason that the borderline patient, given to disorganized and chaotic reactions, is best helped to strengthen his reality-testing by avoiding regression-inducing therapeutic experiences. In all probability, these authors would not have reached the same conclusions if they had used a group-centered approach in which regressive tranferences may become quite intense. Conversely, Ezriel's (1952) observations about indications for group treatment are quite nonrestrictive. He and his colleagues at the Tavistock Clinic believe essentially that any patient who can benefit from individual treatment may also profit from group. Since his groups provide a patient with an opportunity to experience regressive transference reactions in a manner similar to expressive psychotherapy, the intensity of the group experience is limited mainly by the frequency of the sessions.

Another difference in strategies is related to the care taken by the group-centered people to avoid procedures which would interfere with the transference. In order to maximize the use of transference, one must strive to maintain a "sterile operating field." In group terms, this means that the patient's relationship with the therapist and with other members should be confined, as much as possible, to the arena of the therapy sessions. Deviations from this policy will result in some "leakage" of the transference based on a displacement of wishes outside the group. Yet such procedures in many instances are built into the therapeutic structure of individually centered therapy which therefore helps to dissipate group-as-a-whole developments.

One common practice, for example, is to hold a series of individual sessions, often twenty to thirty, with the prospective patient before introducing him into the group. The rationale is that the relationship with the therapist offers the patient a sense of security when entering a new, strange, and sometimes hostile situation. This special tie with the therapist may also tide the patient over some of the rough spots of his therapeutic experience and perhaps contribute to a decreased tendency to drop out. It may give the patient the comfortable feeling that the therapist understands him and knows some of his innermost secrets, even if no one else does. But these therapeutic supports are not entirely unmixed blessings. The patient is encouraged, at least in fantasy, to assume that he has a special relationship with the therapist so that the competitive feelings that ordinarily get aroused in a group will be dampened. Also, the patient may believe it is unnecessary to engage in painful self-disclosure in the group since he has already revealed these matters to the therapist. Such forces tend to divert energy from the group.

A similar, but even more obvious, leakage occurs when the therapist permits, or even encourages, patients to see him in individual sessions when the patient seems to be under special stress. There may be an implicit communication that the group has a limited purpose and usefulness, that the real treatment occurs in a one-to-one contact. It may even encourage patients to become upset or resistant and thus be rewarded with a private interview. Finally, and perhaps most important, it diverts important transference reactions from the group.

For example, a young married woman with three children entered a group because of depression and disabling somatizations. Her immediate response was to seek a private and exclusive relationship with the therapist, mainly by requesting extra time after the regular session. When this behavior was discouraged she sullenly withdrew and it soon became clear that the only real help she believed she could get was in an exclusive contact with the therapist. This need to be the sole and exclusive recipient of parental attention, her greed for more oral supplies than any of her sibling-competitors, was a duplicaton in the therapy of her frustrating life situation. Her marriage was getting along reasonably well until the children began to arrive, at which time she reacted, largely unconsciously, with rivalry and anger toward them, viewing them as intruders and competitors vis-à-vis her husband. If she had been permitted to indulge her wish for an exclusive relationship with the group therapist, her core problem would have gone underground. The neurotic wish would have been gratified rather than interpreted and the therapy might have compromised the patient's opportunity to modify her oral-demanding behavior. Consistent interpretation of her conflict resulted in considerable enhancement of more mature, maternal attitudes.

Of course, the difficulties being described are maximized when the therapist elects to use combined or concomitant individual and group therapy. The problems produced by this approach are similar whether the individual therapist is the same as the group therapist or is a different person, although perhaps somewhat more exaggerated in the latter case. When we hear the story of the patient who decided to have two simultaneous analyses with two different analysts in order to speed up his treatment, we may chuckle at the impossibly ludicrous position he arranged for himself and for his analyst. If we believe that the emotional currents induced in the group should also be confined to the group for interpretation, we would find combined treatment just as unimaginable. If we wish to conduct a treatment based on a transference method, it behooves us to keep all of our transference eggs in one basket. The predisposition to transference-splitting and acting-out is strong in all patients and tends to occur even when the therapist keeps his procedures uncontaminated. The potency of group forces and the need to harness, rather than dampen them is the main point.

OBJECTIONS TO THE GROUP-CENTERED APPROACH

Some writers (Scheidlinger, 1968; Wolf and Schwartz, 1962) have criticized the group-as-a-whole position because its proponents have seemingly embraced a group mind conception, outworn and discredited in most scientific circles. Scheidlinger (1968), in particular, has taken exception to such formulations as group fantasies or group behavior when the group is reacting in unison. Bion's writings are filled with such terminology as group culture, group mentality, and so forth. Scheidlinger (1968: 5) contends that group phenomena are observable, particularly at certain modal points in the life of the group (such as the entry of a new number), but he strongly criticizes any implication that "the group as a group now has a certain fantasy or acts in a certain manner . . . shared fantasies are far from being the same in each individual." Unquestionably, shared fantasies are not identical. While Scheidlinger's observation correctly calls for greater precision in verbal usage, groupwide reactions seem to be observable and hence concepts to embrace these data are undoubtedly needed.

A more pointed objection is the possibility that the individual, the ultimate recipient of our therapeutic efforts, might get lost in our preoccupation with similarities among members. Some have wondered if the group, rather than the individual, is being treated. This question is probably a legitimate one with regard to Bion's writings where the focus upon group trends does not *directly* address the individual and his special, idiosyncratic reactions. But Bion's views were extended by Sutherland and Ezriel (1952) and their colleagues at the Tavistock Clinic to correct this omission. The therapist not only interprets the common group tension but he attempts to comment *on each individual's particular mode of dealing with these impulses and fears.* Thus, he may interpret the group's wish to find a messianic leader who will magically cure them of their symptoms. But Ezriel would not stop at this point. He would go on to describe the special defenses erected to cope with the conflict. For example, patient A is behaving in an ingratiating manner with the hope of finding such help; patient B is assuming a counter-dependent stance, reacting against unacceptable dependence needs; patient C is silently defending against his anger at having such needs frustrated, and so forth. In other words, the complete and ideal interpretation includes the general group problem as well as the individual modes of dealing with this problem.

Finally, we may be asked if the group-centered approach does not adhere too rigidly to a single assumption and method, particularly one about which there may be some uncertainty. To what extent will this orientation dispose a therapist toward forcing his interpretation into some inappropriate and inaccurate mold? If a patient is enmeshed in a reality crisis which he brings to the group, should we expect that the entire group will join him in his current dilemma? How can we be sure that the silent member of a group is quietly concurring in the group's preoccupations? These are legitimate questions for which no easy answers can be readily given. This writer's experience over the past several years using and teaching this method is that its limitations are minor compared to its usefulness. Although the group-centered approach is valuable and makes maximal use of group processes, modifications of the method on the basis of increased experience should not be precluded. A well-conceived rationale and strategy are important for every therapist, but we should certainly keep rigid and stultifying rituals from intruding into our work.

The group-centered approach is based on the assumption that most, if not all, productions in a therapy group are unconsciously guided by a common group tension or an underlying conflict shared by all its members. Although no empirical or theoretical proof is available for this assumption, numerous advantages may be adduced to maximize the shared fantasies, feelings, and conflicts in a group by means of group-centered interventions. Mainly we believe that this method harnesses group processes into a therapeutically useful tool, one which works in the direction of magnifying individual reactions which are the ultimate focus of treatment. In contrast, the individually centered approach attempts to dissipate and dampen groupwide reactions and thus dilutes transference reactions which in turn weakens the curative potential of the group.

REFERENCES

Anthony, E. J. (1968) "Reflections on twenty-five years of group psychotherapy." *International J. of Group Psychotherapy* 18: 277-301.

Arsenian, J., E. V. Semrad, and D. Shapiro (1962) "An analysis of integral functions in small groups." *International J. of Group Psychotherapy* 12: 421-434.

Bion, W. R. (1959) Experiences in Groups. New York: Basic Books.

Durkin, H. (1964) *The Group in Depth*. New York: International Universities Press.

Ezriel, H. (1952) "Notes on psychoanalytic group therapy: II: interpretation and research." *Psychiatry* 15: 119-126.

Foulkes, S. H. (1968) "On interpretation in group analysis." *International J. of Group Psychotherapy* 18: 432-444.

—— and E. J. Anthony (1965) *Group Psychotherapy*. Baltimore: Penguin Books.

Freedman, M. B. and B. S. Sweet (1954) "Some specific features of group psychotherapy and their implications for the selection of patients." *International J. of Group Psychotherapy* 4: 355-368.

Freud, S. (1922) *Group Psychology and the Analysis of the Ego.* London: International Psychoanalysistical Press. (Liveright in Books in Print)

Ganzarain, R. (1960) "'Psychotic' Anxieties in group analytic psychotherapy." *Mental Health Research Newsletter* 2: 15-16.

Heath, E. S. and H. A. Bacal (1968) "A method of group psychotherapy at the Tavistock Clinic." *International J. of Group Psychotherapy* 18: 21-30.

Horwitz, L. (1967) "Training groups for psychiatric residents." *International J. of Group Psychotherapy* 17: 421-435.

—— (1964) "Transference in training groups and therapy groups." *International J. of Group Psychotherapy* 14: 212-213.

Rapaport, D. (1960) "The structure of psychoanalytic theory: a systematizing attempt." *Psych. Issues* 6.

Redl, F. (1963) "Psychoanalysis and group therapy: a developmental point of view." *Amer. J. of Orthopsychiatry* 33: 135-147.

—— (1942) "Group emotion and leadership." *Psychiatry* 5: 573-596.

Scheidlinger, S. (1968) "The concept of regression in group psychotherapy." *International J. of Group Therapy* 18: 3-20.

Slavson, S. R. (1964) *A Textbook in Analytic Group Psychotherapy.* New York: International Universities Press.

Sutherland, J. D. (1952) "Notes on psychoanalytic group therapy: I: therapy and training." *Psychiatry* 15: 111-117.

Whitaker, D. S. and M. A. Lieberman (1964) *Group Psychotherapy Through the Group Process.* New York: Atherton Press.

Wolf, A. and E. K. Schwartz (1962) *Psychoanalysis in Groups.* New York: Grune & Stratton.

A Theory of Group Development
Based on the I CHING

by Anthony G. Banet, Jr.

While a therapy group is in session, the psychotherapist attends to a bewildering series of events. To fulfill his primary leadership function, he periodically intervenes to focus on specific process events that he believes offer the greatest potential for growth and behavior change in group members. The intervention process is comprised of four major elements: (1) accurate observation of the group's content; (2) acute perception of the unfolding group process; (3) appropriate and specific intervention designed to facilitate change; and (4) a follow-through with the diverted process after a change has been initiated.

The psychotherapist perceives the content and process of the group from the perspective of *group structure*. Group structure refers to the therapist's conceptualization of the group, and it includes such components as the group's objectives, the contract between the therapist and group members, and the group's ground rules. The most important component of group structure, however, is the theory of change and group development in which the therapist believes and the intervention stance that this theory prescribes.

Different group structures produce different group phenomena. Therapeutic groups and the phenomena occurring in them vary because different therapists believe in and apply different theories to their work. A forthcoming review of group-development theories (Banet, 1976) concludes that no current theory adequately accounts for all reported group phenomena and that theories of group development vary in a number of critical dimensions, including process focus (on group, personal, or contextual elements), observational base, time perspective, and the role assigned to the leader. In addition, various theories employ different models of change.

Theories using a *linear* model of change view group process as developing in sequential, progressive phases—or stages—toward some goal; for example, see the theories of Schutz (1973) and Tuckman (1965). Theories with a *helix* model of change regard process as a regressive, theme-centered dynamic that moves from manifest to latent levels of significance (Bion, 1959; Whitaker & Lieberman, 1967). Theories employing a *cyclic* change model view process as a dialectic interchange between apparent polar opposites, a dialectic that eventually returns to its starting point. The characteristics of these different change models are detailed in Banet (1976).

The theory presented here, which views psychotherapy group events from the perspective of a Taoist model of change, attempts to bridge the differences between group development theories utilizing different change models. It describes five sequential movements of group process, movements activated by the distribution of *yin* and *yang* energy forces operating in group members, in the therapist, and in the group as a whole.

Taoism is a simple, but foreign, philosophical system that has much to offer to methods that attempt to facilitate behavior change. Maslow believes that Taoism provides the psychotherapist with a "loving perception" of others, a receptive, noninterfering perception that permits the person to "unfold, to open up, to drop his defenses, to let himself be naked not only physically but psychologically as well" (Maslow, 1971). Taoistic objectivity enables the therapist to care for, but not control, the group member; in addition, it views change as a natural process that happens and flowers with a minimum of interference. A synopsis of Taoism's major constructs is presented here to provide a background for the theory of group process and development that follows.

PHILOSOPHICAL ASPECTS OF TAOISM

We live in a world of continuous change. This observation, that all phenomena are dynamic and in flux, dates back to at least 500 B.C., when Heroclitos in Greece and Confucius in China compared the constant movement of experience to the ever-changing flow of a river.

The dynamism of experience has been met with different responses in Western and Eastern thought. Western thinkers have tended to abstract from experience, "freezing" phenomena so that they can be subjected to scientific investigation. Hence, change tends to be seen in a cause-and-effect, linear mode—a static progression from phase to phase.

In contrast, the Eastern mode has been to acknowledge the flow of experience and to search for the law of change, itself unchanging, that governs this flow. The name given to this governing principle is *Tao*. *Tao* defies definition; in the opening sentence of the *Tao Te Ching* Lao Tzu says, "The *Tao* that can be told is not the real *Tao* and the name that can be named is not the real name." And in another place, Lao Tzu says:

> Before the Heaven and Earth existed there was
> something nebulous: Silent, isolated, standing
> alone, changing not, eternally revolving
> without fail,
> Worthy to be the Mother of All things.
> I do not know its name and address it as Tao.
> If forced to give it a name, I shall call
> it "Great."
> The Great Tao flows everywhere.

Taoist scholar Chung-Yuan (1963) states, "The understanding of *Tao* is an inner experience in which distinction between subject and object vanishes. It is an intuitive, immediate awareness rather than a mediated, inferential or intellectual process."

The *Tao* has been characterized as the One that embraces form and matter, being as well as nonbeing, a unification of duality and multiplicity, a wholeness of parts. *Tao* has no opposite. Unchanging in itself, *Tao* is the background of change. From *Tao* flows *ch'i*, vitality or energy; the energy is characterized as *yin* and *yang*.

In the Taoist view, change is the constant flow of experience that is in accord with *Tao*. Events are in a state of flux, but never in a state of chaos: "Change is more than mere movement. It moves to transfer what was to what is and from what is to what will be. It transfers things to create something new from the old, and to create something old from what is new. The opposite of change is not what is unchanging, but movement in an opposite direction. Change is natural movement but the opposite of change is movement against nature . . ." (Lee, 1974). The seasons, the phases of the moon and tides, and life itself—from birth to death—illustrate the phenomena of change in accord with *Tao*. Many commentaries on *Tao* are available; see, for example, Watts (1975).

Taoism is a metaphysical system that grapples with concepts of universal application, such as being, existence, and change. Despite its abstruseness, from *Tao* and the concepts of *ch'i*, vital life energy in the forms of *yin* and *yang*, have come many practical derivatives: acupuncture, T'ai Chi and other martial arts, centering, calligraphy—all are manifestations of and approaches to *Tao*. The text that describes the interplay of yin/yang forces in everyday life is the ancient oracle and scripture, the *I Ching*.

THE I CHING

The *I Ching*, or Book of Changes, applies the Taoist concept of change to human phenomena—individual lives, groups, and social systems. It proposes a cyclic theory of change, change as a movement that returns to its starting point. Although change is orderly, its orderliness is not always perceptible. In human situations, the forces of change produce complex configurations. As a book of wisdom, the *I Ching* guides its reader to achieve *Tao*, a state of resonance with the Oneness of actuality (Dhiegh, 1974), by discovering the proper time for correct action.

The *I Ching* has as its basis the two fundamental principles of *yin*, characterized as the receptive, the responsive, and the docile, and symbolized by the broken line (- -), and *yang*, characterized as the creative, the powerful, and the active, and symbolized by an unbroken line (—). In sets of three, the broken and unbroken lines compose the *pa kua* (eight trigrams), signs associated with natural phenomena and the basic aspects of human experience.

Combined in all possible ways, the *pa kua* produce sixty-four six-line *kua* (hexagrams) that symbolize various elementary aspects of the human condition: primary needs, such as nourishment; personality-development milestones, such as breakthrough, pushing upward, or retreat; social situations, such as marriage, following, and conflict; and individual character traits, such as modesty, grace, or enthusiasm. The sixty-four hexagrams comprise a psychological "periodic table of elements" from which immediate, here-and-now situations are composed.

The eight trigrams provide descriptions of the basic polarities of life:

1. Ch'ien (≡≡≡), the creative, heaven. Associated with energy, strength, and excitement, it represents the pole of creative power.

2. K'un (≡≡ ≡≡), the receptive, earth, is associated with the womb, nourishment, the great wagon of the earth that carries all life. It represents the pole of yielding, docile responsivity.

3. Chen (≡≡ ≡≡), the arousing, thunder. It is associated with movement, speed, expansion, and anger. In terms of human polarities, the sign represents confrontation.

4. Sun (≡≡≡≡), the gentle, penetrating wind. Associated with gentle persuasion, quiet decision making, and problem solving, this sign represents the pole of support.

5. K'an (≡≡ ≡≡), the abysmal, water. It is associated with toil, hard work, danger, perseverance, and melancholy. It represents the pole of body and feeling.

6. Li (≡≡≡≡), the clinging, fire. It is associated with dependency, but also with conceptual clarity and perception. It represents the pole of intellect and mind.

7. Ken (☶), keeping still, the mountain. Associated with fidelity, meditation, and watchfulness, it represents the pole of reflective silence.

8. Tui (☱), the joyous, lake. This sign is associated with the pleasures of the mouth—eating, talking, singing. It represents the pole of joyful interaction.

The eight trigrams are arranged in a circle of opposing characteristics known as "primal arrangement," or "the mandala of earlier heaven" (see Figure 1). This arrangement, which appears in the earliest *I Ching* texts, graphically illustrates a central concept of the Book of Changes: natural reality is an energy field bounded by pairs of opposite forces that produce tension and movement. Change can be understood as the continuous interplay of the yin and yang forces across the energy field.

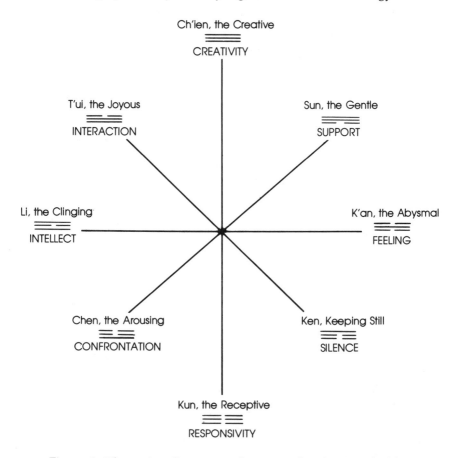

Figure 1. The *pa kua* (hexagrams) arranged as basic polarities, the "primal arrangement," or mandala of earlier heaven.

IMPLICATIONS FOR A THEORY OF GROUP PROCESS

The philosophy of *Tao* and the forces of yin and yang as presented in the *I Ching* have implications for a theory of group process.

The most apparent characteristics of any group are its constant movement and the resistance to this movement by group members. By imposing the *I Ching* concept of movement and change on the group phenomena reported by many group observers, the following process descriptions are generated:

1. The group can be viewed as an energy field demarcated by the basic polarities, as in Figure 1. In each group member, and in the group as a whole, there is tension between the apparent choices of creativity-responsivity, confrontation-support, intellect-feeling, and interaction-silence.

2. Initially, group members attempt to deal with their process by adhering to polar positions. This is an attempt to "freeze" movement, deny change, or place values on the respective polarities.

3. Group process continues as the group develops awareness of its polarized situation. This awareness leads to a struggle to find creative ways to resolve the interplay of yin and yang forces. Paradoxically, this creative struggle develops two new aspects of group life: the appreciation of the now and the potential to transcend the field of apparent opposites.

4. The group process is analogous to a roller-coaster ride (Kahn, et al., 1974). Energy waxes and wanes; it never stops. The process goes up and down; moments of group life are different from one another, but not better or worse, immature or more mature. As Kahn, et al. (1974) suggest: ". . . at any given moment things are as good and important and worth attending to as they are ever going to be. [The model] urges us to attend to the here-and-now because no future here-and-now is going to be any better, just different." Focus on the now (now consciousness) is the dynamic unification of past and future in the present moment (Dheigh, 1974).

5. The group members, by focusing on the now, begin to test out synergistic strategies to deal with the apparent polarities. Synergy is a creative combination of two elements to produce something new or greater than the sum of its parts (the conception of a human being from egg and sperm is the highest form of synergy). In terms of group dynamics, synergy allows the group and its members to free themselves from either/or thinking and to move to a both/and perspective. It is neither compromise nor a golden mean; according to Hampden-Turner (1971), it is "a state of mutual enhancement," an affective and intellectual synthesis. In human relations, the term "synergy" denotes the synthesis of opposites, of group or individual polarities. Sydney Harris

(1972) describes synergy as grasping a paradox and holding it in creative tension, waiting patiently for its evolution into something new.

6. Each group is idiosyncratic. Each group possesses opportunities for growth. Polarities that are critical issues for some groups or group members are nonissues for others. Resolutions or synergy will vary from person to person, from group to group.

The cycle of group process is: (1) a struggle to deny change by clinging to polarities, resolved by (2) appreciation of the now and discovery of the governing principle of change, allowing (3) attempts at synergy to transcend or mutually enhance the apparent polarities, followed by (4) the product of the synergy becoming a new pole, awaiting a new struggle to "freeze" change, thereby completing the cycle. This process is a continuous confrontation of opposites, a dialectic, subtly changing while remaining much the same.

The Taoist concept of change focuses on the individual's cycle of "becoming, begetting and begoning" (Dhiegh, 1974). The human being, seen as the offspring of the creative heaven (*yang*) and the receptive earth (*yin*), is in the center of events: it is the individual's responsibility to know the direction of cosmic change and to move in the direction of change, not against it.

The propositions that follow constitute a theory of group development and provide a synthesis of the important features of several theories. The propositions are based on the author's observations of phenomena in psychotherapy, growth, and task groups, as well as the observations and findings of other investigators of group behavior.

The theory posits a series of continuous confrontations of apparent opposites that occur within group members and within the group as a whole. The dialectic consists of interplay between the forces of yin and yang—energies in opposition with the potential for synergistic fusion. The term "contrapletion," which expresses both the polarity and the capacity of the poles to complete or fulfill each other, can be used to describe the yin/yang relationship. The series of polar confrontations occur within phases or movements, similar to those described by Tuckman (1965) as "forming, storming, norming, performing." These movements repeat themselves, in a spiraling fashion, until some degree of wholeness or integration is reached or until the group artificially terminates or abandons its task.

The ancient Chinese scripture, *The Secret of the Golden Flower* (Wilhelm, 1931), describes a similar, intrapersonal dialectic as an individual moves toward enlightenment. This text details a circular movement in which the union of opposites occurs repeatedly until a higher state of consciousness is reached. The cyclic movement continues until all separate bodily and psychological events are integrated (by transcendence or death) into the oneness of *Tao*.

In this series of movements, the confrontation of polarities occurring within individuals impacts the group as well. The group is not only a theater or an energy field in which individuals struggle to deal with change; it is also an entity in itself that develops and attempts to integrate its energy sources.

The group, as its etymology indicates, is a knot composed of many threads, stronger and more complex than its components.

Basic Premises

1. Change happens naturally. Change is the constant interplay of yin and yang energy and is not the result of frustration, conflict, disequilibrium, or a search for homeostasis; change simply is.

2. The group provides a setting for focused and accelerated change. Groups exist to facilitate, intensify, and enrich the change process.

3. The primary task of any group is to respond creatively to change.

4. The energies of individual members and of the group are distributed as yin and yang forces. (a) *Yin* forces take the form of passivity, docility, receptivity, simplicity. The yin posture of individuals and of groups is one of yielding, accepting, waiting to be acted upon. (b) *Yang* forces take the form of activity, creativity, excitement, firmness. The yang posture of individuals and groups is one of acting, confronting, inviting.

5. Every group presents a unique cluster of yin and yang forces, a composite contributed to by all group members, including the leader.

Propositions Regarding Group Process

The kaleidoscope provides a metaphor for the group process. As yin/yang energies reach interface, they move subtly, delicately, and constantly to form a momentary Gestalt.

These changing arrangements of forces are called *movements;* in each movement the yin and yang forces are specifically manifested as basic polarities. In the first movement, yin and yang appear as an opposition between creativity and responsivity; in the second movement, as a dichotomy between thinking and feeling; in the third movement, as confrontation and support; and in the forth movement as interaction and silence. These basic polarities, illustrated by the mandala of earlier heaven (Figure 1), govern or epitomize the events that occur within a specific movement.

The movements are named for appropriate hexagrams from the *I Ching*. Each movement is described in terms of *process elements, fixation, facilitation, transition,* and *illuminations* from *I Ching* hexagrams. These descriptive categories are defined in the following section.

Process Elements

Process elements refer to events occurring within the group, within individual members, and within the historic context of the individuals in the group.

Group Elements[1]

Group elements are phenomena that occur while the group is meeting. The *interaction system* is the pattern of interpersonal behavior and communication between members; it is *how* interaction happens in the group. It includes how members are addressed, how they cluster or pair off, whether they speak to individual members or to the entire group, etc. The *group emotion* is the feeling tone, the emotional climate: groups may be playful, angry, fearful, hard at work, depressed, excited. The group emotion may be collectively produced or may be the result of the special influence of one or two powerful members. The *normative system* consists of the set of shared ideas about how members should feel, think, and behave. Group norms may be heavily influenced by the psychotherapist, especially if he sanctions certain types of behavior and discourages others. The *group culture* is separate from the set of group norms. It includes preferences and standard operating procedures, such as sitting on the floor, asking permission to go to the bathroom, touching each other, making "inside" jokes: the degree of formality or informality. The *executive system* includes how group leadership is defined and regarded, how or whether leadership functions are shared, members' feelings for (or about) and perceptions of the psychotherapist, his feelings for (or about) and perceptions of members. The group's capacity to develop consciousness of itself, that is, to become its own leader, is also part of the executive system.

Individual Elements

Process events generated by individual group members while they are in the group meeting are member elements. The member's *behavior style* includes his methods of verbal and nonverbal communication, body posture, speech habits; tendencies toward self-disclosure or self-projection,

---

[1]The discussions of group elements, individual elements, and contextual elements are taken from Anthony G. Banet, Jr., "Therapeutic Intervention and the Perception of Process," in J. William Pfeiffer and John E. Jones (Eds.), *The 1974 Annual Handbook for Group Facilitators.* La Jolla, Calif.: University Associates, 1974.

monopolizing or withdrawing, etc. The behavior style may or may not reflect the *personal feeling state*, the *needs, drives,* or *urges* that the member experiences while in the group meeting. There may be considerable variation among individual members in their awareness of body sensations, expectations, comfort level, impluses, wishes, and fears. *Internalized norms* refer to the set of group "shoulds" incorporated by the individual member. For the psychotherapy group member, group norms may conflict with norms gathered from other settings. Norms govern specific behaviors, while *beliefs* and *values* are explicit or implicit definitions of reality (self, the group, outside events) which indicate the ideas or philosophies that the member prizes, prefers, fears, or rejects. The *ego* refers to the member's capabilities for assessing reality, diagnosing his current situation, and altering his style, habits, feelings, and beliefs according to new circumstances. It includes the member's self-concept and self-regard, his strength, intelligence, genetic endowments, defense system, and level of vulnerability.

Contextual Elements

Contextual elements include events that occur among group members when the group is not in session, as well as interactions with persons unrelated to the group. Contextual elements may assume considerable importance in the psychotherapy situation. The "context" is the outside or back-home environment, in which the group member experiences his difficulties and distortions most painfully: it is here that he wants to change his behavior. Because the psychotherapy group meets only periodically, the "back-home" situation of members is an ever-present reality.

   Physical and social contacts refer to interactions with persons (either group members or nonmembers) outside the group setting. *Emotional relations* are the member's feelings about affective relationships with group members or with others outside the group. These include such attitudes as inadequacy and suspicion and ideas of reference. *Contractual relations* are relationships with obligations attached: with spouse, children, parents, employers, or legal authorities, including a member's financial obligations. *Cultural interchange* refers to the member's position in his culture—whether he feels included or alienated; how he feels his membership in the group (i.e., being labeled "sick" or a "patient") is regarded by others outside the group—and the relationship between the culture of the group and the culture of the outside world. Another cultural aspect is the member's inclusion in outside groups (socioeconomic, racial, religious) which may influence his or others' behavior within the psychotherapy group. *Freedom-control relations* represent a member's attitudes toward authority, choice, and responsibility and the influence these perceptions have on his and other members' behavior.

The elements of process are discussed more fully in Banet (1974).

Fixation

Fixation refers to group behavior that attempts to resist the flow of change. A group can retard its development by "movement against nature"—attempting to deny or avoid the change process. Groups may fixate in a given movement and never make the transition to another phase; groups vary in the amount of time it takes to complete each movement.

Facilitation

Facilitation describes the types of therapist interventions that enhance the group's participation in the change process. Primarily, facilitation consists of what Maslow (1971) called "Taoistic listening"—helping the group to hear its own inner voices and to build awareness of the yin/yang energies. Facilitation takes different, specific forms in each of the movements.

Transition

Transition describes the events that conclude a particular movement. In general, when a majority of the group's members have resolved the issues of one movement, the group is ready to make the transition to the next movement. Transition is a group-level event; obviously, not all members of a group achieve synergistic resolution at the same time.

Illuminations from I Ching Hexagrams

The illuminations are excerpts from *I Ching* hexagrams that clarify the dynamics of a particular movement. They are included here for the reader who wishes to discover the *I Ching*'s understanding of group phenomena. The Wilhelm/Baynes translation (1967) is used.[2]

First Movement: Gathering Together

The first movement is governed by the creative/receptive polarity. The psychotherapeutic task—problem resolution, behavior change, growth—is perceived by group members as something external to the group. Yang energy (activity, insight, wisdom, magic) is perceived as residing in the group therapist; the receptive, docile yin force is viewed as within group members. As the group acclimates itself to its setting, there is a clear expectation that the therapist will give and the group will re-

---

[2]*The I Ching or Book of Changes.* Trans. by Richard Wilhelm: rendered into English by Cary F. Baynes. Copyright © 1950 and 1967 by Bollingen Foundation. Reprinted by permission of Princeton University Press.

ceive. The mood of *Gathering Together* is characterized by excitement, waiting, diffused energy, and apprehension.

Process Elements

Group. The group is not yet a visible entity; it is a collection of individual persons plus a leader. Interaction patterns and norms are fragmentary and unformed. Most transactions consist of questions and requests. The predominant group emotion is distrust and a wish for safety and security. There is no group culture as yet and no concept of distributive leadership.

Individual. Group members are preoccupied with concerns of self-identification, comfort, and how they will present themselves to others. There is an immediate awareness of superficial differences among group members, coupled with internal comparisons in many dimensions, e.g., "sickness," sexual attractiveness, age, etc. The prospect of remaining an individual while becoming a member of the group produces confusion and excitement. Inclusion needs are paramount, as are doubts regarding the wisdom of joining the group.

Contextual elements are largely suppressed in the excitement of group formation. Members may make unvoiced comparisons between the immediate situation and previous groups. The confidentiality of group transactions is another unvoiced concern. Members compare the present therapist with authority figures previously encountered.

Fixation

The group will remain in the first movement as long as the perceived yin/yang energy distribution is undisturbed. Irregular attendance or introduction of new group members encourages fixation.

Facilitation

Facilitation of the first movement is enhanced by therapist interventions resulting in clarification of roles and the establishment of trust. As Gibb (1964) and Freidlander (1970) have indicated, trust formation is a prerequisite to all further group accomplishment. Interventions that communicate confidence, leader competence, and the safety of the group initiate a sense of cohesion and involvement in group members. If facilitation is lacking, or if leader proactivity is pronounced, a prolonged fixation of leader/group polarities will occur.

Transition

The movement concludes when all group members indicate at least minimal cooperation with group goals and subscribe to a belief in the distribution of roles and functions among group members and the therapist. There is a relaxation of adherance to polarities, a willingness to stretch and tentatively consider the possibilities of change.

Illuminations from I CHING Hexagrams

1. The Creative: The beginning of all things lies still in the beyond in the form of ideas that have yet to become real. The Creative has power to lend form to these archetypes of ideas . . . the way to success lies in apprehending and giving actuality to the way of the universe (Tao), which, as a flow running through end and beginning, brings about all phenomena in time. Thus each step attained becomes a preparation for the next. . . .

2. The Receptive: The Receptive must be activated and led by the Creative. The Receptive implies action in conformity with the situation . . . since there is a task to be accomplished, we need friends and helpers in the hour of toil and effort. . . .

3. Difficulty at the Beginning: Times of growth are beset with difficulties. They resemble a first birth. But these difficulties arise from the very profusion of all that is struggling to attain form. Everything is in motion: therefore as one perseveres, there is a prospect of great success in spite of existing danger. When it is a man's fate to undertake new beginnings, everything is unformed. Hence he must hold back, because any premature move might bring disaster. It is important not to remain alone; in order to overcome the chaos, the person needs helpers. This is not to say he should look on passively—he must lend his hand and participate with inspiration and guidance . . . the superior man has to arrange and organize the inchoate confusion of such times of beginning, just as one sorts out silk threads from a knotted tangle and binds them into skeins. In order to find one's place in the infinity of being, one must be able to separate and unite.

8. Holding Together: We unite with others, in order that all may complement and aid one another through holding together. This calls for a central figure around whom other persons may unite. To become a center of influence holding people together is a grave matter and [is] fraught with great responsibility. It requires greatness of spirit, consistency, and strength. Therefore let him who wishes to gather others around him ask himself whether he is equal to the undertaking, for anyone attempting the task without a real calling for it only makes [the] confusion worse than if no union at all had taken place . . . But when there is a real rallying point, those who at first are hesitant or uncertain gradually come in of their own accord. Latecomers must suffer the consequences, for in holding together, the question of the right time is important. Relationships are formed and firmly established according to definite inner laws. Common experiences strengthen these ties.

10. Conduct: The situation is really difficult. That which is strongest and that which is weakest are close together. In terms of a human situation, one is handling wild, intractable people. One's purpose will be achieved if one behaves with decorum. Pleasant manners succeed even with irritable people . . . Among mankind there are necessarily differences of elevation; it is impossible to bring about universal equality. But it is important that differences in rank should not be arbitrary and unjust, for if this occurs, envy and class struggle are inevitable.

17. *Following:* In order to obtain a following one must first know how to adapt oneself. If a man would rule he must first learn to serve, for only in this way does he secure from those below him the joyous assent that is necessary if they are to follow him . . . the thought of obtaining a following through adaptation to the demands of the time is a great and significant idea . . . it is implicit in the idea of following and adaptation that if one wants to lead others, one must remain accessible and responsive to the views of those under him . . . once we are ready to listen to the opinions of others, we must not associate exclusively with people who share our views; instead we must mingle freely with all sorts of people, friends or foes. This is the only way to achieve something.

31. *Influence:* All success depends on the effect of mutual attraction . . . this attraction between affinities is a general law of nature . . . through such attraction the sage influences men's hearts, and thus the world attains peace. . . . Every mood of the heart influences us to movement . . . in the life of man, acting on the spur of every caprice is wrong and if continued leads to humiliation . . . a man should not run precipitately after all the persons whom he would like to influence, but must be able to hold back under certain circumstances . . . he should not yield immediately to every whim of those in whose service he stands.

42. *Increase:* When people are devoted to their leaders, undertakings are possible, and even difficult and dangerous enterprises will succeed . . . It is necessary to work and make the best use of time . . .

45. *Gathering Together:* There must be a human leader to serve as the center of the group. In order to bring others together, the leader must first of all be collected within himself . . . People desire to gather around a leader to whom they look up. But they are in a large group, by which they allow themselves to be influenced, so that they waver in their decision. If expression is given to the need for a leader, and if they call for help, one grasp of his hand is enough to turn away distress . . .

48. *The Well:* However men may differ in disposition and education, the foundations of human nature are the same for everyone. And every human being can draw in the course of his education from the inexhaustible wellspring of the divine in man's nature. Two dangers threaten: a man may fail to penetrate to the real roots of his humanity and remain fixed in convention, or he may neglect his own self-development . . . the all-important thing about a well is that its water be drawn. The best water is only a potentiality for refreshment as long as it is not brought up. So too with the leaders of mankind: it is all important that one should drink from the springs of their words and translate them into life.

Second Movement: Standstill

This movement is governed by the thinking/feeling polarity. The awareness of the possibility of change, awakened in the first movement, is countered here by a denial of the possibility and need for change. Group members adhere to one or another polarities, dichotomize their options, and manifest an either/or mentality. Yin/yang polarities are experienced by all group members as splits, compartmentalizations, and a lack of wholeness. A lack of integration between past and present, thinking and feeling, and body and mind is apparent. The feeling level is marked by a clinging dependency, anger, fear, and a resistance to accepting the dangers that work and change involve.

Paradoxically, the group that was called into being to facilitate change becomes the setting for resistance. A series of studies by Myers and Lamm (1975) documents this polarizing impact of early group interaction. After some initial effort to alter previously held positions (symptoms, memories, etc.), group members revert to their previous, pre-group position and fight to maintain it.

This period of resistance is familiar to all therapeutic-group workers. In this second movement, the group regresses and the "basic assumption" group described by Bion (1959) emerges.

Process Element

Group. Members form bonds with each other and against the therapist. Much affect is generated around the therapist; he is alternatively seen as a visionary who demands too much, and as a naive fool who does not live in the real world. There is some attempt to monopolize the yang energy, with the hope that this will render the therapist impotent.

Individual. Group members gain awareness that change involves "letting go" of their past behavior styles. Fearful of the new, they develop feelings of stubborn anger. The prospect of change threatens a whole array of internalized norms, beliefs, and values; group members mistakenly identify their defense structure with their self-concept. The awareness that change involves "letting go" of the past is frightening.

Contextual elements receive the greatest attention during the *Standstill* movement. Focus on contextual elements is a form of flight behavior; as the prospect of change becomes too threatening, the group retreats to the there and then. Attempts are made to depersonalize the therapist and group members, so that the change can be effected on an allegorical, rather than a real level.

Fixation

Standstill can become a long-term movement if the psychotherapist colludes with the flight dynamism of the group by becoming impersonal and distant, thereby encouraging transference reactions. Attribution, projection, scapegoating, and blaming significant others emphasizes a me/not me polarity and avoidance of responsibility. The magnetism of this movement is enormous.

Facilitation

Facilitation of this movement is focused, not on avoiding *Standstill,* but on a constant challenge of either/or thinking. First-person, experiential interventions from the therapist discourage transference. Focus on individual responsibility and teaching the process of letting go promote awareness that the past is not "not me," but a part of the individual's continuum of awareness. Gestalt approaches are particularly helpful in this movement. The therapist must be able to communicate a respect for the past histories of individual members without becoming overwhelmed by the handicaps these histories have generated.

Transition

The movement begins to transition when group members indicate ownership of their polarized position and manifest some willingness to risk letting go of the past. On a group level, there is some excitement about the prospect of future change. It is as though the group is beginning again, this time with a clearer awareness of its task.

Illuminations from I CHING Hexagrams

6. *Conflict:* Conflict develops when one feels himself to be in the right and runs into apprehension. If a man is entangled in a conflict, he must be clearheaded and inwardly strong so that he is always ready to meet the opponent halfway and come to terms. To carry on a conflict to the bitter end has evil effects even when one is right, because enmity is then perpetuated.

12. *Standstill:* Heaven and earth are out of communion and all things are benumbed. What is above has no relation to what is below . . . superior people do not allow themselves to be turned from their principles. If the possibility of exerting influence is closed to them, they nevertheless remain faithful to their principles and withdraw into seclusion . . . the standstill does not last forever. However, it does not cease of its own accord; the right man is needed to end it. The time of disintegration does not change automatically to a condition of peace and prosperity; effort must be put forth to end it.

13. *Fellowship With Men:* True fellowship must be based on a universal concern. It is not the private interests of the individual that create lasting fellowship among men, but rather the goals of humanity . . . there is danger here of formation of a separate faction on the basis of personal and egotistic interests . . . fellowship has changed to mistrust . . . the longer this goes on, the more alienated one becomes.

19. *Approach:* We must work with determination and perseverance to make full use of the time . . . the good begins to prevail and to find response . . . this in turn is an incentive . . . it is well to join the upward trend, but we must not let ourselves be carried away by the current of the time, we must adhere to what is right. . . .

29. *The Abysmal:* If one is sincere when confronted with difficulties, the heart can penetrate the meaning of the situation. And once we have gained inner mastery of a problem, it will come about naturally that the action we take will suceed: in danger, all that counts is really carrying out all that has to be done and going forward, in order not to perish in the danger . . . When we are in danger we ought not to attempt to get out of it immediately; at first we must be content with not being overcome by it.

30. *The Clinging, Fire:* When man recognizes his limitations and makes himself dependent upon the harmonious and beneficient forces of the cosmos, he achieves success . . . By cultivating an attitude of compliance and voluntary dependence, man acquires clarity without sharpness and finds his place in the world.

44. *Coming to Meet:* It is necessary for elements predestined to be joined and mutually dependent to come to meet one another halfway . . . the inferior element is not overcome by violence but is kept under gentle control. Nothing evil is to be feared. . . .

46. *Pushing Upward:* The pushing upward of good elements encounters no obstruction and is therefore accompanied by success. Pushing upward is made possible not by violence but by modesty and adaptability. . . .

49. *Revolution:* Changes ought to be undertaken only when there is nothing else to be done. At first the utmost restraint is necessary . . . when we have tried in every way to bring about reforms, but without success, revolution becomes necessary. The first thing to be considered is our inner attitude toward the new condition that will inevitably come . . . When change is necessary, there are two mistakes to be avoided. One lies in excessive haste and ruthlessness, the other lies in excessive hesitation and conservatism . . . we must be satisfied with the attainable. If we go too far and try to achieve too much, it would lead to misfortune. The object of revolution is the attainment of clarified, secure conditions ensuring a general stabilization on the basis of what is possible at the moment.

Third Movement: Biting Through

Biting Through is governed by the confrontation/support polarity. Yin/yang energy is thoroughly diffused as group members develop greater awareness of the possibilities of change. There is a heightened arousal of intense feeling and a greater need for nourishment. Letting go of polar positions releases power and energy, which is likely to be vaguely directed and potentially explosive. Personal power, choice, authority, competency, and responsibility are major issues. *Biting Through* is marked by the emergence of a both/and attitude and the initial appearance of synergistic fusions.

This period is central in most theories of group development. It is characterized by hard work, pain, trial-and-error behavior, and reports of progress and failure.

Process Elements

Group. Cohesion is marked. Group members assume distributive leadership functions, supporting and confronting one another, relying less on the psychotherapist. Extra-group contacts increase among members. The group assumes the characteristics of a "cultural island"; despite the conflict, the group is perceived as a safe haven from the outside world. Attendance is regular; the next group meeting is eagerly anticipated.

Individual. There is much experimentation with new behavior styles. Feeling states are intense and pendular; highs and lows occur with considerable frequency. Individual beliefs, norms, and values are in flux; the old have departed, the new have not yet arrived. The sense of ego is weakened; identification with the group is strong.

Contextual. Past and future contextual elements have little prominence during *Biting Through.* The current context (life outside the group) becomes a testing ground for experimenting with the new behavior learned in the group sessions.

Fixation

Fixation in *Biting Through* can occur if the insularity of the group becomes preferable to living in the real world. The excitement of dealing with power, competition, anger, and confrontation (for the first time for many group members) can be intoxicating. Fear of such issues as intimacy, love, and affection may prompt members to stay in this movement.

Facilitation

Biting Through is best facilitated by a strong reality orientation in the psychotherapy relationship. Maintenance functions are now shared by many group members, allowing the therapist to closely confront and support the change efforts of group members. The therapist models acceptance of responsibility and power, constructive expression of intense feelings, and strategies of conflict resolution. He prompts group members to awaken their creative powers.

Transition

Transition begins when a majority of group members exhibit a both/and attitude and an increased sense of personal responsibility. Signs of warmth and affection signal that the next movement is about to begin.

Illuminations from I CHING Hexagrams

21. *Biting Through:* When an obstacle to union arises, energetic biting through brings success . . . There are great obstacles to be overcome . . .

The firm yang lines and the yielding yin lines are clearly set apart from one another.

23. Splitting Apart: This is a time when inferior people are pushing forward and are about to crowd out the few remaining strong and superior men . . . it is a time of alternation of increase and decrease, fullness and emptiness. . . .

28. Preponderance of the Great: The ridgepole on which the whole roof rests sags to the breaking point . . . it is an exceptional time and situation . . . it is necessary to find a way of transition as quickly as possible and to take action . . . nothing is to be achieved by forcible measures. The problem must be solved by gentle penetration to the meaning of the situation; then the changeover to other conditions will be successful. It demands real superiority; therefore the time when the great preponderates is a momentous time.

33. Retreat: Conditions are such that the hostile forces favored by the time are advancing, and it is the time for retreat . . . Retreat is not to be confused with flight . . . we must be careful not to miss the right moment while we are in full possession of power and position.

38. Opposition: When people live in opposition and estrangement they cannot carry out a great undertaking in common; their points of view diverge too widely . . . Here success can be expected, because the situation is such that the opposition does not preclude all agreement. Opposition appears as an obstruction, but when it represents polarity within a comprehensive whole, it has its useful and important functions. The oppositions of heaven and earth, man and woman, when reconciled, bring about the creation and reproduction of life . . . the principle of opposites makes possible the differentiation by which order is brought into the world . . . when opposition appears, a man must not try to bring about unity by force . . . as a result of misunderstandings, it has become impossible for people who by nature belong together to meet in the correct way . . . union will resolve the tension, just as falling rain relieves the sultriness preceding a thunderstorm . . . when opposition reaches its climax, it changes over to its antithesis.

39. Obstruction: An individual is confronted by obstacles . . . one must join forces with friends of like mind and put himself under the leadership of a man equal to the situation: then one will succeed in removing the obstacles . . . an obstacle that lasts only for a time is useful for self-development. This is the value of adversity. . . .

41. Decrease: Increase and decrease come in their own time. What matters here is to understand the time . . . anger must be decreased by keeping still, the instincts must be curbed by restriction. By this decrease of the lower powers of the psyche, the higher aspects of the soul are enriched. . . .

51. The Arousing: The fear and trembling engendered by shock come to an individual at first in such a way that he sees himself at a disadvantage . . . in such times of shock, presence of mind is all too easily lost; the individual overlooks all opportunities for action and mutely lets fate take its course. But if he allows the shock of fate to induce movement within his mind, he will overcome these external blows with little effort. . . .

57. *The Gentle:* In human life it is the penetrating clarity of judgment that thwarts all dark human motives . . . penetration produces gradual and inconspicuous effects . . . The ruler's thought should penetrate the soul of the people—this requires a lasting influence brought about by enlightenment and command. Only when this command has been assimilated by the people is action in accordance with it possible.

Fourth Movement: The Taming Power of the Great

This movement is governed by the interaction/keeping-still polarity. There is creative, synergistic resolution of problem situations. Feelings are focused on the enjoyment of the new and the now and the celebration of newly discovered strengths. Reflective, meditative, incorporative silence coexists with playful, productive interaction. Growth and new learning occurs rapidly and with little effort. There is a sense of finishing the task and some awareness that the process of change is continuous.

Yin/yang forces are in balance, with creative energy more prominent. The movement is similar to the affection or work phases described by other theories.

Process Elements

Group. The primary group emotions are feelings of unity, support, and nurturance. A primary group activity is the affirmation of individual members who report and demonstrate new behaviors. The group is accurately perceived for what it is: a temporary stage, a community whose reason for being is declining.

Individual. Individual members experience a sense of newness, perhaps rebirth. Feelings are those of calm, contentment, wholeness. Self-responsibility and the possibility of making free choices produce sober reflections on the future. There is an awareness that the individual is moving in new territory, exploring a revised life with excitement and realistic apprehension.

Contextual. Elements from the past and "back home" context are appropriately woven into the here-and-now process. The immediate future receives considerable attention, and plans for significant life changes are tested out in the group meeting.

Fixation

Fixation occurs when fantasies of union and transcendence become substituted for reality. Perceiving a polarization between the group and the "real world" may result in a reluctance to let go of the benign world of the group. Members may be encouraged to remain in the group long after its purpose (for them) has been achieved.

Facilitation

Facilitation of this movement is largely a matter of not-doing, of letting change flower in individuals and the group. In this movement, the therapist is as role free as he allows himself to be. His final task is to terminate the group; if fixation begins to occur, he will confront the group/real-world polarity.

Transition

Transition of this movement is indicated either by (a) the approach of the termination time, or (b) the slow disintegration of the spirit of *The Taming Power of the Great*. Typically, a group raises new conflicts between polarities and the following *Return* movement quickly dissolves into the situation of the second movement, *Standstill*. One cycle of group development has been completed; the group begins its task again.

Illuminations from I CHING Hexagrams

11. *Peace:* It is a time of social harmony; those in high places show favor to the lowly, and the lowly and inferior, in their turn, are well disposed toward the highly placed. There is an end to all feuds . . . heaven and earth are in contact and combine their influence, producing a time of universal flowering and prosperity. . . .

20. *Contemplation:* Contemplation of the divine meaning underlying the workings of the universe gives to the man who is called upon to influence others the means of producing like effects. . . .

26. *The Taming Power of the Great:* To hold firmly to great creative powers requires daily self-renewal . . . the time of obstruction is past. The energy long dammed up by inhibition forces its way out and achieves great success.

27. *Nourishment:* This is an image of providing nourishment through movement and tranquility. The superior man takes it as a pattern for the nourishment and cultivation of his character.

32. *Duration:* Duration is the self-contained and self-renewing movement of an organized, firmly integrated whole, taking place in accordance with immutable laws and beginning anew at every ending . . . The independence of the superior man is not based on rigidity and immobility of character—he always keeps abreast of the time and changes with it. What endures is the unswerving directive, the inner law of his being, which determines all his actions . . . Whatever endures can be created only gradually by long-continued work and careful reflection.

37. *The Family:* The family is society in embryo; it is the native soil on which performance of moral duty is made easy through natural affection.

40. Deliverance: A time when tensions and complications begin to be eased . . . just as rain relieves atmospheric tension, making all the buds burst open, so a time of deliverance from burdensome pressure has a liberating and stimulating effect on life . . . In keeping with the situation, few words are needed. The hindrance is past, deliverance has come. One recuperates in peace and keeps still.

52. Keeping Still: Past is a state of polarity that always posits movement as its complement . . . True quiet means keeping still when the time has come to keep still, and going forward when the time has come to go forward . . . when a man has become calm, he may turn to the outside world. He no longer sees in it the struggle and tumult of individual beings, and therefore he has that true peace of mind that is needed for understanding the great laws of the universe and for acting in harmony with them.

58. The Joyous: The joyous mood is infectious and therefore brings success . . . Truth and strength must dwell in the heart, while gentleness reveals itself in social intercourse . . . Knowledge should be a refreshing and vitalizing force. It becomes so through stimulating intercourse with congenial friends with whom one holds discussion and practices application of the truths of life.

61. Inner Truth: An echo is awakened in men through spiritual attraction. Whenever a feeling is voiced with truth and frankness, whenever a deed is the clear expression of sentiment, a mysterious and far-reaching influence is exerted. At first it acts on those who are inwardly receptive. But the circle grows larger and larger. The root of all influence lies in one's own inner being: given true and vigorous expression in word and deed, its effect is great.

63. After Completion: The transition from the old to the new time is already accomplished. In principle, everything stands systematized and it is only with regard to details that success is still to be achieved . . . everything proceeds of its own accord, and this can all too easily tempt one to relax . . . after crossing a stream, a man's head can get in the water only if he is so imprudent as to turn back. As long as he goes forward and does not look back, he escapes this danger.

Fifth Movement: Return

The cycle of movement is finished, temporarily. The group either terminates, or is at the point of starting again, on another level of intensity. Members may leave the group, and new members join.

The kaleidoscope is rearranged. If the group continues, the forces of yin/yang move to create a closer resonance with the oneness of *Tao.*

Illuminations from I CHING Hexagrams

24. Return: The old is discarded and the new is introduced. Societies of people sharing the same views are formed . . . the idea of return is based on the course of nature. The movement is cyclic, and the course completes itself . . . everything comes of itself at the appointed time. . . .

34. *The Power of the Great:* An upward movement, in harmony with the movement of heaven . . . true greatness depends on being in harmony with what is right. . . .

64. *Before Completion:* The transition from disorder to order is not yet completed . . . The task is great and full of responsibility. It is nothing less than that of leading the world out of confusion back to order. But it is a task that promises success, because there is a goal that can unite the forces now bending in different directions . . . Before completion, at the dawning of the new time, friends foregather in an atmosphere of mutual trust, and the time of working is passed in conviviality. Since the new era is hard on the threshold, there is no blame in this.

CONCLUSION

Theory serves as a conceptual lens that focuses and sharpens the observer's view of natural phenomena. It alerts the observer to discern events that might otherwise be missed, enables forecasts of future events to be made, and provides a basis for intervention.

The theory of group development described here flows from a Taoist perspective of reality. Its descriptions of group events can be tested against the reader's experience; the theory can then be incorporated or thrown away. Perhaps it will enhance the loving, noninterfering perception a therapist can have of the group with which he works, the perception that Maslow urged all helpers to acquire.

REFERENCES

Banet, A. G., Jr. Therapeutic intervention and the perception of process. In J. W. Pfeiffer and J. E. Jones (Eds.), *The 1974 annual handbook for group facilitators.* La Jolla, Calif.: University Associates, 1974.

Banet, A. G., Jr. Yin/yang: A perspective on theories of group development. In J. W. Pfeiffer and J. E. Jones (Eds.), *The 1976 annual handbook for group facilitators,* La Jolla, Calif.: University Associates, 1976.

Bion, W. R. *Experiences in groups.* New York: Basic Books, 1959.

Chung-Yuan, C. *Creativity and Taoism: A study of Chinese philosophy, art and poetry.* New York: Julian Press, 1963.

Dhiegh, K. A. *I Ching, Taoist book of days, 1975.* Berkeley, Calif.: Shambhala, 1974.

Freidlander, F. The primacy of trust as a facilitator of further group accomplishment. *Journal of Applied Behavioral Science,* 1970, 6, 387-400.

Gibb, J. R. Climate for trust formation. In L. P. Bradford, J. R. Gibb, and K. D. Benne (Eds.), *T-group theory and laboratory method: Innovation in re-education.* New York: John Wiley, 1964.

Harris, S. J. *The authentic person: Dealing with dilemma.* Niles, Ill.: Argus Communications, 1972.

Hampden-Turner, C. *Radical man: The process of psycho-social development.* Cambridge, Mass.: Schenkman, 1970.

Kahn, M., Krocher, T., and Kingsbury, S. The *I Ching* as a model for a personal growth workshop. *Journal of Humanistic Psychology*, 1974, *14*, 39-51.

Lee, J. Y. *Principle of change: Understanding the I Ching*. New York: University Books, 1971.

Maslow, A. *The farther reaches of human nature*. New York: The Viking Press, 1971.

Myers, D. G., and Lamm, H. The polarizing effect of group discussion. *American Scientist*, 1975, *63*, 297-303.

Schutz, W. *Elements of encounter*. Big Sur, Calif.: Joy Press, 1973.

Tuckman, B. W. Developmental sequence in small groups. *Psychological Bulletin*, 1965, *63*, 384-399.

Watts, A. *Tao: The watercourse way*. New York: Pantheon Books, 1975.

Wilhelm, R. (Trans.). *The secret of the golden flower*. New York: Harcourt Brace Jovanovich, 1962.

Wilhelm, R. (Trans.). *The I Ching or book of changes*. (Rendered into English by Cary F. Baynes) (3rd ed.). Princeton, N.J.: Princeton University Press, 1967.

Whitaker, D. S., and Leiberman, M. A., *Psychotherapy through the group process*. New York: Atherton Press, 1967.

Annotated Bibliography: A Guide to the I CHING Literature

The *I Ching* may be the oldest book in the world. Its origins are hidden in Chinese folklore and custom; the mythical emperor Fu-hsi (c. 3000 B.C.) is credited with discovering its underlying principles and symbolizing the concepts of yin and yang as broken and unbroken lines. King Wen (c. 1150 B.C.) is said to have originated the present collection of sixty-four hexagrams, and the commentaries on the individual lines are traditionally ascribed to his son Tan, the Duke of Chou. Additional texts and commentaries, known collectively as the "Ten Wings" were supposedly written by Confucius (c. 460 B.C.), but his authorship is challenged by many scholars.

The *I Ching* was one of the few sacred texts to escape the great book burning of the Emperor Ch'in Shih Huang Ti (c. 213 B.C.). For the next 2000 years, the Book of Changes was a dominant force in Chinese philosophy, literature, and religion.

In the 1700s a Jesuit missionary, Bouvet, introduced the *I Ching* to Western scholars, including Leibniz, who was fascinated by its binary system of mathematics. The first English translation appeared in Shanghai in 1876; James Legge's classic English translation was published in London in 1882.

Richard Wilhelm's German translation was completed in 1924, and was translated into English by Cary Baynes in 1950. The Wilhelm/Baynes translation, with a foreword by Carl Jung, has become widely respected. Together with Herman Hesse's novel, *Magister Ludi*, which sprang from Hesse's study of the *I Ching*, the Wilhelm/Baynes translation has been responsible for the popularization of the ancient book in the contemporary Western world.

The *I Ching* can be viewed as a scripture, as a book of wisdom, as an oracle to be consulted in times of dilemma, or as all of these. Confucius regarded the *I* as the "perfect book"; Emperor Kang H'si, who lived and reigned in accordance with its principles, wrote, "I have never tired of the Book of Changes, and have used it in fortune-telling and as a source of moral principles; the only thing you must not do is to make this book appear simple, for there are meanings here that lie beyond words."

The annotated bibliography that follows is provided for the reader who desires to increase his knowledge of the *I Ching*.

Chuang Tsu. *Inner chapters* (Gia-Fu Feng & Jane English, Trans.). New York: Vintage Books, 1974.
Chuang Tsu developed the doctrines of Taoism. This poetic book expands the basic teachings of Lao Tsu. Beautifully illustrated.

Da Liu. *T'ai Chi Chu'an and I Ching.* New York: Harper & Row, 1972.
A short book of physical exercises and choreography for "mind and body," based on T'ai Chi and selected hexagrams. A good way to wake up in the morning; useful for group work.

Dhiegh, Khigh Alx. *I Ching, Taoist book of days, 1975.* Berkeley: Shambhala, 1974.
This useful volume re-establishes the *I Ching* in one of its earliest formats —as a calendar, with readings for each day. Contains an illuminating essay on the relation of *Tao* to now-consciousness, as well as clear instructions for using the *I* as an oracle.

Dhiegh, Khigh Alx. *The eleventh wing.* Los Angeles: Nash, 1973.
Subtitled "An Exposition of the Dynamics of *I Ching* for Now," this book, by a noted Taoist scholar, provides a catechism and a lucid explanation of underlying principles.

Douglas, Alfred. *How to consult the I Ching, the oracle of change.* New York: G. P. Putnam, 1971.
A simplified guide with some useful definitions. The translation relies heavily on Wilhelm/Baynes, but lacks its grace.

Gardner, Martin. Mathematical games—The *I Ching*. *Scientific American,* January 1974, 108-113.
A sceptical discussion of the mathematical underpinnings of the Book of Changes. Discusses the different sequences and the arrangement of hexagrams.

Gleason, Judith. *A recitation of Ifa, oracle of the Yoruba.* New York: Grossman, 1973.
A fascinating transcription of a Nigerian oracle, handed down through oral tradition. The Ifa uses eight shells to arrive at a variety of signs; provides a useful cross-cultural comparison with the *I Ching*.

Huang, Al Chung-liang. *Embrace tiger, return to mountain.* Moab, Utah: Real People Press, 1973.
A commentary on *Tao*, movement, the *I Ching*, and calligraphy, by a noted T'ai Chi master. He beautifully conveys the simplicity and richness of a life in pursuit of *Tao*, in these transcripts from his T'ai Chi workshops.

Hook, Diana ffarington. *The I Ching and you.* New York: E. P. Dutton, 1973.
Citing Jung's belief that "the meanings of the hexagrams are engraved in the collective unconscious of the human race," the author provides an illuminating discussion of inner, outer, and nuclear hexagrams, as well as descriptions of different methods by which to consult the oracle. Many useful tables and diagrams.

I Ching, the book of change (John Blofeld, Trans.). New York: E. P. Dutton, 1968.
A crisp translation that emphasizes the divinatory aspects of the *I*. Blofeld's introduction is helpful. Combines the text with later commentaries, but lacks the comprehensiveness of Wilhelm/Baynes.

I Ching, book of changes (James Legge, Trans.). New York: Bantam, 1964.
This reprint of Legge's 1882 translation is rather difficult to read. Legge downplays the oracular aspects of the *I* and presents it as a philosophical text. The Bantam edition contains a helpful introduction and study guide by Ch'u Chai.

The I Ching or book of changes (Cary F. Baynes, English trans., from Richard Wilhelm, German trans.) (3rd ed.). Princeton, N.J.: Princeton University Press, 1967.
Without question, the best and most comprehensive translation. Jung's famous foreword discusses the principle of synchronicity and builds appreciation of the oracle. Contains many commentaries and discussions by Wilhelm, whose German romanticism probably makes the *I* more flowery and poetic than it actually is.

Jung, Carl G. The difference between Eastern and Western thinking. On synchronicity. In Joseph Campbell (Ed.), *The portable Jung.* New York: The Viking Press, 1971.
These essays are helpful in approaching the *I Ching* from Jung's perspective. They underscore the intuitive, non-causal stance that is necessary for an understanding of the Book of Changes.

Kahn, Michael, Kroeber, Ted, & Kingsbury, Sherman. The *I Ching* as a model for a personal growth workshop. *Journal of Humanistic Psychology*, 1974, 14, 39-51.
These authors have used the *I Ching* in designing personal growth workshops incorporating meditation, nature study, and group work. Includes a comparison of the "stairstep" model of group process and *Tao*.

Lao Tsu. *Tao te Ching* (Gia-Fu Teng & Jane English, Trans.). New York: Vintage Books, 1972.
A beautiful book. Lao Tsu's work is the principle scripture of *Tao*.

Lee, Jung Young. *Death and beyond in the Eastern perspective*. New York: Gordon and Breach, 1974.
A study of death, afterlife, and reincarnation based on the Tibetan *Book of the Dead* and the *I Ching*. This scholarly discussion is useful for those interested in the religious aspects of the Book of Changes.

Lee, Jung Young. *Principle of change: Understanding the I Ching*. New Hyde Park, N.Y.: University Books, 1971.
The principles underlying change, as depicted in the sixty-four hexagrams, are presented here. A useful, technical discussion of the symbols of *I Ching*, as well as a review of its history.

Merton, Thomas. *The way of Chuang Tzu*. New York: New Directions, 1965.
A poetic synthesis of many translations of Chuang Tzu. Contains a useful introduction on the historical development of Taoism.

Murphy, Joseph. *The secrets of the I Ching*. West Nyack, N.Y.: Parker Publications, 1970.
Murphy attempts to correlate the *I* with passages from the Old and New Testaments. An interesting idea but a spotty book, presenting the Book of Changes as a quickie entrance into the world of fame, riches, and happiness.

Progoff, Ira. *Jung, synchronicity and human destiny*. New York: Julian Press, 1973.
Progoff provides a clear discussion of some difficult concepts. Describes Jung's fondness for the *I Ching* and relates it to other aspects of his psychology.

Siu, R. G. H. *The portable dragon, The Western man's guide to the I Ching*. Cambridge, Mass.: MIT Press, 1968.
To his translation of the Book of Changes, Siu has added excerpts from Western literature to illuminate the hexagrams. A useful compendium of great quotations.

Spence, Jonathan D. *Emperor of China, self-portrait of K'ang-Hsi*. New York: Alfred A. Knopf, 1974.
A rare glimpse into the inner life of the seventeenth-century emperor who loved the Book of Changes. Describes in detail the first contact of Christian missionaries with Chinese culture.

Sung, Z. D. *The symbols of Yi King*. New York: Paragon, 1969.
An unusual book that discusses the *I Ching's* relationship to mathematics, geometry, lunar phases, and the tides. Somewhat obscure, but provides some insights for those who wish to explore such topics.

T'ai Chi Chu'an, A way of centering and I Ching (Gia-fu Teng & H. Wilkerson, Trans.). New York: Macmillan, 1969.
> A gutsy, slangy translation that seems crude and simplistic, but Teng says that's the way it is. An antidote to the poetry of Wilhelm/Baynes.

The secret of the golden flower (Richard Wilhelm, Trans.). New York: Harcourt Brace Jovanovich, 1962.
> A Buddhist classic that incorporates many Taoist principles. Describes a path of individual development and enlightenment. Contains a commentary by Carl G. Jung. The commentaries are very helpful in understanding *I Ching* concepts.

Watts, Alan. *Tao, The watercourse way.* New York: Pantheon Books, 1975.
> Watts's final book and an appropriate summary of his work. Watts emphasizes the nature-base of Tao and the naturalness it encourages.

Wilhelm, Hellmut. *Change: Eight lectures on the I Ching.* Princeton, N.J.: Princeton University Press, 1960.
> An invaluable discussion by Richard Wilhelm's son. Provides a clear understanding of the concept of change and the basic trigrams.

Wilhelm, Hellmut. The concept of time in the book of changes. In Joseph Campbell (Ed.), *Man and time, Papers from the Eranos yearbooks* (3). New York: Bollingen, 1957.
> Helps to understand how "time" as a concept is employed by the *I Ching.* A useful companion to the eight lectures.

Issues

People who offer and receive psychotherapy talk of realizing potential and overcoming obstacles to growth; many people who watch the process and attempt to measure its effects seem unsure whether psychotherapy cures, prevents, or promotes deviance. The social and cultural impact of psychotherapy remains unclear and confused.

Papers in this section discuss the issues that remain unresolved for both traditional and newer psychotherapies: what, if anything, is wrong with people who undergo therapy? What happens in the therapeutic relationship? What is the relationship between psychotherapy and social norms? Does psychotherapy serve society, the patient, or both? What are the values and morals implicit in the psychotherapeutic relationship?

The medical model has been attacked as promoting a myth that mental illness actually exists, a myth that serves the objectives of therapists and not their patients. Beisser discusses the medical model and provides a succinct typology of other helping-relationship paradigms. He warns of the dangers of any one model that becomes a closed system, and reviews the dilemmas that sometimes convert "help" into "training for incapacity" instead. Table 2, based on Beisser's discussion, facilitates the comparison of various models currently used by mental health professionals. The table provides an overview of each model's basic assumptions, goals, strengths, limitations, and the helper role stipulated.

Hurvitz argues that psychotherapy is designed not merely to support the establishment of helpers but also to reinforce the values of a capitalistic society. His view of psychotherapy as a means of social control suggests that not only is psychotherapy not helpful, but that it is actually a harmful process for many.

Table 2. Models of Helping

Types of Models	Evil or Bad Model	Medical Model	Problem-Solving Model
Basic Assumptions	Deviance results from willful "evil" behavior performed by persons who are aware of their motivations and are responsible for their actions.	Deviance results from maladaptive behavior performed by persons who suffer some deficiency— organic, constitutional, psychic, or developmental— that reduces their responsibility.	Deviance results from illogical solutions to personal or situational problems for which persons, although ignorant or unskilled, have some responsibility.
Contemporary Refinement	behavior modification, operant conditioning	psychopharmacology, psychoanalysis	casework, reality therapy, rational-emotive therapy
Goal of Therapy	elimination of undesirable behavior, promotion of desirable behavior	alteration of underlying determinants, prosthesis	scientific thinking, skill building
Strength	clear goals	explanation of behavior	expanded options, reduced confusion
Limitation	justification of cruel behavior	heightened dependency, lessened responsibility	assumption that all "problems" have solutions
Therapist Role	controlling authority	manipulative expert	objective educator

Note. Table is based on A. R. Beisser, "Models of Helping and Training for Incapacity," in this volume.

Crisis Model	Growth or Human Potential Model	Social Issues Model
Deviance results from a combination of temporal, situational, and developmental factors impinging on a responsible person who requires immediate assistance.	Deviance does not exist; all behavior is a celebration of individual uniqueness. Persons make choices and assume responsibility for their behavior.	Deviance results from the behavior of persons victimized by social conditions and cultural institutions that resist change.
crisis intervention	Gestalt, humanistic, experiential therapies	social action, community organization and development
overcoming the crisis and returning to "normal"	self-enhancement, actualization of potential	social change, realignment of social forces
help available when most needed	emphasis on individual responsibility	broad scope and impact, involvement of large groups
no provision for long-term care	denial of deficiencies or limitations	potential infringement of individual rights
supportive parent	facilitative guide	action-oriented planner and advocate

Rachman reviews the evidence to support psychotherapy's claim to be beneficial and finds that the best studies of psychotherapeutic outcome are discouraging, while the inadequate studies are overly optimistic. His view is challenged by Mahrer, who contends that psychotherapy is a multidimensional event for which effectiveness cannot be measured by simple outcome studies.

Few therapists today believe that psychotherapy is value free; Lederer, in his article, indicates his belief that psychotherapy is the proper area in which moral issues may be confronted and resolved.

Models of Helping and Training for Incapacity

by Arnold R. Beisser

I manifest for thee those hundred thousand thousand shapes that clothe my mystery.

Bhagavad Gita

Since the beginning of time men have been appointed by society and chosen to be helpers of others. Helping tasks have gradually been refined and codified into a wide range of service fields. Before professions were delineated, those in helping positions likely made judgments and did their helping *ad hominem*. But increasingly, as professions have become refined, the security of helpers has become based on the model that they employ. The models have changed over the years, first with one in ascendance and then another. But remnants of each major model have been present throughout most of history and continue today.

As the community has become more dispersed and values have become more ambiguous, those in the helping fields have come to cling with greater determination to a single model, often deriving their security from a narrow set of concepts. Tracing the mental health field from the time of Zilboorg's (3) "first Psychiatric Revolution," we see evidence of this all inclusive adherence to a single model, even though in subsequent revolutions more sophisticated and rational models have been proposed. In each case it appears that the new model was embraced so thoroughly that any use of its predecessor was precluded. This paper will describe the models currently available, and the social and professional interferences with their full utilization.

From *American Journal of Orthopsychiatry*, July 1973, 43(4), 586-594. Copyright © 1973, the American Orthopsychiatric Association, Inc. Reproduced by permission of the publisher and the author, Dr. Arnold R. Beisser.

The helping model is a way of conceptualizing what is wrong with the person to be helped, and what needs to be done in order to help him. The model is an explanatory theory of human behavior, and at the same time it implies the necessary control approaches and preventative measures; that is, it contains elements of a normative theory as well. Six such models can be identified that have been employed extensively in the psychiatric, mental health, social welfare, psychological, and other related fields.

THE EVIL OR BAD MODEL

The evil model holds that deviant behavior has been performed by someone who is willfully bad. The doctrine reached its quintescence under Pope Innocent VIII in the Malleus Maleficarum (12) written by the two monks, Sprenger and Kramer. This doctrine explained that evil was the source of deviance, and resulted from willful acceptance of the devil or demons. Treatment measures employed were attempts at exorcism; preventative means were exercised through religious practices. The residue of the evil model is still present, though the doctrine is less dramatic and the source often concealed. In its contemporary guise, it deems some behavior simply unacceptable; of course, some behavior is "bad" for most people and measures are used to control it—it is repressed or suppressed by society, by groups, and ultimately by the individual himself.

Perhaps because of the many abuses in the service of the evil or bad model throughout history, increasingly large segments of the population, especially the sophisticated, eschew it. It is rejected so thoroughly that many people take a neutral stance on various forms of criminal behavior, including killing, by ascribing its origins to either the "sick" or the social issues model. The natural organismic revulsion against such crime is repressed by some adherents of the "sick" or social issues models. (The revulsion returns, however, in distorted form, displaced or projected onto others than the criminal. For example, the police, the people responsible for crime control and protection of society, have become the very symbols of evil to some people. This is not to say that the police may not deserve such criticism under some circumstances, but by projecting all blame on them, individuals or groups who do "bad" things are absolved of the responsibility for them.) Bad behavior continues in spite of a belief commitment to a concept that rejects it. To deny this may make it impossible for one to experience realistically his own or others' behavior.

THE SICK MODEL

In this model the individual is viewed as the helpless victim of physical or chemical influences, or of psychic traumata, that determine his behavior. "He can't help it," and the assumption is made that if he were able to "help it" he would choose not to be sick (1). In recent years, this has been called the "medical model," usually by non-medical professions with pejorative intent. Nevertheless, the model has been employed by all of the helping professions and continues to have preemi- nent importance.

The person who has considered himself or his behavior "bad" or "evil" is often greatly relieved when he thinks of it as "sick." It provides him with an acceptable explanation. Of course, this acceptance is contingent upon an accepting attitude by the helping professional and others with whom he is in contact. The label "sick" often makes behavior comprehensible, and therefore absolves the person of responsibility.

THE PROBLEM-SOLVING MODEL

This is a rational scientific approach to deviance. It assumes that a helper may work with someone in need of help by objectifying the experiential components towards rational solution. Options are considered and alternatives listed, with the best solution finally made. It conceives of deviance as a "problem" and emphasizes the intellect in its solution. It may or may not employ the concept of unconscious determination. It is *the* method of the Industrial Revolution and the Technological Age. It is, first, an approach that implies that what is faced is a problem for which there is a logical solution.

THE CRISIS MODEL

The crisis model (17) asserts that as the individual traverses the epigenetic scheme, he encounters a series of nodal points of tumultuous change. These periods, which are ordinarily time-limited, are considered developmental transition points from one stage of life to another. In addition to developmental points, certain situational events may occur that are not necessarily a part of the epigenetic scheme but may also produce a crisis within the individual. For example, getting married may precipitate a developmental crisis, while an automobile accident with serious injury also changes the balance of life. This is a significant concept to the helper as it defines the periods of appropriate helping and the focus of the personal experience to be dealt with.

THE GROWTH AND HUMAN POTENTIAL MODEL

This model (15) is a reaction against seeing life as evil, sick, a problem, or a crisis. Rather, it seeks to celebrate the uniqueness of the individual in *whatever* he experiences. It views all human behavior in terms of its strengths and advantages. It redefines experiences within other models into a "eupsychian" concept. The helper's task is to provide a forum for self expression and to employ skills that liberate the individual's latent capacities. A person is considered responsible for whatever he does. His behavior is not bad or sick, and he is free to do whatever he chooses so long as he accepts responsibility for his choices.

THE SOCIAL ISSUES MODEL

The responsibility in the social issues model is placed not on the individual, as in the other models, but on society or other people. It assumes that the individual is a helpless victim of social influences. Useful change cannot be made within the person except in reflection of social change. The only change necessary is in the improvement of societal forces that affect people. Individuals are not bad or sick, society is. Individuals don't have problems, society does. Within a mental health context, Michael Tanzer (20) identified illness as the product of a "sick society." R. D. Laing (13) has furthered this concept, and has written that the schizophrenic is simply an epiphenomenon of a contradictory disturbed society, that he sees the duplicity surrounding him more clearly than those who are defended against it. The helper seeks social change by any one of many methods.

Each of the methods used by mental health professionals falls roughly within one of the models described above, although some methods can be extended to include several of them. Of course the highly skilled and experienced practitioner has often been able to transcend the constricting limitations of a single model. He has learned that a person is more than a model or a concept. Nevertheless, contemporary helping methods can be approximately classified in the following way.

Evil or Bad Model

Behavior modification (21) and operant conditioning are contemporary refinements of this model. They provide methods of eliminating undesirable behavior and promoting desirable behavior.

Sick Model

Psychopharmacologic, electrical, surgical, and other physical agents are directed toward altering or removing the somatic cause of an illness. The analytic therapies may operate similarly in the psychological sphere, seeking unconscious causes and determinants.

Problem-Solving Model

Traditional casework and counseling are such rational objective methods. Reality Therapy (9) and Rational Therapy (6) have similar approaches.

Crisis Model

Crisis Therapy.

Human Growth and Potential

Gestalt Therapy (18), Experiential Therapy, Client-centered Therapy (19).

Social Issues

Social action, community organization and development.

Each of the above models has application to work with individuals, families, groups, organizations, and communities. Each is dependent on the conceptual sets used by the helper and those he seeks to help.

WHICH MODEL IS THE APPROPRIATE ONE?

Each of these models has its place. Each is partial, with its meaning in a particular figure/background constellation. The reality is that there sometimes *are* evil acts, *are* people who "can't help it," *are* problems, *are* crises; the individual does have the potential for growth, and there *are* social influences. Taken all together, these models roughly approximate the issues of human deviance and the range of perspectives of the human condition and suffering. Taken individually, however, they are easily applied inappropriately to many situations.

One of the problems in the use of any model, individually and selectively, is that there is an evolutionary refinement of its essential characteristics. Among those who use the model, diagnostic skills improve to include subtle clues so that each model finally becomes all inclusive in the eyes of its proponents. For, if one looks hard enough, he may find some elements of *evil, sickness, problems, crises, growth* or *social influence* in almost any piece of human behavior. Therefore, as an example, in the witch hunts carried out within the procedures of the Malleus Mallificarum, diagnosis was so thorough that no one accused could escape. Under torture, nearly everyone confessed to evil. Those who

296 Creative Psychotherapy

would not confess were assumed to be protected by the devil and to require more stringent torture-diagnostic measures. Only if the accused died in the process of diagnosis was it inferred that he was innocent. Similarly, utilizing the sick model with an eye to finding evidences of psychopathology, no one can escape. The same may be said of each model.

In this sense, each concept contains the seeds of its own demise. For each is a partial model useful only within its own ecological context. To apply a model as an ideology, in all situations, may serve as a security measure for the professional, but inevitably will have procrustean effects on the persons being "helped."

The limitations of each model are apparent in our experience. Let me list some of them:

The Evil Model

The evil model has served as justification for cruel treatment throughout man's history. In order to "help" the evil person, torture, burning, and all sorts of cruel punishment have been utilized.

The Sick Model

The sick model has the potential to allow the person to abdicate responsibility for his behavior, since it assumes "he can't help it." Moreover, the dedicated helper may actually, unwittingly, teach the person he helps how to be helpless, for "how can one be a helper if there is not a person to be helped?" Mowrer (16) has compared the sick and evil models in this respect and has concluded his own preference in the title of his essay, "Sin, the Lesser of Two Evils."

The Problem Model

The problem model, the ultimate in rational objective approaches, is extremely useful in appropriate circumstances. However, there are many life experiences that simply are not problems to be solved in a rational way. Instead, one must learn to accept and live with them. To "go with" the experience has been one of the elements of Eastern philosophy for centuries but alien to the West. Viewing some life experiences as problems to be solved may do little more than to create an insoluble problem.

The Crisis Model

The difficulty with the crisis model is that, like the problem model, there are many life situations that are not crises. Some cities have seen the development of clinics, dedicated to crisis intervention, that will not work with a patient after six visits; after that period of time, the theory says, the crisis should be over. Rigid adherence to this model makes no provision for long-term problems or illnesses that transcend crises.

The Growth Model

When carried to its extreme, the growth model may become a denial of sickness or of a problem. As such, it may serve as a justification for anything or for any act. One may act out any piece of behavior with the justification that he is only "actualizing" himself. This is the basis of some abuses from the human potential movement.

The Social Issues Model

While the growth model may be used to deny social responsibility, the social issues model may allow denial of individual responsibility. It can serve as a justification for infringement on the rights of others. If one conceives of himself as the helpless victim of society's influence, why should he exercise his personal responsibility? If he assaults, robs, or kills someone, he simply projects the responsibility onto society or those "others" who caused him to do it.

Many years ago, John Stuart Mill observed that every concept is correct in what it affirms, but wrong in what it denies or ignores. We can see the verity of this observation in the employment of the above models when they are carried to a reductionist position for all cases. Contemporary society is varied and changing, and produces individualized needs that can be met only by a helper who can flexibly select the appropriate model from the variety available. Despite this, professionals often function as though they were part of a closed system.

CLOSED SYSTEM MODELS IN A PLURALISTIC SOCIETY

In the 1950s a group of studies began to emerge that describe how social institutions unwittingly train people for incapacity. Although designed to be helpful, these institutions established rigid closed systems with firm means of control. Those encased in the system learned roles that were functional only within that closed system. Goffman (10) and Gruenberg (11), in studying mental hospitals, prisons, and similar institutions, observed that in these "helping institutions" the inmates were socialized in a way that allowed them to "get along" within the institution but made them almost completely incapable of effectively caring for themselves in the larger, more complex open system, outside. The role behavior they learned was only effective when complemented by certain kinds of role behavior of the controllers of the organization.

Elsewhere they were lost, and would seek to reestablish these kinds of complementary roles with the people encountered. Leonard Duhl found that many other public facilities, for example public housing, had a tendency to create the same kinds of limitations in role behavior, effective only within a closed system.

While the studies have dealt with the recipients of helping institutions, in one way or another, all contemporary men and women face a similar issue. We have been educated in the family and in schools toward models that are effective in a relatively stable society. It is as though we have been trained to live in a more nearly closed system of the Gemeinschaft community in the preindustrial society. In a stable society, a person could be taught a role that would hold him in good stead throughout life. However, in a changing society, these same roles provide him with discomfort and a set of behaviors that are ineffective in many of the situations faced by contemporary individuals. The anomie and alienation that have characterized our society are, in themselves, reflections of this.

As it has traditionally been done, the training of psychiatrists and other mental health professionals has produced the same kind of limited individual as in the hospital patient or prison inmate—one who is trained to function only within a role restricted closed system (his office or hospital). He draws his security for personal functioning and the leverage for his therapeutic efforts from the rigidity of his structure. Elsewhere in the community or on the street he is helpless or panicked in confrontation with life problems, and if faced there with a helping task he will do his best to return it to the rigidities of the familiar structure.

Even in this era of community mental health, with professionals besieged by even louder voices to work in the community, mental health programs have great difficulty in recruiting professionals willing or able to work in the community. It is even hard to staff well delineated services that are not traditional, such as emergency services, consultation activities, and various after-care functions. Professionals do not feel able, or do not wish to function in these new and pressured settings. Instead these functions are often delegated to the lesser trained, or non-professionals, in the agency, presumably under the supervision of the professionals. But how can professionals supervise a task in which they themselves are not competent?

THE PROFESSIONAL DILEMMA

A professional can hardly be expected to make diagnostic and treatment decisions matching the needs of his client or patient with all available modalities, if his personal security and professional competence are rooted in a single model. For example, if the professional's personal *Weltanschaung* is based on a commitment to the human growth and potential position of self-actualization, he may find it difficult to find common purpose with a patient whose concept of what he wants and needs is the elimination of "bad behavior." Similarly, if a professional's personal commitment is to the "sick" model, ferreting out subtle psychopathological conflicts, his patient's request for facilitation of his need to actualize some aspect of his potential may fall on deaf ears. A professional's theoretical commitments may blind him to alternatives other than his own, for their recognition would produce cognitive dissonance (7), and professional dysfunction inevitably would result.

One may wonder what factors create mental health professionals who cling so tenaciously to a single modality. Although it is popular to speculate about the high level of psychopathology of those in the helping professions, it is not necessary, and perhaps even unjustified, to look here for reasons. The nature of the work—the intense relationships formed with disturbed individuals—would be reason enough. Added to this is the observation that because of high social and geographic mobility, relatively small differences in social classes, and weakly structured nuclear families, American society produces individuals who derive a large part of their personal stability and security from occupations and occupational reference groups. That is, rather than being able to take their bearings and sense of security from other aspects of their lives and build their professional activities upon these, the American professional reverses the process: his personal security is based on his professional role and sense of competence (4).

Repeatedly, studies have shown that a high degree of commitment by a professional to his psychotherapeutic method has potent therapeutic effects. The "true believer" is more likely to have influence over his patient than the detached scientist (8). Yet the detached scientist's position is often the only alternative presented by professional education to the "true believer." Eclecticism has developed a "bad name" in American psychiatry precisely because it has implied an uncommitted professional.

The dilemma may be stated simply. To be an effective therapist, one must believe in his model; yet there is an advantage in utilizing the variety of models available. It is difficult at this time for one to have a strong sense of professional identity without narrowing one's therapeutic commitment to a single methodology.

THE EDUCATIONAL DILEMMA

The problem is not unique to mental health professionals and may in part be traced to the split in American education between cognitive and affective learning. Education has focused on technical skills and cognitive learning. In professional education, the ideal has been to be "objective." The technician whose emotions do not interfere with his professional activity has been the ideal presented. The affective components have been systematically screened from education.

Because in the mental health field it is impossible to screen out the affective and emotional components, educational programs for professionals in these fields have struggled mightily to find means of making it possible for professionals to feel firmly grounded. Personal psychotherapy and psychoanalysis have had their place, sensitivity training has seen its day, supervision has played a central role, and, more recently, the human potential movement has been a factor. All of these and others have been valuable adjuncts in learning to be a mental health professional. Yet the problem has been that each has also required the student to commit himself to the concepts of the helping method. Thus the cure has created its own kind of dysfunction.

It is an erroneous assumption that the means for finding professional identity and security is identical with the means necessary to treat *all* patients, yet this seems to be implied in much of clinical practice. The admission of the affectional components of a professional's experience into the understanding of the therapeutic process was a giant step forward, but to assume that this awareness is congruent with treating the needs of a patient is to carry a good thing too far. For the mental health professional to understand himself and to be aware of his needs is a necessary component of effective therapy; it is not, however, *sufficient* to insure that what he does will be in the interest of the patient.

Recent developments in education have incorporated many of the techniques derived from psychotherapy, psychoanalysis, Gestalt therapy, reality therapy, client-centered therapy, and others. Education utilizing elements of these methods has attempted to resolve the division between cognitive and affective learning and knowledge (5). Curiously, the very fields (psychotherapy and mental health) that have been the source of these new educational methods have been slow in utilizing them in professional education. In large part this has been due to the problem of distinguishing between educational intent and psychotherapy. The confusion has not been helped by those who have declared that such a distinction is irrelevant.

The methods used for educational intent need not acquire a narrow conceptual commitment to a single therapeutic method. Rather they can be used as a means for teaching the would-be professional where and how to look for his own stability, how to be aware of his own needs, and as a means to enhance his sense of identity. With these means, any and all effective treatment technologies can be incorporated into the professional's functioning.

With each technique and with each model the professional has a range of feelings and needs. He must have an opportunity to identify with these as part of the learning of any technique. This would allow him further to develop a central core of personal and professional integrity that is *not* dependent upon a single model. Such opportunities must be made available in pre-service training and in continuing education (2).

THE RESEARCH DILEMMA

Differential research designed to determine the effectiveness of various means in treating individuals with different conditions is technically difficult. But the major drawback to this much needed research is the narrow theoretical commitment of professionals, which causes a lack of interest in carrying out cross-model research. Moreover, since most professionals are proficient in only one or two models, comparative outcomes are confounded by personality factors: either different therapists must be used for each model, or a single therapist with different degrees of commitment to each.

Although selecting the appropriate model for an individual patient is a complicated diagnostic problem, the principal problem seems to lie in the nature of the mental health professional's identity and security. This identity is too often based on commitment to a narrow set of concepts and his security on support from a like-minded reference group.

Within the six models described in this paper there are many technologies presently available. Some of these have been listed. Ideally, these could serve as cognitive scripts to be followed to meet a particular patient's needs under appropriate circumstances. The challenge to professional education is the same as the one to differential research on psychotherapy. Progress in one is likely to result in progress in the other. The time is ripe for these developments.

REFERENCES

1. Beisser, A. 1965. The paradox of public belief and psychotherapy. *Psychotherapy: Theory, Research and Practice.* 2(2).
2. Beisser, A. 1971. Identity formation within groups. *J. Humanistic Psychol.* 2(2).
3. Beisser, A. and Green, R. 1972. *Mental Health Consultation and Education.* National Books Press, Palo Alto, Calif.
4. Bennis, W. and Slater, P. 1968. *The Temporary Society.* Harper & Row, New York.
5. Brown, G. 1971. *Human Teaching for Human Learning.* Viking Press, New York.
6. Ellis, A. and Harper, R. 1961. *Guide to Rational Living.* Wilshire Book Co., North Hollywood, Calif.
7. Festinger, L. 1957. *Theory of Cognitive Dissonance.* Stanford University Press, Stanford, Calif.

8. Frank, J. 1961. *Persuasion and Healing*. Johns Hopkins Press, Baltimore.

9. Glasser, W. 1965. *Reality Therapy*. Harper & Row, New York.

10. Goffman, E. 1962. *Asylums*. Aldine, Chicago.

11. Gruenberg, E. 1967. The social breakdown syndrome: some origins. *Amer. J. Psychiat.* 123:12.

12. Kramer, H. and Sprenger, J. 1969. *Malleus Maleficarum*. (Translated by Montague Summers.) The Hogarth Press, London. (Reprint of edition published 1948, The Pushkin Press, London.)

13. Laing, R. 1967. *Politics of Experience*. Pantheon Books, New York.

14. Leonard, G. 1969. *Education and Ecstacy*. Dell Publishing Co., New York.

15. Maslow, A. 1968. *Toward a Psychology of Being* (2nd ed.). Van Nostrand Reinhold Co., New York.

16. Mower, O. Sin, the lesser of two evils. *Amer. Psychol. 15*:301-304.

17. Parad, H. 1965. *Crisis Intervention: Selected Readings*. Family Service Association of America, New York.

18. Perls, F. et al. 1965. *Gestalt Therapy*. Dell Publishing Co., New York.

19. Rogers, C. 1951. *Client Centered Therapy*. Houghton Mifflin, Boston.

20. Tanzer, M. *The Sick Society*. Holt, Rinehart & Winston, New York.

21. Wolpe, J. 1969. *Practice of Behavior Therapy*. Pergamon Press, Elmsford, N.Y.

Psychotherapy as a Means
of Social Control

by Nathan Hurvitz

Despite considerable evidence that traditional psychodynamic psychotherapy is not helpful and may actually be harmful, psychodynamic psychotherapy persists. The failure of the manifest purpose of such psychotherapy suggests that it has a more important latent purpose, one that is in accord with the values of American capitalist society. It is proposed that this latent purpose is to serve as a means of social control. This control is exercised through the ideological and clinical practice aspects of such psychotherapy, with each aspect reinforcing the other.

Since World War II there has been a growing concern about mental health and a greater acceptance of psychotherapy as a means of treating "mental illness." However, there are serious questions as to whether the many psychotherapists who practice in various settings according to psychoanalytic or psychodynamic theories and concepts play a significant part in alleviating the widespread mental health problem that exists.

There is no agreed-upon, objective evidence based on experimental studies that use appropriate measures and control groups which indicate that any school or method of psychotherapy based on psychodynamic principles, theories, or concepts helps people to overcome disordered, inappropriate, or deviant behavior that is presumed to have a psychological basis any better than any other school or method or any more than their own life experiences (Eysenck, 1960; Frank, 1963; Koegler & Brill, 1967; McPartland & Richart, 1966; Schofield, 1964; Schorer, Lowinger, Sullivan, & Hartlaub, 1968). Testimonials are not evidence—whether they are offered on behalf of psychotherapy, prayer, or voodoo.

Some researchers and therapists, like Mowrer (1959), consider psychodynamic psychotherapy to be "non-therapeutic [p. 161]." Hersch

Reprinted from *Journal of Consulting and Clinical Psychology*, 1973, 40(2), 232-239. Copyright 1973 by the American Psychological Association. Reprinted by permission.

(1968b), who regards psychodynamic theory highly, nevertheless stated that the focus on psychodynamic concepts and the neglect of physical and biological factors "led to the frequent misdiagnosis of children with some degree of brain damage, since dynamic formulations could always be found to encompass the symptomatology [p. 500]." This problem is illustrated by Kysar (1968), who reported that his autistic and retarded child was denied proper medical assistance because of psychodynamic interpretations of the child's disabilities. According to Eberhardy (1967) and Veach (1971), psychodynamic formulations place a tremendous guilt load on and create problems for the parents and especially for the mothers of children who have psychological disorders, and also alienate them from working on behalf of others who have similar problems.

Bergin's (1967) explanation that studies of psychotherapy do not show changes between an experimental and a control group because positive and negative changes cancel each other out may suggest that as much psychotherapy is as valueless or harmful as it is valuable or helpful. The possible harmfulness of psychotherapy for some people may be due to inappropriate behavior which is precipitated by "regression in the service of the ego," by manipulating transference and countertransference experiences, by weakening instead of strengthening moral standards and demands of conscience (Mowrer, 1967), and by destroying relationship that could help clients (Hurvitz, 1967). Freeman (1967), in an effort to explain the high suicide rate of psychiatrists stated that

> The current emphasis upon personal psychoanalysis for . . . the young psychiatrist has dangers that have not been adequately recognized. It is suggested that the insistence upon thorough insight into one's own personality cannot be endured by all who would essay it [p. 155].

The "medical model" on which psychodynamic psychotherapy is based may contribute to the very problems it proposes to "cure" (Szasz, 1960). According to Noyes (1968), many ancient peoples regarded suicide as honorable. Suicide subsequently came to be regarded as a disgrace which is lessened in contemporary times if the suicide is caused by the "illness" of "madness." Noyes concluded that identifying suicide as an illness weakens the suicide taboo and "may paradoxically result in a rise in its incidence [p. 183]." The medical model fosters a mystique about who can perform psychotherapy by setting forth requirements regarding education, supervised clinical training, a personal psychotherapy experience, certification or licensing, etc., that are irrelevant to effective behavior change activities (Brown & Long, 1968; Hurvitz, in press; Spray, 1968; Stachyra, 1969). The "disease ideology" inhibits mental health research (Taber, Quay, Mark, & Nealy, 1969), and it is used to support reactionary policies such as incarceration and neglect of emotionally disturbed poor and the use of public funds to train psychiatrists who enter private practice and leave public institutions without professional help (Albee, 1971).

Desired changes in behavior and attitudes are achieved with people with psychological problems for much less money and in a much shorter time by nonprofessionals such as students (Ellsworth, 1968; Poser, 1966), housewives (Rioch, Elkes, Flint, Usdansky, Newman, & Silber, 1963; Verinis, 1970) and by their participation in voluntary peer self-help psychotherapy groups such as Recovery, Inc., Alcoholics Anonymous, Synanon, etc. (Hurvitz, 1970). Sechrest and Bryan (1968) suggested that the mail-order advice of astrologers who serve as marriage counselors "may actually be a great bargain [p. 34]."

Despite the growing awareness that traditional psychotherapy is no more effective than any other type of therapy, that it may be harmful, that there are serious limitations to the medical model on which it is based, that it is used for reactionary purposes, and that nontraditional and nonprofessional psychotherapy may be more effective in some instances, psychodynamic psychotherapy continues to spread. Thus, the persistence of the theory and practice of psychotherapy is puzzling and disturbing. One explanation states that psychotherapy has achieved "functional autonomy" (Astin, 1961). The present author proposes that psychodynamic psychotherapy, which is in accord with the individualistic and competitive mobility system and the ideology of liberal democracy of American capitalism, has a latent purpose that is more important than its manifest purpose (Merton, 1957); and this latent purpose is to serve as a means of social control (Halleck, 1971; Keniston, 1968; Leifer, 1969; London, 1969; Szasz, 1963). This is accomplished through the ideology and practice of psychotherapy.

THE IDEOLOGY OF PSYCHOTHERAPY

The psychodynamic psychotherapy ideology states that people are "inherently" or "instinctively" aggressive and hostile, that "unconscious" biological or instinctual forces are the causes of individual behavior, and determine interpersonal relations, social interaction, and social forms. This ideology regards inappropriate behavior or emotional disorder as the "acting out" of putative "unconscious conflicts" associated with concepts such as the "Oedipus complex," "infantile sexuality," "death instinct," and others. Psychotherapy is thus based on and fosters an ideology that accepts the status quo and its institutions, and it proposes that changing individuals is the way to change the society. According to Simon (1970), the psychodynamic "way of conceptualizing various problems represents an avoidance of their social sources, and the large rewards to psychologists represents an attempt to divert attention from more basic sources of difficulties [p. 338]." The psychodynamic ideology makes personal problems of political issues (Horowitz, 1968; Mills, 1963).

The most serious aspect of the social control function of psychotherapy is the belief of some political scientists, social philosophers, legal pundits, literary critics, motivation researchers, and other intellectual opinion makers who identify with the existing order that psychodynamic theories and concepts offer a meaningful way to understand and change individual and group behavior and social institutions. This perspective permeates the culture and is an aspect of the world taken for granted (Berger, 1965; Riessman & Miller, 1964). Psychodynamic theories and concepts have also entered the middle- and low-brow culture of the movies, television, popular songs, comics, etc., and affect the lives of people who do not understand the function of the psychotherapy enterprise.

The psychotherapy ideology identifies success with personal worth and failure with one's own inherent limitations (Davis, 1938). This ideology contributes to the belief that the failure of the poor is their own fault (Hersch, 1968a), aggravating their problems. Psychotherapists tend to treat middle- and upper-class members who are dissatisfied with their place and achievement within the social system, but not with the system itself (Rangell, 1968). They enable their clients to live in the problem-causing society and to use socially approved means to achieve their own and society's goals. They foster their clients' belief that they can live fulfilling lives without making basic social changes.

Associated with the ideology of success and personal worth is the concept of adjustment in psychotherapy. Goldman and Mendelsohn (1969), reported that adjustment "seems to be the main emphasis [p. 171]" in psychotherapy. A diagnosis of maladjustment or mental illness, according to Tedeschi and O'Donovan (1971), "constitutes control of information consistent with general societal norms about what kind of social relationships and behavior are appropriate and normal [p. 61]." The adjustment concept can thereby be used to legitimatize "the prevailing normative system." Goffman (1961) stated that "inappropriate behavior is typically behavior that someone does not like and finds extremely troublesome [p. 363]. . . ." Therefore, the diagnosis of mental illness or maladjustment is a political decision "in the sense of expressing the special interests of some particular faction or person rather than the interests that can be said to be above the concerns of any particular grouping [p. 364]. . . ." The psychotherapy ideology is used by the legal system to justify the doctrine of Parens Patriae, the state in the role of parents, and force upon a resisting defendant what it regards as the kind of adjustment that is in his own best interests, based on the value system of those in power (Stone, 1971).

The psychotherapist and the psychodynamically oriented social philosopher maintain the status quo by proposing that the feminist movement is based on an ideology that is the "expression of emotional sickness, or neurosis . . . [and] was at its core a deep illness [Lundberg & Farnham, 1947, p. 143]." The current students' movements, according to a psychoanalytically oriented social philosopher, are largely dominated by unconscious drives and the will to revolt against the deauthoritized father (Feuer, 1969), and his interpretation agrees with that of many others identified with the psychodynamic viewpoint.

Political and other opponents are deprecated and their ideologies dismissed by psychodynamic interpretations of their motives. When an individual commits a bombing or assassination that is "senseless" or "crazy" according to our prevailing normative system, the psychodynamic psychotherapists explain that his behavior is caused by unconscious, irrational motives, as exemplified by the newspaper headline (Smith, 1969): "Sirhan Saw Kennedy as 'Replica' of His Hated Father, Expert Says [p. II 1]"—and not by another ideology. Sociologists explain movements for social change on the basis of the emotional instability of their participants; and they propose that "Most of the extremely violent diatribes against government, against business, against the church, and so on, are the products of neurotic, paranoid or otherwise maladjusted personalities [Horton & Leslie, 1970, p. 54]." McLean (1967) divides critics of pesticides into two types, purposeful and compulsive. The purposeful, according to McLean, include those who gain some personal profit from their criticism; and the compulsives, McLean said, were described by Freud as "neurotics, driven by primitive, subconscious fears to the point that they see more reality in what they imagine than in fact [p. 616]."

The psychodynamic ideology fosters and gives credence to the value of idealist, spiritualist, and occult concepts in psychotherapy (Ansell, 1966; Eisenbud, 1970; Nelson, 1969). Some therapists espouse esoteric Eastern religions that encourage withdrawal and resignation, others encourage self-understanding through astrology, others profess a belief in reincarnation and discuss the part played by a client's experiences in a previous life in his present problems, and still others seek the "significance of suffering" in a mishmash of psychology and theology.

The psychodynamic ideology uses psychological constructs to explain anti-Semitism in terms of the Oedipal drama wherein the Christians' sons must destroy the Jews' fathers (Van den Haag, 1969) and by the denial of sociohistoric-economic factors as pointed out by Neff (1948). This ideology also leads to confusion about American blacks, white racism, and black militants. Although Grier and Cobbs (1969) presented a sociohistorical analysis of "black rage" in America, their allegiance to psychodynamic concepts leads them into confusion about the sources of this rage (Collins, 1968), how it will cause change, and to the disparagement of black militants who are the vanguard change a-gents. In accord with the slogan "A good therapist helps a man change his inner life so that he can more effectively change his outer world, [Grier & Cobbs, 1969, p. 151]" [sic] are more concerned with uncon-scious motivations. Thus, they do not attempt to analyze class dynamics in American capitalist society and its effect on race relations or to de-velop an action program against racism.

Psychotherapy serves as a means of social control because it is based on and fosters an ideology that accepts the status quo and proposes that changing individuals will improve the society. This ideology, which is fostered by intellectuals who identify with the existing order, permeates the common culture and lives of people who do not understand the nature of our society, and fosters a "false consciousness" among them; it protects the status quo against those who would change it; it psychologizes, personalizes, and depoliticalizes social issues; it iden-tifies success with personal worth; it fosters a concept of adjustment which often implies submission; it is used in ad hominem arguments to disparage others; it gives credence to idealist, spiritualist, and occult concepts that deny a scientific basis for theories and practices for solving problems and changing behavior and society; and it leads to misunder-standing the position, aspirations, and ways of changing the conditions of oppressed ethnic and racial groups in America.

THE PRACTICE OF PSYCHOTHERAPY

The ideology of psychotherapy is demonstrated in its practice. This prac-tice fosters the individual's self-involvement and personalizes his per-spective. The analysis of his "unconscious conflicts" by investigating his dreams, slips of the tongue, etc., trains the individual in continuing introspection and in the interpretation of people, processes, and events in methods associated with investigation of the unconscious and away from concern with the social causes of self-defeating behavior, depres-sion, etc., since it is known that clients tend to assume the values of their therapists (Rosenthal, 1955).

Most clients of psychotherapists are women (Chesler, 1971). They seek psychotherapy because of depression, various psychosomatic ail-ments, feelings of aimlessness and lifelessness, and frigidity—among other complaints and problems. Psychodynamic psychology with con-cepts such as "Electra complex," "penis envy," "vaginal orgasm," etc., has fostered a view of women as appendages to men, as less developed human beings, and as "natural" or "instinctive" mothers and homemakers, fostering conditions and attitudes that create problems for many women. Psychotherapy thus presumes to help these women overcome their problems by inducing them to accept the very conditions that give rise to their complaints (Chesler, 1971; Friedan, 1963). Psychotherapists who regard sexual competence as the sine qua non of the effective adult may exploit women clients by being sexually intimate with them (Masters & Johnson, 1970; McCartney, 1966; Shepard, 1971).

Bruno Bettelheim, who is identified with the psychodynamic approach which states that militant students are dominated by unconscious drives and the will to revolt against the deauthoritized father, is quoted (Lerner, 1969) as saying that student activists at the University of Chicago are "very very sick [and] need not action by the police but psychiatric care [p. II 9]." Bettelheim makes this charge despite the finding of a study by Joseph Katz of the Institute for Study of Human Problems at Stanford University that student activists tend to be psychologically "healthy" (Leo, 1967). When students are labeled sick, they are belittled, their principles and the movement in which they participate to effect social change is disparaged, and they are denied the ability to function on their own behalf. They must therefore participate in some kind of psychotherapeutic program to be made "well."

Similar labeling is applied to welfare recipients who may be required to submit to a psychological and/or psychiatric evaluation or endure a "rehabilitation program" as a condition of receiving public welfare; and private welfare agencies may require their clients to participate in a psychotherapeutic (casework) experience in order to receive financial aid (Cloward & Piven, 1967).

Political activists and militants who are labeled sick and in need of psychiatric care are compared with mental hospital patients (Anonymous, 1968). This anonymous writer stated that the erratic and lawless behavior of participants in riots, peace marches, protest marches, sit-ins, and other similar activities need to be studied just as patients are studied in order to help them. "In this regard the soundly-organized, treatment-oriented hospital . . . [p. 237]" offers lessons on how to temper, rechannel, or control behavior. In addition to the anonymous writer who proposes to treat political activists like mental hospital patients, Bellak (1970) proposes a program of prevention of emotional disturbance such as that expressed in political activism "by large scale and often legally controlled measures [p. 3]," in which a "jury of psychologists, psychiatrists, and social workers would determine each case [p. 3]."

The therapist's function to modify the deviant in accord with the requirements of the "well" society in hospitals, clinics, offices, etc., may require him to lie (Halleck, 1963) and to serve as a "double agent." Although the therapist's primary responsibility is to the society, the patient believes that the therapist functions on his behalf, thus serving as a double agent, as Szasz (1967) has pointed out in relation to the college psychiatrist. Szasz's position has been challenged by Seeley (1968); however, it is reported by Daniels (1969) and by Levy (1970), who stated there is "a contradiction of serious consequences between the psychiatrist's benevolent aspirations and the real role required of him by prison authorities [p. 6]." This role is defended by Lerner (1968), who stated, in relation to the psychiatrist in the armed forces, that "no amount of rationalization or sophistry can justify serving the best interests of the individual to the direct and clear-cut detriment of the organization or of society [p. 96]."

The requirement that draft resisters, student rebels, black militants, political extremists, draft-eligible young men, delinquents, criminals, welfare recipients, social agency clients, and others who are dependent on the community, such as the senile elderly and unemployable alcoholic—or who otherwise disturb or offend those who hold middle-class values (Davis, 1938; Gursslin, Hunt, & Roach, 1960)—must participate in a psychotherapy program as a condition of receiving something else: a draft deferment (Isay, 1969), lighter sentence, freedom, eligibility for assistance, financial aid, etc., means that they may be labeled mentally ill. Such a label may have continuing damaging consequences throughout the individual's life despite efforts to educate people to the fact that there is nothing shameful about mental illness because it is an illness just like any other illness (Sarbin & Mancuso, 1970). Szasz (1961) stated that mental illness is a convenient term of derogation, denigration, or thinly veiled attack, and "even psychoanalysts have been unable to resist adopting this usage [p. 59]." Szasz (1963) also pointed out that such a label may result in the denial of civil rights.

Psychotherapists have created a community mental health movement and have established programs, facilities, and activities designed to quiet restive neighborhoods (Harper, 1969; Piercy, 1969; Zegans, Schwartz, & Dumas, 1969). Leifer (1969) characterized this movement as follows:

> Described in nonmedical terms, community psychiatry is a quasi-political collectivist movement that, by means of social interventions supported by state-sanctioned social power, attempts to palliate personal troubles, to foster the orderly and productive functioning of individuals in their communities and organizations, to alleviate certain disturbances of domestic tranquility, to organize and integrate community action programs, to implement the dominant social ideology . . . [p. 240].

This movement accepts the society which established it and by enabling the society to maintain itself, perpetuates the problems it was planned to abolish (Statman, 1970). An illustration of Leifer's (1969) most damaging charges was reported in a *Los Angeles Times* article which stated that a mental health center will be built in the black ghetto with $3.7 million from state, federal, and private sources. The medical director of the projected center is reported as saying that the "center will help people live in their surroundings 'of continual crisis' [Jones, 1968, p. II 1]," an objective that institutionalizes present evils.

The community mental health program, facilities, and activities are used to co-opt indigenous community leadership to assist professionals to preserve the social structure. Billington, Munns, and Geis (1969) reported that a former narcotics addict in a community treatment program for present addicts complained that the project was inculcating a mood of passivity and complacency among Mexican-American clients instead of serving "the group's need for political awareness and restiveness [p. 462]." Richards (1968) reported that clients who participated in a mental health movement changed their allegiance from their fellow members of the community to the professionals whose values they assume.

The practice of psychotherapy personalizes the client's perspective and fosters an individualistic instead of a social effort to change the causes of the clients' psychological problems. Aspects of psychodynamic theory with regard to women create their problems; and the practices based on these theories exacerbate their problems. Psychodynamic concepts are used to label political activists, welfare clients, deviants, and others who do not conform with middle-class values as mentally ill. On the basis of such a label, clients are required to submit to incarceration in a mental hospital and/or to a program of psychotherapy to cure them. The mental illness label has many damaging consequences. The therapist may serve as a double agent to fulfill his role. The community mental health movement that psychotherapists have established accepts the society of which it is a part, it is designed to quiet restive neighborhoods, it offers individual solutions to social problems, and it co-opts indigenous community leadership into maintaining the status quo.

CONCLUSION

The persistence of psychotherapy that does not succeed in fulfilling its manifest purpose suggests that it may have a more important latent purpose. This latent purpose is to serve as a means of social control. This purpose is achieved in two ways—by the ideology of psychotherapy and by its practice. Each aspect of the ideology and practice reinforces the other aspects; and ideology and practice reinforce each other. In this way, psychotherapy creates powerful support for the established order—it challenges, labels, manipulates, rejects, or co-opts those who attempt to change the society. It may be suggested that every society uses the means of control available to it—the mass media, educational institutions, police, courts, etc., including theories and practices of psychotherapy which are in accord with the prevailing value system of the society.

REFERENCES

Albee, G. W. In reply. *Professional Psychology*, 1971, *2*, 142-144.

Anonymous. Dealing with irresponsible acting-out behavior in these United States. *Journal of Psychiatric Nursing and Mental Health Services*, 1968, *6*, 237-238.

Ansell, C. The unconscious: Agency of the occult. *Psychoanalytic Review*, 1966, *53*, 164-172.

Astin, A. A. The functional autonomy of psychotherapy. *American Psychologist*, 1961, *16*, 75-78.

Bellak, L. Enforced prevention, treatment of emotional ills recommended. *Roche Report: Frontiers of Clinical Psychiatry*, 1970, *7*, 3.

Berger, P. L. Toward a sociological understanding of psychoanalysis. *Social Research*, 1965, *32*, 26-41.

Bergin, A. E. Further comments on psychotherapy issues. In D. Arbuckle (Ed.), *Counseling and psychotherapy: An overview*. New York: McGraw-Hill, 1967.

Billington, B., Munns, J. G., & Geis, G. Purchase of conformity: Ex-narcotic addicts among the bourgeoisie. *Social Problems*, 1969, *16*, 456-463.

Brown, B. S., & Long, S. E. Psychology and community mental health: The medical muddle. *American Psychologist*, 1968, *23*, 335-341.

Chesler, P. Women as psychiatric and psychotherapeutic patients. *Journal of Marriage and the Family*, 1971, *33*, 746-759.

Cloward, R., & Piven, F. F. The weapon of poverty: Birth of a recipients' militant movement. *The Nation*, 1967, *204*, 582-588.

Collins, C. W. Review of W. H. Grier & P. M. Cobbs', *Black rage*. *Shalom*, 1968, *17*, 14-15.

Daniels, A. K. The captive professional: Bureaucratic limitations in the practice of military psychiatry. *Journal of Health and Social Behavior*, 1969, *10*, 255-265.

Davis, K. Mental hygiene and the class structure. *Psychiatry*, 1938, *1*, 55-65.

Eberhardy, F. The view from the couch. *Journal of Child Psychology and Psychiatry*, 1967, *8*, 257-263.

Eisenbud, J. *Studies in the psychoanalysis of psi-conditioned behavior*. New York: Grune & Stratton, 1970.

Ellsworth, R. B. *Nonprofessionals in psychiatric rehabilitation*. New York: Appleton-Century-Crofts, 1968.

Eysenck, H. J. The effects of psychotherapy. In H. J. Eysenck (Ed.), *Handbook of abnormal psychology*. New York: Basic Books, 1960.

Feuer, L. S. *The conflict of generations: The character and significance of student movements*. New York: Basic Books, 1969.

Frank, J. D. *Persuasion and healing*. New York: Schocken, 1963.

Freeman, W. Psychiatrists who kill themselves: A study in suicide. *American Journal of Psychiatry*, 1967, *124*, 846-847.

Friedan, B. *The feminine mystique*. New York: Norton, 1963.

Goffman, E. *Asylums*. Garden City, N.Y.: Anchor Books, 1961.

Goldman, R. K., & Mendelsohn, G. A. Psychotherapeutic change and social adjustment: A report of a national survey of psychotherapists. *Journal of Abnormal Psychology,* 1969, *74,* 164-172.

Grier, W. H., & Cobbs, P. M. *Black rage.* New York: Bantam Books, 1969.

Gursslin, O. R., Hunt, R. G., & Roach, J. L. Social class and the mental health movement. *Social Problems,* 1960, *7,* 210-218.

Halleck, S. L. The impact of professional dishonesty on behavior of disturbed adolescents. *Social Work,* 1963, *8,* 48-56.

Halleck, S. L. *The politics of therapy.* New York: Science House, 1971.

Harper, T. S. The Lincoln hospital protest: Community mental health leadership as the agent of ghetto imperialism. *Something Else.* 1969, *2,* 10-11.

Hersch, C. Child guidance services to the poor. *Journal of the American Academy of Child Psychiatry,* 1968, *7,* 223-241. (a)

Hersch, C. The discontent explosion in mental health. *American Psychologist,* 1968, *23,* 497-506. (b)

Horowitz, I. L. *Professing sociology.* Chicago: Aldine, 1968.

Horton, P. B., & Leslie, G. R. *The sociology of social problems.* (4th ed.) New York: Appleton-Century-Crofts, 1970.

Hurvitz, N. Marital problems following psychotherapy with one spouse. *Journal of Consulting Psychology,* 1967, *31,* 38-47.

Hurvitz, N. Peer self-help psychotherapy groups and their implications for psychotherapy. *Psychotherapy: Theory, Research and Practice,* 1970, *7,* 41-49.

Hurvitz, N. Peer self-help psychotherapy groups: Psychotherapy without psychotherapists. In H. M. Trice & P. M. Roman (Eds.), *Therapeutic sociology.* Science House, in press.

Isay, R. A. The draft age adolescent in treatment. *Psychiatric Quarterly,* 1969, *43,* 203-210.

Jones, J. "Mental health center planned at Wrigley Field." *Los Angeles Times,* September 10, 1968, p. II 1.

Keniston, K. How community mental health stamped out the riots (1968-1978). *Trans-action,* 1968, *5,* 21-29.

Koegler, R. R., & Brill, N. Q. *Treatment of psychiatric outpatients.* New York: Appleton-Century-Crofts, 1967.

Kysar, J. E. The two camps in child psychiatry: A report from a psychiatrist-father of an autistic and retarded child. *American Journal of Psychiatry,* 1968, *125,* 103-109.

Leifer, R. *In the name of mental health.* New York: Science House, 1969.

Leo, J. "Studies agree that most campus activists are comparatively intelligent, stable and unprejudiced." *New York Times,* June 19, 1967, p. L29.

Lerner, J. The psychiatrist's dilemma. *Journal of American Geriatric Society,* 1968, *16,* 94-98.

Lerner, M. "The militants overreach." *Los Angeles Times,* February 7, 1969, p. II 9.

Levy, H. Prison psychiatrists: The new custodians. *Health PAC Bulletin,* 1970, *3,* 6-11.

London, P. *Behavior control.* New York: Harper & Row, 1969.

Lundberg, F., & Farnham, M. F. *Modern woman, the lost sex.* New York: Harper, 1947.

Masters, W. H., & Johnson, V. E. *Human sexual inadequacy.* Boston: Little, Brown, 1970.

McCartney, J. Overt transference. *Journal of Sex Research,* 1966, *2,* 227-237.

McLean, L. A. Pesticides and the environment. *BioScience,* 1967, *17,* 613-617.

McPartland, T. S., & Richart, R. H. Social and clinical outcomes of psychiatric treatment. *Archives of General Psychiatry*, 1966, *14*, 179-184.

Merton, R. K. *Social theory and social structure.* Glencoe, Ill.: Free Press, 1957.

Mills, C. W. *Power, politics and people: The collected essays of C. Wright Mills.* New York: Ballantine, 1963.

Mowrer, O. H. *The crisis in psychiatry and religion.* New York: Van Nostrand, 1959.

Mower, O. H. Communication, conscience and the unconscious. *Journal of Communication Disorders*, 1967, *1*, 109-135.

Neff, W. S. Psychoanalysis and anti-Semitism. *Jewish Life*, 1948, *2*, 7-11

Nelson, M. C. Contributions on parapsychology: Introduction. *The Psychoanalytic Review*, 1969, *56*, 3-8.

Noyes, R., Jr. The taboo of suicide. *Psychiatry*, 1968, *31*, 173-183.

Piercy, M. The Grand Coolie dam. *Leviathan*, 1969, *1*, 16-22.

Poser, E. G. The effect of therapists' training on group therapeutic outcome. *Journal of Consulting Psychology*, 1966, *30*, 283-289.

Rangell, L. Broadcast 7934-U.E. 2047. University of California, Berkeley, October 20, 1968.

Richards, H. Rehabilitation and role innovations—To bridge the paper gap. Paper presented at the annual meeting of the American Orthopsychiatric Association, Chicago, March 1968.

Riessman, R., & Miller, S. M. Social change versus the "psychiatric world view." *American Journal of Orthopsychiatry*, 1964, *34*, 29-38.

Rioch, M. J., Elkes, C., Flint, A. A., Usdansky, B. S., Newman, R. G., & Silber, E. National Institute of Mental Health pilot study in training mental health counselors. *American Journal of Orthopsychiatry*, 1963, *33*, 678-689.

Rosenthal, D. Changes in some moral values following psychotherapy. *Journal of Consulting Psychology*, 1955, *19*, 431-436.

Sarbin, T. R., & Mancuso, J. C. Failure of a moral enterprise: Attitudes of the public toward mental illness. *Journal of Consulting and Clinical Psychology*, 1970, *35*, 159-173.

Schofield, W. *Psychotherapy, the purchase of friendship.* Englewood Cliffs, N.J.: Prentice-Hall, 1964.

Schorer, C. E., Lowinger, P., Sullivan, T., & Hartlaub, G. H. Improvement without treatment. *Diseases of the Nervous System*, 1968, *29*, 100-104.

Sechrest, L., & Bryan, J. H. Astrologers as useful marriage counselors. *Trans-action*, 1968, *6*, 34-36.

Seeley, J. R. In defense of the college psychiatrist. *Trans-action*, 1968, *5*, 47-50.

Shepard, M. *The love treatment: Sexual intimacy between patients and psychotherapists.* New York: Wyden, 1971.

Simon, L. J. The political unconscious of psychology: Clinical psychology and social change. *Professional Psychology*, 1970, *1*, 331-341.

Smith, D. "Sirhan saw Kennedy as 'Replica' of his hated father, expert says." *The Los Angeles Times*, March 13, 1969, p. II 1.

Spray, S. L. Mental health professions and the division of labor in a metropolitan community. *Psychiatry*, 1968, *31*, 51-60.

Stachyra, M. Nurses, psychotherapy, and the law. *Perspectives in Psychiatric Care*, 1969, *7*, 200-213.

Statman, J. Community mental health as a pacification program. *Radical Therapist*, 1970, *1*, 14-15.

Stone, A. A. Psychiatry and the law. *Psychiatric Annals*, 1971, *1*, 19-43.

Szasz, T. S. The myth of mental illness. *American Psychologist*, 1960, *15*, 113-118.

Szasz, T. S. The uses of naming and the origin of the myth of mental illness. *American Psychologist*, 1961, *16*, 59-65.

Szasz, T. S. *Liberty, law and psychiatry.* New York: Macmillan, 1963.

Szasz, T. S. The psychiatrist as double agent. *Transaction*, 1967, *4*, 16-24.

Taber, M., Quay, H. C., Mark, H., & Nealy, V. Disease ideology and mental health research. *Social Problems*, 1969, *16*, 349-357.

Tedeschi, J. T., & O'Donovan, D. Social power and the psychologist. *Professional Psychology*, 1971, *2*, 59-64.

Van Den Haag, E. *The Jewish mystique.* New York: Stein & Day, 1969.

Veach, F. H. California foundation makes gains for mentally ill. *Schizophrenia*, 1971, *5*, 1.

Verinis, J. S. Therapeutic effectiveness of untrained volunteers with chronic patients. *Journal of Consulting and Clinical Psychology*, 1970, *34*, 152-155.

Zegans, L., Schwartz, M., & Dumas, R. A mental health center's response to racial crisis in an urban high school. *Psychiatry*, 1969, *32*, 252-264.

The Effects of Psychotherapy

by Stanley Rachman

With few exceptions, psychologists appear to have accepted the need for satisfactory evidence to support the claim that psychotherapy is beneficial. Most writers also appear to accept the view that in the absence of suitable control groups, investigations cannot provide a conclusive result. Working within these terms of reference, several writers (Cross, 1964; Dittmann, 1966; Kellner, 1967; Bergin, 1970) have concerned themselves primarily with the evidence emerging from studies incorporating control groups. In most instances it is concluded that there is now modest evidence to support the claim that psychotherapy produces satisfactory results. It is, however, a little dispiriting to find that with successive reports, the claims appear to become increasingly modest.

Although there is a continuing theme in these discussions on the outcome of psychotherapy, the writers concerned are by no means in agreement. Discussing the earlier reviews, Bergin says "Cross (1964), for example, reviewed 9 control studies and determined that 6 were favourable to therapy, whereas our own review of the same reports yielded only 1 that approximated adequacy and even that one is subject to criticism (Rogers and Dymond, 1954). Dittmann (1966) added 5 more studies to Cross's group, considered 4 of them to be positive evidence, and concluded that 10 out of 14 controlled outcome studies were favourable to psychotherapy. Actually, only 2 of the studies indicate that psychotherapy had any effect and neither of them would be generally acceptable as evidence. Thus, these authors claim *strong* support for the average cross-section of therapy, whereas I would argue for a more modest conclusion." While I agree with Bergin's assessment of these reviews, it should in fairness be pointed out that both Cross and Dittmann were more tentative and cautious than Bergin allows. For example,

Reprinted from *The Effects of Psychotherapy* (Chapter 5), by Stanley Rachman. Oxford; New York: Pergamon Press, 1971.

Cross mentions that some important "cautions must be kept in mind." The work referred to in his review consisted of "quite brief or superficial" treatment, the measurement techniques were "of questionable or unproven validity," and for some of the studies "the method of control itself is questionable." For these reasons he specifically urges caution: "even though the reviewed studies are the most careful which have been done, various limitations prescribe any strong conclusions" (p. 416). It should also be remembered that 4 of the largest and best-designed studies produced *negative* results—Teuber and Powers (1953); Barron and Leary (1955); Fairweather and Simon (1963); Imber *et al.* (1957). In regard to the last-mentioned study, Cross placed a more optimistic interpretation on the data than did the authors themselves. As will be shown below, the authors made no claims for psychotherapy, and their findings were sometimes contradictory, often fluctuating and, finally, inconclusive. Cross himself points out that the Rogers and Dymond study uses a questionable method of control, and this investigation is also discussed below.

Bergin's rejection of the conclusion reached by Dittmann is understandable. Even Dittmann, however, has his reservations: "My impression is that studies of the outcome of psychotherapy have finally allowed us to draw conclusions on other bases than intuition, but the conclusions, themselves, are modest, and are, moreover, diluted by confusion." All the same, he felt that 1966 was "a year of bumper crop in outcome studies." Dittmann claims that 4 out of the 5 control studies described by him were favourable to the position that psychotherapy is effective. Two of these studies can be dismissed immediately. The first is the study by O'Connor *et al.* (1964). It deals with 57 patients with colitis who also received psychiatric treatment. Their 57 so-called control subjects, like the treated ones, received medical and even surgical treatment during the course of the study. Moreover, the treated patients were said to have psychiatric problems while only a minority of the controls were so described. A second study quoted by Dittmann used as the criterion for improvement after psychotherapy a measurement of "time perspective" as interpreted on the basis of TAT stories (Ricks *et al.*, 1964). The study by Seeman and Edwards (1954) involved very small numbers of children and, in any event, on one of the major outcome criteria (teacher ratings) no differences emerged. The report by May and Tuma (1965) showed that patients given drugs improved more than those who did not receive drugs; it produced no evidence that psychotherapy was effective. The study by Ashcraft and Fitts (1964) cannot be assessed satisfactorily because they used an unpublished test as their criterion of outcome. As Dittmann allows, "the results are complicated because of the many subscores of the test and the methods of analysis, but clearly favour the treatment group."

As measurements of the self-concept feature prominently in out-come studies and the notion of changes in self-concept is also a central feature of non-directive therapy, it seems desirable to examine the idea and its measurement in detail. Such an examination may also be thought of as being instructive insofar as the assessment of assessment is concerned.

SELF-CONCEPTS

Wylie (1961) has neatly summarized the predictions which flow from theories of self-concept psychotherapy. It is to be expected that success-ful therapy will produce various changes in self-concept, such as the fol-lowing: "increased agreement between self-estimates and objective es-timates of the self . . . increased congruence between self and ideal-self, if this congruence is very low at the outset of therapy . . . slightly de-creased self-ideal congruence if this congruence is unwarrantedly high at the outset of therapy . . . increased consistency among various as-pects of the self-concept" (p. 161).

Wylie mentions, among other difficulties, many of the problems in-volved in attempts to relate changes in self-concept to psychotherapy. Two of the major problems are the possibility of mutual contamination between measures of improvement and measures of self-concept (p. 165) and the serious problems of scaling. (For example, "neither can one say that equal numerical changes involving different scale ranges are psychologically comparable" [p. 166].) Like Wylie, Crowne and Stephens (1961) draw attention to the large variety of tests which have been evolved to measure self-regard, self-acceptance, and the like. They comment unfavourably on the assumption that these tests are equiva-lent "despite their independent derivation and despite the relative lack of empirical demonstration that there is a high degree of common vari-ance among them" (p. 107). They point out that there is a serious absence of information on both the reliability and validity of these tests. For exam-ple, "criterion validation of self-acceptance tests is, of course, logically impossible . . . face validity, however, has apparently been assumed without question (and this) implies adherence to a further assumption . . . that of the validity of self-reports. In terms of these assumptions, a self-acceptance test is valid if it looks like a self-acceptance test and is similar to other tests and what a person says about himself self-evaluatively is accepted as a valid indication of how he 'really' feels about himself" (p. 106). Another major difficulty with these tests is the often dubious assumption that the items chosen represent a fair sample of the possible parameters. They argue that it is "of importance to draw one's sample of test items in such a way as represent their occurrence in the population." Although they are not entirely consistent on this subject, writers generally assume that the self-reports given by subjects are valid. Crowne and Stephens draw attention to reports of extremely high correlations between self-concept rating scales and social desirability scales. In one study, for example, the correlations between Q-sort and social desirability score were found to be 0.82, 0.81 and 0.66. Social desirability correlated 0.82 with the ideal-self rating scale score and 0.59 with the ideal-self Q-sort. In a study conducted on students, correlations of 0.84 and 0.87 were found between items on a Q-sort and a social desirability scale. In a psychiatric sample the correlation was found to be 0.67. Another study quoted by them produced what is probably a record correlation of 0.96 (between social desirability and an ideal-self score). They conclude quite firmly that "failure to control for social desirability in the self-acceptance assessment operations would make the results, no matter what the outcome, uninterpretable in terms of self-acceptance" (p. 116). They even go so far as to suggest that in the absence of suitable controls, the tests in question "may better be interpreted as a measure of social desirability than of self-acceptance."

In all, Crowne and Stephens were unimpressed. "The failures of self-acceptance research can be traced, at least in a large part, to neglect of several crucial psychometric and methodological principles: the unsupported assumption of equivalence of assessment procedures, the absence of any clear construct level definition of the variable, failure to construct tests in accord with principles of representative sampling, and questions concerning the social desirability factor in self-report tests" (p. 119). Although not as harsh in their judgements, Lowe (1961) and Wittenborn (1961) are also critical of self-concept procedures.

Moving from a consideration of the general status of self-concept research, we may now examine its specific application in the assessment of abnormal behaviour and the effect of psychotherapy. We strike an immediate difficulty in attempting to define the relationship between the self-concept and adjustment. Although there is fairly good agreement that low self-regard is related to maladjustment, high self-regard may indicate one of *three* things. It may be a sign of good adjustment or of denial of problems or, yet again, of "unsophisticated conventionality" (Wylie, 1961). For example, Crowne and Stephens mention a study by Bills in which subjects with high self-acceptance scores were found to be more maladjusted than low scorers. Summarizing a good deal of the literature, Wylie concluded that "there is much overlap between groups" (i.e., neurotics, non-psychiatric patients, normals). Comparisons between psychotics and normals have been contradictory with at least "3 investigators reporting no significant difference between psychotic and normal controls" (p. 216). Considering the range from normal through various types of abnormality, she concludes that "a clear linear downward trend in self-regard is *not* found" (p. 216). In 4 studies, in fact, a curvilinear relationship between self-regard and severity of maladjustment was observed. An important aspect of this research was the finding that subjects who were judged to be the best adjusted in various studies had high self-regard, "but their self-regard was not necessarily significantly better than that of the most poorly adjusted subjects." Wylie concluded that "we can see that the level of self-regard is far from being a valid indicator [of] degree of pathology" (p. 217).

Although therapeutic claims on behalf of psychotherapy have sometimes been made on the basis of changes in self-concept scores, the omission of control groups is a crucial deficiency. In addition to the general inadequacies of the self-concept notion and its measurement (some of which have been enumerated above), it is necessary to draw attention to one further limitation. Dymond (1955) observed that a small group of 6 subjects who showed spontaneous remission and decided not to undertake therapy after being on a waiting list "appeared to have improved in adjustment, as measured from their self-description, about as much as those who went through therapy successfully" (p. 106). Their Q scores increased from 33 to 47.3 (significant at the 2% level). A comparison group of 6 apparently successfully treated patients (although there are some confounding variables here) showed changes from 34.8 to 48.3. The two groups were "not initially differentiable in terms of adjustment status at the beginning of the study." Instead of drawing what would appear to be the obvious conclusion, however, Dymond states that "no deep reorganisation appears to take place" (in the untreated patients). "The 'improvement' appears to be characterized by a strengthening of neurotic defences and a denial of the need for help" (p. 106). If Dymond's attempted explanation is correct, then presumably one would be entitled to conclude that a similar process occurs when the self-concept changes after psychotherapy. That is, can psychotherapy also be "characterized by a strengthening of neurotic defences"?

Further evidence that significant changes in self-concept occur without psychotherapy was provided by Taylor (1955). He found that subjects who were required to do self and self-ideal reports repeatedly showed the changes usually attributed to psychotherapy. The subjects showed an increase in the correlation between the descriptions of self and self-ideal, increased consistency of self-concept, and an increase in positive attitudes towards the self. Although these improvements are said by Taylor to be smaller in magnitude than those reported for cases of psychotherapy, this is doubtful. The comparisons which he made are between his experimental group of 15 subjects and 3 single case reports of disturbed patients. Either way his conclusion is consistent with Dymond's and interesting in itself: "significant increases in positiveness of self-concept, and in positive relationship between the self and self-ideal, may be valid indexes of improvement wrought by therapy, but increased consistency of self-concept is achieved so readily by self-description without counselling that it would seem a dubious criterion, especially when self-inventories or Q-sorts are used in conjunction with therapy."

Writers on the subject have expressed the following views. "When such tests are used in further research as if they had been carefully and adequately constructed, little can ensue but error and confusion. And such seems to be the case in self-acceptance research. Perhaps it is true that these tests are not yet used commonly in clinical settings where their inadequacies could lead to disservice to the client . . ." (Crowne and Stephens, 1961). Lowe (1961) cautiously concluded that "there is, in short, no complete assurance that the cognitive self-acceptance as measured by the Q-sort is related to the deeper level of self-integration that client-centred therapy seeks to achieve" (p. 331). Concluding her analysis of 29 research studies, Wylie (1961) said: "of course nothing can be concluded from these studies concerning the role of therapy in causing the reported changes" (p. 182).

Kellner (1967) has argued that the case for the effectiveness of psychotherapy is a sound one, and supports his conclusion by a reasonably detailed consideration of several studies. Many other studies are mentioned in passing and will not be taken up here. Here I will confine myself to those studies (other than with children or by counselling) on which Kellner bases the main force of his argument, but will not take up his discussion of those studies in which psychotherapy failed to produce results more satisfactory than the improvements observed in controls. It should be mentioned, however, that Kellner's attempts to explain the negative results which have frequently been reported are less than satisfactory. In his discussion of the Barron–Leary study, for example, he suggests that the untreated patients were probably less disturbed than their treated counterparts—despite evidence to the contrary contained in the study itself. On the other hand, his reservations about the use of various outcome criteria appear to be well grounded. He notes, for example, that MMPI scores are generally inappropriate and that "self-acceptance, if used as the only measure, is at present an inadequate criterion of improvement" (p. 345). He also notes a number of studies in which this type of assessment has failed to pick up therapeutic changes.

Kellner attaches significance to the 2 studies reported by Ends and Page (1957, 1959) in which they assessed the effects of various types of psychotherapy on hospitalized male alcoholics. As I feel that these studies fail to support the notion that psychotherapy is effective, it is necessary to consider them with care. Kellner describes the first of these studies in some detail and points out that 63 patients (out of an original group of 96) completed the programme: each of 4 therapists had 15 sessions with 4 different groups of patients. The methods of therapy were client-centred, psychoanalytic derivation, learning theory (an inappropriate designation), and, lastly, a social discussion group which served as control. In addition to the specific therapy, all patients participated in other presumably therapeutic activities during their stay in hospital. These included AA meetings, lectures, physical treatments, and so on. The outcome of therapy was evaluated by changes occurring in the self-ideal correlation. As Kellner points out, the MMPI which was used initially was discontinued, and the evaluation of therapy depended almost entirely on Q-sort analysis. He states that "1½ years after discharge from hospital the degree of improvement was judged by independent raters" (p. 345). He goes on to say that the "ratings 1½ years after discharge showed a significant improvement in the 2 groups which had shown changes in the Q-sort." On the Q-sort analysis itself there were greater "reductions in the discrepancy between self and ideal in the client-centred group and in the psychoanalytic group." The second study (Ends and Page, 1959) is referred to briefly, and Kellner points out that although the self-ideal correlation again "discriminated significantly between treated patients and untreated controls," only the paranoia scale of the MMPI discriminated significantly. As Kellner regards MMPI scores as an unsatisfactory measure of outcome (and in any event these scores failed to show therapeutic changes) we will confine ourselves largely to a consideration of the other two measures, i.e. Q-sort analyses and follow-up ratings.

The Q-sort analyses are fairly complex and will be discussed at some length below. The follow-up data which appeared to have influenced Kellner's judgement of these studies are scanty and can be discussed fairly briefly. Ends and Page claim that the follow-up data show significant success for the psychotherapy groups but point out that the "results are by no means unequivocal" (p. 275). We might add that they are by no means clearly described. Although it is implied that follow-ups were carried out on 3 occasions, the results are all presented in a single table so that it is impossible to sort out the patients' progress at various stages. To make matters worse, it is not at all clear how the follow-ups were conducted or the data analysed. They say: "follow-up data from county welfare officers, from the hospital's own follow-up clinic, and from hospital admission records were analysed. The initial follow-up was made 6 months after discharge by county welfare officers using a standard interview form. The 1-year and 1½-year follow-ups were made through the hospital follow-up clinic and hospital admission records" (p. 275). The results are presented in 5 categories but unfortunately the categories deal with different types of data and different time periods. For example, a rating of "greatly improved" was given when there was no evidence of further alcoholic episodes during the 1½-year period. The rating of "possibly improved" was given when there was evidence of one or two brief episodes within the *first 3 months* following discharge and, "as far as could be determined no evidence of a reversion to the former pattern during the follow-up period." They define recidivism as "readmission to *the same* hospital for alcoholism" (our emphasis). It is in no way made clear that the patients were actually interviewed; in the context of the discussion it seems unlikely, but one cannot be sure. Secondly, it would appear that the follow-ups at the 1-year and 1½-year periods were carried out by examining the information which happened to be present in the hospital's clinic and records. On the basis of their criterion for recidivism, it seems quite possible that their 1-year and 1½-year follow-ups did not include the full sample—but only those patients who made contact with the hospital after discharge. If this is the case, the most that one can conclude is that patients who had undergone psychotherapy did not return to the same hospital and *not* that they were necessarily improved or abstinent. In view of their description of the composition of the category "possibly improved" there appears to be no certainty that the patients did not resume drinking after 3 months. As Kellner puts it, "fewer patients from the client-centred group had been readmitted to the hospital." His description of the follow-up procedure may, however, be slightly misleading. We cannot be sure that "the degree of improvement was judged by independent raters" at 1½ years "after discharge from hospital."

In dealing with the first study, we feel that Kellner might have drawn attention to the extremely high defection rate—no fewer than 33 of the original 96 patients failed to complete the programme, i.e. a 30% loss rate. It is not stated whether the defections were more common in one or other of the groups, not whether the defectors were comparable in initial status to the patients who completed the programme. Kellner might also have noticed that although Ends and Page excluded the MMPI data from their first study because "preliminary analysis revealed that physical and psychological treatment effects were confounded in the MMPI profiles," scores from the same test *were included* in the second study. The authors' inclusion of the MMPI data in the later study is doubly puzzling in view of their stated reason for excluding it, i.e. physical and psychological treatment effects were confounded. It is nowhere explained how they reached this conclusion or how they were able to decide that the Q-sort analysis "held such confounding to a minimum." In any event, they appear to have changed their minds in the second study.

Their Q-sort analyses are atypical and sometimes difficult to follow. Certainly their justification for using some of the analyses is doubtful.

324 *Creative Psychotherapy*

They carried out a large number of comparisons between different variations of the self and ideal-self correlations and found a number of significant "movement indexes." The client-centered group show 2 significant changes, the analytic group 3 significant changes, the learning theory group 2 significant changes and 2 negatives, and the controls 1 negative. A conclusion drawn from the comparisons is that the patients who received psychotherapy showed significant improvements, the control subjects showed little change and the "learning therapy" patients deteriorated slightly.

This conclusion appeared to be supported in their second study when they compared 28 patients who received twice as much client-centered therapy (i.e. 30 sessions) and 28 control patients who were simply assessed at the termination of the 6-week therapy period. In this comparison, however, the control patients were found to show some degree of improvement although not as large as the treated patients. One curious factor to notice here is that this second control group showed statistically significant improvements on 5 of the 8 comparisons, whereas the control group in the earlier study showed only 1 positive change and 1 negative change. The improvements observed in this second control group are, however, explained by Ends and Page as having been "gained minimally in self-acceptance only by a defensive manoeuvre that appears to be unstable at the outset" (p. 12). The matter is made even more intriguing by comparing the control patients in the second study with the treated patients of the first study. The treated patients showed significant improvement on only 4 of the indexes. The major surprises, however, occur when the authors compare the patients who had 30 sessions of therapy with an additional control group of 28 patients who were simply re-tested after a 2-week wait period. "In general, figure 6 reveals that the control group made greater gains on 5 of the indexes than did the therapy group" (p. 23). Apparently these improvements represent "a defensive reaction" otherwise known as a "flight into health." This interpretation, we are told, is "supported by a wealth of clinical observation," and a "flight into health" is distinguished from "truly integrated therapeutic change." The difference in improvement scores between the treated and untreated groups is explained by the claim that group therapy "retards the flight into health" (p. 27). This flight into health apparently occurs "as a defence against self-examination and criticism" and on average occurs between the tenth and fifteenth therapy sessions. However, "this phenomenon seems to occur with or without therapy" (p. 24). We might note, incidentally, that if it occurs between the tenth and fifteenth therapy sessions the successful results obtained in the first study (in which 15 treatment sessions were given) appear to be fortunate.

On the MMPI results (considered in the first study to be confounding) the treated and untreated patients were found to produce significantly different results on only 2 of the 13 comparisons. The treated group showed significantly greater decreases in the paranoia scale, and the untreated patients showed significantly greater decreases in the Hy scale. We are also informed in the *second* study that the patients who received 15 treatment sessions, i.e. those in the first study, "demonstrated no significant change from pre- to post on any of the MMPI scales" (p. 14). Moreover, only one significant difference on the MMPI scales was observed between those patients who received 15 and those who received 30 treatment sessions. This is explained by Ends and Page on the grounds that the pre-treatment scores "suggest that the [first treated] group were somewhat healthier to start with as far as scale elevation is concerned. One would, therefore, expect less change on the MMPI scales simply because this group needed to move less, and, indeed, had less room in which to move since they began closer to the normal means for the scale" (p. 14). However, the same comment could be made about the untreated patients as they also show consistently lower MMPI scores than the patients who received 30 treatment sessions. We may even extend the argument to the analysis of the Q-sort data as the control group had a z score of 0.406 prior to treatment while the treated group had a score of 0.303.

Almost all of the conclusions reached by Ends and Page are doubtful. Conclusion number 6 is particularly misleading. They state that "the flight into health phenomenon occurs in those not participating in group psychotherapy. Following the inevitable collapse, those not receiving group therapy show no indications of reintegration in a therapeutic sense but instead recover by re-erecting a structure only superficially different from the initial one" (p. 29). As the so-called flight into health phenomenon (i.e. improved self-acceptance) was most clearly observed in the group which was re-tested after two weeks, it is hard to see how they can speak of an "inevitable collapse." This control group was *not* re-tested after the second week. It is not possible to say whether or not they "collapsed" or whether they "re-erected superficial structures" or showed no indication of "re-integration." On the contrary, when last tested they were showing considerable improvement.

It can be seen, then, that the studies by Ends and Page have serious shortcomings. The defection rate is extremely high and contains possible biasing factors. The selection of outcome measures, Q-sorts, and MMPI scores is unfortunate. The follow-up data are scanty and confounded. The Q-sort and MMPI scores suggest quite different conclusions. One of the untreated control groups shows considerable improvement after a

2-week wait period—greater than that seen in treated patients. Their exclusion of MMPI data from the first study is inconsistent. Their explanation of improvement in the untreated controls is unconvincing and, even if accepted, could be applied with equal significance to the improvements observed in some of the treated patients. As a great deal of time and effort was put into these studies it is a pity that the authors did not pay more attention to the accumulation of "hard" information such as status at follow-up determined by direct interview and by external informants. The total absence of follow-up data in the second study is particularly unfortunate. Overall, this research is devalued by implausible special pleading.

The study by Shlien *et al.* (1962) is frequently quoted as evidence in support of the effectiveness of psychotherapy. They compared the effects of unlimited client-centred therapy with time-limited client-centred therapy and time-limited Adlerian therapy. They included, in addition, 2 control groups. One control group consisted of normal people and can be dismissed as irrelevant. The other control group consisted of patients who requested therapy but did not recieve it. These untreated controls were re-tested after 3 *months.* The sole criterion of therapeutic effectiveness was a self-ideal Q-sort.

The authors claimed to have demonstrated the effectiveness of psychotherapy and drew attention to the effectiveness of time-limited therapy. Apart from weaknesses in the experimental design, the authors reported their results in brief form and, regrettably, omitted vital details. For example, *all* of their results are presented as averages (mean or median?) and these are shown in the form of a graph. No actual figures are provided. It is nowhere stated what sort of patients they were dealing with. They do not indicate why the untreated group remained untreated. Nor do they state whether the allocation of patients to the treatment or no-treatment conditions was random—in the context of the report, it seems highly unlikely.

In regard to the experimental design used, one of the control groups is irrelevant. The other control group comprised untreated patients who may or may not have been re-tested at the follow-up period 12 months later. In any event they appear to have carried out the Q-sort on only 2 occasions as compared with 4 occasions for each of the treated groups. The sole criterion on which the effects of therapy are based is the Q-sort—generally agreed to be inadequate (e.g. Kellner, 1967). We are provided with no information about the psychiatric status of the patients either before or after treatment, nor are we told anything about their actual behaviour. In regard to the results themselves, the treatment groups appear to have shown substantial increases in self-ideal correlations. The untreated control group, on the other hand, shows a surprisingly unchanging course. Prior to treatment the self-ideal correlation for this group is precisely zero, and at the end of the 3-month waiting period it is still precisely zero. In the graph containing the results of the study they appear to be precisely zero at the 12-month follow-up period as well —but this may be misleading because it is by no means certain that they were re-tested at the follow-up occasion. In any event this remarkable stability is somewhat unusual. Ends and Page, for example, found that their 2-week waiting control patients showed an increase in self-ideal correlation of 0.25, i.e. they improved from 0.35 to 0.60 on re-test after 2 weeks. As mentioned earlier, other workers have found similar "spontaneous" changes in this type of correlation. In sum, the Shlien study will do as an exploratory investigation, but as evidence in support of the effectiveness of psychotherapy it is unconvincing.

Although Kellner's appraisal of the evidence appears to be over-optimistic, some of his comments on the problems of research into psychotherapy are well taken. In particular, he argues the case for increased specificity in a persuasive manner. Certainly, the treatment of a mixed bag of patients with a mixed bag of techniques is unlikely to further our understanding of the nature and possible effects of psychotherapy.

PHIPPS CLINIC STUDY

The by now well-known study of the effects of psychotherapy on psychiatric out-patients carried out at the Phipps Clinic has celebrated its tenth birthday, and the status of 34 of the original group of patients at the 10-year follow-up period had now been described by Imber *et al.* (1968). The patients were originally assigned at random to 1 of 3 forms of treatment: "individual psychotherapy, in which a patient was seen privately for 1 hour for once a week: group therapy, in which groups of 5–7 patients were seen for 1½ hours once a week: and minimal contact therapy, in which the patient was seen individually for not more than one half hour once every 2 weeks" (p. 71). The treatment was carried out by second-year psychiatric residents who took no part in the evaluations of their patients. These evaluations took place at the end of 6 months of treatment and again 1, 2, 3, 5, and 10 years from the time of the initial treatment contact. A variety of assessments was carried out and the two main criteria were personal discomfort and social effectiveness. Significant improvements were observed in all 3 groups but some fluctuations occurred during the 10-year period, particularly among those patients who had minimal treatment. The main changes occurred within the first 2 years after treatment outset and, with some exceptions, tended to hold up at the 10-year follow-up period. As the authors remark, "it does seem somewhat improbable that differences consequent to a brief therapeutic experience a decade earlier should persist in such a striking fashion." Their argument is supported by a number of points, the most prominent of which is that some of the differences between treatments were absent at the 5-year follow-up period and then reappeared at the 10-year follow-up period. An overall evaluation of this admirably persistent investigation is complicated by fluctuations in the results and by an unfortunate lack of correspondence between the two major criteria. The omission of an untreated control group is understandable but unfortunate as it precludes any conclusions about the effect of psychotherapy *per se.* In view of the earlier discussion of possible events contributing to the spontaneous remission of neurotic disorders, the authors' findings on their patients' explanation of their improvements are interesting. "Although improved patients tended to associate their better current condition to a change in their socio-economic situation or to their adaptation to general life circumstances, including symptoms, it cannot be determined whether psychotherapy fostered these changes or whether they occurred quite independently of the treatment experienced. In any event, it is clear that, in retrospect, patients conceive of improvement as a function of adjustment to their lot in life or to a change in external socio-economic circumstances" (p. 80). It is tempting to conclude from this study that psychotherapy was effective and that more psychotherapy was more effective (even when administered by inexperienced therapists). However, in view of the limitations of the study and the unclear outcome, I share the authors' caution. Although the results are inconclusive they do encourage the possibility that psychotherapy may be beneficial—even if it is provided in a brief and limited form by inexperienced therapists.

UCLA STUDY

Despite some unfortunate inadequacies in the analysis and reporting of their data, the study by Brill *et al.* (1964) contains interesting information. They carried out a long-term double-blind study of the use of placebos, prochlorperazine, meprobamate, and phenobarbital, "in conjunction with brief visits" in the treatment of 299 predominantly neurotic out-patients. The selection of patients was carried out in a systematic fashion, and on acceptance for the trial they were randomly allocated to 1 of the 3 drug treatments or to psychotherapy (given weekly for 1 hour's duration) or to a placebo control or to a no-treatment waiting list control. The authors conclude that the "patients in all 5 groups showed a tendency to improve, in contrast to a lack of improvement in the patients who were kept on a waiting list and received no treatment" (p. 594). They add that "the lack of any marked differences would suggest that neither a specific drug nor the length of the psychotherapeutic sessions was the crucial factor in producing improvement in this sample of patients" (p. 594). We may add that the patients receiving placebos did as well as the treated groups.

One of the most interesting findings was the resistance encountered by the investigators when the study was introduced and carried out. They comment on the "prejudice in favour of psychotherapy among patients and therapists" and point out that the "extent of the bias in favour of psychotherapy, even in beginning residents who had had very little experience with it, was quite startling" (p. 591). This was particularly surprising as "all of this took place at a time when, in fact, no one knew how effective or ineffective drug treatment was."

The effects of the treatment were assessed by a variety of procedures. The therapists rated the improvements on a symptom check list and a 16-item evaluation form. The patient was required to complete a similar item evaluation and one relative or close friend did likewise. In addition, a social worker carried out an evaluation of each patient —unfortunately the value of this information is limited by the fact that the valuation was carried out after the social workers had read the reports on each patient. Lastly, the patients were required to complete MMPI tests. The before and after profiles for each patient were drawn on the same profile sheet, and two independent psychologists sorted the profiles into degrees of improvement or lack of improvement. Although their evaluations agreed rather well ($r = 0.85$), their conclusions differed on one of the most crucial comparisons, i.e. whether the treated groups were improved to a significantly greater extent than the untreated controls.

It will be realized that this study required a great deal of effort and careful planning. It is particularly unfortunate, therefore, that the handling of the resulting information was inadequate. In fact it is extremely difficult to evaluate the information provided because they rarely give the actual figures obtained and rely almost exclusively on graphic presentations. The absence of basic information such as the means and standard deviations on the various measures before and after treatment is particularly serious. Matters are further confounded by their failure to give adequate descriptions of many of the assessment procedures employed. For these reasons and because they were almost exclusively concerned with inter-group comparisons, we are not able to say with certainty whether any of the groups was in fact significantly improved. In order to reach a conclusion on this point one would need to have the means and standard deviations of the pre- and post-treatment assessment (subject, of course, to the usual tests of significance). The study is also limited by the unfortunately high rate of drop-outs—43.5% of the selected subjects either dropped out of the treatment or were not reassessed—or both. Despite some reassuring remarks made by the authors, there are indications that the drop-outs were somewhat different from the treated subjects. In their own words, "the drop-out group may be characterized as less intelligent, less passive, and more inclined to act out their problems" (p. 584). As the data for the groups are not provided, the matter remains in a degree of doubt except for the IQ scores, which are presented graphically. This shows the completed subjects to have a mean IQ of approximately 125. They were a group of superior intelligence and the drop-outs were of high average intelligence (approximately 115).

One of the major drawbacks to this study is the doubt which surrounds the degree of improvement, if any, shown by the treated and placebo groups. In some of the graphical presentations (e.g. fig. 5) they appear to have made "doubtful" to "slight" improvement. In other representations the changes seem to be slightly larger. Bearing in mind all these shortcomings, one can probably agree with the general conclusion reached by Brill and his colleagues to the effect that the treated (and placebo) groups showed slight improvement over a period of 1 year. They could detect no differences between the improvements registered by the 3 drug-treated groups, the placebo group, and the psychotherapy group. All of these groups, however, appeared to do better than the untreated waiting-list controls. Taken at face value, the main conclusion regarding the effects of psychotherapy would appear to be that it may have produced a slight improvement overall and this degree of improvement was neither smaller nor greater than that observed in patients who received placebos. The conclusion that psychotherapy is no more effective than an inert tablet can be avoided, however, by drawing attention to the shortcomings enumerated above. And one may also add that the psychotherapy was given for only 5 months and that much of it was conducted by trainee psychotherapists. As an attempt to evaluate psychotherapy the study must be regarded as inconclusive.

The information discussed so far is based on the condition of the patients at termination of treatment (mean duration 5.5 months). Koegler and Brill (1967) later reported their condition after a 2-year follow-up period. Their findings are striking: "The most marked improvement is in the rated status of the waiting-list (i.e. untreated) patients" (p. 77). At follow-up there were no significant differences between any of the groups. This suggests that at very best, treatment (by drugs, psychotherapy, or placebo) achieves improvement more quickly. The authors quote Jerome Frank's notion that ". . .the function of psychotherapy may be to accelerate a process that would occur in any case."

In regard to the question of spontaneous remissions, it will be recalled that Bergin was quoted as giving a zero rate for this study. In fact it is impossible to work out a percentage remission *rate* from the information given. The results are reported for the no-treatment waiting-list control group *as a group,* and while it is true that at termination they had shown relatively little change as a group, there is no way of determining whether any of the 20 remaining patients concerned (14 of the original 34 were lost) remitted spontaneously. Nevertheless, they caught up *within 2 years* and were then no different from the other groups of patients.

In the study by Greer and Cawley (1966), the relationship between treatment and outcome was also examined. It will be recalled that all of the patients were sufficiently ill to require in-patient care and they had the following types of treatment. Sixty-three received supportive treatment, 42 had physical treatment, 10 underwent leucotomy, 28 had psychotherapy, and 19 had psychotherapy combined with physical treatment. Thirteen patients received no treatment "as they remained in hospital less than 2 weeks and in most cases discharged themselves against medical advice." At discharge, the group of patients who had received psychotherapy "had a significantly more favourable outcome than the remainder." The mean outcome score for the 20 patients concerned was 1.96; The mean score for the 19 patients who had psychotherapy and physical treatment was 2.11 and the mean outcome for those 13 patients who received no treatment was 2.15. The worst outcome was recorded by the patients who underwent leucotomy, and they had a mean score of 2.60. Although this trend was seen to continue at "final outcome" (i.e. the follow-up), the difference between the patients who had psychotherapy and those who had no treatment was no longer significant. The significant advantage for the psychotherapy patients in relation to those who had received supportive treatment or physical treatment was maintained. The patients who had undergone leucotomy had the worst outcome of all, but their numbers were small. The more favourable outcome for psychotherapy patients when discharged from hospital may be misleading. Although no direct information is provided on the selection procedures in operation at the time of the patients' stay in hospital, there are significant indications that the patients who received psychotherapy were unrepresentative of the total patient sample. Greer and Cawley examined the significance of the factor of patient selection by carrying out some comparisons between the patients who received psychotherapy and the remainder. It was found that the psychotherapy patients "differed from the other group in several important respects." All of the patients receiving psychotherapy had a history of precipitating factors, and none of the 16 patients whose symptoms were regarded as being of life-long duration had received psychotherapy. In addition, a significantly higher proportion of psychotherapy patients were married and significantly fewer of them had an unfavourable pre-morbid personality. All of these features had previously been demonstrated by the authors to relate significantly to outcome, "so patients who had received psychotherapy would be expected to have had a more favourable prognosis, irrespective of treatment." They concluded that it would not be justifiable to ascribe the difference in outcome between the psychotherapy group and the rest of the sample to the effect of the particular treatment. Having noted that the patients selected for psychotherapy had a favourable prognosis irrespective of the particular treatment given, they go on to point out that "this argument does not necessarily demonstrate that psychotherapy was *ineffective* in these patients. From the findings of the present study we are not entitled to draw any conclusions regarding the efficacy of psychotherapy" (p. 83). As we have already seen, however, the Greer–Cawley study contains a considerable amount of useful information on the course of neurotic illnesses. In regard to improvement rates and eventual outcome they unearthed a disconcerting finding. The correlation between immediate outcome (i.e. condition at discharge) and final outcome is very low—$r = 0.19$.

To sum up, it is disappointing to find that the best studies of psychotherapy yield discouraging results while the inadequate studies are over-optimistic.

REFERENCES

Ashcraft, C. and Fitts, W. (1964) Self-concept change in psychotherapy, *Psychother. Theor, Res. Pract. 1*, 115-18.

Barron, F. and Leary, T. (1955) Changes in psychoneurotic patients with and without psychotherapy, *J. Consult. Psychol. 19*, 239-45.

Bergin, A. E. (1970) The evaluation of therapeutic outcomes, in *Handbook of Psychotherapy and Behaviour Change* (eds. A. E. Bergin and S. Garfield), Wiley New York.

Brill, N., Koegler, R., Epstein, L., and Forgy, E. (1964) Controlled study of psychiatric outpatient treatment, *Arch. Gen. Psychiat. 10*, 581-95.

Cross, H. J. (1964) The outcome of psychotherapy, *J. Consult. Psychol. 28*, 413-17.

Crowne, D. and Stephens, M. (1961) Self-acceptance and self-evaluative behaviour: a critique of methodology, *Psychol. Bull. 58*, 104-21.

Dittmann, A. (1966) Psychotherapeutic processes, in *Annual Review of Psychology* (eds. Farnsworth, McNemar and McNemar), Ann. Rev. Inc., Palo Alto.

Dymond, R. (1955) Adjustment changes in the absence of psychotherapy, *J. Consult. Psychol. 19*, 103-7.

Ends, E. and Page, C. (1957) A study of 3 types of group psychotherapy with hospitalized male inebriates, *Q. J. Stud. Alcohol. 18*, 263-77.

Ends, E. and Page, C. (1959) *Group Psychotherapy and Concomitant Psychological Change*, Psychol. Monogr. 73.

Fairweather, G. and Simon, R. (1963) A further follow-up comparison of psychotherapeutic programs, *J. Consult. Psychol. 27*, 186.

Greer, H. and Cawley, R. (1966) *Some Observations on the Natural History of Neurotic Illness*, Australian Medical Association.

Imber, S., Frank, J., Nash, E. and Gleidman, L. (1957) Improvement and amount of therapeutic contact, *J. Consult. Psychol. 77*, 283-393.

Imber, S., Nash, E., Hoehn-Saric, R., Stone, A. and Frank, J. L. (1968) A 10-year follow-up of treated psychiatric outpatients, in *An Evaluation of the Results of the Psychotherapies* (ed. Lesse), Thomas, Springfield.

Kellner, R. (1967) The evidence in favour of psychotherapy, *Br. J. Med. Psychol. 40*, 341-58.

Koegler, R. and Brill, N. (1967) *Treatment of Psychiatric Outpatients*, Appleton-Century-Crofts, New York.

Lowe, C. (1961) The self-concept: fact or artifact?, *Psychol. Bull. 58*, 325-36.

May, P. and Tuma, A. H. (1965) Treatment of schizophrenia, *Br. J. Psychiat. 111*, 503-10.

O'Connor, J., Daniels, G., Karsh, A., Moses, L., Flood, C. and Stern, L. (1964) The effects of psychotherapy on the course of ulcerative colitis, *Am. J. Psychiat. 120*, 738-42.

Ricks, D. *et al.* (1964) A measure of increased temporal perspective in successfully treated delinquent boys, *J. Abnorm. Soc. Psychol. 69*, 685-9.

Rogers, C. R. and Dymond, R. (1954) *Psychotherapy and Personality Change*, Chicago Univ. Press, Chicago.

Seeman, J. and Edwards, B. (1954) A therapeutic approach to reading difficulties, *J. Consult. Psychol. 18*, 451-3.

Shlien, J., Mosak, H., and Dreikurs, R. (1962) Effect of time limits: a comparison of two psychotherapies, *J. Counsel. Psychol. 9*, 31-34.

Taylor, D. (1955) Changes in the self-concept without psychotherapy, *J. Consult. Psychol. 19*, 205-9.

Teuber, N. and Powers, E. (1953) Evaluating therapy in a delinquency prevention program, *Proc. Ass. Nerv. Ment. Dis. 3*, 138-47.

Wittenborn, J. (1961) Contributions and current state of Q-methodology, *Psychol. Bull. 58*, 132-42.

Wylie, R. (1961) *The Self Concept*, Univ. Nebraska Press, Nebraska.

Some Known Effects of Psychotherapy and a Reinterpretation

by Alvin R. Mahrer

THE DEFINITION OF PSYCHOTHERAPY

Research tends to redefine psychotherapy through selection of certain person interactions as the focus of study. Thereby, research has quietly redefined psychotherapy to an extent that it is far broader than previously understood. The studies of psychotherapy now provide the following definition: (a) Psychotherapists include hospital aides, counselors, physicians, agency workers and volunteers (Frank, 1961; Gurin, Veroff & Feld, 1960; Powers & Witmer, 1951) in addition to clinical psychologists, psychiatrists and psychoanalysts. The new meaning includes a highly liberalized range of training and experience (Kiesler, 1966). (b) Psychotherapy refers to ". . . counseling, guidance, placement, and recommendations to schools, as well as deeper level therapies" (Levitt, 1967, p. 41), warm friendship from a paid volunteer as well as intensive treatment by clinical psychologists and psychiatrists. (c) Psychotherapy includes a frenetic dispersion of goals as well as theories of psychopathology, personality development and psychological change (Mahrer, 1967a). (d) Psychotherapy patients cover the spectrum of degrees and kinds of psychological problems and distresses, expectancies about therapy, and demographic characteristics (Colby, 1964; Kiesler, 1966). Since research studies have quietly but effectively redefined psychotherapy far beyond the traditional boundaries, we are faced with the options of accepting the results as adding to the body of known facts about psychotherapy, or sorting out the results on the basis of whether they were really studying psychotherapy at all. In either case, what is known about psychotherapy is established by research employing an extremely broad definition of psychotherapy.

Reprinted from *Psychotherapy: Theory, Research and Practice,* 1970, *7*(3), 186-191. Used with permission of author and publisher.

RATED IMPROVEMENT

Eysenck (1952) and Levitt (1967) summarized the findings of 59 studies totalling approximately 16,000 cases and found a stable 65–70 percent of cases judged as having improved. Both writers concluded that 65–70 percent of cases treated by psychotherapy improved; that is psychotherapy is "effective" in 65–70 percent of the cases. These same results lend themselves to another conclusion: professional persons directly or indirectly involved in psychotherapy demonstrate a readiness to rate 65–70 percent of patients as having improved under such treatment. In other words, we are proposing two sets of interpretative conclusions to research results on rated improvement under psychotherapy.

UNIDIMENSIONAL EFFECT

The effects of psychotherapy are predominantly measured by a single dimension: improvement (cure, recovery, remission of illness). No other effects are permitted because there are so few research results on other dimensions proposed by recent advances in behavior modification, existential, humanistic and experiential psychotherapies (Mahrer, 1967b). Out of all potential meaningful effects of psychotherapy, research studies have leaned almost exclusively on those which lend themselves to a traditional medical-psychiatric dimension of improvement or worsening of condition. Thus the known effects of psychotherapy have been largely confined to a single dimension of change.

LENGTH OF TREATMENT

Succinctly summarizing many studies on length of treatment and effects of psychotherapy, Luborsky punctuates a definitive trend: "Those who stay in treatment improve . . ." (1959, p. 324); the longer a patient remains in treatment the greater is the likelihood of positive outcome. However, another conclusion is also relevant: professional persons directly or indirectly involved in psychotherapy tend to give lower ratings of improvement to patients who terminate prematurely and higher ratings of improvement to patients who remain with the psychotherapist. This line of research may have penetrated a human foible in psychotherapists. The results may shed light on the actual effects of psychotherapeutic processes over varying treatment durations, however, the same results may be reinterpreted in terms of varying rater tendencies as a function of patient willingness or unwillingness to remain in treatment.

RELATIVE EFFECTIVENESS

The effectiveness of psychotherapy has been compared with that of sheer hospital custodial treatment (Eysenck, 1952, 1965). Rates of improvement under psychotherapy were compared with Landis' (1938) report that approximately 70 percent of New York state hospitalized psychiatric patients were discharged as improved from 1917 to 1934, according to the case summaries of the hospital physicians. Eysenck carefully observes: ". . . we may thus say that of severe neurotics receiving in the main custodial care, and very little if any psychotherapy, over two-thirds recovered improved to a considerable extent" (1967, p. 24). Comparing this improvement rate with those of psychotherapeutic treatment, Eysenck draws the following provocative conclusion: "They fail to prove that psychotherapy, Freudian or otherwise, facilitates the recovery of neurotic patients. They show that roughly two-thirds of a group of neurotic patients will recover or improve to a marked extent within about two years of the onset of their illness, whether they are treated by means of psychotherapy or not . . . The figures fail to support the hypothesis that psychotherapy facilitates recovery from neurotic disorder" (1967, p. 28-29). Led by DeCharms, Levy and Wertheimer (1954), Kiesler (1966), Cartwright (1955a), Luborsky (1954), Rosenzweig (1954), Stevenson (1959) and Strupp (1964a, 1964b), a crescendo of protest focused upon the design and the obtained *results* (without demonstrating stable refutory findings). We fully accept the results, but focus upon an alternative *conclusion:* Hospital physicians, utilizing essentially custodial treatment, judge their psychiatric patients as improving at a rate commensurate with and even exceeding that of patients rated by psychotherapeutically oriented professionals. The relative effects of psychotherapy are a function of the relative tendencies for hospital physicians and psychotherapists to judge patients as having improved under their respective treatment regimes. In other words, Eysenck's reported findings may be interpreted as evidence of the ineffectiveness of psychotherapy relative to sheer hospital custodial treatment; taken in this light, it is understandable that his results have aroused so heated an opposition. But the results also lend themselves to reinterpretation as evidence of the relative confidence and commitment of both hospital physicians and psychotherapists in the effectiveness of their respective programs, hardly a startling conclusion.

CONGRUENCY WITH THERAPIST VALUES

The effects of psychotherapy may be partly a reflection of the degree of congruency with the therapist's value system. Rosenthal (1955) found that patients rated as "improved" changed in the direction of the moral values of their therapists in such areas as sex, aggression and authority, whereas patients rated as unimproved failed to adopt their therapists' values in these areas. At least two conclusions are consistent with these results: (a) Improvement means adopting the value system of the therapist; lack of improvement means failing to adopt his value system. (b) Therapists tend to rate as improved those patients who adopt the therapist's value system; therapists tend to rate as failing to improve those patients who do not adopt their value systems.

POSITIVE AND NEGATIVE EFFECTS

Until recently, the research answer to the question of whether psychotherapy patients improved was a simple "no." Spearheaded by Bergin (1963) and Truax (1963), a closer look at these negative findings revealed them as the resultant of equal but opposite improvement and deterioration effects. These canceling-out effects were found by Rogers (1961), Truax (1963) and Truax and Carkhuff (1967) on measures of adjustment-maladjustment; by Cartwright (1957, 1961) on self-consistency measures; by Barron and Leary (1955) and Fairweather et al. (1960) on MMPI scales, Rogers and Diamond (1954) and Butler and Haigh, (1954) on self-ideal scores, Cartwright and Vogel (1960) on Q scores, and Mink (1959) on measures of social adjustment. Under closer scrutiny, the effect of psychotherapy leaped from a glum "no effect" to two equal but opposite effects. Psychotherapy may improve or deteriorate patients; it may be for better or for worse, conclude Bergin (1967) and Truax and Carkhuff (1967). These studies set the stage for an understanding of psychotherapy as potentially a positive or negative experience.

THERAPIST CHARACTERISTICS

High or low therapist loadings on the following characteristics were found to be associated with better or worse outcome: (a) The therapist's degree of empathy, sensitivity and accuracy in understanding the patient's inner experiences, coupled with a facility in communicating this understanding in the patient's feeling language; (b) The therapist's unconditioned positive regard, nonpossessive warmth and caring for the patient; and (c) The therapist's own authenticity, mature integration, genuineness and congruence (Barrett-Lennard, 1962; Gardner, 1964; Strupp, Wallach & Wogan, 1964; Truax, 1963; Truax & Carkhuff, 1967). Bergin (1966) and Truax and Carkhuff (1967) have drawn the significant conclusion that across the various approaches, these therapist variables are associated with positive and constructive or negative and deteriorative therapeutic outcome.

These data are also consistent with a reinterpretation of psychotherapy as a highly valued experience with a maturely integrated, genuine, authentic individual who offers sensitive understanding and empathy within a context of unconditioned positive regard and warm, non-possessive caring. The experience is positive and constructive or negative and deleterious as a function of the degree to which the therapist fulfills this needed role and the patient seeks such a valued relationship. According to such a reinterpretation, what is now commonly accepted as psychotherapy is a means of undergoing an experience in which one individual (the therapist) typically fulfills a role of provider, and another individual (the patient) is the receiver of mature genuineness, sensitively empathic understanding and warmly unconditioned caring.

PATIENT CHARACTERISTICS

Such a highly valued experience will have a greater likelihood of occurrence when patients are psychologically minded (Gallagher, Levinson & Ehrlich, 1957; Hiler, 1959; Sharaf & Levinson, 1957), have a high desire to reveal personal feelings (Hiler, 1959), a high need for self-understanding and self-confidence (Feifel & Eells, 1963; Garfield & Wolpin, 1963), expectations congruent with the therapist's own role image (Heine & Trosman, 1960), and an ability to establish a positive, empathy-eliciting "homophilic" relationship with the therapist (Levinson, 1962; Strupp, 1958, 1964a, p. 6; Strupp & Williams, 1960; Wallach & Strupp, 1960).

Patients not described by the above characteristics or motivated toward undergoing something other than the above highly valued experience are variously labeled as poor risks, unable to profit from psychotherapy, of poor prognosis or inadequately motivated. Accordingly a known effect is that psychotherapy is not appropriate for individuals described as less intelligent, less anxious, less educated, less verbal and insightful, less appealing and attractive, more concrete and action-oriented, more severely disturbed, more sociopathically impulsive and more inclined to find the therapeutic procedure meaningless (Bergin, 1966; Barron, 1953; Cartwright, 1955b; Fulkerson & Barry, 1961; Garfield & Affleck, 1961; Hollingshead & Redlich, 1958; Kirtner & Cartwright, 1958a, 1958b).

PSYCHOTHERAPY: THE RESULT OF PERSONALITY CHANGE

Gurin, Veroff and Feld (1960) and Frank (1961) have found that those persons culminating in formal psychotherapy comprise a segment of a larger class of individuals undergoing an active process of seeking help from a large variety of agencies, institutions, friends, teachers, clergymen, attorneys, physicians, relatives and others. Reviews by both Eysenck (1952, 1960, 1967) and Bergin (1963) testify that psychotherapy patients and controls alike are part of an overriding ongoing process of personality change. Psychotherapy may be reinterpreted as merely one outcome of a larger process of motivated help-seeking.

SOME KNOWN EFFECTS AND A REINTERPRETATION

What are some known effects of psychotherapy? The above results are open to at least two lines of interpretation. According to the first interpretation, psychotherapy is occurring when a research investigator defines a professional or semi-professional person as a psychotherapist, and this includes a volunteer spending time on a hospital ward, a counselor making a recommendation to a school, or a hospital physician giving some advice to a psychiatric patient. On the basis of this first line of interpretation, some of the known effects of psychotherapy are as follows:

    1. Psychotherapy effectively "improves" patients in approximately 65–70 percent of the cases.

    2. Psychotherapy, in general, as compared with other change conditions in general, does not uniquely facilitate the recovery from neurotic conditions.

    3. Psychotherapy may either improve or deteriorate patients' conditions.

    4. Psychotherapy is accompanied with improvement (constructive personality change) or deterioration as a function of the therapist's degree of (a) empathy and sensitive understanding, (b) authenticity and genuineness, and (c) unconditioned positive regard and nonpossessive warmth.

    5. Psychotherapy tends to effect improvement in patients who are psychologically minded, able to reveal personal feelings, need self-understanding and self-confidence, have congruent therapeutic expectation, tend to remain in psychotherapy and can establish a therapeutic relationship. Psychotherapy increases this congruence between the value systems of therapists and patients.

6. Psychotherapy does not tend to effect improvement in patients who are less intelligent, less anxious, less educated, less verbal, less insightful, less appealing, more concrete and action oriented, more severely disturbed, more sociopathically impulsive, more inclined to terminate treatment without the therapist's full approval and more inclined to find the whole therapeutic procedure rather meaningless.

The above conclusions represent only one mode of interpreting the research findings. A second line of interpretation understands the research as providing information about a broad class of persons called patients or clients, another broad class of persons called therapists, and the nature of the interactions between these two classes of persons. The emphasis here is upon the complex of motivations among two or more persons in interaction. Accordingly, the above research findings lend themselves to the following reinterpretations concerning the known effects of psychotherapy:

1. Persons seeking psychotherapy are already engaged in an active process of personality change involving the seeking of a relationship with a help-providing external agent. An ongoing process of personality change motivates persons toward a number of help-providing situations, including psychotherapy. The effects of psychotherapy are in part a function of a larger process of personality change which activated the person toward the psychotherapeutic situation.

2. Therapists and patients utilize psychotherapy as a means of undergoing specially valued human relationships typically involving (a) a special relationship with a highly valued individual representing maturity, integration, authenticity and genuineness; (b) the providing and receiving of empathic, sensitive understanding of one's innermost experiencings; and (c) the providing and receiving of unconditional positive regard, warmth and caring. The effect of psychotherapy is, typically, to provide two or more persons with a special and highly valued relationship along the above lines. The implications are that the psychotherapeutic situation (a) is a function of the conjoint motivations of therapists and patients, and (b) may utilize a larger spectrum of motivations and therapist-patient relationships.

3. Patients for whom psychotherapy is a means of undergoing a specially valued human relationship tend to be psychologically minded, desirous of revealing personal feelings, needing self-understanding and self-confidence from the therapist, congruent with the therapist's role image, and motivated toward establishing a positive, empathy-eliciting relationship. The implication is that the psychotherapy situation may be extended to other persons undergoing other kinds of personality changes.

4. Patients for whom psychotherapy is not a means of undergoing such a specially valued human relationship tend to be described as less

intelligent, less anxious, less educated, less verbal, less insightful, less appealing, more concrete and action-oriented, more severely disturbed, more sociopathically impulsive, more inclined to terminate treatment without the therapist's full approval and more inclined to find the whole therapeutic procedure rather meaningless. The implication is that the psychotherapy situation may be revised and reconstructed to provide a meaningful change experience for persons presently considered inappropriate for treatment.

5. Professional persons directly or indirectly involved in psychotherapy have a tendency of rating 65–70 percent of patients as having improved under such treatment; hospital physicians have a somewhat greater tendency to rate non-psychotherapeutic hospital treatment programs as effecting improvement in roughly analogous patients.

6. Professional persons directly or indirectly involved in psychotherapy tend to give higher ratings of improvement to patients who adopt the therapist's value system, remain in the therapeutic relationship until it is dissolved by mutual agreement and are motivated toward experiencing the idealized human relationship in therapy. Lower ratings of improvement are given to patients who fail to adopt the therapist's value system, whose discontinuance of the relationship is considered premature by the therapist and who are not motivated toward experiencing the specially valued human relationship in therapy.

There are at least two meanings of psychotherapy. According to one meaning, psychotherapy occurs when at least one person is designated as a psychotherapist, regardless of his professional training, implicit model of personality change, psychotherapeutic approach, treatment goals, and the nature and motivations of the person with whom he is interacting. According to the second meaning, psychotherapy is to be identified in terms of given training experiences, given sets of psychological principles, given aims and goals, and given interacting individuals. Research findings based upon the former definition are inappropriate for assessing the known affects [sic] of psychotherapy according to the latter definition.

The medico-psychiatric dimension of improvement-deterioration simply is not enough to scale the multidimensional effects of psychotherapy. It is difficult to justify the use of an improvement-worsening dimension, appropriate for a single model of personality and approach to psychotherapy, for research on all approaches to psychotherapy. The implication and proposal is that research utilize a broad array of dimensions consonant with behavior modification, experiential and existential approaches. For example, Butler (1968) reports findings in which psychotherapy was accompanied with increased self-ideal congruence and increased self-actualizing individuality. The further implication is that whole classes of persons, formerly classified, under the old dimension, as unimproved or worsening, may be reunderstood as changing along dimensions better suited to contemporary approaches to psychotherapy.

REFERENCES

Barron, J. Some test correlates of response to psychotherapy. *Journal of Consulting Psychology,* 1953, *17,* 235-241.

Barron, F. & Leary, T. Changes in psychoneurotic patients with and without psychotherapy. *Journal of Consulting Psychology,* 1955, *19,* 239-245.

Barrett—Lennard, G. T. Dimensions of therapist response as causal factors in therapeutic change. *Psychological Monographs: General and Applied,* 1962, *76,* No. 43 (Whole no. 526).

Bergin, A. E. The effects of psychotherapy: Negative results revisted. *Journal of Counseling Psychology,* 1963, *10,* 244-255.

Bergin, A. E. Some implications of psychotherapy research for therapeutic practice. *Journal of Abnormal Psychology,* 1966, *71,* 235-246.

Butler, J. M. Self-ideal congruence in psychotherapy. *Psychotherapy: Theory, Research and Practice,* 1968, *5,* 13-17.

Cartwright, D. S. Success in psychotherapy as a function of certain actuarial variables. *Journal of Consulting Psychology,* 1955, *19,* 357-363. (b)

Cartwright, D. S. Effectiveness of psychotherapy: A critique of the spontaneous remission argument. *Journal of Counseling Psychology,* 1955, *2,* 290-296. (a)

Cartwright, D. S. The effects of psychotherapy. *Journal of Counseling Psychology,* 1957, *4,* 15-22.

Cartwright, D. S. The effects of psychotherapy: A replication and extension. *Journal of Consulting Psychology,* 1961, *25,* 376-382.

Colby, K. M. Psychotherapeutic processes. *Annual Review of Psychology,* 1964, *15,* 347-370.

DeCharms, R., Levy, J. & Wertheimer, M. A note on attempted evaluation of psychotherapy. *Journal of Clinical Psychology,* 1954, *10,* 233-235.

Eysenck, H. J. The effects of psychotherapy: An evaluation. *Journal of Consulting Psychology,* 1952, *16,* 319-324.

Eysenck, H. J. The effects of psychotherapy. In H. J. Eysenck (Ed.) *Handbook of abnormal psychology.* New York: Basic Books, 1960, pp. 697-725.

Eysenck, H. J. The inefficacy of therapeutic processes with adults. In B. G. Benenson and R. R. Carkhuff (Eds.) *Sources of gain in counseling and psychotherapy.* New York: Holt, Rinehart & Winston, 1967, pp. 22-31.

Frank, J. D. *Persuasion and healing.* Baltimore: Johns Hopkins Press, 1961.

Fulkerson, S. D., & Barry, J. R. Methodology and research on the prognostic use of psychological tests. *Psychological Bulletin,* 1961, *58,* 177-204.

Gallagher, E. B., Levinson, D. J. & Erlich, I. Some sociopsychological characteristics of patients and their relevance for psychiatric treatment. In M. Greenblatt, D. J. Levinson & R. H. Williams (Eds.) *The patient and the mental hospital.* Glencoe, Ill.: Free Press, 1957.

Gardner, G. The psychotherapeutic relationship. *Psychological Bulletin,* 1964, *61,* 426-437.

Garfield, S. L. & Affleck, D. C. Therapists' judgments concerning patients considered for psychotherapy. *Journal of Consulting Psychology*, 1961, 25, 505-509.

Garfield, S. L. & Wolpin, M. Expectations regarding psychotherapy. *Journal of Nervous and Mental Disease*, 1963, 137, 353-362.

Gurin, G., Veroff, J. & Feld, S. *Americans view their mental health*. New York: Basic Books, 1960.

Hiler, E. W. The sentence completion test as a predictor of continuation in psychotherapy. *Journal of Consulting Psychology*, 1959, 23, 544-549.

Hollingshead, A. B. & Redlich, F. C. *Social class and mental illness*. New York: Wiley, 1958.

Kiesler, D. J. Some myths of psychotherapy research and the search for a paradigm. *Psychological Bulletin*, 1966, 65, 110-136.

Kirtner, W. L. & Cartwright, D. S. Success and failure in client-controlled therapy as a function of initial in-therapy behavior. *Journal of Consulting Psychology*, 1958, 22, 329-333. (a)

Kirtner, W. L. & Cartwright, D. S. Success and failure in client-centered therapy as a function of client personality variables. *Journal of Consulting Psychology*, 1958, 22, 259-264. (b)

Landis, C. Statistical evaluation of psychotherapeutic methods. In S. E. Hinsie (Ed.) *Concepts and problems of psychotherapy*. London: Heinemann, 1938, pp. 155-165.

Levitt, E. E. The undemonstrated effectiveness of therapeutic processes with children. In B. G. Berenson and R. R. Carkhuff (Eds.) *Sources of gain in counseling and psychotherapy*. New York: Holt, Rinehart & Winston, 1967, pp. 33-45.

Luborsky, L. A note on Eysenck's article "The effects of psychotherapy: An evaluation." *British Journal of Psychology*, 1954, 45, 129-131.

Luborsky, L. Psychotherapy. *Annual Review of Psychology*, 1959, 10, 317-344.

Mahrer, A. R. The goals and families of psychotherapy: Summary. In A. R. Mahrer (Ed.) *The goals of psychotherapy*. New York: Appleton-Century-Crofts, 1967, pp. 259-269. (a)

Mahrer, A. R. The goals and families of psychotherapy: Implications. In A. R. Mahrer (Ed.) *The goals of psychotherapy*. New York: Appleton-Century-Crofts, 1967, pp. 288-301. (b)

Powers, E., Witmer, H. *An experiment in the prevention of delinquency*. New York: Columbia University Press, 1951.

Rogers, C. R. A theory of psychotherapy with schizophrenics and proposal for its empirical investigation. In J. G. Dawson and N. P. Dellis (Eds.) *Psychotherapy with schizophrenics*. Baton Rouge: Louisiana State University Press, 1961, pp. 3-19.

Rosenthal, D. Changes in some moral values following psychotherapy. *Journal of Consulting Psychology*, 1955, 19, 431-436.

Rosenzweig, S. A transvaluation of psychotherapy: A reply to Hans Eysenck. *Journal of Abnormal and Social Psychology*, 1954, 49, 298-304.

Sharaf, M. R. & Levinson, D. J. Patterns of ideology and role-definition among psychiatric residents. In M. Greenblatt, D. J. Levinson & R. H. Williams (Eds.) *The patient and the mental hospital*. Glencoe, Ill.: Free Press, 1957.

Stevenson, I. The challenge of results in psychotherapy. *American Journal of Psychiatry*, 1959, 116, 120-123.

Strupp, H. H. The outcome problem in psychotherapy revisted. *Psychotherapy: Theory, Research and Practice*, 1964, 1, 1-13. (a)

Strupp, H. H. The outcome problem in psychotherapy: A rejoinder. *Psychotherapy: Theory, Research and Practice,* 1964a, *1,* 101. (b)

Strupp, H. H., Wallach, M. S., & Wogan, M. Psychotherapy experience in retrospect: Questionnaire survey of former patients and their therapists. *Psychological Monographs: General and Applied,* 1964, *78,* No. 11 (whole no. 588).

Truax, C. B. Effective ingredients in psychotherapy: An approach to unraveling the patient-therapist interaction. *Journal of Counseling Psychology,* 1963, *10,* 256-263.

Traux, C. B. & Carkhuff, R. R. New directions in clinical research. In B. G. Berenson and R. R. Carkhuff (Eds.) *Sources of gain in counseling and psychotherapy.* New York: Holt, Rinehart & Winston, 1967, pp. 358-391.

Some Moral Dilemmas Encountered in Psychotherapy

by Wolfgang Lederer

It is a classical distinction between the preacher and the therapist that the former preaches, and the latter does not; will say: [sic] the former professes himself to be an advocate of a formal morality, whereas the latter, theoretically at least, considers matters pertaining to morals and ethics as irrelevant to his detached and scientific pursuit of psychological understanding.

In the actual practice of psychotherapy I have long found this classical distinction to be both irrelevant and inapplicable to the chief business at hand, namely: the assistance demanded by the patient and required of the therapist. I say "assistance," and not "cure," for most patients in therapy are not, medically speaking, "sick"; they are perhaps stuck, or lost, or hung up, or confused, and most likely anxious and depressed—but they are essentially hale and intact, and need assistance to get unstuck, or unhung, or whatever one may call it.

Of course, for anyone properly trained (or currently in training), the very thought of giving assistance causes a distinct shudder: assistance is given by friends and relations, by old-fashioned social workers, and by the Salvation Army; whereas any reputable therapist would rather say nothing than be caught giving advice; and especially so, if such advice pertains not to practical things such as the proper dosage of aspirin or a streetcar schedule, but—I hesitate to mention the word—to morality.

Indeed, it can be argued—and of course has been—that there is no such thing as morality, but only a vast number of differing moral codes or standards; so that it may well be asked whose morals the moralizing psychiatrist would dispense. His own? Those of his wife? His children's? Those morals codified in secular law? Or in ecclesiastic law? And in the latter instance, of which ecclesia?

Reprinted by special permission of The William Alanson White Psychiatric Foundation, Inc. From *Psychiatry*, February 1971, *34*, 75-85. Copyright © The William Alanson White Psychiatric Foundation.

I have an answer to all this; but rather than advancing it immediately (thus opening myself to immediate demonstration of my answer's limited applicability), I shall proceed to introduce a number of exemplary case histories, and so try to build up my thesis bit by bit.

My first case is a woman of middle years, a professional person of high competence and good reputation in a field closely related to my own, proud mother of three pre-teen children, two boys and a girl; and she came to consult me because of violent and drunken scenes of jealousy being enacted almost daily between herself and her current lover, an older woman with whom she and her children were sharing a house.

The past history told of a tyrannical and highly successful father, an industrialist; of a sickly mother and of a younger brother, equally sickly. My patient grew up as her mother's nurse, because father so wanted it; when her brother's incompetence became apparent, she changed role and became her father's son and office manager, because he so wanted it; and when, with Olympian anger and selfishness he made her his slave and forbade her all life of her own, she fled by night and escaped clear across the continent.

She was a plucky girl, supported herself and got a good postgraduate education. She was pretty and sought after, but could tolerate only weak men: in due course, though rather late, she married, and divorced, three of them; and was left alone with three kids to feed.

Though she now badly needed help, she had lost all confidence in the so-called stronger sex, which, whenever it lacked her father's brute temper, also seemed to lack his strength. And so, to her own greatest dismay, it worked out that her next companions, one after the other, were women. Moreover, however much they differed in other respects, these women had two features in common: they were older than my patient, and they had some sort of ailment, most commonly alcoholism.

My patient nursed them, and often supported them, lovingly; her lovers returned her love with drunken stupors and brawls; because of the children—they could not always be ushered to bed in time to avoid these ugly scenes—the situation became, over and over again, untenable. On the third or fourth go-round she consulted me.

In the course of therapy—and without my urging—she evicted, for the sake of the children, her latest lover. She settled down to what she thought would become a lifetime of loneliness, and in therapy discussed the question of her homosexuality: was this her "true" orientation, or was it not?

She learned then—and without my urging—that she had loved her terrible father as much as she had feared him; that she had nursed her mother to please him; that she had slaved in his office to please him; and that she had fled because it was impossible to please him. She learned that she had married second-rate men because she thought this was all she deserved; and that she had avoided strong men from fear—not from fear of their strength, but from fear of being unable to please, from a deep conviction of not being good enough. She had absorbed this contempt of herself and of her femininity from the father she could never please; for she realized that to please him she would have had to be a boy.

At that point in her therapy she met a retired pilot, widowed three or four years; a man in strapping good health, except for his eyesight; and a man who, since the death of his wife and the near simultaneous grounding by the airlines, had turned impotent. He was older than she, and depressed; but despite his gray mood, he had set out, dutifully (he too had children), tenaciously, and with ingenuity, to build for himself a second career.

They approached each other hesitantly; they came closer against grave misgivings, each fighting an inner panic. They became lovers. Gentle and strong, he valued her, and helped her value herself, as a woman; and how much of a woman she was he attested to her by his renewed potency. Naturally, they were planning to marry.

And now my patient posed me an urgent question:

She was, she said, in seventh heaven, and in hell, both at once. That she had found, so late in the day, such a good man, was nothing short of a miracle. That she had been able, with him and for his sake, to pass the archetypal test of womanhood, in that her love had restored to him his manhood intact—that too was a miracle. Before her was a totally unexpected, for years no longer hoped-for state of blessedness, a unique chance. And yet—at the gates of this paradise there stood, like an angel with raised sword, the secret she had not told him, had not been able to get herself to tell him—the secret of her years of homosexuality.

This was her question: Dare she tell? How would he react if she did? Would he reject her? And how, if she did not tell him, could she manage to live with him?

She agonized, and had some grounds for agonizing, because he had been raised within strict and narrow limits. He was simple of heart and, when it came to the byways of love, totally uninformed. Behind him, it seemed, stood a fundamentalist and wrathful God.

She agonized and, so help me, I do believe I asked her, and not only once: "Well, what do you think?"

She answered, and when she almost screamed: "For Christ's sake, tell me what I should do!," it was not so much like swearing, but more like a true plea for charity, charity in the original sense of *caring* participation in the existence and the suffering of fellow man.

So, because she obviously *needed* me to care and to participate, I said, with all the emphasis I could muster: "You have got to tell him."

You have got to tell him, not because I think it necessarily bad to tell a lie, or to suppress a truth, but simply because *you*, the way I see *you*, the way I think *you* are built—(and this perception of you is all I can go by)—*you* are incapable of living with a lie or of sitting on an imprisoned truth. You have got to tell him, because *for you* it is wrong to lie.

You have got to tell him, because if you don't, you are still afraid of him, just as you were always afraid of your father, and could never face him, but had to run from him to save yourself. You cannot run from your husband, and you cannot live with him in fear.

And you have got to tell him, so that you shall not deprive him of the chance to prove to you his humanity, and his love, and his strength; so that you may finally, and fully, trust him, and feel finally, and fully, accepted by him.

Obviously, I would not have told this story—and endangered my professional reputation by engaging in what could be called sheer melodrama—if my patient had not promptly taken my advice, and told the truth, and been told by her white-haired groom that he could not care less; and if she had not shortly married him and for several years now lived happily ever after.

Or rather:

I hope I would have had the honesty to tell the story even if—as could easily have happened—all had ended badly. It could indeed have ended very badly, and I, part-responsible, would have had to shoulder another quantum of karma for my journeys through the eons.

Did I say ". . . part-responsible"? Is it not our easy faith that only the patient, solely and alone the patient, is responsible for his or her actions? And that we, uninvolved, go scot-free?

How comfortable that would be.

Like blaming it all on God.

I am afraid I cannot do that.

I find that from time to time patients, just like the one above, ask for, and need, and deserve the "charity" of our participation. In the full awareness of our own fallibility, it is incumbent upon us that we must not fail the patient dangling at the end of a frayed rope; but we must say: "Put your foot here, and your hand there . . ."; and hope that our judgment is correct.

Correct for whom? Correct for the patient.

This complicates matters further. We cannot simply base ourselves on our own feelings of right and wrong, we cannot say, as a good friend would say: "In your place, I would do such-and-so." What *we* would do in the patient's place is, strictly speaking, irrelevant. And the patient would be quick to correct us if we attempted such personal counsel: "I could not care less," the patient might say, "what *you* would do. I am not you. But I need to know, and I need for you to tell me, what *I* should do."

And so, out of whatever understanding and intuition our training and our native talent may give us, we must try to determine, and venture to propose, what would serve the patient best: what would do the least harm, and the most good, to him and to others. And because, no matter how careful we are, the "I would do such-and-so" cannot ever be totally eliminated from our conscious and unconscious calculations, therefore we counsel never quite *un-self-ishly*, and therefore we assume, therefore in all charity we must be prepared to assume, if things do not go well, a burden of guilt.

But perhaps, in this moral discourse, I have already shocked a moral reader—by my cavalier attitude toward lying in the case I have just presented. Did I not state there that lying is not necessarily wrong, but only wrong for that patient in that instance? But is not lying *always* immoral?

Well, let us take the following situation, one that I have encountered many times:

A student did well for a year or two at, let us say, Cornell, but then ran into one of the many shattering experiences and conflicts that youth is heir to; and in consequence, grades nose-dived and the student eventually quit—or had to quit—Cornell. There followed a series of attempts at various other colleges, all of which similarly ended prematurely and in disaster. He (or she) now entered therapy, supporting both self and therapist by working at some measly job. After some months, or a year or two, the crisis is over, and the student is ready to go back to school. The chances are that he will try an entirely new college, let us say U.C.-Berkeley; and in the normal course of admissions proceedings the student will be asked to send in transcripts of all previous academic work.

He can submit the transcript from Cornell without fatal damage to his chances: the nose-dive in the third year, against the background of two successful lower-division years, will not necessarily be held against him. But what about the intervening failures at other schools? Would they not show him up as totally disorganized, incapable of academic work, and hence a bad risk? And how could he possibly explain to the Berkeley Dean of Admissions that because he has been in therapy he is now a new man? How, in fact, can he himself be sure that he is now well until *after* he has proven himself at Berkeley? And what if, because of such justifiable doubt, Berkeley should refuse to take the risk of accepting him? Then how can he ever prove himself?

Obviously, the question is—and the patient will ask it of his therapist—"Must I mention my failures since leaving Cornell? Can I not try to obtain admission strictly on the strength of my good performance during the first two years?"

The therapist can of course now say, "This is up to you," and wash his hands of the dilemma. In so doing, he is likely to convey to his patient: "Do what you think you can get away with." And that, I think, misses the point.

My answer would be a discourse on what could be called "essential truth." This is a precarious and dangerous concept, and it derives whatever legitimacy it may have from the implied belief in the fullest responsibility of each individual for every one of his actions.

In the case of the student in question it would present itself as follows: The Dean of Admissions needs to decide on the suitability of applicants who are totally unknown to him. He quite legitimately bases his decision on their past scholastic record as the best indicator of their future scholastic performance. When this past record indicates repeated failure, he is quite within his rights if he rejects the applicant. However, in some instances, he may be willing to listen to special pleas, such as the assertion that the student has meanwhile been in therapy and therefore considers himself once again fit to study. He may even be willing to consider a letter of recommendation from the psychotherapist. However, none of this will place him in a position to formulate a genuinely competent opinion of his own; his specialty is grades, not psychopathology; and even after reading the reports he has no true grasp of the applicant's present qualifications. Still, he must make a decision; and he may, after soul-searching, admit the student on a probationary basis, or reject him as an unwarranted risk; and he would most likely have misgivings either way.

As to the student, he could now take the position, and quite correctly, that his admission or rejection is entirely based on a decision made by the dean—hence, with all consequences, the dean's responsibility. Otherwise put: the student, having complied to the letter with all admission requirements, submits himself to judgment, and whatever happens happens to him as to a passive, hence not responsible, party.

By contrast, I would suggest the following point of view: What the dean really needs to know is not all the facts—many of which he cannot properly evaluate—but simply whether the student is now ready to resume his studies. In view of past complications, only the student and the therapist can form a halfway valid opinion in this regard. Therefore, if the student, after due consideration, decides that he is ready and able to resume his studies, then he may take it upon himself to submit the Cornell transcripts only, and not to make mention of the intervening failures. If, however, he does decide not to tell the whole truth (which surely amounts to telling a lie, in the formal sense) but confines himself to telling the essential truth—namely, that he was once a good student and can be a good student again—then he is also fully responsible for the consequences: then it is up to him to prove that he was right in taking the decision into his own hands.

Yes, this is a precarious doctrine, easily abused. But it is necessary to point out that the opposite, an absolute and unthinking loyalty to truth—in the formal, literal sense—is subject to as much abuse as absolute and unthinking loyalty to any concept or dogma.

In our own lifetime it has been formally and legally established, at the Nuremberg trials, that loyalty, in the form of obedience to orders, does not relieve one of responsibility: if an order, issued by no matter how high an authority, is flagrantly inhuman and immoral, then it must be disobeyed. We are currently being reminded, by certain events in Viet Nam, that not only German, but also American (and all other) soldiers must at times take upon themselves the responsibility for disobeying orders, if they are not to become criminals.

Similarly, it will not do to be blindly, irresponsibly honest. But whether, and to what extent, a man tells the truth, is a matter for his own soul-searching integrity. He must ask, not only why he should presume to lie, but also to what end he may be telling the truth—for a literal truth is often spoken to convey a totally false impression, and may be false in its essence.

For instance: I know of a man who, himself of a hot and sensual nature, had married a lovely woman of aristocratic reticence. For reasons of her upbringing, she could not offer him the sexual abandon he craved. His solution was to have affaires, concerning which he felt guilty. To relieve his guilt, he told his wife all about his extramarital adventures. He did this, he said, because he did not wish there to be any secrets between them, because he wanted to prove both their closeness and his honesty.

True, he did want to be honest and close, but only for the purpose of cruelty. The *essential truth* of the matter, which he failed to face, was that he had married his wife for reasons of prestige in the first place; that he resented her for depriving him sexually; that he blamed her for the guilt her mere presence caused him to feel; and that he meant to punish her by flaunting his infidelity and the sexual attractions of other women. What he really needed to be truthful about—and primarily toward himself—was not the affaires, but his marriage. Because he was not, the marriage—not necessarily a hopeless venture otherwise—broke up.

Or again, consider the following example:

A college student consulted me because he was disturbed by homosexual fantasies; after several months of therapy he entered upon an affaire with an emotionally highly compatible girl and, his presenting complaint having vanished, he stopped therapy.

A year or so later he was back. The draft board was breathing down his neck, and his call-up seemed imminent. He was ideologically opposed to the war in Viet Nam, and felt he could not permit himself to be sent there. On the other hand, the thought of going to jail for several years, or of expatriating himself permanently, seemed equally unbearable. He could claim no physical defect which would disqualify him from the service, nor any psychological impairment except perhaps one: it had occurred to him that he could profess to be homosexual, and he wanted me to write him a statement saying that I had treated him for that condition.

It was of course true that I had. It also seemed likely that my having treated him for homosexual preoccupations would be taken to mean that he was actively or potentially homosexual, and that this might well keep him out of the draft.

But in essence, it was quite untrue. He had never been an active homosexual, nor had such inclinations ever had the upper hand. It was not at all likely that he would turn homosexual in the service. But above all, by using homosexuality as an "out," he was side-stepping all the moral and ideological issues which supposedly were so dear to him: the *essential truth* of the matter seemed to be that he was afraid to live up to his own convictions.

It was the latter consideration which made me feel entitled to bawl him out good and proper: how dare he, a young man of illustrious promise, scuttle his moral self? How dare he, by such spurious use of a fact—namely, that he had been in therapy because of homosexual fears—give the lie both to the draft board and to his own integrity?

He left me in a fury. Shortly thereafter he joined the Peace Corps and was sent to some remote and inhospitable nook of South America, there to help improve the lot of an incredibly wretched people. In his letters, since then, he has conveyed to me his sense of profound satisfaction and inner calm, a never-before experienced well-being which he ascribes to being at peace with his own convictions and deeply attached to the gentle people he is serving. "For the first time in my life," he wrote, "I wake up happy every morning."

To be at peace with one's convictions—I suppose that is merely another way of putting the ancient truth that one must know oneself, and be true to oneself. For to know oneself, that means, above all, to know one's convictions, one's standards and values; and without knowing them, one has no sense of self and, to paraphrase Polonius, one cannot then be true to any man.

Such inability to be true to oneself or others can form a psychiatric condition in its own right. I say *condition* rather than *complaint* for the patient may not be at all aware of it.

For example:

A married woman, a Catholic, entered therapy because of a general sense of discontent with herself, her marriage, and her occupation. She soon began to speak in mocking and derogatory terms of her faith and of the Catholic Church, but indicated that she went to mass fairly regularly, and on occasion even to confession. I asked whether she had ever discussed her doubts and criticisms directly and openly with a priest, so as either to resolve them and become at one with her faith, or to find them valid and to quit the Church: either course was compatible with integrity, but her present position, it seemed to me, was not. She thereupon dropped the subject, and went on to speak of her marriage.

Her husband, according to her, was a good man but dull, and she had long ceased loving him. They had no children, and presumably would never have any. I asked: "What do you mean—'presumably'?" She explained that even though her husband had never satisfied her sexually—a fact she had carefully dissimulated so as not to wound his pride—she was still having intercourse with him when he demanded it; but she was not using contraception—the pill made her fat, and other methods were too messy; and considering that under these conditions she had never become pregnant, she presumably never would. On further questioning she explained that she had gone off the pill two or three years ago—without telling her husband. He had then been a student and poor, and would have panicked at the thought of an offspring he could not afford; so it had seemed better not to worry him. Now of course, when he had decided they should try to have children so as to give their marriage more meaning, she could not tell him why she had reason to think herself sterile. I asked, "You cannot tell him?"—and she changed the topic.

Shortly thereafter she took an office job. The new boss was attractive and attentive, and clearly very interested in her. Of course, what with being Catholic and married, she could not even think of an affaire—or so she said.

Within weeks she was sleeping with her boss. "He is," she said, "separated from his wife. I think he said he'll be getting a divorce." I asked: "You *think* he said?" But I did not really expect an answer.

When last heard from, this woman was separated from her husband, carrying on some sort of an affaire with someone or other, and still wondering why she continued to be haunted by that nagging sense of discontent. I suppose she thinks herself reasonably honest, in that she has uttered very few outright lies in her life; but as to suppressions of truth—these are legion. That they connect with her sense of discontent, with her whole approximate, wishy-washy, evasive style of life—this has still not occurred to her.

In fact, she is not a great deal worse, in this regard, than most of us. Facing up to essential truths is difficult, and not only for patients. We therapists, for example, are by and large social- and public-minded citizens, but we much more often feel the call for civic action than we actually bestir ourselves. When it comes right down to it, we plead family obligations, and obligations to patients, and our professional need for self-effacement, and God knows what else; in actual fact we are simply afraid of a realm of action which is to us so unfamiliar.

And yet, it is our own proclivity to excuses that makes us often blind to the excuses of our patients—and to their detriment. For instance:

A middle-aged man, underdog both at his office and at home, eventually confesses to his therapist, a young woman resident in psychiatry, that he has never learned how to drive a car. He explains that cars make him nervous: as a boy of fourteen he had once been induced by a friend to take the wheel of a stolen car, and he had promptly wrecked it. No great harm was done to himself or his friend, but ever since the thought of driving has given him goose pimples.

This kind of explanation appeals to therapists no end: what might one not make of it in terms of the Oedipus complex and castration fear! And how plausible it must seem, particularly to the resident, a young lady who, as it happens, suffers from a strabismus so severe that freeway signs are a blur to her, and also has a sadly deficient sense of orientation; she feels that she has her own reasons to leave the driving to others. Therefore, confirmed in her own aversion, she listens contentedly as the patient reels off further arguments against driving: Is not the private automobile a social evil at best? Is not traffic ever more congested and slowed, is not the air ever more polluted, and are not children stunted by being driven wherever they must go?

But too much justification is suspect. And so the resident, at last alerted, asks why the topic seems to bother him. Are there reasons why he *should* be able to drive?

It now turns out that his inability to drive stands in the way of a promotion at work—a promotion he needs both financially and in terms of morale; and it turns out that weekends are a misery because so much of the countryside, whither he and his family would like to travel, is accessible only by private car.

This being so—the resident gently suggests—then why not take driving lessons after all, and brave the pangs of an ancient trauma?

But now it comes out: what horrifies him is not the past at all; what horrifies him is to have to go to a driving school. Not the driving—he supposes he could manage that—but literally: the going to the school, the walking in at the door—at his age!—and the admitting that he never learned to drive. To confess this to a sympathetic physician is one thing; but he imagines—has often imagined—the one brief upward glance of the receptionist at the driving school, her almost imperceptible gesture of disbelief, her silent "Is it possible—at his age?" He admits to foolishness, but he cannot bear to be so exposed—almost, as it were, caught redhanded; he cannot bear to reveal his shame to the receptionist. And yet—he also knows: he will never be able to respect himself unless he faces this panic.

What is he, in truth, afraid of?

It is hard to define, and different schools of psychiatric thought will put it in different ways: the revelation of social inadequacy, of his castrated state, of his passive-aggressive defense mechanisms, of his existential guilt—it does not really matter. What matters is that, being aware of his fear, being aware of his list of shameful excuses, he cannot step back from this challenge and still respect himself. The moral aspect here takes the form: it is wrong to be less than you could be.

What is wrong, what is immoral about that?

Indeed—what is moral? What is morality?

Here I am clearly outside of my competence: I am not a moral philosopher, I have not studied ethics. Perhaps I should have. I suppose it is part of my load of guilt that I have not. But such is our world: philosophers do not treat patients, and psychiatrists generally do not study ethics.[1] And yet, if my concern for moral problems in therapy has any validity, then I need some sort of definition of the term.

Morality, then, to put it simply, by way of a working hypothesis, is the concern for good and evil—the same concern, incidentally, that is the peculiar province of the superego. And what is "good," what "evil"? Only an approximate definition seems possible to me: "good" is that which, in the overall and in the long run, furthers the survival of the human community.

Whatever helps me, as a single individual, to survive better, that is *useful;* but whatever I, as an individual, can do to enhance the welfare of the community, that is *good.* Morality, negatively expressed, is then also the concern that nothing I do shall harm the human community.

A code of ethics, such as the one attributed to Moses, is a set of dos and don'ts designed to enable numerous people to live together without destroying each other. It is—as is its little brother, the code of manners—a manifestation of moral concern; but morality, which gave

---

[1]After completing this paper I eventually took my own admonition to heart and read *Situation Ethics,* an essay on "The New Morality" by the Episcopalian former Dean of St. Paul's Cathedral, Cincinnati, Joseph Fletcher (Westminster Press, 1966). There, to my great satisfaction, I found a formulation of morality which, though couched in religious terms, coincides essentially with the views presented here.

rise to it, also stands above it, and must continue to scrutinize the code of ethics to see whether, in this day and in this instance, it truly serves the professed ends. A code of ethics, a code of conduct, is an aid and guide to the individual but it does not, it must not absolve him of his personal moral concern and responsibility. In our complicated age, more than ever before, to live by a fixed code of ethics is just not good enough.

And furthermore: while any code of approved conduct is always experienced as an artificial structure imposed upon humanity from above—whether by a human lawgiver or by a God—moral concern itself is, I believe, of the human essence; it is part of the genetic-biological heritage of the human animal, who *must* live in communities to be truly human.

Moral code and moral concern, in their relationship to each other, resemble the relationship between a lifesaving device such as a lifeboat and the safety-mindedness that caused the lifeboat to be built and installed. The boat is admirably suited to secure survival in one specific situation, namely, a shipwreck; but the underlying safety-mindedness will, for other predicaments, think up other devices, such as fire escapes or parachutes. Similarly, a code of ethics assures community survival only under the conditions for which it was designed; moral precepts, like laws, become obsolete; only moral concern, asserting itself over and against the code, can modify and innovate so as to safeguard the community here and now.

Because a community safeguarded by a high degree of moral concern is likely to outlive, and therefore to outbreed, less cohesive groups, we can assume that morality, in the million or so years since the first hominids, has actually been bred into us; it now sticks ineradicably in our bones, and today as ever we ignore it only to our own peril and detriment.

This is not to say that we do not try our best to circumvent it. Both the Id and the Ego, comprising respectively our instinctual needs and our instrumental capabilities, have still more ancient genetic foundations and claims; but because we are the social animal *par excellence,* the superego with its nagging concern for communal welfare, for good and evil, cannot be slighted without our knowing in a deep-down and thoroughly irritating and depressive way that we are alienating ourselves from humanity.[2] By the same token, because we are, ourselves, human, any disregard for morality must also lead to an alienation from ourselves.

With this, I can return to the man who was afraid to learn to drive, and to the resident who treated him. She found out, by further questioning, that he was letting himself down in many other ways as well, that

---

[2]For a more explicit treatise on positive superego functions, see Wolfgang Lederer, "Dragons, Delinquents and Destiny," *Psychol. Issues,* Monogr. No. 15, 1964.

he had, in fact, once almost obtained a Ph.D., but had surrendered the whole effort a few months short of completing his course requirements because of some panic or other. The inability to drive, it appeared, was only a symbol for his numerous shortcomings, and with this recognition the resident, I suspect, began to question herself: Were her own strabismus and disorientation really sufficient reason not to drive—or was it in truth more rewarding for her to be able to enlist the services of others?

But her thoughts, I hope, did not stray long from the patient: the issue he presented was indeed trivial; to him, however, his failure to learn to drive at the proper time seemed to signify that he had somehow fallen out of step with his age; and ever since, in this regard as well as in his studies, his job, and his role as father and husband, he could not be counted on to do what would normally be expected of him. His minor and apparently purely personal shortcoming came to stand, in his mind, for a generally delinquent attitude toward his social obligations. And because this shamed him so, he compounded his debt by continuing, day by day, not to learn; in the end, the fear of discovery and of having to admit his failing presented in itself an insuperable obstacle.

But then—fear is not really insuperable; once we know that nothing stops us but fear, or, to paraphrase a great man, that we are fearing nothing but fear itself, then there are no more excuses, and fear becomes superable. In the end, the possible has a way of becoming mandatory.

I sense, at this point, an uneasiness, almost a wish to apologize: Am I not preaching, after all? And was it not my introductory statement that therapists don't preach?

But it is so hard to discuss moral questions without sounding preachy. At least I find it hard. On the other hand, I also find this a risk that I have to take: for if desertion of morality indeed causes a sense of alienation, and if alienation is the chief psychic ailment of our times, then is it not the duty of the alienist, the psychiatrist, to concern himself with morality, or rather, the lack of it, as, at the very least, one of the possible causes of the ailment?

We do still recall, most of us, the one big and general upsurge of the public mood since VJ-Day, when freshly inaugurated President Kennedy asked us what we could do for our country: a call to moral concern which promised, for one brief shining moment, to gather the stray and alienated under one banner of the common good. We also know, and see with great hope, that while some of our youngsters are trailing off into romantic isolation, the very best of them show today a deep concern for the communities of man which, on this shrinking globe, are ever closer to becoming one community. New terms, new values, are quickly superseding the old; in place of religion, and patriotism, and glory, strangely dry words become inspirational: ecology, the ecosystem

—conservation, pollution control, population control—are for the first time moral concerns bonded to hitherto purely instrumental science, making the young scientists ask, not what is possible, but what is humanly permissible or impermissible, what will benefit the community as a whole and what will harm it, what, in short, is good and what is evil.

Why this excursion into the big world? What is its relevance to the psychiatric consulting room?

Perhaps this: if the community at large is hungering for a new morality, then perhaps our patients are, too. Perhaps we have underestimated the importance of morality to the individual.

But which morality?

Here we return to the beginning, and now we can answer: the morality of moral concern. Unlike the preacher, we do not advocate any particular code of ethics nor, by and large, are we to prescribe any particular course of action. But we must, I think, insist with our patients that they consider the right and the wrong of their actions carefully in the light of their own standards; that they expose their standards to the buffeting of diverse opinion; and that they try hard to identify and to dispel excuses and rationalizations and to arrive at the essential truth of their position. We must then help them to spot the exact point where they are stopped by fear alone, and encourage them to wrestle with their fear as Jacob wrestled with the angel.

The result, optimally, will be the opposite of alienation, that union with the self which we call integrity.

Integrity is, I submit, the goal of all therapy. In its attainment, moral issues, far from being treacherous bogs to be avoided, are the proper arena for our therapeutic battles—battles which will require of the therapist on occasion a far more active intervention than is provided for in the psychoanalytic model.